Reform in China
Huang Tsun-hsien and the Japanese Model

HARVARD EAST ASIAN MONOGRAPHS
95

REFORM IN CHINA

Huang Tsun-hsien

and the Japanese Model

NORIKO KAMACHI

Published by COUNCIL ON EAST ASIAN STUDIES, HARVARD UNIVERSITY, and distributed by HARVARD UNIVERSITY PRESS, Cambridge (Massachusetts) and London   *1981*

The Council on East Asian Studies at Harvard University publishes a monograph series and, through the Fairbank Center for East Asian Research and the
Japan Institute, administers research projects designed to further scholarly understanding of China, Japan, Korea, Vietnam, Inner Asia, and adjacent areas.

Library of Congress Cataloging in Publication Data

Kamachi, Noriko.
Reform in China.
(Harvard East Asian monographs ; 95)
Originally presented as the author's thesis.
Bibliography: p.
Includes index.
1. Huang, Tsun-hsien, 1848–1905. 2. Politicians
—China—Biography. 3. China—Politics and government—
19th century. I. Title. II. Series.
DS764.23.H8K35   1981   951'.03'0924 [B]80–28520
ISBN 0–674–75278–3

To the Memory of My Father

Contents

Acknowledgments

I should like to express my gratitude to Professors John K. Fairbank and Benjamin I. Schwartz, who guided me into graduate study in the field and have given me constant support to shape this work first into a dissertation and then into a book. I am indebted to Professor Chūzō Ichiko and a number of friends who directly or indirectly helped me to write it. Among them I should like to acknowledge the generosity of Paul Cohen, Albert Craig, Irene Eber, Joseph Fletcher, Marius Jansen, S. T. Leong, Charlton Lewis, Masanori Nakamura, Don Price, John Schrecker, Beatrice Spade, Philip West, and Ernest Young, who read the entire manuscript or parts of it at various stages and gave me valuable criticisms and suggestions. I am especially grateful to Dr. Yen-yu Huang, who provided me with important information on the Huang family and on his grandfather, Huang Tsun-hsien. I owe an enormous debt to Marian Wilson for her assistance in editing my draft manuscript over many years, and to Florence Trefethen, who not only edited the final drafts but also helped to refine my translations of poems. Teruko Craig provided calligraphy for the Bibliography and Glossary, and Katherine Frost Bruner provided the Index. Of course, all the mistakes and interpretations are mine. While I was writing the dissertation, the American Association of University Women and the Philanthropic Educational Organization gave me generous support. The University of Michigan, Dearborn, supported my preparation of the manuscript for publication, and the Fairbank Center for East Asian Research at Harvard University provided me with office space.

Preface

One of the most challenging questions for historians of East Asia has been how to explain the contrast between China and Japan in their responses to the modern West. After the Western Powers forced Japan to end its seclusion policy in the mid-nineteenth century, it emerged as a major world power within half a century, while China's full-scale industrialization was delayed until after the socialist revolution in the mid-twentieth century. Juxtaposing these developments in the two countries, Marius Jansen wrote the most comprehensive account of the relationship between Japan and China since the late nineteenth century.[1] Seeking to learn why China's response was so painfully slow, scholars of Chinese history have devoted much of their attention to the intellectual-ethical problems that accompanied the transformation of China's traditional society. The present study is concerned with this large question.

Joseph Levenson phrased the problem in the 1950s this way: "In large part the intellectual history of modern China has been the process of making *kuo-chia* [a nation-state] of *t'ien-hsia* [a universal empire]."[2] Unlike the Japanese, who had a clear sense of national identity from very early times, the Chinese lived with the "sense of being a universe unto themselves"[3] until that universe was shaken by the modern West in the mid-nineteenth century. Thereafter, dramatic changes in intellectual outlook took place and, by the end of the century, a new perception of the world emerged. In this process, the major problem of the Chinese intellectuals was how to reconcile the concepts of modernity with China's traditional values.

During the 1860s and 1870s, only a small number of officials and scholars were convinced of the need for Western technology, and they directed their primary efforts to the restoration of Confucian order and the dynastic institutions which Western intrusions and large-scale rebellions had seriously endangered. Since what they tried to defend was the traditional Confucian culture, their orientation has been identified as "culturalism" as opposed to nationalism, which developed later. The intrinsic contradictions between their goals and the means (Western technology) have been demonstrated in the work of Mary C. Wright.[4] Our knowledge of the Confucian statesmen known as the "Westernizers" and early reform advocates, such as Tseng Kuo-fan (1811–1872), Li Hung-chang (1823–1901), Feng Kuei-fen (1809–1874), and Cheng Kuan-ying (1842–1923), has since then expanded, most notably through the works of K. C. Liu.[5]

In the process of intellectual transformation, the most conspicuous development during the 1880s and 1890s was the emergence of nationalism, which was based on the newly conceived idea of national sovereignty. In the field of foreign policy, the national-sovereignty concept was firmly established by the late 1890s. By then, the Chinese officials in charge of foreign affairs were conversant with the Western concept of international relations and were able to handle imperialist demands tactfully in a conscious effort to defend their national sovereignty. This point has been convincingly demonstrated by John Schrecker in his case study of the German concession in Shantung.[6] After the Sino-Japanese War of 1894–1895, an acute awareness spread among Chinese intellectuals that China was a vulnerable country in a competitive world. This Social Darwinian image of the world as a struggle for survival was popularized by the writings of Yen Fu (1853–1921). The intellectual implications of his interpretive translations of the works of Herbert Spencer, Thomas Huxley, Adam Smith, Montesquieu, and John Stuart Mill have been scrutinized by Benjamin Schwartz, who pointed out how single-mindedly

Yen Fu concerned himself with the need to enrich and strengthen the state.[7] Achieving wealth and power for the state was unanimously accepted as the goal of reform in China. Hao Chang defined the decade from the mid 1890s to the early 1900s as an important watershed in the intellectual transition from traditional to modern China and pointed out that the most crucial developments during this decade were not only "a turning away from the universal moral community (*t'ien-hsia*) and acceptance of the state as the terminal community" and "the transformation of the moral goal of the state into the political goal of collective achievement," but also the emergence of the concept of modern citizenship.[8] By the turn of the century, nationalism had become the keynote of the political ideas of the educated elite inside and outside the bureaucratic establishment. "Bureaucratic nationalism" directed the decision-making of the powerful Governor General Chang Chih-tung (1837–1909), and "mercantile nationalism" motivated the treaty-port merchant Cheng Kuan-ying to propose far-reaching institutional reform.[9] Indeed, the Reform Movement of the late 1890s was the intellectual elite's most vociferous expression of nationalism.

As a sub-theme to the major theme of nationalism, there was a strain of universalistic utopianism among the reform advocates of the late nineteenth century. It was a quiet but continuous stream of thought beneath the raging billows of nationalism. K'ang Yu-wei's (1858–1927) *Ta-t'ung shu* (The book of the great community) was the most articulate expression of late Ch'ing utopianism. Kung-ch'üan Hsiao has suggested in his study of K'ang Yu-wei that K'ang's nationalist concerns and his utopian speculations developed on two different levels and that the latter hardly bore any relationship to the real situation in China.[10] Even so, K'ang's universalist orientation influentially shaped his reform ideas. Hō Takushū's comparative studies of reformist thought in China and socio-political thought in early Meiji Japan have demonstrated this point. The contrast between K'ang and Fukuzawa Yukichi (1834–1901) in their perception of the economic thought of Adam Smith is particularly revealing. Both men admired Smith

and the idealized capitalist economic system. However, while Fukuzawa fully accepted the capitalist economic philosophy and
positively encouraged the rich to pursue profit, K'ang did not regard the capitalist society as an ideal and expounded, instead, his
view of the ideal society as a kind of utopian socialism.[11] During
the 1900s, revolutionary intellectuals translated the universalist
ideal into political action. Don Price has illuminated how the
leaders of the 1911 Revolution were motivated by universalist
inspirations as well as nationalist commitment. They perceived
the revolution as "part of an inexorable universal moral drama"
in the process toward a "universal moral order of equality and
liberty."[12]

The reform ideas of nineteenth-century Chinese intellectuals
reflected not only their intellectual inclinations but also their
situation in the socio-political hierarchy. The reform ideas of
Wang T'ao, for example, would have been different had he not
led a life of exile in Shanghai and Hong Kong as a "treaty-port
intellectual" alienated from the orthodox establishment. In his
study of Wang T'ao, Paul Cohen has depicted the late Ch'ing
cultural landscape as a spectrum between two poles, the littoral
and hinterland. In his scheme, one pole, the hinterland, was the
center of the orthodox tradition, and the other pole, the littoral, the cultural waterfront which faced the most direct impact
of Western civilization.[13]

In imperial China, the most decisive factor determining the position of an individual in the socio-political hierarchy was his
academic status earned through the civil service examinations.
In the late nineteenth century, however, the holding of a high
academic degree did not necessarily assure a respectable position
in the establishment, because of the saturated bureaucracy. Moreover, the competition for higher degrees became increasingly
keen in the nineteenth century, because of the growth of the population and the spread of literacy.[14] The frustration of the intellectuals who had degrees but no offices or who had offices but
were kept in minor positions combined with their nationalist fer-
vor helped fuel the Reform Movement.

This study of Huang Tsun-hsien (1848–1905) is addressed to the same broad questions that have been asked in previous works. But it places special emphasis on the question of how the Chinese perceived the modernization in Japan before the Sino-Japanese War of 1894–1895. Huang Tsun-hsien was the first Chinese to make serious efforts to comprehend the great changes that were taking place in Japan after its encounter with the modern West. He was interested not only in Japan's modernization along Western lines but also in Japan's history and culture, including the everyday life of the people. He wrote fascinating books on Japan, based on his personal observations of the country from 1877 to 1882. He urged his countrymen to take a serious look at Japanese accomplishments as early as the 1880s and hoped that his books would serve as a reference for reform in China. His account of Meiji Japan, especially of the Meiji Restoration, had a significant impact on the Reform Movement in China after the Sino-Japanese War, and Huang emerged as an important leader of that movement.

In Paul Cohen's socio-cultural topography, Huang Tsun-hsien was located in the middle of the hinterland-littoral spectrum and was identified as a "pioneer reformer of the hinterland." As a holder of the *chü-jen* degree, Huang was a qualified member of the orthodox elite. But he chose to start out his official career by serving as a staff member in an overseas legation. By doing so, he placed himself on the fringe of the imperial bureaucracy. In his subsequent efforts to make his way to a more central bureaucratic position, he had to follow a route similar to that of the intellectuals in the littoral; that is, he followed the route of recommendation by powerful officials who needed the services of foreign experts. Eventually he was received in audience by the Emperor as a candidate for a high position; but no sooner had he made his way to the center of power than his official career was cut short by the coup d'état of the Empress Dowager in 1898.

Huang's career reflected a new pattern of mobility in the bureaucracy in late Ch'ing China. How he integrated his efforts to develop his own career and at the same time promote reform in China is a sub-theme of the pages that follow.

The approach of this study is biographical. I have attempted to portray Huang Tsun-hsien as an independent-minded intellectual. His distinctive ethnic background as a Hakka, his intellectual inclinations which foreshadowed those of the May Fourth generation, and his experiences in China and abroad shaped his nationalism and reformist thinking.

Reform in China
Huang Tsun-hsien and the Japanese Model

ONE

Huang Tsun-hsien's Native Home

> *Towering over the abundant woods,*
> *A giant t'ung tree stands before the gate,*
> *My home is on the north side of the brook.*[1]

Eastern Kwangtung in the T'ang and Sung dynasties was a lonely place of banishment abounding in poisonous insects but, by the beginning of the Ming dynasty, emigrants from north and central China had given it a dense population. Among these emigrants was a group called the Hakka (guest people). They were of the same Han race as the majority of Chinese, but they maintained their own distinctive dialect and customs.

By all accounts, the Hakka had moved from north China in successive waves following each major disorder in the north, the invasion of Inner Asian tribes in the fourth century, the ninth-century Huang Ch'ao Rebellion which ended the T'ang dynasty, and, most significant of all, the occupation of north China by the Jurchens and Mongols in the twelfth and thirteenth centuries. The original settlers, referring to themselves as "hosts" (Punti), named the Hakka "guest people" as latecomers to the south, but it is not clear when the Hakka themselves adopted this name and began to develop their distinct ethnic consciousness underpinned by a fierce pride in being descendants from the original homeland of Chinese civilization in the north. Such feelings became most visible in the nineteenth century.

The Hakka were widely distributed in China's southern provinces, namely Kwangtung, Fukien, Kiangsi, Kwangsi, Hunan, and Szechwan, but their main concentration was in northeastern Kwangtung, particularly the Ch'ing-dynasty administrative district of Chia-ying. Chia-ying department was almost exclusively inhabited by Hakka and was their cultural and spiritual center, so that the dialect of this area came to be regarded as standard Hakka.[2]

From the densely populated areas of eastern Kwangtung, thousands of Hakka migrated to the Canton region and further westward to Kwangsi province during the seventeenth and eighteenth centuries. They settled first in the mountainous areas that had been left unoccupied, or else started out as tenants of the early settlers. They did not bind their women's feet, and both men and women worked hard tilling the land, planting fruit trees and bamboos, and weaving cloth out of grass. By toil and thrift, the Hakka improved their conditions, increased in number, and became tough competitors with the indigenous groups. Feuds between the Hakka and their hostile neighbors broke out frequently, and tension between the Hakka and other ethnic groups in Kwangsi eventually helped ignite the great Taiping Rebellion in 1851. The Taiping leader, Hung Hsiu-ch'üan, was a member of a Hakka lineage in the Canton area whose ancestors had migrated from Chia-ying in the eighteenth century.[3]

Huang Tsun-hsien was born in 1848 into a distinguished Chia-ying Hakka family. The clan name Huang was assumed to have derived from the name of a state where the ancestor of the Huang clan had been enfeoffed in ancient times. This had been in Kuang-chou of Honan province, a part of the Central Plain, the cradle of Chinese civilization during the earliest three dynasties, Hsia, Shang, and Chou. The remote ancestors of Huang Tsun-hsien had moved south in the tenth century and settled in several districts in Fukien province. At the time of the Mongol invasion, they had moved again, this time to Kwangtung, and had settled in the southern part of Mei-chou which was renamed Chia-ying during the Ch'ing. At the end of the Ming dynasty, Huang's ancestors had established their residence to the east of the walled city of Chia-ying, a place called P'an-kuei-fang. They had lived there for eight generations by the time Huang was born.[4]

The Huang family was prosperous and influential in the locality. Some seventy family members lived together in their compound when Huang was a child—a most positive sign of the family's prosperity. Their family fortune had been built on moneylending by Huang Tsun-hsien's great-great-grandfather, Huang Jun. Huang Jun began his career as a poor scribe at the local marketplace and achieved success as a pawnbroker. Describing the life of Huang Jun, Huang Tsun-hsien wrote:

> His family was very poor. He commuted to the fair wearing a bamboo hat and straw sandals. There he wrote contracts for transacting cattle business for people who came to the fair. At the time, foreign coins began to circulate in the Fukien and Kwangtung areas. He was good at detecting counterfeit coins by examining the color, sound, and quality of the metal. He sat at his desk in the marketplace all day, and came home only after the people at the fair dispersed. In this way, he gradually accumulated wealth, and by the time he was thirty he owned a pawnshop. By the end of his life, he owned four or five pawnshops.[5]

Huang Jun's wife, Chung t'ai-shu-jen, joined the Huang family as a child-bride (*t'ung-yang-hsi*).[6] It was a widely practiced custom among poor families to adopt a female child as the fiancée for their young son. The girl was brought up by her parents-in-law and was a domestic servant in the household until the marriage was consummated. Such an arrangement enabled poor families to avoid paying the exorbitant bride price that was customarily required for obtaining a grown-up bride.

Huang Tsun-hsien's great-grandfather, Huang Hsueh-shih, studied the classics and took civil service examinations, although he never succeeded in becoming an official and remained a merely local notable.[7] His wife, Li t'ai-fu-jen, came from a respectable official's family. She lived until 1858, when she was eighty-five and Huang Tsun-hsien was ten years old. She was a remarkable woman and exerted great influence on Huang Tsun-hsien. After the death of her husband, she supervised the management of the family business and became the matriarch of the large household.

Huang Tsun-hsien's grandfather, Huang Chi-sheng (1804–1891), was the sixth son. Like his father, he remained a member of the local gentry, although two of his elder brothers gained academic degrees and served as magistrates in Yunnan and Fukien respectively.[8]

Huang Tsun-hsien's father, Huang Hung-tsao (1828–1891), was successful in the provincial examination of 1856 and obtained a *chü-jen* degree. He was appointed to a minor official post at the Board of Revenue and served in Peking for almost twenty years. In 1878, he was appointed the Magistrate of Kuei-lin department of Kwangsi province. Then he was charged with the supervision of the Transit Tax (likin) Bureau, first in Nan-ning and later in Wu-chou of Kwangsi province. While he was in Wu-chou, the Sino-French War broke out, and he was made responsible for supplying provisions for the imperial troops fighting on the Vietnamese border. His performance was recognized by Imperial Commissioner Li Hung-chang. In 1889, he was awarded a promotion in official rank and an appointment as the Magistrate of Ssu-en department of Kwangsi province. There he gained a reputation as a conscientious and competent administrator. He was also a well-known poet and published three volumes of poems and essays.[9] Undoubtedly, Huang Tsun-hsien inherited not only his father's ability as a practical-minded official but also his talent as a poet.

When Huang Tsun-hsien was born, Li t'ai-fu-jen, his great-grandmother, was seventy-five. When he was one year old, his brother was born, and in the following year his sister. Because Li t'ai-fu-jen could not bear to see them competing for their mother's milk, she took Tsun-hsien under her wing. She cared for him day and night, cooked special food for him, bathed him, and sewed silk clothes for him. She dressed him like a girl in a red skirt and blouse, powdered his face with sweet-smelling powder, and adorned him with earrings—a charm against bad luck. When he began to talk, she taught him poems, and soon he had memorized all of the poems in the collection by one thousand poets which was widely used for the instruction of children. When he was three and a half years old, she took him to the family school and asked the teacher to give special care to this unusually young student. He was very

attached to his great-grandmother; his admiration for her was almost worship. A touching story handed down in the Huang family
demonstrates how great was the influence of this admirable woman on the youthful Huang Tsun-hsien. The story was set down by
Huang Yen-yü, a grandson of Huang Tsun-hsien, who heard it
from his mother:

> Our grandfather [Huang Tsun-hsien] was greatly disturbed in his youth
> when he learned that his great-grandmother, once standing outside the
> room where a concubine of his great-grandfather's was in labor, spoke
> out loudly, invoking the evil spirit to harm the newly born. He knew
> how devoted and kindhearted his great-grandmother was to the family.
> Yet, just because of her jealousy, she could be so unkind and such a dif-
> ferent person. The revelation of the episode shocked him. So he swore
> he would never engage a concubine. And he did not.[10]

In his poems, Huang Tsun-hsien expressed his love toward his
mother, his sister, his wife, and his daughter, as well as his great-
grandmother. In fact, those of his poems most praised by literary
critics were the ones dedicated to the women in his family. A
contemporary poet, Ch'en San-li, exalted Huang's "Now, in
Separation" as the best poem ever written in the past thousand
years. It was written for his wife, née Yeh, who remained at
home while Huang served at the Chinese Legation in London.[11]
In "A visit to the grave of my great-grandmother, Li t'ai-fu-jen,"
Huang reminisced about his childhood which had centered around
her. Another famous poem, "Farewell to a sister," depicts a
mother's love and her toil to support the family during difficult
times. In poems that refer to his mother, every line is deeply moving.
While she was alive, he watched over her with loving concern for
her well-being; she was selflessly dedicated to the family despite
hardships. After her untimely death, he remembered her and
regretted her loss.[12]

Huang also wrote some romantic love poems, though the practice was not acceptable among scholars. "A poem on a new bride"
is a long colloquial poem about a newlywed couple, presumably
written when his first son was born one year after his marriage. He
described love in the newly decorated chamber, subtle expressions

of affection between the wife and husband in the everyday life of a large family, and the psychology of pregnancy and childbirth.[13] He wrote a series of colloquial poems entitled "Mountain Songs" (*shan-ko*) based on the Hakka ballads.[14] They included love songs that a man and woman chanted in exchange, according to the folk tradition of the Hakka. These poems of Huang were hailed by the new generation in the early Republican period when liberation from old morals was the spirit of the time. In the days of Huang, however, erotic love had no place in respectable literature. Since the poems on the new bride and the mountain songs were so unconventional, Huang himself did not include them in his collected poems. In any case, he treated women with sympathy and respect in his poems. As a reformer, he advocated education for women. He raised the question that, if half the four hundred million population were to remain illiterate, (that is, the female half), how could China survive?[15] Perhaps his respectful attitude toward women was nurtured in his early childhood under the influence of his great-grandmother, as well as by the Hakka tradition in which women shared hard work and responsibility with men.

The childhood of Huang Tsun-hsien was peaceful and happy under the loving care of his great-grandmother inside the compound of the powerful family. The prosperity of the Huang family, however, did not last. The widespread social unrest and the great rebellion, symptoms of the decline of the dynasty, began to affect the family when Huang was eleven years old. In 1859, the year following the death of Huang's great-grandmother, Chia-ying was attacked by the Taipings. A force of 50,000 or 60,000 men led by Shih Chen-chi, who had been under the command of Shih Ta-k'ai, the Wing King of the Taipings, surrounded the walled city of Chia-ying and broke into it by setting off explosives under the city wall. During the defense, the Magistrate Wen Sheng and his son were killed, along with 4,000 men and women.[16] The atrocities left the young Huang with dreadful memories.

Though the Taiping Rebellion had started as a Hakka movement, the Hakka in Chia-ying suffered greatly at the hands of the Taiping troops. In 1865, almost a year after the fall of the Taiping capital in Nanking, the remnants of the Taiping forces attacked Chia-ying. Led by Wang Hai-yang and Hu Yung-hsiang, this group fought desperately against the pursuing imperial troops in the border areas between Hunan and Kiangsi and between Kiangsi and Kwangtung. Pressed closely by the imperial forces under the command of Tso Tsung-t'ang, more than 100,000 Taipings entered the western part of Kwangtung, and some occupied the city of Chia-ying. Tso Tsung-t'ang mobilized the troops in Fukien, Kiang-si, and Kwangtung, including the battalion of Pao Ch'ao, who had been known as a ferocious fighter against the Taipings. It took two months for the imperial troops to recover the city. During the siege, the city and its suburban areas suffered heavy damage. Tso Tsung-t'ang stated in his report to the throne that, in his many years of campaigns against the rebels, such bitter combat as he had experienced at Chia-ying had been rare. The fighting was tough because the Taipings had recruited veteran fighters from among disbanded local militia and local bandits. It was the final battle against the remnant forces of the Taipings.[17]

The attack on Chia-ying came a few days after Huang Tsun-hsien's wedding. Huang, then seventeen years old, took refuge on a boat with his bride and some thirty members of his family. They sailed westward to San-ho hsu in the Ta-p'u district. All night long they heard the noise of the Taiping soldiers crossing the river and the cries of people fleeing in confusion. Huang's poems on this trip reflect his intense fear and resentment of the Taipings:

> *Parents, brothers, sisters wondered in whispers,*
> *South, north, east, west? Which way to flee?*
> *Thirty of us all packed into one boat,*
> *Made our escape from death in the tiger's den.*[18]

No sooner had they anchored than San-ho hsu also became unsafe. They moved on to Ch'ao-chou through the waterways, and once they were surrounded by a gang of Taipings. Their treasures hidden in the bottom of the boat were taken, and they narrowly escaped being slaughtered. Huang described the frightening event in "Going to Ch'ao-chou":

The north wind blew cold.
Our oars plied the flat river.
Our boat was just nearing a city
With smoke rising up from its chimneys
When we were abruptly surprised
By robbers who loomed out of ambush.
Their onrush filled us with terror.
Their oars hit the water like rainfall.
Our boatmen tied up our boat
To challenge the bandits with lances.
But our boatmen were not a strong match,
And would merely enrage the aggressors,
So we beat on the hull "Stop! Stop fighting!"
Let the bandits steal what they wanted.[19]

Huang's poem "Extracts of what I overheard from the bandits' conversation" reveals his abhorrence of the evil conduct of the Taipings. They drank one hundred gallons of wine in the morning and ate one thousand sheep in the evening. They gambled all the time and took new women every night.[20]

When Taipings in Chia-ying were suppressed, Huang expressed relief in a poem called, "Rejoicing to hear that Tso Tsung-t'ang's government troops recovered Chia-ying and conquered the bandits." He was also concerned, however, over the harshness of the suppression, because he thought of the Taipings not as enemies but as children of the Emperor. In later years, he denounced Tseng Kuo-fan, the commander-in-chief of the campaigns against the Taipings, for his brutality.[21]

Upon returning home, Huang found the house looted and his bride's luggage emptied. The Huang pawnshops had also been pilfered and the buildings destroyed. The damage was enough to cause a sudden decline in the family fortunes.[22] The difficult situation was described in Huang's poem written for his sister who was married into the Chang family of Chia-ying in 1867:

Father sent us a letter
To warn that our fortunes had fallen,

To tell us the bridal clothes
Would make just a small trousseau—
Four chests, or five at the most.
Opening the chests, our mother
Sighed before looking inside.

Our family used to be wealthy
Before these disasters shook us.
Those riches piled up through the years
Were taken, leaving us nothing.

Once the shelves of our pawnshop
Were filled with the raiment of others.
Today, we must pawn our own clothes
But do not know where to take them.
We add fallen leaves to our firewood.
We eke out our thin gruel with water.
No scrap of cloth is too trifling
For Mother to piece into garments.[23]

In referring to his family's history, Huang glorified its Hakka origins. The Hakka, he emphasized, were descendants of respectable clans which had lived in centers of Chinese civilization and were therefore true bearers of such ancient virtues as hard work, thrift, and the simple life:

Those ancient clans from China's Central Plain
Were called "guests" wherever they wandered.
They crossed the Long River, came to Fukien;
After many moves, sank roots along the coast.

Thrifty as the ancients of Wei and of T'ang,
Direct as the people of the Three Dynasties.
Their women toil from dawn till the setting sun,
Keeping their ancient round of work alive.

Cock crow finds them at the water well.
Dark catches them hauling their loads of wood.

> *Rarely with powdered faces, formal dress,*
> *They pass their days in garments of grass-green.*[24]

Huang's high-spirited expression of pride in the Hakka was reflected in the strong sentiment that fermented among the Hakka during and after the Taiping era. During the period, the Hakka were generally identified as rebels and bandits, and there were implications that they were descendants of non-Chinese aboriginals.[25] The Hakka protested against these abusive charges, and intellectuals among them advocated their cause in writing. In 1867, Ting Jih-ch'ang, a prominent official from a Hakka family, wrote to the Governor of Kwangtung explaining the background of the Hakka and asking him for unprejudiced treatment of them in case there were conflicts with the Punti.[26] Lin Ta-ch'üan, a Hakka intellectual from Ta-p'u, wrote a treatise on the history of the Hakka, which became a familiar expression of Hakka consciousness in the late Ch'ing period. Lin identified the Hakka as descendants of the subjects of the ancient Three Dynasties, emphasizing the affinities between the Hakka dialect and the ancient language; he asserted that they had maintained the legacies of their ancestors. The compiler of the gazetteer of the district of Chia-ying (1898 edition), Wen Chung-ho, also discussed the history of the Hakka along those same lines.[27] As a result, the Hakka problem attracted the attention of officials and intellectuals, and between 1851 and 1904 over thirty people, including Westerners, published books or articles on that issue.[28]

The circumstances of Huang's education, as well as his Hakka background, influenced his attitude toward contemporary intellectual life. As the son of a gentry family, Huang was naturally expected to study Confucian classics, to gain academic degrees by passing the civil service examinations, and to embark on a career as a government official. Huang began his primary education at the family school before he was four years old. His teacher, Li Hsueh-yuan, early recognized Huang's talent in poetry. When he was nine, Huang surprised Li with a poem that showed unusual gifts. Word spread among the local people, and Huang gained a reputation as a poetic prodigy. It was a memorable event for Huang; he recalled the poem and recorded it later in an autobiographical note.[29] It appears that Huang had no other teacher. Beyond the level of the family school, he studied alone and grew up as a man of great self-confidence. This rather unconventional background amazed K'ang Yu-wei, the intellectual leader of the Reform Movement of 1898, who noted that Huang was so gifted and independent-minded from an early age that he was able to attain an admirable level of scholarship through self-education. Huang himself regretted that, because his home was in a remote region, he did not have an opportunity to study under a great master.[30] Moreover, his education was disrupted by the disturbances of the Taiping Rebellion. The books in the family library went up in flames when the house was raided, and thereafter financial crisis in the family made it difficult to purchase books.[31] Also, the stringent financial situation of the family precluded Huang's concentrating on his studies. On his twentieth birthday, he lamented that, during the past ten years, he had been forced to give up half his studies under the pressure of matters essential for survival.[32]

In the spring of 1867, Huang took his first examination.[33] By passing it, he gained the status of a department student and was qualified to take the provincial examination. In the summer of the same year, he traveled to Canton to take the triennial provincial examination, which he failed. It was his first long trip and the experience was traumatic. He described his agony in "My trip to Lake Feng":

> In all my twenty years, that was the first
> Time my face got soiled with dust from the road.
> I journeyed long, a weary thousand li
> In hope the examination would bring success.
>
> I took my seat in a hot, cramped cubicle
> With others, packed in like bees in a hive.
> I felt like a minnow trapped in a dry cart rut.
> My hungry bowels rumbled; my lips felt parched.[34]

The competition for obtaining academic degrees was intense

toward the end of the dynasty. While the population of China more than doubled during the period between the early eighteenth century and mid-nineteenth century, the quotas for the higher degrees (*chin-shih* and *chü-jen*), which were fixed in 1702, remained the same. Because the literate population undoubtedly expanded during this period of stability and economic prosperity, the competition in the civil service examination increased enormously. Competition for *chü-jen* degrees was especially keen because the number of *sheng-yuan* degree-holders is believed to have been increased about 20 percent after the Taiping Rebellion. The total numbers of holders of *sheng-yuan* and *chü-jen* degrees in the empire were estimated to have been 600,000 and 10,000 respectively.[35]

He tried again in 1870 but failed once more. In the following year, at the annual examination which every *sheng-yuan* (licentiate or one who had passed the district-level examination) was required to take, he was awarded the status of *lin-shan-sheng* (salaried student). Two years later, in 1873, he was selected as a *pa-kung-sheng* (senior licentiate of the first degree). Most of the *pa-kung-sheng* were selected from among the salaried students, and the quota was one per district or department. They were entitled to take the *t'ing-shih* (court examination) given in Peking, and those who passed the court examination were qualified for minor posts in the central or local government. In the summer of 1873, Huang for the third time tried the provincial examination, but without success.[36]

In the following year, Huang went to Peking in order to take the court examination, but he failed. By this time, he was weary of the strenuous study in preparation for the examinations and was disgusted with his embarrassing image as an unsuccessful official career aspirant. A poem written in 1874, "Now I am about to take the court examination," expresses his frustration:

> *I am twenty; those years have rolled away*
> *And my fat thighs remind me I am weighed*
> *Down with studying, my wings clipped by care,*
> *My steps trudging the examination stair*

> *Towards an official post, a future joy!*
> *Why should I shun the life of the hoi polloi?*
> *Why should I memorize prices for rice*
> *Instead of making friends in the marketplace?*[37]

In order to meet the requirements of the examinations, one had to expend tremendous time and energy on uncreative study, which tended to shrivel a person into intellectual impotence. It was frightening for Huang to witness examples of this. A moving poem about a friend he met at the examination in Canton in 1870 tells us how he felt about the studies for examinations:

> *The examination papers rustled*
> *Like ten thousand silkworms munching*
> *Mulberry. Three red candles glowed*
> *And a voice boomed from the next cubicle.*
>
> *I peeped in, saw a man*
> *In a white shirt, heard his chant*
> *Rattling the roof tiles, felt his bright eyes*
> *Watchful as tigers' eyes.*
>
> *How could I guess he would become my friend?*
> *We shook hands, changed greetings.*
> *He was a general's son,*
> *Had memorized the Classics,*
> *Had stored in memory the ins and outs*
> *Of military tactics, strategies.*
>
> *I felt at peace, at pleasure*
> *As the full moon rose over the eaves.*
> *This man, this moon, this tower—*
> *How could I go to sleep!*

So he went out with this man, Lo Shao-shan, and his old friend from home, Liang Chü-shih. They climbed to the top of the high tower in front of the examination hall. The moonlight revealed millions of houses in the city below them, and in the distance they could see the sand bars at the seashore. The exuberant trio engaged in witty repartee till late at night.

Three years later, Huang chanced to see this intelligent man again. To his great dismay, Lo Shao-shan had changed completely:

> *In a voice shrunk to a whisper*
> *He told of the past sad years,*
> *Dull spirited and pitiful*
> *Curled up in his cocoon.*

Filled with pity and indignation, Huang continued:

> *Shao-shan, Shao-shan, let us climb the tomb of King Yueh*
> *And watch the clouds go floating overhead*
> *And recall heroic deeds of that ancient king.*
> *Or else, shall we sail into the Southern Ocean,*
> *Facing our boat into the winds, the waves?*
> *We two can land the leviathan, taste its meat.*

> *You with your rare gifts, why grow heavy*
> *With plodding, pedestrian prose and poems?*
> *Shake your head, beat your wings, soar, escape!*
> *You will never learn to love your shabby cage.*[38]

Unlike other reformers in the late Ch'ing era, Huang did not propose to modernize the examination system, since he placed no hope at all in it. He wrote to a friend in 1902 that school education and the examination system were incompatible because the examination system was a device for restricting human ability, not for developing it.[39]

Huang denounced not only the examination system but also the general conditions of scholarship prevailing at the time. He was indignant to find that most scholars indulged in a hidebound exegesis of Confucian Classics and were totally insensible of contemporary problems. A long poem, written when he was about seventeen, expresses his disapproval of contemporary scholars:

> *Humdrum scholars recite the* History, *the* Odes
> *Showing off their learning.*

Noses in the air, they allude to antiquity.
Clapping hands, they long for the ancient order.
Ah, the splendor of the Three Dynasties,
And the Sage who came thereafter!
What a decline to this present chaos!
They wail. They weep.
They churn out drawings, copies
Of old chariots. Their fingers grow calloused.
They hold picture books of the "well field"
And think of living that utopian dream.
Their impossible dreams are not the ancients' fault.
These scholars cannot see that times have changed.[40]

Huang placed this poem on the opening page of his collection of poems, *Jen-ching-lu shih-ts'ao,* (Collected poems of the master of Jen-ching-lu) which he began compiling in 1890. This poem set the tone for the assertion he reiterated in his poems throughout his life. In a poem written when he was twenty, he criticized Confucian scholars for their subjugation to the myth of antiquity:

All men are fashioned out of yellow mud.
So why are ancients wise and moderns not?
Even today will soon become the past.
Where is the line that marks antiquity?[41]

Huang's questioning of the authority of the past was later echoed by T'an Ssu-t'ung, a young activist in the Reform of 1898, who said: "If antiquity is so admirable, what is the point of being a modern man?"[42]

Huang's criticism of those scholars who depended on the authority of the Classics did not imply a denial of ancient learning. On the contrary, he had intimate feelings toward the ancients and took genuine pleasure in their books:

We cannot live in the days of the ancients,
And I regret that I was born too late.
Yet, through their books, I can communicate
Every day with those venerable ancients.

> *Of all my life, reading I like the best;*
> *For this I'm called a madman by the rest.*[43]

The relativity of antiquity in the unending stream of time was the theme of Huang's earliest known poem, "Farewell to the passing year," written in 1865:

> *At last year's end I wrote a poem*
> *To bid that passing year farewell.*
> *The time since then—a finger's flick.*
> *Now goodbye to this year as well.*
>
> . . . . . .
>
> *Those living fade into the past*
> *And people change as years pass by.*
> *Staying alive a hundred years*
> *One says a hundred times goodbye.*[44]

Of the cults of the past, the most rampant was a rigid adherence to the ancient style of writing. Huang pitied mediocre scholars for their painful efforts to imitate the ancient writers and despised them for their pretentiousness about their mastery of the Classics. Caricaturing them, he wrote:

> *The pedants love antiquity,*
> *Read ancient books day after day,*
> *Use no words when composing poems*
> *Not found in the Six Classics tomes.*
> *Even a scrap that's dull or trite,*
> *If old, can whet their appetite.*[45]

Huang daringly suggested that the ancient writings revered by present-day scholars had once been nothing but records of the common speech of ordinary people. The gap between the written and spoken languages increased; while the ancient form of writing was retained, the spoken language changed in the course of time. By the same token, he argued, the vernacular of the present day would be cherished as a classic by future generations. Deciding to compose spontaneous poems in the vernacular, free from the restrictions of the classical forms, he wrote:

I am sitting in a room in the light of bright windows.
I burn incense in a censer,
place my best inkstone on my left,
My finest writing tablet on my right.

If I let my thoughts flow, my writing hand follow,
how can antiquity hem me in?
If I write in the everyday language of now,
After five thousand years, readers will admire
The grandeur of these ancient words.[46]

It is remarkable that Huang was making such iconoclastic statements against the authority of the ancient style of writing as early
as the 1860s. Indeed, his assertions foreshadowed the vernacular
literature movement of the late 1910s. Until then, it was taken for
granted that respectable writings had to be in classical forms, and
it was not acceptable for scholars to write in a colloquial style. As
we have noted, Huang himself excluded his colloquial poems from
his collection. Most of his poems were in the classic style, though
he boldly adopted unconventional vocabulary to refer to contemporary events and to introduce new concepts. Huang's early advocacy of vernacular literature was supported by his awareness that
the Hakka dialect was closely related to the ancient Chinese language. There were similarities between the two in pronunciation,
rhyme, and word usage.[47] Thus, it was relatively easy for the Hakka to learn the rules of rhyming, which were based on ancient
pronunciation; in other words, for Hakka there was a closer relationship between the spoken and the written language. In this
respect, Huang's Hakka background gave him the confidence to
denounce the contemporary scholars' rigid adherence to the ancient style.

Huang's criticism of contemporary scholarship was not limited
to the general attitudes of scholars, but extended to the prevailing
schools of Confucian learning—the school of Han learning and the
school of Sung learning. He maintained that both these schools
failed to transmit the whole teaching of Confucius. As for the
scholars of Sung learning, who had been noted for their inclination

toward metaphysical speculation, Huang characterized them this way:

> *They flaunted esoteric sophistry,*
> *Slavishly copied Tsu-ssu, Mencius,*
> *Oddly bizarre in their philosophy,*
> *Discussing world affairs, capricious.*[48]

As for the school of Han learning, which had been identified as the school of exegesis, Huang admitted that there had been some great scholars in the early Ch'ing who made major contributions in clarifying the obscurities in the Confucian texts. However, he criticized the tendency among the scholars of Han learning to limit themselves to exegesis. Huang proclaimed that only Confucius himself was great and deserved reverence:

> *Great was the Way of Confucius,*
> *Epitome of all the hundred schools.*
> *Even Yen Yuan and Min Tzu-ch'ien,**
> *Could not grasp wholly his philosophy.*
> *How can Confucius ever be revealed*
> *Through nitpicking scholarship of Han and Sung?*[49]

*The supreme disciples of Confucius.

After the Taiping disaster, scholars became more and more dissatisfied with the established doctrines of Han and Sung learning. Moreover, there was an increasing tendency among them to attempt eclectic syntheses of Han and Sung learning in an effort to establish a new philosophical and moral discipline which could meet the needs of the time. For example, Ch'en Li, a scholar of great reputation who taught at the famous Hsueh-hai t'ang Academy in Canton, maintained that the quarrel between the Han and Sung schools was not well grounded. Shortly before his death in 1871 he wrote: "[Contrary to the general belief], scholars of the Han period were good at discussing principles, and they were not behind the scholars of the Sung in this respect. The Sung scholars made a mistake in slighting the Han scholars.

As for present-day scholars, they are also mistaken; they respect the Han scholars but do not discuss principles."[50]

Tseng Kuo-fan, the prominent scholar-statesman who achieved a great reputation for his successful campaign against the Taipings, was another scholar who attempted to combine various schools of thought. His thought centered on the Neo-Confucian philosophy of the Ch'eng-Chu school (that is, the Sung learning); but he showed an earnest interest in the teachings of the school of statecraft and the moral teachings of the T'ung-ch'eng school, and at the same time did not want the Han school to be obliterated. By combining the thought of various schools, he developed what he called the "philosophy of social usage" (*li-hsueh*). It was based on the concept of *li*, which for him included laws and institutions as well as ceremonial rituals, rites, and rules of proper social conduct.[51] Huang admired Tseng and recognized him as the greatest scholar of the time, though he criticized Tseng for his harshness in suppressing the Taipings. In his own poems, Huang frequently adapted passages from Tseng's poems. Moreover, Huang used copies of the Tseng family letters as a text for instructing his children in writing; they, in turn, used the letters to instruct their children.[52]

The influence of these scholars probably accounts, at least partly, for Huang's critical attitude vis-à-vis the established schools of Confucian learning. Moreover, the fact that he did not have a master to follow contributed greatly to his development as an anti-authoritarian intellectual. In lamenting his misfortune in not having had a teacher, he stated. "I studied by myself in a clumsy way. I read at random in all sorts of books on classical studies, but I was not pleased with either Sung or Han learning. As a result, I could not make any distinguished contribution to scholarship."[53] His preference for independence rather than belonging to any school or faction characterized Huang's thinking and behavior throughout his life, not only as an intellectual but also as an official.

During the years when he was studying for examinations, Huang's eyes were opened to the realities of the world outside

China. He realized that China was facing a major crisis unprecedented in its history. Anxiety over foreign affairs was his central
concern and remained a dominant theme in his writings for the
rest of his life. In fact, his interest in foreign affairs soon led him
to decide to serve his country as a diplomat. The development
of his patriotism was significantly hastened by his trip to Hong
Kong in 1870.

Hong Kong was the first Westernized city Huang visited. He
was struck by the sight of high-rise buildings, illuminated streets,
stores filled with luxury goods, and busy entertainment centers.
He called the city a secular paradise. For him, Hong Kong was a
revelation because it was concrete evidence that rich and powerful
Europeans had advanced to China's waterfront. His patriotism
was aroused by the realization that this city was governed by
foreign officials and dominated by "blue-eyed and red-bearded"
merchants. It was shocking that the main streets were named for
British sovereigns and that the tallest building was dedicated to
the worship of the Christian god. Lamenting the presence of a
foreign city on Chinese soil, he wrote:

> *At the height of the Ch'ien-lung Emperor's glorious reign,*
> *Barbarian envoys demanded this terrain.*
> *I weep for the loss of this sweep of landscape.*
> *Who could so foolishly have given it up?*
> *The hillside was opened up, and the city grew.*
> *Tall building suddenly loomed, a dread mirage.*
> *On the hilltop, the wind flutters the Union Jack,*
> *Mistaking it for a Yellow Dragon flag.*[54]

For many years, Huang had criticized Confucian scholars for
indulging in the pedantic investigation of the past while remaining
indifferent to the problems of the present. Denouncing scholars
who limited their efforts to book learning, he wrote in 1865:

> *Scholars who never dare to venture out of doors*
> *Should not presume to talk about the questions of the day.*
> *To help us grasp the present is the point of history.*
> *To know the world around us, practice is the only way.*[55]

After his trip to Hong Kong, his criticism of conservative scholars centered on their ignorance of the world beyond China and their indulgence in petty competition for official positions. In a poem presented to a friend soon after his trip to Hong Kong, he wrote: "[Confucian scholars] do not realize that beyond the great oceans that surround China there are still more continents."[56]

Huang was keenly aware that the advancement of the Westerners undermined China's traditional prestige. When he traveled to Canton in 1873, he wrote a poem regretting that the tributary relationship between China and neighboring countries had been upset by the Western intrusion:

> *Once our coasts and inland fields were opened,*
> *Visiting Westerners came to frighten us.*
> *Long ago we built a border tower*
> *Dividing China from barbarians.*
> *There at the tower they paid homage and tribute*
> *To the Emperor of China, as the stars*
> *In all galaxies salute the great North Star.*
> *But the ocean currents shift from east to west.*
> *The tide keeps tribute missions from our shores.*
> *The only visitors that reach us now*
> *Are Western steeds descending from the sky.*

He then narrated the fateful events related to the Western advance, highlighting the British attack on the fort of Humen during the Opium War. He praised Admiral Kuan T'ien-p'ei, who died in defense of the fort, and Governor-General Yeh Ming-ch'en, who resisted the British entry to the city of Canton, was taken prisoner and sent to India, where he died. Huang's poem concluded with lamentation over the foreigners in Canton:

> *Kapok blossoms fall and their fuzz flies*
> *After a night rain on the hill of Ko-wu.*
> *Pheasants call sadly on the hillside paths.*
> *The city's buildings stand like hollow ghosts.*
>
> *Oh, Yang-c'heng,* city of sheep, named after*
> *A hermit who came to town on the back of a sheep.*

Han Yü cleared the land of hostile crocodiles,
But the Western whales will not be turned away.[57]

*Canton

In this poem, he presented the Western intrusion as an uncontrollable disaster which had fallen on China without warning. Probably it reflected the general opinion of the intellectuals in the Canton area who witnessed the Western aggression but were little informed of its background. In the early 1870s, the sources of information on Western countries were severely limited. The Translation Bureau of the Kiangnan Arsenal began publishing translations of Western books by 1871, but most of the subjects were science, engineering, and military technology. Although, at the T'ung-wen kuan, a printing press was established in 1873 to publish translations of foreign books, they were for distribution to officials, and the quantity was very limited. Missionary publications were essentially on Christianity. Among them *Chiao-hui hsin-pao* (*Church News*), a weekly magazine published by an American Protestant missionary beginning in 1868, contained some news on international affairs aside from Christian commentary. After his trip to Hong Kong, Huang began to read this magazine as well as translations from the Kiangnan Arsenal.[58]

Huang lived in Peking from 1874 through 1876. It was his first trip to north China, and this visit marked an important turning point in his life in many respects. In the early spring of 1874, he arrived at Tientsin by sea and traveled by land to Peking. The topography of north China, the homeland of his Hakka ancestors, was stern. On the dry, dusty land, poor villages were scattered, and the sight of the desperate beggars who swarmed around him was disheartening.[59] In Peking, he took the court examination without success, and stayed with his father, who at the time held a position in the Department of Agriculture of the Board of Revenue. He was acquainted with high-ranking officials in the metropolitan area who assisted him in developing his career. Ting Jih-ch'ang, a Hakka from Kwangtung province, when appointed Governor of Fukien, offered Huang a position on his staff. Huang declined because he was preparing for another examination in Peking. Among the officials Huang met during his visit to the north, Chang Yin-huan impressed him more than anyone else.

Chang was an unusual official who had trained himself to become an expert on foreign affairs. After failing a district examination, he never took another and spent much of his time in the study of foreign relations. He purchased the title of a student of the Imperial Academy and later the rank of Magistrate. In 1875, he was called to Chefoo to assist the Financial Commissioner of Shantung in coastal defense. While he was supervising the fortification project, Li Hung-chang came to the city to negotiate with Sir Thomas Wade, the British Minister to China, over the settlement of the Margary affair, an incident of anti-foreign hostility by the Chinese living on the China-Burma border which had resulted in the murder of a British Vice-Consul, August Margary.[60] Chang ably assisted Li in the negotiations, for which he received Li's praise.

During the summer of 1876 when the negotiations over the Margary affair were in progress, Huang chanced to travel to Chefoo, accompanying his father who was making an official trip to the city. There he met Li Hung-chang and Chang Yin-huan for the first time. Li recognized Huang as having unusual talent, and the admiration was reciprocated.[61] By that time, Li had established himself as the most powerful statesman in the empire and had been performing functions as the de facto Foreign Minister of China. Shortly after succeeding Tseng Kuo-fan as the Governor General of Chihli province in 1870, Li was concurrently appointed the Imperial Commissioner for the Northern Ports and then Grand Secretary. From his office at Tientsin, he exerted unprecedented influence over the national politics and foreign relations of China to the end of the century. Huang's entire official career was concurrent with the years of Li's prominence.

Huang established close personal ties with Chang Yin-huan. While in Chefoo, he often visited Chang and presented him with poems expressing his views on social and intellectual issues.

According to the contemporary practice, candidates for official positions had to secure recommendations from high-ranking officials. In addition to gaining Chang's recognition and support, Huang was undoubtedly influenced by Chang to implement his desire to serve China as a diplomat. An opportunity to make such a decision awaited Huang within a few months after his encounter with Chang. After Huang entered government service, Chang extended invaluable assistance to him to advance his position. Their close association lasted until Chang's tragic death in 1900.

Huang's experiences in the north enabled him to discuss international affairs from a broader and more realistic point of view. In the poems written while in the north, he no longer described the Westerners' intrusion as a calamity that had fallen on China out of the blue. Sadly, but with excitement over the broadening horizon, he accepted the reality that Westerners could come to China freely. After all, he reasoned, the Chinese and the barbarians lived on the same globe. "Arriving at Tientsin by boat" expressed his new view of the world:

> How separate and remote the Milky Way!
> How vast the sea that borders China's coast!
> Yet between China and barbarian lands
> No barrier. Barbarians and Chinese both
> Share the chances of this earth, this sky,
> People of hostile countries all afloat
> In one same sea, China a millet grain
> Among bushels.* When the giant phoenix
> Strikes the water, the south wind will blow
> And we'll be quickly covered in red dust.[62]

*Chuang-tzu: "China in a large ocean is like a millet grain in a granary."

In another poem on Tientsin, he noted that all men (Chinese and barbarians) were created out of yellow mud.[63] Thus, he perceived the world as a universal human community and recognized that relationships between East and West were inevitable.

While accepting the fact that the Westerners could not be

stopped from coming to China, Huang was worried over the Chinese handling of diplomatic problems. He was frustrated to realize that the Chinese were not adequately coping with the current realities of the world. In a poem on the Margary affair, he condemned the anti-foreign violence because it simply brought further humiliation to China. His criticism was directed not only against the xenophobic local populace who laid hands on the British diplomat, but also against the officials and intellectuals at large who indulged in the arrogant notion of the Middle Kingdom. "Stop clamoring 'Expel the barbarians',￼" he wrote; "The East and the West are one family."[64] Huang's words were obviously leveled at those who criticized Li Hung-chang's diplomacy as compromising. In fact, strong opinions had been voiced by officials who demanded a hard-line approach in diplomatic negotiations. They upheld idealistic Confucian principles and appointed themselves the guardians of the government's moral integrity. This trend among officials was later identified as the *ch'ing-liu* (pure current) and was even developed into a political clique.[65] Huang sympathized with Li Hung-chang, who had to confront the foreign negotiators with a realistic solution.

"Now the world is one," Huang wrote in 1876, in the poem on the Margary affair. "Stop being self-important about the Middle Kindgom."[66] He was among the earliest to challenge openly the concept of the Middle Kingdom, the self-image of China from antiquity. Around 1879, Hsueh Fu-ch'eng, then on the secretarial staff of Li Hung-chang, and Cheng Kuan-ying, a treaty-port intellectual, also expressed doubts about the Sinocentric world view. Hsueh wrote: "It has been two thousand years since the time of the Ch'in and Han dynasties. The world in which Chinese and barbarians were absolutely separated has turned into a world to which both China and the foreign countries belong."[67] Cheng Kuan-ying urged the Ch'ing government to abandon its claim to be the only legitimate ruler on the earth when he wrote: "The globe being round, since all live between heaven and earth, why should there be the forced distinction between barbarian and Chinese."[68]

Huang took the provincial examination given in Peking (*shun-t'ien hsiang-shih*) in the fall of 1876 and passed as the 141st. Thus, he finally acquired a *chü-jen* degree at the age of twenty-eight. He immediately purchased an official title of Intendant (*tao-yuan*, 4th rank) the highest position that could be purchased out of the capital. In view of the fact that there was a long waiting list of qualified candidates for official appointment, Huang did not expect to obtain an official position quickly through the regular route.[69] Toward the end of the Ch'ing, opportunities for official appointment for qualified candidates were not readily available. The total number of the holders of *chü-jen* degrees was estimated to have been around 10,000 at any time in the nineteenth century. The total number of local government positions filled by the officials between the 4th and 7th ranks (including circuit intendants, prefects, and chou and hsien magistrates) was always less than 2,000. To make the situation worse, the government resorted to the much-criticized practice of sales of official positions as a way to get through the financial crisis caused by the Taiping catastrophe. As a result, as many as about half the local posts in the empire designated for officials between the 4th and 7th ranks were occupied by those who qualified themselves through monetary contributions to the government. Under the circumstances, even those who qualified by passing the civil service examinations often facilitated their appointments and promotions by making contributions.[70]

In early 1877, Ho Ju-chang, a Hanlin editor and a Hakka from Ta-p'u, Kwangtung, was appointed Minister to Japan. He was a close friend of Huang's father, and Huang called him uncle. Before accepting the appointment, Ho recommended that Huang accompany him to Japan as a counselor. Ho accepted the post only after Huang consented to go with him. Around the same time, Ch'en Lan-p'in, a native of Kwangtung, was appointed Minister to the United States, and he also tried to persuade Huang to be his assistant. Huang's father did not approve of his son's going to the United States because of the distance; he preferred to have Huang go with his old friend, Ho Ju-chang.[71]

Huang's decision to join the diplomatic mission to Japan disappointed his relatives and friends, particularly Ho Ti-shan, the Provincial Director of Education who had selected Huang as a salaried student and then as a senior licentiate of the first degree. In the eyes of these people, Huang was a promising man capable of acquiring the highest degree in the examination system and of eventually becoming a Hanlin academician. It was a pity, they felt, for Huang to give up his promising future by going abroad.[72] In fact, in those days when the diplomatic service was not respected, an overseas assignment was regarded as a political dead end for a bureaucrat.[73]

In terms of formal official rank, the overseas positions were not low. The minister's post was for 2nd to 4th rank, and the counselor's for 4th to 6th rank, while a provincial governor was 2nd (B) and a district magistrate was 7th[74]. The ranks for overseas positions were, of course, regulated by considerations of diplomatic protocol and did not carry much prestige within China's internal bureaucratic system.

From the financial point of view, overseas service was very rewarding. Following the advice of Sir Robert Hart, the Inspector General of the Maritime Customs, the Ch'ing Government decided to finance the overseas legations amply. According to the regulation of 1877, the monthly salary of the Minister to Japan was 1,000 taels. The exact amount of Huang's salary is not clear, but the monthly salary of a counselor was between 240 and 400 taels.[75] In addition to salary, staff members of the legations were given an extra allowance for preparation for the trip to and from China, which amounted to approximately three months' salary each way.[76] Their stipends were very liberal in comparison to those of local government officials and their administrative assistants. According to the study of Ch'ü T'ung-tsu, the range of annual salary of a district magistrate was from 400 to 2,259 taels for the entire period of the Ch'ing. The salaries of administrative experts hired as private secretaries by magistrates were relatively high, and in the areas near Canton around 1800, varied from 1,500 to 1,900 taels per year.[77]

Financial advantage was certainly a major consideration when Huang accepted the appointment; his family had been in difficulties since the Taiping catastrophe. The salary of his father as a minor official in Peking was not high enough to support their large family. Being the eldest son, Huang anticipated the responsibility of supporting the entire household; hence it was important for him to secure an official post as soon as possible. If he had chosen to pursue the highest degree, he would have had to spend an indefinite expanse of time in preparing for the examination. Moreover, his chance of success was small because of the excessive competition. In addition, Huang was afraid his handwriting did not conform to the officially required style, which called for fine, restrained strokes, the outline of each character forming a uniform square. Huang's syle was after the fashion of Su Shih, a Sung dynasty poet, and was characterized by rhythmic, bold strokes that stretched out freely.[78]

The most crucial reason Huang chose to serve as a diplomat, however, was his conviction that diplomacy was of first importance for China. Like Chang Yin-huan, who did not follow the conventional route for success in bureaucracy, Huang did not put primary emphasis on the pursuit of a successful career as a scholar-official. Instead, he chose to serve his country in the way he felt was the most useful. From an early age, he had been critical of the narrow-minded careerism of Confucian scholars and had admired realist statesmen of the past, such as Chia I of the Han and Chiang T'ung of the Western Chin, who offered practical solutions to the problems of their times.[79] Huang's decision grew from his disenchantment with conservative scholarship, his disappointment with the examination system, and his strong sense of patriotism, as well as from his concern over the financial need of his family.

For a Chinese official, acceptance of a position abroad meant a great disruption in family life. Huang had to leave his wife, who was obliged to look after his parents and children at home. Thereafter, except for short periods, his wife lived separately from Huang most of the time until his retirement from official life.

Huang wrote a poem addressed to his wife, expressing his feelings when leaving home for Japan:

> *Ten years together without strife or sorrow,*
> *Today we part. Tomorrow I'll be far.*
> *Do you know the famous Azuma Bridge*
> *From which a traveler looked back toward home?*
> *How many autumns shall I long for you*
> *From that bridge, seeing nothing except*
> *Willows swaying in the twilight breeze?*[80]

TWO

Discovery of Japan: The Eastern Frontier of the Chinese World

Japan was the first Asian country to establish diplomatic relations with China on the principle of the modern multi-state system. By the time the two countries concluded the Friendship Treaty in 1871, each had already signed treaties with Western nations. The Sino-Japanese Friendship Treaty, modeled after those concluded with the Western Powers, was undertaken at the initiative of the Japanese, who were eager to Westernize their domestic institutions and foreign relations. The Chinese rather reluctantly responded to the Japanese proposal. Based on the provisions of the treaty, Japan sent its Minister, Yanagiwara Sakimitsu, to Peking in 1874; however, not until late 1877 did China's diplomatic representative arrive in Japan. The exchange of diplomats was a significant indication of China's willingness to renew diplomatic exchanges with Japan (once a part of the traditional Chinese world) in accordance with the European concept of international relations.

As a member of China's first delegation to Japan, Huang Tsun-hsien sustained various kinds of cultural shock. Japan's adoption of Western-style diplomatic protocol greeted him the moment he disembarked. Japan's determination to Westernize all facets of its national life astonished and disturbed him, primarily because the Chinese still regarded Japan as part of their cultural world, although they were well aware of pervasive differences. In ancient times, Japan had adopted the Chinese writing system, calendar, and Confucianism; the continued demand for Chinese books, fine arts, handicrafts, and silk at the Nagasaki trade center was surely a sign that the Japanese still shared Chinese cultural values. That Japan had not been China's tributary state for many centuries did not seem to have affected the Chinese perception of Japan's position in the world prior to the mid-nineteenth century.[1]

Huang's writings on Japan provide us with a firsthand impression of Japan by a man whose own culture stemmed from a common root, a root that included indigenous elements and those borrowed from outside. He was a fluent writer, able to set down his observations in detail and with amazing speed; his first book on Japan was published within two years after his arrival. What were his sources of information? With whom did he associate in Japan? As a Confucian literatus, how did he react to the state of Confucianism in Japan? How did his background as a Hakka affect his views of Japanese culture? How did he evaluate the modernization process in early Meiji Japan? What was his reaction to the constitutional movement in Japan during the late 1870s and early 1880s? To what extent did he understand Japanese problems in modernizing ethical as well as material life? How did he feel about China's neighbor becoming a powerful nation? In particular, how did he react to Japanese aggression in China's border regions? The answers to these vital questions are the subject of this chapter and the two following.

THE FIRST CHINESE LEGATION IN TOKYO

China's first diplomatic mission to Japan was headed by Minister Ho Ju-chang (Imperial Commissioner to Japan) and Vice-Minister Chang Ssu-kuei. A thirty-nine-year-old scholar who had held a prestigious position at the Hanlin academy, Ho had no experience as a diplomat, but he had been recommended by Li Hung-chang, whose influence in the management of diplomatic affairs in China was great. Li regarded Ho's interest in foreign affairs as unusual for a Hanlin academician. It was reported that, whenever Ho traveled to Shanghai or Tientsin, he visited missionaries in order to learn about Western countries.[2]

Chang Ssu-kuei came from a wealthy gentry family in Ningpo who had engaged in trade. He was among the first to use steamships for business inside China. During the Taiping Rebellion, his ships were requisitioned by the imperial troops, and thereafter he established contact with high-ranking government officials. He purchased an academic degree in 1863 and joined the secretarial staff of Tseng Kuo-fan, who directed the campaign against the Taipings at Anking. Chang's name was well known to the Japanese; he had contributed a preface to W. A. P. Martin's Chinese translation of Wheaton's *Elements of International Law*, published in China in 1864 and reprinted in Japan the following year. Chang was sixty-one years old at the time he arrived in Japan.[3]

Huang Tsun-hsien's post as Counselor (*ts'an-tsan*) ranked next to the Vice-Minister.[4] His duties were perhaps comparable to those of a private secretary in the local government. He wrote most of the letters sent in Ho Ju-chang's name to the Tsungli Yamen and Li Hung-chang. Liao Hsi-en was the correspondence secretary who copied Huang's draft letters, and Shen Wen-ying was in charge of handling books and literary writings. Most of the seventeen staff members of the legation came from Kwangtung or Chekiang province, as did the Minister and the Vice-Minister. Aside from the staff in Tokyo, there were consuls who would be stationed at Yokohama and Kobe. The relatives of some delegates followed them to Japan. Huang brought his younger brother Tsun-k'ai and his relatives Liang Chü-shih and Huang Hsi-ch'üan; Ho Ju-chang brought his younger brother and a thirteen-year-old son; Chang Ssu-kuei was accompanied by his grandson. No one brought a wife or a daughter or any female member of his family.[5]

Among the staff members was an American, Dr. Divie Bethune McCartee (1820–1900), who had been in China more than twenty years. He had originally come as a medical doctor under the auspices of the Board of Foreign Missions of the Presbyterian Church; later, he became the United States Consul at Ningpo and Chefoo and the Vice-Consul at Shanghai. From 1872–1877 he taught at Kaisei Gakkō, the government school of foreign languages in Tokyo, and was the English-language interpreter at the Chinese Legation until May 1880.[6]

The Chinese delegation left Shanghai aboard the *Hai-an* on November 27, 1877, and arrived at Nagasaki on November 30. They were greeted with a 21-gun salute, their introduction to Western-style ritual as performed in Japan. Ho Ju-chang recorded the event in his diary with a special note. They stayed in Nagasaki for three days, where they were enthusiastically welcomed by the Overseas Chinese. There were about 1,000 Chinese living in Nagasaki. Some were said to be descendants of the Ming loyalists who had taken refuge there at the time of the Manchu conquest in the seventeenth century, but most had come after the port was opened to Western traders in 1859. The leaders of the community entertained the diplomats at their guild house, and used these social occasions to inform their guests about conditions in Sino-Japanese trade, Japanese social customs, and the recent rebellion of Saigō Takamori.[7]

En route to Yokohama, the *Hai-an* passed Hirado, Shimonoseki, and Matsuyama. The passengers enjoyed the scenery of the Inland Sea area. At this time, Ho Ju-chang noted that this region was the home of the well-known historian, Rai Jō (San'yō, 1780–1832). Rai's books were read in China for their excellent classical Chinese. The envoys went ashore at Kobe, where they and a large crowd viewed an ancient ritual performed by local Chinese residents. The city was decorated with flags and lanterns in honor of the guests. From Kobe, the envoys made short trips to Osaka, Kashiwabara, and Minatogawa to visit historical sites. They were particularly interested in the shrines: one was dedicated to Toyotomi Hideyoshi (1536–1598), a man the Chinese considered evil because he attempted to conquer Korea and China; another shrine honored Sugawara Michizane (845–903), a Confucian scholar-statesman who was deified as a god of scholarship; and last, the shrine to Kusunoki Masashige (?–1336), the epitome of a loyal minister. Huang was much impressed by the story of Kusunoki Masashige and compared him to Yueh Fei of the Sung dynasty. On December 16, the party arrived at Yokohama, where they were welcomed by the enthusiastic Chinese residents.[8]

Despite the detailed instructions and briefings they had received from Li Hung-chang and the Japanese Minister in Peking, the envoys were surprised to discover how every aspect of diplomatic protocol in Japan was Westernized. When Ho, Chang, and Huang were given a royal audience on December 28 to present their credentials, they found the Emperor in Western dress. Furthermore, he was attended by only the three officials who participated in the ceremony of audience. They noted that the audience hall in the temporary palace in Akasaka was very small and had little furniture or decoration. The ceremony itself was quite short and informal. The delegates bowed to the Emperor and presented their credentials; he, in turn, handed the letter to an official. Then the Emperor read aloud a prepared statement from a paper he took out of his pocket. The Chinese thought his voice was rich and resonant, but they understood nothing he said. That afternoon, they were introduced to Sanjō Sanetomi, Iwakura Tomomi, Ōkubo Toshimichi, and other government officials. On New Year's Day 1878, Ho, Chang, and Huang visited the palace again, in company with Western diplomats. The New Year's greeting was also simple; it consisted of bowing and the reading of messages. The Chinese noted especially that, at the banquet given by the Foreign Minister, Western food was served and Western music played.[9] On these formal occasions, the Chinese delegates wore their official gowns of silk damask embroidered in bright colors. It is said that their costumes stood out vividly against the black and white attire of the rest of the diplomatic corps.[10]

The Chinese rented an old Buddhist temple in the Shiba district of Tokyo for the legation office and the living quarters for the staff. After about a year, they moved to a larger building in Kōjimachi (present-day Nagata chō).[11] The legation became the center for Sino-Japanese cultural exchanges and attracted many Japanese literati. Since this was the first group of scholar-officials from China, the Japanese literati welcomed them enthusiastically.

Huang and his colleagues regarded their cultural association with the Japanese as an important part of their mission. They enjoyed socializing with the Japanese and gave generously of their time in commenting on their visitors' use of classical Chinese.

THE JAPANESE FRIENDS OF HUANG TSUN-HSIEN

During the early Meiji period, there was a growing tendency in Japan to denigrate traditional learning; however, the authority of classical Chinese studies (*kangaku*) was still great. Throughout the Meiji period, the ability to write in classical Chinese was a basic requirement for educated men, including those who studied Western subjects. Commenting on the continuing importance of Chinese studies in Meiji Japan, the literary critic Kinoshita Hyō wrote:

> The prestige of *kangaku* was not easily shaken. For the educated people, the only acceptable poetry and prose were those written in classical Chinese. The great masters of Chinese learning like Yoshino Kinryō, Shimada Kōson, Nakamura Keiu, Shigeno Seisai, Kawada Yōkō, and Shinobu Joken were respected as the authorities on literature . . . Even though numerous schools for Western learning appeared all of a sudden like mushrooms after a rain, traditional private schools for classical Chinese learning continued to enjoy prosperity. Most of the students were enrolled in such schools, although they were commuting to Western-style schools.[12]

Ōmachi Keigetsu, another contemporary writer, regarded the Meiji era as the greatest in the history of classical Chinese poetry (*kanshi*) in Japan. "Ever since Chinese books were imported to Japan a thousand years ago," he wrote, "there has been no era like the Meiji, when the art of composing Chinese poems reached very high standards."[13]

Most of those closely associated with Huang were established historians, scholars of the classics, distinguished poets and writers, calligraphers, Shinto priests, and some former feudal lords who led leisurely lives in Tokyo. All were well-versed in classical Chinese literature. As Huang confessed later, his contacts were mostly limited to the circles of the old-style literati. Because of their urge to associate with the Chinese literati, visitors were found in the living quarters of the legation almost every day. The common literary culture shared by the Japanese and Chinese made their social interchanges lively. No similar gatherings occurred in the European or American legations, despite a great curiosity about Western culture among the Japanese.

Huang and his colleagues were often invited to join the literati at a favorite restaurant or in a private dwelling. For large banquets, Nakamuraya at Ryōgoku or Kōyōkan at Shiba were popular. For lesser occasions, they patronized small restaurants that offered a more intimate atmosphere. Most of these were in Ueno, Asakusa, and near the elegant residential areas along the Sumida River, where many of the literary men and retired daimyo lived. Shinobazu Lake in Ueno was called "Small West Lake," after the famous lake in China, because of its scenic beauty and romantic atmosphere. It was one of Huang's favorite places to spend the long, hot summer nights. On the banks of the Sumida, which they called "Ink Water" (its name is a homonym of ink from inkstone), there were hundreds of cherry trees. Huang felt that it was like strolling in paradise to walk under the tunnel of cherry blossoms. Sometimes he and his friends held parties on a boat on the Sumida.[14]

Conversations between the Chinese and Japanese literati were conducted mostly in writing. The Japanese were highly trained in reading and writing classical Chinese, but they did not understand spoken Chinese. Although there were interpreters in the legation, the Japanese preferred to communicate in writing. They disapproved of the young Chinese interpreter who had learned his Japanese in Tientsin; he had a heavy Nagasaki accent and lacked a proper classical education. Writing brush in hand, the Chinese and their guests "conversed" on paper, and so highly did the Japanese value Chinese calligraphy that fragmentary bits of handwritten conversations were preserved by many of the visitors. However, only Ōkōchi Teruna (1848–1882), the former lord of Takasaki, was so devoted to his Chinese friends that he systematically saved all the records of his conversations with them. After each visit, he noted in red ink on the conversation sheets the date

and place of the meeting and identified the participants and their
writings. He bound the sheets of the conversations held between
1875 and 1882, which totaled about 100 volumes (each volume
contained about 60 sheets). These volumes were preserved at
Heirinji, Ōkōchi's family temple in Tokyo, where they were discovered by Sanetō Keishū in 1943. They provide valuable first-
hand information on the talks between Huang and his Japanese
friends who happened to belong to Ōkōchi's literary circle.[15]

What kind of man was Ōkōchi, the major recorder of Huang's
friendly association with the Japanese? As lord of Takasaki,
Ōkōchi had been eager to modernize the military system of his
domain and was interested in becoming acquainted with Westerners. He studied military art with a French adviser who had been
hired by the *bakufu*. But after he retired, Ōkōchi preferred to
share the pleasures of wine and poetry with the Chinese literati.[16]
Beginning in 1875, he kept the records of his conversations in
classical Chinese held with the Korean residents in Tokyo. In
1877, he met Wang Chih-pen, who had come from the Ningpo area
to Tokyo about 1875 as a Chinese-language instructor at a private
school. His relative Wang Jen-kan owned a trading firm in Asakusa
that dealt in books and stationery. When the Chinese delegation
arrived, Wang Chih-pen was recruited for the legation's staff and
served for a short period. Through Wang's introduction, Ōkōchi
met Shen Wen-ying on December 23, 1877, Ho Ju-chang and
Chang Ssu-kuei on February 25, 1878, and Huang Tsun-hsien on
March 3.[17]

Having been given a peerage then put on the shelf, Ōkōchi was
not interested in politics. He had few acquaintances among the new
leaders in the government, nor was he in the circles of established
scholars. He often requested his Chinese friends to introduce him
to the well-known literary figures who visited the legation. For example, through Shen Wen-ying he met a master of Chinese poetry,
Mori Shuntō, and the historian Aoyama Nobutoshi. Obviously,
Ōkōchi was not the best recorder for Huang on political or scholarly
subjects.

Huang's conversations with Ōkōchi were mostly on such topics as the change of seasons, poetry, calligraphy, food, parties, manners and customs, and wine and women. Ōkōchi liked to talk about sex and romance and enjoyed teasing his Chinese friends about their relationships with Japanese women, mostly their maids. He frequently urged a reluctant Huang to engage a concubine and wrote a treatise on Japanese concubinage for him. Huang collected a great deal of information from this romantic man on Japanese women's lives and on the customs of everyday life.

Ōkōchi's records of conversations give us a little information about some of Huang's visitors. On one occasion, Ōkōchi rescued a few conversation sheets used by Huang and Aoyama Nobutoshi from a wastebasket and preserved them among his own records.[18]

Of his Japanese friends, Huang most highly esteemed Aoyama Nobutoshi (1820–1906) and Shigeno Yasutsugu (1827–1910). Huang's understanding of Japanese history and the interpretation of the Meiji Restoration was decisively influenced by these historians who served in the Bureau of the Compilation of History of the Meiji Government. Aoyama's family had been official historians in Mito for generations. His father, Aoyama Nobuyuki (1776–1843), had been president of the Shōkōkan, the institute for the compilation of the *Dai Nihon shi* (History of great Japan, begun in 1657 by order of Tokugawa Mitsukuni, lord of Mito). Aoyama greatly esteemed Rai San'yō, whose *Nihon gaishi* (Unofficial history of Japan) and *Nihon seiki* (Record of the governments of Japan) followed the same ideology as the *History of Great Japan*. Both San'yō and Mito historians discussed the legitimacy of the imperial line as the central theme of Japanese history, basing their assumptions on the Neo-Confucian doctrine of "great righteousness." Later writers interpreted their work as veiled criticism of the Tokugawa regime; hence these volumes became the source of inspiration for the loyalists in the restoration movement. Huang's conversations with Aoyama concentrated on scholarly topics, as the fragmentary records indicate. Huang once told Ōkōchi that Aoyama was the greatest scholar he had met in Japan, that his personality was austere, and that he was very different from a versatile man of letters like Ōkōchi.[19]

Shigeno Yasutsugu from Satsuma studied at the Shōheikō, the most prestigious academic institution under the *bakufu*. After the restoration, he served in the Ministry of Education. In 1875, he was appointed Vice-President of the Bureau of Historical Compilation and directed the compiling of the *Dai Nihon hennenshi* (Chronological history of great Japan). Later, in 1888, he was appointed professor at Tokyo University, where he played an important role as a founder of modern historical studies in Japan. As an active participant in literary circles, Shigeno organized the Kyūusha (Old Friends Society), which comprised about ten literati, including Oka Senjin. In 1879, he founded another group, the Reitakusha (Mutual Benefit Study Society), whose members met for the purpose of improving their literary style. The Chinese diplomats participated in the monthly meetings of this society.[20]

An official of the Bureau of Historical Compilation, Miyajima Seiichirō (1838–1911), lived next door to the legation after it moved to Kōjimachi. As a bureaucrat in the central government, he was closely associated with Ōkubo Toshimichi. As early as 1872, he submitted a draft constitution in line with Ōkubo's idea of gradual progress toward constitutional monarchy.[21] Undoubtedly, Huang's understanding of the constitutional movement during the 1870s and 1880s was structured by the information he received from officials like Miyajima. Huang supported the basic approach of the government leaders in this matter. Also, Huang appreciated Miyajima's artistic sensibilities, noting in a poem that Miyajima had studied Chinese painting with Shen Nan-p'in in Nagasaki and that he and Huang frequently discussed poetics.[22]

Aside from the above-mentioned scholars who were engaged in compiling histories for the government, there were other scholars and men of letters whom Huang saw frequently and with whom he enjoyed light-hearted conversation. Oka Senjin, Gamō Shigeaki, Ishikawa Ei, and Kametani Kō were all older than Huang and had come from samurai families who held hereditary positions in their feudatories. Some had been active loyalists but did not gain positions in the new government. On the whole, their political views were conservative and they disliked the social changes caused by Western influences after the restoration. Huang sympathized with their sentiments. Because of their education in Confucian learning and their respect for Chinese scholarship, they were congenial associates for him.

Oka Senjin (1833–1914) from Sendai was a well-known scholar of Chinese learning who had studied at the Shōheikō and had participated in the loyalist movement. His history of the Meiji Restoration centered on the loyalists' activities. He was concerned with the contemporary international scene and advocated strengthening Japan as a protection against aggression by the Western powers, particularly Russia. He emphasized the importance of military power over economic well-being and embraced a rudimentary pan-Asian ideology. While admitting the value of Western technology, he maintained that the Confucian ethic should be the spiritual basis of the government and society. He was indignant that his contemporaries scorned Confucian learning as outdated. Huang agreed with Oka on this point and often told him, "In the spiritual realm [*hsing-erh-shang*], the teachings of Confucius and Mencius are perfect; in the material realm [*hsing-erh-hsia*], the scholarship of Europe and America is comprehensive."[23]

Gamō Shigeaki (1833–1901) was another scholar of the Chinese classics. In an essay on the Japanese spirit, he lamented the process of Westernization and praised the spirit of the loyalists who had brought about the Meiji Restoration. He was one of those who most frequently saw Huang.[24]

Ishikawa Ei (1833–1918) was a poet and a scholar of the Chinese classics. He published several textbooks on the art of writing and drawing. His *Nihon bunshō kihan* (Examples of good writing by Japanese) was a popular textbook of writing in classical Chinese. Ho Ju-chang wrote the preface for this book, and Huang Tsun-hsien and Shen Wen-ying also contributed.[25]

Kametani Kō (1838–1913) was highly regarded by Huang for his talent as a writer. Huang once told Ishikawa and Ōkōchi that he esteemed most the writings of Kametani; in his opinion, the work of Shigeno Yasutsugu and Kawada Yōkō would not change much after ten years, but Kametani's literary future was very promising. Kametani had come from Tsushima to join the loyalists in Kyoto and had followed Sanjō Sanetomi to Tokyo at the restoration. Thereafter, he studied briefly under Yasui Sokken (1799–1876), then taught at Tokyo University for a short time before retiring to become a private teacher.[26]

Huang was impressed with the literary achievements of the Japanese; he wrote that some of their poems were good enough to stand alongside those of the T'ang and Sung poets.[27] His close friend Mori Rochoku (1818–1888) was regarded by many people as the undisputed master of Chinese poetry. Beginning in 1875, Mori had published *Shimbun shi* (Modern poetry), the most prestigious journal of Chinese poetry in early Meiji Japan. Huang thought highly of Mori's son, Mori Kainan (1868–1911), who was about sixteen when Huang first met him. Huang believed that he possessed qualities of poetic genius and expressed great expectations for his future. Actually, Kainan did become one of the great poets of the Meiji era.[28]

Nakamura Masanao (Keiu, 1832–1891) and his associates in his literary society, Dōjinsha, entertained Huang at their gatherings. Their journal, *Dōjinsha bungagu zasshi,* published Huang's writings and commentary on them.[29] The society included a number of established scholars and well-known literary figures: Shigeno Yasutsugu, Mukōyama Kōson, Kametani Kō, Kawada Yōkō, Mishima Chūshū, Naitō Chisō, and Oka Senjin. Other members were the journalist Kurimoto Joun, editor of the daily newspaper *Yūbin hōchi,* and Takezoe Shin'ichirō, a diplomat who was later a key figure in Japanese diplomacy in Korea and China. We shall discuss Huang's relations with Nakamura Keiu later in some detail because of his unique position as the only scholar of Western learning with whom Huang was closely associated.

Huang met many other literary figures. Those who either conversed with Huang and Ōkōchi (to become part of the latter's records) or received mention in Huang's poems were Uemura Seigi, Uchimura Nobuyuki, Kihara Genrei, Ōnuma Atsushi,

Namma Kōki, Ono Chōgen, Ro Gempō, Iwaya Shū, and Kusakabe Tōsaku. Huang singled out these men for their excellence in poetry and calligraphy. Naruse On was especially praised for his calligraphy; his tablet was chosen to be hung in Huang's studio, Jen-ching-lu.[30] Katō Ki, the chief priest of the Minatogawa shrine and an authority on imperial court music of Japan, had studied under Aizawa Seishisai in Mito. He was an ardent supporter of the loyalist movement.[31]

Some top leaders of the government also met socially with the Chinese literati. Itō Hirobumi was remembered by Huang as a chain smoker and a clever man who was well versed in both old objects of art and contemporary world affairs. When Huang visited the house of Ōkuma Shigenobu, he was shown a Sung period painting. At Ōkubo Toshimichi's (assassinated in 1878) house, he saw a hanging scroll that was supposedly the work of Yueh Fei of the Southern Sung. Soejima Taneomi, who held a titular office in the Ministry of the Imperial Household, often attended social affairs with the Chinese.[32]

Some junior officials in the foreign ministry became Huang's friends. Among them was Miyamoto Shōichi, the major negotiator for the supplementary treaty with Korea in 1876. The terms of this treaty, which took advantage of the Korean officials' lack of sophistication in conducting high-level diplomatic negotiations, made harsh demands on Korea. No customs duties would be exacted from the Japanese, and their currency would be the medium of exchange for commercial transactions between the two countries.[33] Whether or not Huang knew these details, he did not mention them in his poem in reminiscence of Miyamoto. He only noted that Miyamoto had been his companion on the annual visit to the Chōkaen garden during the cherry blossom season. They always took along a bottle of sake and enjoyed stimulating conversations. Miyamoto's discussion of the Crimean War impressed Huang with the imminent danger of a Russian advance on East Asia.[34]

Huang praised the writing skills of Ishihata Tei, a staff member of the Foreign Ministry. In 1871, when Ishihata and Yanagiwara

Sakimitsu went to China, he had kept a travel diary that provided valuable information on the negotiation of the first Sino-Japanese treaty.[35]

Among the young government officials who were Huang's close friends was Narahara (Inoue) Nobumasa (1863–1900), with whom Huang would have a later and fateful encounter. By government order, Narahara studied Chinese with Ho Ju-chang and Huang at the Chinese Legation from January 1879 to 1882. When Ho left Japan in 1882, Narahara followed him to China, where he studied under the great T'ung-ch'eng scholar Yü Yueh for several years. Thereafter, he conducted a field survey and compiled a comprehensive report on China's geography, economy, and social conditions. After the Sino-Japanese War, he was a member of the Japanese delegation that negotiated with the Chinese government for the concession in Soochow, which Japan obtained as a result of the war. During the negotiations in Shanghai, Narahara found Huang on the other side of the table. In 1898, when the coup d'état against reformers endangered Huang's life, Narahara, now a staff member of the Japanese Legation in Peking, endeavored to rescue him. Narahara was one of the most promising China specialists in the Japanese government. He met an untimely end in Peking while defending the legation during the Boxer uprising.[36]

Miyajima Daihachi, a son of Miyajima Seiichirō, also studied Chinese at the legation. Later, he continued his studies in China at the prestigious Lien-ch'ih Academy at Pao-ting and at the Liang-Hu Academy in Wu-ch'ang. After returning home in 1898, he opened an institute of Chinese language, Zenrin Shoin, which remained the largest center of Chinese language education in Japan until 1941.[37] Thus, the Chinese Legation in Tokyo provided language-training opportunities for Japan's first-generation China experts.

The Chinese Legation also attracted a new generation of Sinophiles who embraced pan-Asian ambitions. They were precursors of the adventurers who attempted to make their careers by promoting Japanese expansion in China in later decades. Among the frequent visitors to the legation was Sone Toshitora (1847–1910), the principal organizer of an early pan-Asian organization, Kōakai (Raise Asia Society), in whose activities Huang participated to a limited extent. Although Sone was not quite accepted by Ōkōchi Teruna as a true literatus, the Chinese did not reject him. Later, we shall discuss the involvement of the Chinese diplomats in this organization and their reaction to the pan-Asian movement in early Meiji Japan. Another Sinophile, Kawashima Naniwa (1865–1922), a hero among the Japanese adventurers on the Chinese continent, began his practical training in Chinese by frequenting the legation, where he appears to have started as a messenger boy carrying notes from one room to another.[38]

It is ironic that the Chinese Legation educated the future agents of Japanese imperialism in the Chinese language. Until the early 1880s, however, the pan-Asian ideology in Japan was so vague that it was difficult to distinguish the pan-Asian radicals from serious students like Narahara Nobumasa.

No survey of Huang's acquaintances in Japan would be complete without mention of his contact with the Chinese community. The status of the Chinese in early Meiji Japan reflected the balance of power between China and Japan and Japan's inferior position in international trade. Before 1894, the Chinese in Japan were among the privileged foreigners who enjoyed extraterritoriality under consular jurisdiction. (The Japanese in China had the same privileges.) In Japan's treaty ports, Chinese merchants shared prosperity and prestige with Westerners. During the first decade of the Meiji period, 95 percent of the export-import trade of Japan was handled by foreign traders, since the inexperienced Japanese traders were unable to compete with them. Most of the European and American merchants who came to Japan had been trading in China's treaty ports; thus, when they extended their operations to Japan, they brought their Chinese compradors with them. In the wake of the compradors came merchants, artisans, and laborers to live in the foreign settlements in the treaty ports. As a result, the Chinese population in the foreign settlements outnumbered the Westerners. In Yokohama in 1880, there were 2,169 Chinese in a total alien population of 3,280. Chinese merchants prospered as middlemen between Western traders and Japanese dealers. In addition, they monopolized the trade between Japan and China, which had a long history. The Chinese merchants' trading network between Japan and the central and south China coast had been established during the days when Nagasaki was the only port open for trade. The wealth and high social status of the Chinese merchants in Yokohama were illustrated in the colored wood-block prints depicting the scenes of banquets at fancy restaurants where Westerners, geisha, and Chinese in colorful silk gowns mingled.[39]

There was another side to the Chinese community. The majority of Chinese residents in Yokohama were laborers or were unemployed. The crowded Chinatown that developed inside the foreign settlement was associated with filth, noise, and crime, with an abundance of opium-smoking, gambling, prostitution and the purchase of children from poor Japanese for sale in China. The scenes in Chinatown fanned up feelings of contempt toward the Chinese among the Japanese populace, who at the same time envied and resented the prosperous Chinese merchants. However, there was no serious racial antagonism yet, and intermarriage was quite common.[40]

Huang and his colleagues visited Yokohama from time to time. At the festival of Kuan Yü, the central deity in the Chinese guild house, the Minister and the Vice-Minister attended the celebration. Since the community in Yokohama was predominantly Cantonese, the leaders of the guild house were also Cantonese, which facilitated their association with the legation staff, who came from the same province. The leaders of the Yokohama community, in turn, visited the legation and occasionally participated in the conversations with the Japanese literati. Ch'en Yü-ch'ih, one of the founders of the guild house in 1868, did calligraphy for the tablet of the Mimeguri shrine, which was in the neighborhood of Ōkōchi Teruna's residence on the bank of the Sumida.[41] The fragmentary records indicate that the contact between the Chinese diplomats and the Chinese residents of Yokohama was close. Perhaps Huang gained information on Japanese traders and Japan's export-import business from them. No doubt the position of the overseas Chinese in early Meiji Japan supported Huang's view of Japan as a part of the world that was congenial to the Chinese.

MISCELLANEOUS POEMS ON JAPAN *AND* TREATISES ON JAPAN

No sooner was Huang settled in Toyko than he began to collect information on various aspects of Japanese society and culture for the purpose of writing a book. He was motivated by a sense of mission to report on Japan to his countrymen. In addition, it was his considered opinion that the Chinese could no longer afford to indulge in their arrogant indifference to the outside world, especially to that country separated from China by no more than a narrow stretch of water. Pointing out how insufficient China's knowledge of Japan had been, Huang wrote:

> Japan was already mentioned in the *Shan-hai ching* (The classic of mountain and sea). Nevertheless, descriptions of the geography of Japan in the dynastic histories are very inaccurate: out of ten statements, barely one is correct. As to monographs on Japan, we have only the *Ch'ou-hai t'u-pien* (Illustrated treatises for defense of the coast), but its description of Satsuma is based on hearsay. After the T'ang, there are many poems which were written for Japanese monks who were departing for home after studying in China, but nothing about Japanese life is mentioned in these. The Japanese have had written history since ancient times, but the Chinese could not get copies, owing to the strict ban on overseas trade. Only Chu Chu-ch'a acquired a copy of the *Azuma kagami* [History of the eastern provinces]. This ban is one of the reasons why the Chinese did not have the opportunity to learn about Japan.
>
> Men of letters in our country never traveled to Japan, and those who did could not read Japanese. In view of this fact, there is little wonder that Chinese books on Japan are full of mistakes.[42]

In contrast to the scarcity of Chinese writings on Japan, Huang pointed out, Japanese books on China were numerous enough to fill a room. To provide his countrymen with reliable information on Japan, Huang decided to compile *Jih-pen-kuo chih* (Treatises on Japan). In the preface to this work, Huang compared

his duties as Counselor of the legation to those of the officials in
the ancient Chou court who were responsible for compiling
gazetteers on feudal principalities:

> The duty of the Director of Emissary Affairs [*hsiao-hsing-jen*] de-
> scribed in *Chou Rites* was to go to various countries and in one book
> report to the King on the condition of the people's lives. Another
> book would concern the propriety or lack of propriety in their observa-
> tion of rituals, government, education, and administration of punish-
> ments. The Court Historian of the Exterior [*wai-shih-shih*], who
> belonged to the Spring Official, was in charge of compiling treatises
> on various countries. . .
>   I would assume that a Counselor of the present day would be [equiv-
> alent to] the Director of Emissary Affairs or the Court Historian of
> the Exterior of ancient times. The Ambassador, who holds the imperial
> flag and rides in a four-horse carriage, has to attend to his duties and
> has no time to spend on such matters as writing. Unless his subordinates
> engage in the task of collecting information on the country, how can
> the court's aim to investigate the country be fulfilled?[43]

The form Huang adopted to organize his report on Japan
was a well-established tradition in Chinese historiography.
Treatises on Korea, Ryukyu, and Vietnam had been compiled
by imperial commissioners who visited these tributary states of
China.[44] In general, Huang followed the pattern of those
treatises. Nevertheless, the content of Huang's book was quite
different fron any of the previous compendia. The first piece
in Huang's book, the "Treatise on Royal Succession," was a
standard entry in traditional words on China's tributaries.
However, in this treatise, Huang discussed not only the lines
of imperial succession but also the political history of contemporary Japan. In place of a treatise on investiture and
tributes, the most important of the treatises on a tributary
state, Huang originated the "Treatise on the Relationship with
Neighboring States" to discuss Japan's relations with China
and Western countries. The rest of his treatises dealt with
Astronomy, Geography, Government Offices, Food and Money
(economy), Military Systems, Criminal Codes, Scholarship,
Rites and Customs, Products (agricultural), and Handicrafts.

These were standard titles of treatises in the dynastic histories of China and were not usually used for treatises on tributaries. Perhaps Huang's adoption of these titles for his treatises on Japan indicated his serious commitment to thorough research on Japanese institutions and culture, which he treated with respect.

At first glance, Huang's treatises appear to be following the conventions of traditional historiography. Compared with previously written treatises on tributary countries, however, the modernity of Huang's approach is striking. While the compilers of the treatises on tributary states were primarily concerned with the fulfillment of their tributary obligations to China, their progress in Confucian scholarship, and perfection in Confucian rituals, as well as distinguished individuals and peculiar local products, Huang attempted a comprehensive survey of historical, political, economic, military, and cultural aspects of Japanese society. Moreover, Huang valued quantitative information.

Huang skillfully organized his observations on contemporary Japan, including its modernization, into the traditional form of a treatise. He added critical comments as the introduction or conclusion for each treatise, after the style of Ssu-ma Ch'ien (145?–90? B.C.), who wrote comments at the end of each chapter of his *Shih chi* (Records of the historian). Just as Ssu-ma Ch'ien began his comments with "The Grand Historian says," Huang used an introductory phrase, "The Court Historian of the Exterior says." His extensive comments are the most valuable source of information on Huang's views of modernization as well as of his views of Japan.

Although Huang had a model in Chinese historiography on which to pattern his treatises, there was no Japanese work arranged in the form of a treatise. Huang complained that Japanese historians had not compiled treatises on Japan. At the time he was in Japan, the treatises in the *History of Great Japan* were not completed, except for those on the military system and on justice. In the past, Huang noted, Gamō Shūjitsu (1768–1813) had attempted a compilation, but he was unable to carry out his project. Arai Hakuseki (1657–1725) had only titles of treatises listed in his writings. The

absence of a tradition of compiling treatises in Japanese historiography made Huang's work difficult.[45] His major source
materials were books by Japanese scholars, especially those
written in classical Chinese, and publications by the Meiji Government. He cited numerous statistical tables compiled by the
government and the regulations and laws it had issued.

While preparing *Treatises on Japan,* Huang wrote another
book on Japan, using materials he had collected for the treatises.
Jih-pen tsa-shih (Miscellaneous poems on Japan) consisted
of 154 poems on various Japanese topics, each with explanatory
notes and comments. All the poems were in the traditional form
called "seven words stop short," that is, four verses with seven
words in each. The topics of the poems and the organization of
the book were roughly identical to those of *Treatises on Japan.*
In his explanations of the poems, Huang often noted that detailed
discussion would be found in the forthcoming *Treatises on Japan.*
In a sense, *Miscellaneous Poems* was a by-product of the *Treatises,*
planned as a full compendium on Japan. Reminiscing in later years
on the circumstances surrounding the compilation of *Miscellaneous
Poems,* he wrote:

> After having stayed in Japan for almost two years, I had become ac-
> quainted with some Japanese scholars, read some Japanese books, and
> learned about Japanese manners and customs to some extent. Antici-
> pating my compilation of *Treatises on Japan,* I had collected old
> stories and studied about new institutions. Selecting some miscellaneous
> topics, I wrote brief notes on them and put them together, using my
> poems as connective material.[46]

Huang's poems were an excellent expression of his poetic insight, which made his observation of Japan more than an anthropologist's report. He emphasized, however, that his primary purpose in writing the poems was to convey accurate information on
Japan; he was less concerned with literary quality. As he said in
the preface to the first edition of the book:

> I am not good at "stop short." My purpose in writing this book is to
> state the facts. Following the examples of *Nan Sung tsa-shih shih*

[Miscellaneous poems on the Southern Sung] and *Luan-yang tsa-yung* [Miscellaneous songs on Luan-yung], I managed to shape my writing into a form of poetry. My Japanese friends who might perchance see these poems would be amused because they are very clumsy.[47]

Huang's poems were certainly unconventional and did not always follow the rules of "stop short." However, he was proud of the fact that his work was different from previous Chinese writings on Japan, which were mostly based on hearsay: "Even though my writing is not very refined in style, I have consulted Japanese books and asked Japanese scholars to correct my errors of substance. Therefore, my accounts are not based on groundless imagination. Nevertheless, since I do not understand the Japanese language, I am afraid I may have made many mistakes."[48] Huang acknowledged the assistance of Shigeno Yasutsugu, Oka Senjin, Aoyama Nobutoshi, Gamō Shigeaki, and others who corrected errors in his manuscripts. He remarked that their marginalia covered every page and that he had had to rewrite the manuscript four times.[49]

Since Huang did not understand Japanese, he had to depend on written conversations, which were in classical Chinese. He did learn many Japanese words well enough to use in written communications with the Japanese literati. He also learned *kana* and understood their general functions in written Japanese. At the same time, he knew how difficult it was for a Chinese to read Japanese, since the parts of sentences written in *kana* were crucial to understanding. In later years, Chou Tso-jen (1885–1967) praised Huang's grasp of the principles of the Japanese writing system and his humble acceptance of the fact that it was impossible to understand written Japanese, even if one were conversant with the Chinese characters.[50] Despite his difficulty in reading Japanese books, Huang relied on them as his main source of information. He confirmed and supplemented this information through conversations with his friends. It was unavoidable, however, that many of Huang's explanations of things Japanese contained inaccuracies. One of his Japanese friends expressed annoyance over the misstatements in Huang's books, saying that Huang did not accept all the corrections suggested by friends.[51]

In *Treatises on Japan,* Huang frequently cited government announcements and regulations and some proposals and petitions which were originally written in Japanese. In the "Treatise on the Criminal Code," for example, he cited the entire criminal law in Chinese translation. Although many Chinese characters were used in the original documents, they were written in Japanese. Huang probably did not understand their precise meaning. No doubt he had someone make a translation into Chinese for the purpose of citation.

Huang began *Miscellaneous Poems on Japan* in the fall of 1878 and finished it in the spring of 1879.[52] He celebrated its completion with a poetic interment of the manuscript. Ōkōchi Teruna, eager to have Huang's handwriting, asked for the first draft of the manuscript. Huang said he preferred to imitate Liu T'ui of the T'ang who buried his writings, and Huai Su, a T'ang calligrapher who did the same with his writing brushes. Then Ōkōchi offered to make a tomb in his garden for Huang's manuscript. He had Huang's inscription, "Tomb of the first draft of the Miscellaneous Poems on Japan," carved on a four-foot-high stone tablet. To celebrate the completion of the tablet in the fall of 1879, Ōkōchi invited Huang and four mutual friends to a banquet at his house. When everyone was in a high mood after drinking, Huang put the manuscript in a bag, which he buried in a hole at one corner of the garden. After performing a libation, he chanted a poem as an invocation:

> *A volume of poems, a mound of earth;*
> *Commingle poems and earth forever.*
> *Gods and goblins, guard the souls*
> *Of poems at rest in peace forever*
> *Here by the Sumida River.*

Ōkōchi chanted his own poem in response, and the rest of the participants chanted theirs in turn. Ōkōchi had these poems and a narrative of the occasion carved on the reverse of the tablet.[53]

As soon as he finished the manuscript of *Miscellaneous Poems* in the spring of 1879, Huang presented a copy to the Tsungli Yamen (Foreign Office), which published it from the T'ung-wen kuan (foreign language school) in the winter of the same year.[54] In the same spring, Wang T'ao (1828–1897) visited Japan by invitation of the Japanese literati. Huang participated in parties for Wang and became a close friend. When Wang was about to depart, Huang showed him the manuscript. Finding it an important work, Wang asked permission to publish it; accordingly, Wang's newspaper *Hsun-huan jih-pao* in Hong Kong brought out the work in 1880.[55] This edition was reprinted in Japan during 1880. The text was punctuated by Iijima Yūnen, a postscript was contributed by Ishikawa Kōsai, and the original prefaces by Wang T'ao and Hung Shih-wei were included. According to Huang, other publishers in Tokyo and Kyoto and the Chung-hua Press in China published the same edition.[56]

Treatises on Japan was written over a long period of time. By the spring of 1879, Huang had drafted fourteen chapters.[57] By December he thought it would be finished within one year, but, by the time he left Japan in 1882, he still had not completed it. While he was in Japan, he had collected all the source materials and drafted a substantial portion of the text. However, it was not until 1887 that Huang finally completed the work at his home in Kwangtung. Publication took a long time, and it was not until after the Sino-Japanese War ended in 1895 that copies were finally circulated. The first edition, printed at the Fu-wen-chai Press in Canton, was dated 1890, but a preface by Hsueh Fu-ch'eng, written in Paris, was dated the third month of 1894. To explain the discrepancy in these dates Huang Tsun-keng (Yu-fu) stated that, although printing was begun in 1890 at Fu-wen-chai, it was not completed until around 1895.[58] During 1898, two reprint editions of the *Treatises on Japan* were published. For the new edition published in Shanghai, Huang added some comments in small type. Since he did not date any of the treatises or his comments, it is difficult to determine when they were written, except for the parts added in the 1898 edition. Because of the book's long gestation, there are some conflicting ideas reflecting changes in Huang's thinking.

In the following analyses of Huang's views of early Meiji Japan, I relied primarily on *Miscellaneous Poems on Japan* (1880 edition) as my source of information. I supplemented this with his statements in *Treatises on Japan* insofar as they expressed the same views in more detail as *Miscellaneous Poems.*[59]

Huang hoped his works would serve as a stepping stone to further studies of Japan and that newer books would soon replace his own. As he expressed it, "In the present world, civilization progresses day by day, and our knowledge increases every day. Therefore, what we think novel and exciting today will become commonplace in a few decades. For this reason, my book will serve merely as a forerunner and, whenever better books come out, this book can be discarded."[60] Contrary to his hope, Huang's writings remained the most comprehensive accounts of Japan during the Republican era. Tai Ch'uan-hsien (1890–1949), a Nationalist Government functionary who in 1928 wrote *Jih-pen lun* (A discussion of Japan), stated that he had not seen any Chinese book that analyzed Japan so extensively as Huang's *Treatises on Japan.*[61] Chou Tso-jen, a celebrated writer in Republican China and a dedicated student of Japanese literature, also praised Huang's writings. He was impressed by Huang's sensitivity and insight into Japanese culture; according to him, Huang was the first Chinese who really understood Japan.[62] Both Tai and Chou were unique among Chinese intellectuals in giving serious thought to Japanese culture. The Japanese literary critic Takeuchi Yoshimi wrote that he recommended Huang's *Treatises* and *Miscellaneous Poems,* Tai's *Discussion of Japan,* and the essays by Chou Tso-jen as the best analyses of Japanese culture ever written by Chinese.[63]

JAPAN AS A CULTURAL PROVINCE OF CHINA[64]

All the dancers here are wearing
Gold and purple fish-shaped pendants.

As the hand-drum beats are muted,
Notes from bamboo pipes take over.
"Grand Peace" played by these musicians—
The great T'ang Court's own ritual music.
Here preserved in sound, in costume
Formal styles of ancient China.[65]

Huang's basic view of Japan was that biologically and culturally its people stemmed from the same roots as the Chinese. He used the phrase "the same culture and the same race" (*t'ung-wen t'ung-chung* or, in Japanese, *dōbun dōshu*) to describe the close ties between the two peoples.[66] This phrase was frequently used by the Japanese; to them it meant that both Japanese and Chinese belonged to the same category as opposed to the white race in the West. Huang's interpretation of "same race" was slightly different; he believed that the Japanese, especially the ruling house, were descended from Chinese ancestors. In his discussions of the ancient history of Japan, he commented on the legend of Hsu Fu recorded in *Hou Han shu* (History of the Later Han dynasty). According to that legend, Hsu Fu, a Taoist hermit (*fang-shih*), migrated to Japan with 3,000 boys and girls to escape the tyranny of the Ch'in. They settled in the Kumano area and became the ancestors of the Japanese Emperor. Referring to the tomb of Hsu Fu in Kumano and the shrine dedicated to him in Kii, Huang maintained that it was quite possible that Hsu Fu was a historical figure and that the Sujin Emperor, the first emperor for whom there are detailed accounts in the historical records, was descended from Hsu Fu or one of his followers. In connection with the legend, Huang pointed out that the regalia of imperial succession—sword, bronze mirror, and jade—came from Ch'in China and that the important rituals in Japan were similar to the Taoist rites of purification. He criticized Japanese historians who neglected to mention the legend in their writings. According to Huang, they were afraid that acknowledgment of the Chinese origins of the Japanese ruling family would imply Japan's position as subordinate to China. Such a fear was groundless, Huang argued;

after all, many great European nations were of Germanic origin but were not thereby dependencies of Germany. Even if Hsu Fu was not a historical figure, Huang argued, the very existence of the legend strongly suggested the possibility that the Japanese imperial family was of Chinese descent.[67]

There was no question about what "the same culture" meant. Huang recognized the trace of Chinese influence in every aspect of Japanese life from the court ceremonies to the everyday life of the commoners. He suspected that even Shintoism, the most important "indigenous" element in Japanese culture, had originated in China. He recognized the powerful influence of Shintoism in every Japanese institution—the military system, the legal administration, taxation, the treasury, rites and decorum, and the rituals of the imperial court. While admitting that religion was a powerful force in any ancient society, he thought there was no other country where religion and government were so closely integrated as in Japan, where for centuries every major political event had been accompanied by Shinto rituals. He pointed out the similarities between Taoism and Shintoism and the affinity between the purification rites in Shintoism and the Taoist practices in Chou, Ch'in, and Han China. In addition, he argued that, while the Japanese had adopted the major philosophies and religions of China—namely, Confucianism, Buddhism, even Christianity—it was strange that only Taoism was missing in Japan. Therefore he suggested that Shintoism might have developed from Taoism, which had been transmitted from China around the time of the Ch'in.[68]

Huang's theory concerning the Chinese origins of Shintoism was significant as an antithesis to the doctrine of the Mito scholars, who upheld the uniqueness of Japan as a divine land. Modern scholars in Japan and the West agree that there were undoubtedly important influences from China in the formation of Japanese Shintoism.[69] The weakness of Huang's argument lay in his assumption that all cultural elements in Japan (he meant high culture) had been transmitted from China, if not from the West. In his treatise on scholarship in Japan, he dwelt only on Chinese and Western learning, ignoring the existence of national learning (*kokugaku*). Consequently, he did not mention Kamo no Mabuchi or Motoori Norinaga in his list of prominent scholars in Tokugawa Japan. Toward the end of his life, Huang maintained that there was no national learning in Japan;[70] in his opinion, Japan was a province of China insofar as its culture and formal social ethics were concerned.

In Japan, Huang found traces of ancient Chinese legacies that had long been lost in China. For him it was a delightful surprise to encounter these, which were at the same time reminders of his Hakka ancestors: for example, the Japanese way of squatting on the floor and offering stools only to honorable visitors conformed with the etiquette described in *Han shu* (History of the Han dynasty). The interior finish of Japanese houses with pillars and beams in plain wood pleased Huang. (In contemporary China, pillars were painted and heavily decorated with carvings.)[71] He admired the taste of the Japanese, who valued simplicity and natural beauty. He was impressed with the cleanliness of Japanese houses: "They clean the house every day; not a speck of dust can be found on the floor." Also, the Japanese liked fresh air and kept their doors open even at night. However, comfortable as Japanese dwellings were in summer, they were cold in winter. Visitors to Japan, including anthropologists, continue to comment on these features of Japanese life.[72]

Huang was taken by surprise at the ceremonial music and dance (*gagaku*) performed by the Imperial Court orchestra at a banquet given by a high-ranking official. He had never dreamed of hearing the music of the T'ang dynasty, long extinct in China. The dancers' costumes, their accessories, and the dance itself were exactly how he had pictured them in his reading.[73] There were many other things in Japan that he had read about but never seen in China. Clogs, the most common footwear in Japan, had been worn in China during the Six Dynasties.[74] Huang found that the Japanese customs at banquets—the way they drank, sang, danced, and put aside some food to take home to their families—were exactly like the ancient Chinese customs described in *History of the Han Dynasty*. He noted the Japanese fondness for excursions and picnics.

On beautiful days in spring and autumn, clad in gay *kimono* and with flowers in their hair, the Japanese loved to go on outings, taking along a bottle of wine. As they walked, their clogs made cheerful tapping sounds, and the colorful lining at the hems of their *kimono* fluttered in the breeze. Huang was reminded of Chinese paintings.[75]

Huang's observation of the everyday life of the Japanese was as detailed as that of a cultural anthropologist. He portrayed the lives of women with deep insight and sympathy. His poems depicted female infants, school girls, housewives, maids, concubines, entertainers, and prostitutes, and evinced pleasure in the simple and unpretentious appearance of Japanese women. Unlike contemporary Chinese women, they were not loaded with earrings and bracelets; but their greatest virtue was that they had not adopted the custom of foot-binding. Their simple and healthy appearance resembled the women of ancient China, whose virtues were maintained in modern China only among the Hakka women. Huang found that Japanese women's behavior also resembled that of the idealized women in ancient China: "When a married couple go out together, the wife walks behind her husband, and the husband is at ease and full of confidence. When a visitor comes to their house, the woman comes out to greet him without showing hesitation. She would not flirt with him either. This was the way in ancient China."[76] On the whole, he found Japanese life simpler and more frugal than life in China. By noting the flavor of the ancient Chinese legacy in the Japanese life style, Huang subtly criticized the majority culture in Ch'ing China, especially opium-smoking and foot-binding, and, at the same time, expressed his pride as a Hakka.

Huang's delight in finding ancient Chinese legacies in Japan was shared by many other Chinese visitors. In particular, Chinese students who studied in Japan during the last decade of the Ch'ing dynasty glorified the legacies of China prior to the Manchu and Mongol conquests. Among the most devoted students of Japanese culture was Chou Tso-jen, who translated Japanese literature into Chinese, married a Japanese, and chose to remain in Japanese-occupied Peiping during the Sino-Japanese War. He was attracted to

Japanese culture, which was free from the evils in China, namely, eunuchs, foot-binding, opium-smoking, and the eight-legged essay which was required for the civil service examination and which was the cause of the deterioration of Chinese literature. Reminiscing on his first impressions of Japan, Chou wrote: "For me, Japan was half foreign country and half ancient China. It seemed to me that ancient China continued to live on in that foreign land."[77]

Huang recognized the Japanese modifications of Chinese culture. The most conspicuous was their use of Chinese characters. He encountered many words written in Chinese characters that did not make sense to him, since they were transliterations of Japanese words. The Japanese also created some characters that did not exist in China. Huang listed examples, many of which he found on outdoor signboards. He was amused by them and was generous toward such deviations. The most important development in the Japanese writing system had been the creation of *kana,* the Japanese syllabary system. Huang took great interest in the two sets of phonetic symbols that were created from Chinese characters. The symbols were simple, easy to learn, and made it possible for the masses to become literate. It was a practical and commendable innovation, Huang noted. In later years, Huang stressed the need for simplifying the Chinese writing system in order to raise the literacy rate of the nation.[78]

Confucianism was the most important element of Chinese culture to be transmitted to Japan. Huang emphasized the fact that the scholarly tradition in Japan began with the introduction of the Chinese writing system and the Confucian classics. Had Japan not accepted them, he wrote, it would have remained an island with a primitive culture. Since he did not recognize the development of national learning in Tokugawa Japan, to him Chinese learning was *the* scholarship until the introduction of Western learning. He acknowledged the scholarly achievements of the Japanese by listing the names of prominent scholars and their works.[79] He esteemed their ability to compose Chinese poems, and stated that they wrote far better than the Koreans or Vietnamese.[80]

Although Huang praised the literary accomplishments of the
Japanese, he criticized them for neglecting the core of Confu-
cianism, namely, government service and the maintenance of
Confucian order:[81]

> What the Japanese acquired was only the trivial part of Chinese learn-
> ing, its lees and dregs. The fundamentals of statecraft and self-cultiva-
> tion were never put into practice or even learned by the Japanese.
> Ever since the T'ang, the Japanese have learned merely how to compose
> poems and prose. Since the Ming, they have added the Records of the
> Conversation of Chu Hsi [to their curriculum]. The trivial art of writing
> and the empty talk on human nature are, as a matter of fact, the trivia
> of Confucianism.[82]

Huang admitted that Japanese scholars were not given the opportunity to participate in government because Confucian government was never realized under the Japanese emperors. Why was
this so? In his view, the first problem for Japanese government
was that the imperial in-laws, particularly the Fujiwara family,
usurped political power. Then the military leaders founded *bakufu*
(military government). "Because the military men monopolized
political power," Huang wrote, "the Imperial Court was unable
to give scholars prestigious positions and responsibility in the
government."[83] He did not mention the differences in the power
bases of Chinese and Japanese emperors, and took for granted the
possibility of realizing a Confucian bureaucracy under a Japanese
emperor.

Nevertheless, Huang still blamed Japanese scholars for neglecting their political responsibilities, saying they consigned themselves to ivory towers: "They buried themselves in the irrelevancies
of literature and labored over trifling exegeses or engaged in
fruitless pure talk." As a result, the scholars were naturally
slighted and Confucian studies were regarded as impractical.
People satirized the scholars, saying, "Let them recite their classical canons to defend us from bandits; let them take up their
writing brush to defeat enemies." After the country was challenged by the arrival of the Westerners, the scholars of Chinese
learning were regarded as even less worthwhile; there was even

talk of abolishing Chinese learning. To Huang's way of thinking, the scholars themselves were primarily responsible because of their failure to fulfill Confucian duties.[84]

In relation to the limited success of Confucianism in Japan, Huang noted the great influence of Buddhism. It was precisely because Confucianism in Japan lacked vigor that Buddhism was allowed to prosper, Huang commented. He stated that Buddhism in Japan owed its success to the fact that there was no Duke of Chou or Confucius, not to mention Han Yü, to refute Buddhism and defend the *tao* (truth). He emphasized the negative aspects of Buddhism in Japanese history, such as the extravagant use of state funds for constructing temples and the interference of powerful Buddhist monasteries in government affairs. In this respect, he compared Japanese Buddhism to the Buddhism of T'ang China condemned by Confucian scholars.[85]

Huang lamented the neglect of Confucian studies after the Meiji Restoration. During the first decade of the Meiji, valuable old books were shipped to foreign countries in large quantities. Confucian scholars were impoverished and neglected. ''The Five Classics were abandoned in high pavilions; Confucian scholars maintain only their school buildings. While living in poverty, they still wear scholars' gowns. They grow old in mountain schools writing books and sweeping fallen leaves.''[86]

Huang was especially indignant with those people who forgot the great contribution of Chinese studies to the Meiji Restoration. He maintained that Confucian learning had provided spiritual guidance to the loyalist movement that brought forth the restoration. Huang understood that the principal accomplishment of the restoration lay in bringing about an end to the hegemony of the military usurpers and restoring the government to the legitimate ruler in the wake of the national crisis caused by the Western advance. He emphasized that the restoration was accomplished by the selfless devotion of the loyalists, who had been awakened to the sense of "great righteousness" (*taigi*), and that the loyalist spirit had been nurtured by Confucian studies.

As an example of loyalty demonstrated by a Chinese scholar,

Huang exalted Chu Chih-yü (Shun-shui, 1600–1682, known as Shu Shunsui in Japan). Leaving China at the time of the Manchu conquest, he eventually settled in Japan to become a Confucian tutor to Tokugawa Mitsukuni (1628–1700), the lord of Mito. His tombstone bore the engraving "a scholar of the Ming," in accordance with his will. Huang stated that his loyalty surpassed that of Po I and Shu Ch'i, who refused to eat grain grown in the territory of the Chou, the conquerors of their state. Chu Chih-yü would not eat even wild grasses grown on the land of the conquerers. Since Chu's biography had not been written in China, Huang ordered Shen Wen-ying to collect materials for the purpose.[87]

In promoting the cult of loyalty as the moral basis for the anti-*bakufu* movement, books written by the Mito scholars in the late Tokugawa period played decisive roles. In the earlier period, however, the major efforts of the Mito scholars centered around the compilation of *History of Great Japan*, which was begun in 1657. The work was carried out at the Bureau of History of the Mito *han* by generations of historians and was finally completed in 1906 under the auspices of the Meiji Government. One of its major purposes was to clarify the legitimate line of the imperial succession based on the Neo-Confucian doctrine of the "great righteousness."[88]

Rai Jō (San'yō, 1780–1832), a powerful source of inspiration to the late Tokugawa loyalists, heavily depended on *History of Great Japan* as a source of information. His *Nihon gaishi* (Unofficial history of Japan, 1827), which became a bible of the loyalist movement, was renowned for the beauty of its style. The book, written in classical Chinese, was known among Chinese intellectuals, too.[89]

For his chapters on Japanese history in *Treatises on Japan*, Huang extensively borrowed from Rai's *Nihon seiki* (Record of the governments of Japan, 1832) and in general followed the framework of *History of Great Japan*. Moreover, Huang copiously adopted Rai's comments on major historical events with little modification. Huang's narrative of Japanese history up to the early nineteenth century was no more than a summary of Rai's book. However, Huang included the mythological era preceding the Jimmu Emperor, whereas Rai and the Mito historians had begun with the Jimmu. Also, Huang did not regard the contest for legitimacy between the Northern and Southern Courts in the fourteenth century as very important, while it was a matter of central concern for the Mito historians. Nevertheless, Huang highly commended the loyalty of the ministers of the Southern Court, particularly Kusunoki Masashige (?-1336), as the epitome of the loyal subject.[90]

Huang exalted the spirit of the loyalists not only in his comments on Japanese history, but also in his poetry. His eulogistic poem "Patriotic Heroes in the Modern Age" praised the late Tokugawa loyalists and their predecessors. He commemorated such patriots as Yamagata Masasada, who questioned the legitimacy of the Tokugawa rule and was arrested and died in prison; Takayama Hikokurō (Seishi, 1747-1793), who openly protested against the Tokugawa rule by prostrating himself toward the imperial palace on Sanjō Bridge in Kyoto and later committed suicide out of indignation over the Tokugawa *bakufu's* neglect of national defense; Gamō Shūjitsu (Kumpei, 1763-1813), who was famous for scorning the tombstone of Ashikaga Takauji, a military usurper of the fourteenth century; Hayashi Shihei (1738-1793), who was persecuted for criticizing the *bakufu's* defense policy by warning that the water under the Nihonbashi Bridge was connected with the water under London Bridge; Watanabe Kazan (1793-1841), a scholar of Dutch learning who was imprisoned and ordered to commit suicide for advising that Japan open its doors to the West; Sakuma Shōzan (1811-1864), another scholar of Dutch learning who advocated the opening of the country and the union of the *bakufu* and the imperial house, and was assassinated by the radicals; Yoshida Shōin (1830-1859), a disciple of Sakuma Shōzan, who educated many leaders of the restoration movement at his private school and died a martyr during the great persecution of the loyalists; Monk Gesshō (1813-1858), a supporter of the loyalist movement in Kyoto and an associate with Saigō Takamori (1827-1877) of Satsuma, with whom he

fled during the persecution of 1858, was refused admission to
Satsuma, and tried with Saigō to drown himself, after which
Saigō was rescued.

All these loyalists were devoted patriots. Huang emphasized the
fact that they rose against the *bakufu* when it demonstrated in-
competence in handling the national crisis. In his poem, Huang
related the anecdote of a peasant woman in Mito who protested
against the house arrest of her lord by the *bakufu* and begged for
a pardon for him at the risk of her own life. Another anecdote
concerned the legendary Sakura Sōgorō, the hero of a peasant
rebellion, who ventured his life by making a forbidden petition to
the shogun for rent reduction for an entire village. These popular
heroes were commemorated for their selfless devotion.[91]

Among the leaders of the restoration, Saigō Takamori received
Huang's special attention. He dedicated a poem to this tragic hero
who, after resigning from the new government, eventually perished
as the leader of the great rebellion against the Meiji Government.
When a comet appeared in the southern sky soon after Saigō's
death, people believed it to be his spirit and called it the star of
Saigō. Huang concluded his poem with these words: "Bright
star, accept my toast! Great hero of our age, rare genius in the
wide world!"[92]

The cult of loyalism was promoted by the government in the
early Meiji years. The government officially honored the martyrs
of the restoration and enshrined earlier loyalist leaders, such as
Kusunoki Masashige, who had been honored by the late Tokugawa
loyalists. Among other examples, the most popular figures were
the 47 retainers of Akō who dedicated their lives to avenging
the death of their lord in the early eighteenth century. Plays
based on their lives and deeds attracted large audiences throughout
the Tokugawa era. After the restoration, the 47 became more
popular than ever. In the first year of the Meiji, when the Emperor
moved his residence to Tokyo, he made an offering at the Senga-
kuji temple where the 47 were buried. In 1872, the government
decreed that the real names of the historical figures in the play
might now be used.[93] Huang was greatly impressed by the story

of the 47 and wrote a long narrative poem describing the event and praising the courage of these men who accomplished their righteous cause under tremendous hardships.[94]

Huang's veneration for acts of loyalty and martyrdom had been expressed in his earlier poems. While he was still in Peking he had eulogized a horse of the T'ung-chih Emperor which was believed to have died of grief at the Emperor's death.[95] At about the same time, Huang wrote a eulogy on T'ien Heng, a hero of the early Han, and his 500 retainers who refused to shift their loyalty to the new ruler and committed suicide at the news of their master's death.[96] Perhaps it was because Huang cherished the sentiment of loyalty that he was particularly moved by the stories of loyalists in Japan.

The spirit of martyrdom was the central theme in Huang's accounts of the Meiji Restoration. He discussed the history of the restoration, beginning with the enthronement of the Kōmei Emperor in 1848 and ending with the year 1878, focusing on the Japanese reaction to Western demands for opening the country, the growth of the anti-Tokugawa movement, and the establishment of the new regime. Huang argued that the conciliatory policy of the Tokugawa toward the Westerners gave impetus to the loyalists, who had become aware of the illegitimacy of the Tokugawa rule, and that the anti-foreign movement was actually anti-Tokugawa. He gave great credit to Rai San'yō's books and to Minamoto Shōbyō's *Kokushi ryaku* (Brief history of Japan) and to *History of Great Japan* for their contribution to awakening the spirit of "Revere the Emperor and punish the hegemon." When the loyalists voiced criticisms against the Tokugawa Government in 1858, the government harshly persecuted them. However the government's action only aroused greater indignation among many others who followed in the footsteps of the slain loyalists. Thus, Huang concluded, the fall of the Tokugawa was brought about by the unemployed samurai (*ch'u-shih*), who read history widely, had high ideals, were free from hereditary positions or family bonds, and were willing to dedicate their lives to the struggle against the military regime.[97]

Huang's exaltation of the spirit of martyrdom was shared by those Chinese intellectuals who attempted to reform the government in China under the leadership of the Kuang-hsu Emperor. K'ang Yu-wei and Liang Ch'i-ch'ao, the most eloquent advocates for reform, praised the loyalists in Japan and attributed the success of the Meiji Restoration to their efforts. The effect of their talk about the heroic spirit of the Japanese loyalists on their younger followers was tremendous. T'an Ssu-t'ung and T'ang Ts'ai-ch'ang, who sacrificed their lives in 1898 and 1900, had been convinced of the need for selflessness in the cause of reform. After the failure of the Reform of 1898, Liang continued to advocate the loyalist spirit and wrote a book on *bushidō* (way of the warrior) in China to remind the younger generation that such spirit had existed in ancient China and to urge them to revive that spirit.[98] It appears that, of all the Japanese topics about which Huang wrote, the stories of the loyalists had the most immediate impact on contemporary Chinese intellectuals.

THREE

Westernization in Early Meiji Japan

That ancient land has willed itself new birth,
Steers itself toward the mainstream of the earth.
Idle their looms yet opulent their dress.
East-neighbors look like strangers from the West.[1]

APPRAISALS OF EARLY MEIJI MODERNIZATION

Huang depicted traditional Japan as a peaceful island country, comparable to the peach-blossom paradise in Chinese legend. Once the bliss of tranquility was broken by the Western advance, he observed, the Japanese began vigorous efforts to make their country a world power. He was amazed by the Japanese zeal for nation-building and the adoption of modern Western institutions. In general, he admitted that Japanese accomplishments in modernization were admirable, especially in view of the fact that only about ten years had elapsed since the Meiji Restoration. He recognized, however, that there were some serious problems facing the new leaders of Japan: the economy of the country was under strain and the government was threatened with bankruptcy; a disheartening trade deficit was plaguing the nation's economy; the prospect of treaty revision was remote; and the leadership of the new government was challenged by the advocates of the "People's Rights."

Huang's initial reaction to the modernizing of Japan was amazement. The scenes in Tokyo in the late 1870s were a curious mixture of tradition and newly imported European fashions in public buildings, dress, and various technological innovations. Within a decade after the Meiji Restoration, Japan acquired railways, gaslights, a telegraph system, modern schools, a modern army and navy, and a centralized bureaucracy. Soldiers and policemen wore Western-style uniforms. Government functionaries dressed in Western clothes. Even among those who preferred traditional garments, it was fashionable to add an imported object, such as a European-style umbrella, pocket watch, or leather shoes. The flood of Western fashions was so spectacular that the Japanese themselves were dazzled by it. To express their mixed feelings of excitement and bewilderment, numerous novels and songs satirized the new trends in hairdressing, clothes, Western-style restaurants, and other innovations. Of such literature, *Tōkyō shin hanjōki* (A new prosperity in Tokyo, published in 1874–1876) was the most popular.[2] Its author, Hattori Seiichi (Bushō, 1841–1908), was a young samurai from Fukushima who came to see Tokyo soon after the restoration. He was excited by the scenes in the new capital and put down his impressions of things that amazed him—new-style schools, rickshaws, newspaper offices, photography, restaurants where beef was served, fire brigades, eyeglasses, girls' schools, trade fairs, as well as the old establishments for entertainment at Yoshiwara. These topics were mostly identical with those of Huang's poems on Japan, which suggests that Huang's amazement over Westernization was shared by the Japanese themselves.[3]

Huang's poem about a coachman (coach-driving was a new occupation) depicted a street scene in Meiji Japan:

> *Swinging his whip from the high driver's seat,*
> *The coachman makes his way along the street.*
> *Wool jacket, leather boots, his style of dress*
> *And haircut are imported from the West.*
> *Half naked tatooed coolie just last year*
> *Today rides proudly in his new career.*[4]

The horse-drawn coaches carrying upper-class men and women in Western-style dress added to the exotic atmosphere in the center of Tokyo. A Japanese innovation, the rickshaw (a kind of sedan chair on two large wheels), soon became popular in Japan and in China's treaty ports. Huang thought the rickshaw was one of the marvels of Japan. Rickshaw men "can run as fast as the wind and can compete with coaches pulled by two horses. Most of them cover as much as two or three hundred *li* a day. Their skill is most astonishing."[5]

In the downtown sections, photographers' studios attracted attention with their displays of pictures of popular entertainers, and even upper-class women did not hesitate to have their photographs on view. Photography was immensely popular in Japan.[6]

Tokyo's residential districts impressed Huang with the regularity of their streets and the system of numbering houses. The ward, the town, and even the street numbers were marked on maps. Each house had a tablet with the names of its occupants posted at the entrance.[7] Today, Japanese cities are notorious for the irregularity of their street numbers, but in the early Meiji era Tokyo impressed Huang with the ease with which a house could be located.

Huang the diplomat was in a position to observe the lifestyle of the new upper class, the bureaucrats. This class was the first to adopt Western dress and customs. The bureaucrats lived in Western-style houses or at least had Western-style drawing rooms, complete with imported carpets and stoves. Huang observed that they competed with each other in acquiring imported furniture and that they entertained guests with imported wine.[8] They now took summer vacations in resort areas, a Western custom.[9] On appropriate occasions, they wore Western formal clothes enhanced by insignia. They greeted foreign envoys by shaking hands. But Huang noted that even Westernized officials slipped into Japanese *kimono* at home.[10]

"Western method" (*hsi-fa*) was Huang's label for everything the Japanese borrowed from the West, that is, institutions, manners and customs, technology and skills. There were many practical modern devices—the train, the telegraph, postal service, hospitals, fire brigades, and police stations. Huang praised them unreservedly.

For example, when he visited a hospital, he was struck by the cleanliness and the pleasant atmosphere; medicines and equipment were arranged in an orderly way, and there were even plants in the hallways. He thought that Western surgery was far superior to the traditional Chinese method of diagnosis by feeling the pulse.[11]

Aside from his generally favorable impressions of Westernization, how did Huang assess Japanese achievements in the economic and military strengthening of their country? He was keenly interested in gathering statistical data on the economy, for example, agricultural production, state revenue and expenditure, national and foreign bonds, and other measures that reflected Japan's economic condition. Confessing his fascination with statistics, he wrote, "Statistics is one of the best methods Japan has adopted from the West. It provides essential information on population, taxation, education, and all other aspects of society and serves to indicate the progress toward national goals in every month and year."[12] He stated that statistical tables revealed the power of the nation (*kuo-shih*) and extensively cited statistical tables in the *Treatises on Japan.*

Huang's view of the economic situation in early Meiji Japan was pessimistic. He noted that the financial foundation of the Meiji Government was precarious. First of all, Japan was a poor country with scant resources. While its population was one-twelfth of China's, its land area was only one twenty-fifth. Although the government imposed heavy taxes on land and collected various other kinds of taxes, state finances were strained. He emphasized the problems caused by the deficit in foreign trade and over-issuance of currency.[13]

Huang noted some positive effects of the overseas trade in the increase of agriculture and handicraft products, especially tea and silk, for export. However, he was aware of its negative aspects, which brought on a severe financial crisis. In his opinion, Japan's gains from opening the country were very small in comparison with its losses, the greatest loss being Japan's becoming dependent on foreign goods as a result of a Westernized living style. He deplored the universal Japanese urge to Westernize all aspects of life, from state ceremonies to food and drink. Huang understood that the principal cause of Japan's trade deficit was excessive imports of the consumer goods necessary for Westernization. Disdaining what he felt was superfluous luxury, Huang attributed Japan's problems to foreign trade, even though the country was spared the evils of opium-smuggling which had caused such trouble to China.[14] In fact, Western-style living and clothing was not as widely spread as Huang emphasized, and those who could afford expensive imports were very limited. Nevertheless Westernization was indeed costly. Japan had to import not only woolen textiles and leather that were needed for Western-style clothing, but also machinery and equipment for industrialization. Moreover the government hired many foreign advisors with very high salaries. The problem of payment to foreign countries was recognized by government leaders.[15]

Huang also identified another reason for Japan's trade deficit as the inferior position of Japanese traders in international competition. He was informed of many cases of bankruptcy in Japanese firms that engaged in foreign trade, and he was pessimistic about Japanese merchants' ability to compete with foreigners because of their inexperience in overseas trade.[16] In fact, Japan's foreign trade was dominated by Westerners, who took full advantage of their privileges of fixed tariffs and extraterritoriality, their superior capital endowment, and Japan's lack of an information network on overseas markets. The foreigners' domination of Japan's trade was a matter of serious concern to the contemporary Japanese and was believed to be a major cause of trade imbalance.[17]

Huang discussed the disastrous effects of the unequal treaties on Japan, emphasizing that the Western nations forced Japan into an exploitative trade relationship for their own benefit. He argued that the flow of gold abroad was more harmful to a country than any other kind of economic disaster and that it was a new form of invasion in the modern world:

> Nowadays the weak have become prey to the strong. Those who subjugate others do not want to take over their lands or enslave their

people; rather, they force them into making disadvantageous treaties and seek to take their wealth. Like the fox-fairies that possessed men, they daily suck their blood; like harmful insects that continuously inject poison, they relentlessly exploit the limited resources of others to satisfy their unbounded greed. Indeed, this is far more harmful than the loss of territory.[18]

He noted that China and Japan were fellow sufferers from unequal treaties and the consequent trade relationships with the Western nations. He observed, however, that Japan suffered more because it was a smaller and poorer country. Expressing his sympathy for Japan, he wrote, "I cannot but shed tears to see the extreme hardship of this brother country."[19]

In connection with Japan's fiscal crisis, Huang took up the problem of inflated paper currency. He admitted the advantages of issuing paper currency in maintaining government finances, particularly for paying the cost of suppressing the rebellions, building new industries, and financing transportation and communication systems. He pointed out, however, that the excessive issuance of paper money caused inflation in the price of commodities and generated tremendous anxiety among the populace. The inflationary situation seemed so serious that Huang wondered whether the Meiji Government could sustain its currency system. Quoting from the *Odes,* Huang compared the uncertain financial situation to "a boat adrift; where it will go you know not."[20]

As a matter of fact, the Japanese economy was at subsistence level during the early decades of the Meiji era, and the government was in the throes of a financial crisis. This fact was keenly felt by contemporary Japanese and has been substantiated by the researches of economic historians. The government was crippled financially by the burden of the campaigns to quell the rebellions in southwest Japan, which posed a serious threat to the new regime. By the time the campaigns ended in 1877, the government had borrowed 15 million yen and had issued 27 million yen in paper currency, a total that amounted to more than 80 percent of the revenue in the 1877 budget. These governmental measures led to high inflation; moreover, the international trade balance was in the red from the first year of the Meiji through 1881, except for the years 1868 and 1876. Consequently, a large amount of gold was shipped abroad, which further accelerated inflation. The paying out of gold was regarded by contemporaries as the most dangerous threat to Japan's economy.[21]

Heavy taxation was another source of popular discontent in early Meiji Japan. Huang expressed compassion for the Japanese people, who had to pay a very high land tax in comparison with their Chinese counterparts. The Meiji government fixed the land tax at 3 percent of the assessed land value in 1873. Although it was reduced to 2.5 percent in 1877, the tax amounted to more than 30 percent of the yield during the early years of the Meiji period. In contrast, the central government in China shared in a very small portion of the yield, as Huang stated that the Ch'ing government collected less than one fortieth of the yield from poor districts. It has been estimated that the land tax during the last quarter-century of the Ch'ing fell within the range between 2 and 4 percent of the land produce in most districts and provinces. In Japan, in addition to the land tax which was the primary source of the revenue, the government collected numerous kinds of direct and indirect taxes: revenue stamps, on brewing sake and soy sauce, on boats and carts; corporation taxes; the mining tax; taxes on government employees' salaries, on products in Hokkaido, and on tobacco. In addition, local governments collected taxes to cover their expenses. Huang noted that the only item that was tax-exempt was salt, a major source of government revenue in China. He realized that it was technically impossible to control salt production in Japan because the country was surrounded by an ocean.[22] By the Confucian criteria of good government, heavy taxation was a negative sign. Huang generally followed the Confucian criteria in his *Miscellaneous Poems of Japan.* When he wrote the conclusion to his discussion on taxation in *Treatises on Japan,* however, he changed his viewpoint and emphasized the positive aspects of heavy taxation by the central government for the purpose of financing government projects.[23]

Huang praised the Japanese government's efforts to promote

the native cotton and sugar industries because these products were major import items, and to assist technological improvements in the silk and tea industries. He reported in detail on the Tomioka silk factory—built in 1870 with French technological aid—and on the Maebashi silk-yarn factory, founded by the former *han* official of Maebashi with the aid of Italian technicians. He was also impressed by the government-sponsored exhibitions aimed at improving the quality of products for export. In 1879, a nationwide contest among tea, silk-yarn, and cocoon producers was held in Yokohama with over 1,000 participants. He judged that government initiative and incentive were key factors in improving agricultural and manufacturing industries, especially for export goods.[24]

Although Huang recognized the importance of technological change, he did not comprehend industrialization as a crucial process headed toward modern transformation. Lack of positive understanding kept him from discussing industrialization as a whole. He dealt with railways and mining, which were under the jurisdiction of the Ministry of Industry (Kōbushō), in his "Treatise on Government System." His discussions in "Treatises on Products" were limited to agricultural products, including silk and tea. In the "Treatise on Industry" (*kung-i*), he confined himself to traditional handicraft products—silk-weaving, swords, copper ware, ceramics, lacquer ware, fans, paper, paintings, and miscellaneous items—as well as a discussion of the history of medicine and agricultural technology. Obviously, Huang did not foresee the change in economic structure which was to follow industrialization. In this matter Huang was no more farsighted than most of his contemporaries in Japan.[25] It is small wonder because, at the time when Huang stayed in Japan, the results of the Japanese efforts for economic development were not yet visible.

In their study of modern economic growth in Japan, Kazushi Ohkawa and Henry Rosovsky defined the years 1868 to 1885 as a period of transition. During this period, a policy for economic growth was set up as a national objective, but a concrete beginning was not yet possible. There was as yet no recognizable development with the attributes of modern economic growth suggested by Simon Kuznets. (1) There was no concrete evidence to indicate that real product per capita was rising in a rapid or sustained manner in the 1860s; in the late 1870s, 75 to 80 percent of the gainfully occupied population were engaged in agriculture, and the agrarian sector produced about 65 percent of the national product. (2) Rapid population growth was not observable, the rates of increase in population in the 1870s being 0.75 or 1 percent. (3) High rates of transformation of the industrial structure could not be recognized in the fairly typical pre-modern manufacturing pattern, which was heavily concentrated in handicraft-type textile and food production. (4) The Japanese-Dutch studies were far from meeting the criteria of the application of modern scientific thought and technology to industry, transport, and agriculture. (5) The only one of Kuznets's criteria to be met was international contacts, a result of the reestablishment of diplomatic and trade relations with the West during the 1850s and the most important force pushing Japan in the direction of rapid economic growth.

As to the financial aspect of the transitional period, Ohkawa and Rosovsky have divided it into sub-periods. From 1868 to 1876, the economic situation was relatively stable, despite political instability. The years 1876 to 1885 were a period of great upheaval, subdivided into two parts: the years of inflation from 1876 to 1881, and the years of deflation from 1881 to 1885. Huang's stay in Japan coincided with the years of inflation. According to Ohkawa and Rosovsky, the number of national banks allowed to issue bank notes rose from about 4 to 148 between 1876 and 1880, and in 1880 note issuance reached 34 million yen, the legal maximum. Ohkawa and Rosovsky have pointed out that this inflation led to a distortion in the economy which affected the government most adversely in terms of its preparation for modern economic growth.[26] Their study endorses Huang's conclusions about Japan's economic situation during the period when he was there.

As for Japan's new military forces, Huang was impressed by the discipline, equipment, organization, and general education in the military academies. Considering the accomplishments of the eight years since the establishment of the conscription system in 1873, he thought that Japan's military power would soon be formidable. He was especially impressed by the large areas where soldiers drilled every day, even without the incentive of military emergency.[27]

At the same time, Huang noticed the difficulties inherent in building a modern army. Resistance to conscription was widespread. Because military service had been restricted to the hereditary samurai families during the Tokugawa era, Huang noted, ordinary peasants knew nothing of what army life entailed, and they feared it. Moreover, the term "tax in blood," used in the official announcement of the conscription law, was exploited by demagogues who spread a rumor that soldiers would literally have to shed their blood. Popular resentment against conscription developed into peasant uprisings in many areas. Household registers were falsified, some people fled from their registered domiciles, and some even mutilated themselves. One problem with the original conscription law was the many provisions for exemption; the revised law of 1879 was improved in this respect and was much more effective. Despite these difficulties, Huang thought the Japanese were making steady progress in building a modern army.[28]

To explain Japan's military capacity, Huang cited many statistics, including detailed reports of the number of men enlisted in 1880, the organization of the military bureaucracy, the size of the standing army at each army post (*chindai*) and of the imperial guards, the organization of the army, the curriculum at the military academies, the budget, the laws and discipline, and the army and navy medical services. Huang paid special attention to the development of military technology and industries. He noted the new-style rifle invented by Murata Tsuneyoshi in 1880, which was adopted as the standard army weapon in 1885 and remained in use for many years. Over 100 arsenals were planned for construction by the late 1880s. Eighty percent of the equipment of the arsenals consisted of up-to-date models imported from Europe, with only 20 percent being outmoded.[29] Huang was aware that the Japanese were endeavoring to attain self-sufficiency in the manufacture of armaments. Indeed, "Self-reliance in the production of weapons" was the major goal of the military in Japan during the 1880s.[30]

In his appraisal of the Japanese naval forces, Huang was less optimistic. "The history of the Japanese navy is very short," he remarked. "Only after the purchase of the *Fusō*, *Kongō*, and *Hiei* from England in 1878, accomplished by making use of every resource from various tax funds, is the Japanese navy in better shape so that it now looks somewhat like a [real] navy. Those who are in charge of the navy want to expand it; however, Japan can hardly afford naval expansion."[31] In fact, the three gunboats mentioned above were Japan's major acquisitions after the Meiji Restoration and were the only iron or composite ships of over 2,000 tons that Japan possessed before 1885. Naval leaders proposed plans for expansion in 1881, only to have them rejected for financial reasons. In 1883, an eight-year plan to increase the number of warships from 10 to 32 was approved. By 1887, when Huang had completed the *Treatises on Japan,* the navy had acquired the cruisers *Naniwa* (3,650 tons) and *Takachiho* (3,650 tons) and 7 other new ships. Huang's report was accurate insofar as it concerned the period of his stay in Japan, and he was quite accurate in pointing out the financial obstacles to naval expansion.[32] In concluding his discussion of Japan's naval capacity, Huang stated that the Japanese navy was much inferior to that of China: China had more than 10 ironclads and many lesser ships. In fact, despite Japan's frantic efforts toward naval expansion during the 1880s and early 1890s, foreign observers of the two navies in 1894, when the Sino-Japanese War broke out, assessed Japan's navy as the weaker.[33] Commenting on Japan's ambition to become a world naval power, Huang stated: "Japan, the three-island country, seems to have the ambition to become as powerful as England. It is obviously impossible." Nevertheless, he continued, in view of the situation in the world, where the great powers cast covetous eyes on their potential prey, the Japanese were right in building up their military strength, regardless of the cost.[34]

As for the Japanese effort toward treaty revision, Huang noted that Japan realized the problems inherent in the treaties only after their disastrous effects became apparent. He condemned the treaties, not only because of their economic consequences but also for their injustice. He especially emphasized the wrongs perpetrated by extraterritoriality, which gave foreigners in treaty ports special privileges that allowed them to exploit the native populace.[35] At the time Huang completed *Treatises on Japan,* he was still doubtful about any amelioration of the treaties in Japan's favor. It was mostly in the additions he inserted for the reprint edition of 1898 that Huang commended the nationwide zeal of the Japanese for effecting treaty revision.[36]

Among the Japanese efforts for treaty revision, Huang was greatly interested in the promulgation of the new criminal codes, the *chizaihō* (criminal prosecution law, 480 articles) and the *keihō* (criminal law, 430 articles) which were promulgated in July 1880 and remained in effect from January 1, 1882, through November 1, 1890. The *chizaihō* was the first codified regulation governing criminal prosecution, drafted with the aid of a French jurist, Boissonade, based on the French criminal code of 1808. Prior to it, the Meiji Government issued the *shinritsu kōryō* (the outline of the new statutes) in 1870, based on the Ming statutes and containing such archaic penalties as slow death. Pressed by the need for treaty revision, the Japanese adopted a modern Western code. It was a large step toward modernization of the Japanese legal system. Huang cited the entire texts of the *chizaihō* and *keihō* in his treatise on criminal codes.[37]

Since education was an important foundation of national strength, Huang paid great attention to the school system in Japan. At all levels of education, he noted, practical subjects were taught. The nationally standardized curricula and the uniform school hours and schedule were new to him. He was also struck by the efficiency of Western methods of pedagogy: in contrast to the traditional Chinese school where each student received instructions from a teacher individually, one teacher could simultaneously instruct many students. Referring to a statement in a government announcement of the establishment of the modern school system in 1872 that "there should be no person without education, and no village without a school," Huang commented that the realization of such a goal was the secret of creating a strong nation, as proved by Germany. He paid special attention to women's education. He visited the Tokyo Normal School for Women, which had been founded in 1875 under the patronage of the Empress. He noted that the curriculum consisted mostly of Western subjects, although women's traditional skills like sewing were included. At the kindergarten attached to the women's normal school, he was impressed by the military-like discipline.[38]

Education was not limited to schools. Huang found that newspapers and museums were playing important roles in spreading new knowledge to every corner of the country. He recognized that all newspapers were devoted to promoting civilization and enlightenment and served as essential media for public education.[39] He was amazed when he visited the National Museum in Ueno to find all kinds of interesting displays, among them the famous gold seal of the Han, which had been unearthed in Kyushu. According to the record in the *History of the Later Han Dynasty,* the king of Wa (Japan) sent an envoy to China in A.D. 57, and in return a seal was bestowed upon him by the Kuang-wu Emperor. The unearthed gold seal has been assumed to be that seal.[40]

For all the achievements following the Meiji Restoration, government leadership was essential. Huang recognized that the Japanese had created an efficient bureaucracy by cleverly combining the ancient official system Japan had adopted from China with the modern Western system. The Meiji bureaucracy was "well ordered and full of vigor."[41] At the same time, he observed that during the first few years the Meiji Government issued new laws and ordinances one after another, some of which conflicted with each other and created confusion. After the return of the Iwakura mission from Europe and the United States, he noted, government ordinances were more consistent and were based on efficient Western principles.[42] In the "Treatise on Government Offices," Huang listed the major official posts in the central and local governments, indicating official ranks, grades, and salary scales, which ranged from 800 yen per month for the Minister of the Dajōkan to 12 yen for a clerk of the 8th rank.[43] He described the development of government organizations during the first decade of the Meiji era and listed the Ministers and Councillors from 1868 to 1879, most of whom came from Satsuma, Chōshū, Tosa, and Hizen. Commenting on the contemporary criticism of the monopoly of top government positions by men from these feudatories, Huang wrote that it was natural that meritorious leaders of the restoration should hold powerful positions in the new government:

> When the shogun returned the government [to the Emperor], the Emperor was too young [to assume personal rule]. Consequently, hereditary nobles in Kyoto and men from powerful feudatories participated in the government. For this reason, the authority of the Dajōkan (Council of State) was great . . . Even though the Emperor was the head of the council, his power was very restricted. Petitioning to establish a parliament by popular vote, Soejima and Itagaki complained that the political power was neither in the hands of the Emperor nor in the hands of the people; it was monopolized by the oligarchs. Once this voice was raised, many people joined the chorus, demanding a parliament according to the Western example. They denounced the government by men from the powerful feudatories, saying that it was residue of the feudal past.
>
> Although these voices were raised by jealous and resentful men, [the fact remains that] Satsuma, Chōshū, Hizen, and Tosa had contributed much to the state. It is natural that the power of the government should fall into the hands of the men from these feudatories.[44]

During Huang's stay in Japan, the nationwide Freedom and People's Rights movement reached its apogee. The movement began in early 1874, when the former State Councillors, Soejima Taneomi and other leaders from Tosa and Hizen, jointly petitioned the government for an elected legislature. They had resigned from the government as a result of the conflict of opinion with leaders from Satsuma and Chōshū over the proposed expedition against Korea. Their movement gained support from former samurai, a frustrated group who had lost their social and economic status after the restoration and were discontented with the new regime dominated by men from Satsuma and Chōshū. The movement went into a new phase when these samurai were joined by rich farmers and village headmen, as well as rich merchants who had been politicized in the course of their opposition to the new taxation system. They began to assert their right to participate in decision-making on matters of taxation and the expenditure of public funds. They organized political associations, which later developed into political parties. Among these, Aikokusha (Patriots' Society) and Risshisha (Society of Men with High Purposes) were the most important national organizations. Numerous local groups were loosely affiliated with the national organizations. They published magazines and newspapers for popular enlightenment and sponsored public lectures that spoke out against severe government suppression. Freedom (*jiyū*) from the oppression of the feudal past was the most cherished ideal among the supporters of the People's Rights movement. Translations of Rousseau's *Social Contract*, Samuel Smiles' *Self Help*, John Stuart Mill's *On Liberty*, and Herbert Spencer's *Social Statics* were among them.[45] Books on the American Revolution were popular; the American struggle for independence was an inspiring example, since it not only embodied the spirit of freedom and independence but marked the first step toward the founding of a powerful state. While advocating freedom and the rights of individuals, the leaders of the People's Rights movement were strongly motivated by national aspirations and believed the parliamentary system was the best means for achieving national unity and strength under the Emperor.[46]

Huang's initial reaction to the People's Rights movement was astonishment and suspicion. In the beginning, he understood the movement to be basically political opposition to the new regime. "No sooner had the imperial rule been restored," he wrote in a poem, "that the people began to clamor for democracy." In the note to the poem, he wrote:

> After the Genji and Heike rose, the Emperor held only a nominal position like the Emperor of the Eastern Chou dynasty. In the first year of the Meiji, the Tokugawa rule was abolished and the imperial

government restored. Great were the accomplishments of the restoration! In recent years, however, Western thought has gained tremendous popularity, and there are even those who propagate the United States's theory of people's rights and freedom.[47]

Huang disapproved of the ideology of the movement, primarily because it conflicted with the Confucian norm of social order, which he regarded as immutable. In conversation with Ōkōchi Teruna in late 1878, he stated: "In recent years the attitudes of learned men have become more and more frivolous and shallow. When one person advocates the American theory of freedom, everyone joins the chorus. They will eventually consider the ruler and father to be as useless as worn-out sandals."[48] He expressed his belief in the immutability of the Confucian social order in a brief piece he contributed to the literary magazine of the Dōjinsha in 1882. "Those things that can be changed are steamships, railways, telegraphs, and all that would benefit finance, agriculture, commerce, and handicrafts. Those things that cannot be changed are relationships between ruler and subjects, father and son, husband and wife, and all that are related to ethical norms."[49]

Later, while still in Japan, Huang became more sympathetic toward the People's Rights movement after he began to read Japanese translations of Rousseau and Montesquieu. In 1902, he wrote to Liang Ch'i-ch'ao, a trusted friend who was in exile in Japan, that he had experienced a great revelation about the ideal political system after reading these authors:

> When I was in Japan, most of the people I associated with were conservative scholars, many of whom were disciples of Yasui Sokken. Around 1879 and 1880, the idea of People's Rights became very popular. When I first heard of it, I was astounded and suspicious. After a while, I read the writings of Rousseau and Montesquieu. Then I changed my views and thought that the world of Grand Peace (*t'ai-p'ing*) must be democracy (*min-chu*). However, I did not have anyone with whom I could talk about it.[50]

Huang's comments on the People's Rights movement in the "Treatise on Royal Succession" reflected his sympathy for the movement. He understood that it was a legitimate popular protest against autocratic government and that the people's frustration was rooted in the social and economic as well as the political oppression accumulated from the Tokugawa past:

> For the past few years, those who petitioned for opening a parliament arose one after another, and their vigor seems to exceed even that of the loyalist movement in the past. I wondered what the reasons were, and came to the following conclusion. After all, under the feudal rule, the distance between the rulers and the ruled was extremely great: commoners were not allowed to marry into a samurai family; they were forbidden to carry a sword, to wear silk, and to ride on horseback; the taxes were extremely heavy . . . there was no standard rule in handling criminal cases, and commoners were at the mercy of judicial officials . . . It was indeed an extreme case of autocracy. When oppression reaches an extreme, the natural reaction is an explosion.[51]

Even after the Meiji Restoration, Huang realized, the people's lives did not become easier; the government continued to demand great sacrifices for the sake of strengthening the state. Huang pointed out that the government was zealous in adopting all sorts of Western institutions except the parliamentary system and that it suppressed popular demands for representation:

> The government established a new taxation system after the Western model in order to squeeze money from the people; it imposed a conscription law to collect a "tax in blood" from the people in accordance with the Western system; it promulgated a Western-style penal code to punish wrongdoers; it built Western-syle schools to enlighten the masses. The only thing the government has not adopted from the West is a parliament, the most important institution in Western countries. The pretexts used by the government leaders were that the national polity of Japan differed from that of the West, that the people were not educated enough, and that the people did not want it.[52]

Furthermore, the government's many new laws and orders caused great confusion and inconvenience. To justify these new laws and regulations, the government termed them "Western methods." Thereupon the people used the identical justification in demanding a parliamentary system because it is a "Western method."[53]

Although government leaders attempted to suppress the agitation by the advocates of the People's Rights movement, especially the all-out attack on the government in newspapers, they were aware that adoption of some form of representative government was inevitable and were preparing for a gradual transition toward a constitutional monarchy. In April 1875, the Council of Elders (Genrōin), a consultative body, was established by imperial edict, which assured gradual progress toward constitutional government. In the same year, the first meeting of the assembly of prefectual governors was convened. In 1878, the government instituted elected prefectural assemblies. The prefectural assemblies were empowered only with the right to discuss matters concerning the finance of the prefectural government and the method of taxation; the governor retained the power to make final decisions. The voting rights in the election of the assembly were restricted by the amount of tax payment.[54] Huang witnessed the election and wrote a poem on elected assemblies, expressing his great curiosity.[55]

Commenting on the local assemblies in the "Treatise on Government Offices," Huang emphasized the limitations of their prerogatives and the restrictions that served to enfranchise only a small number of the local elite. After Huang read the minutes of a local assembly meeting held in 1879, he became doubtful whether government by elected representatives was any better than government by appointed officials. After all, he wrote, the prefectural assemblies were the cleverest camouflage of an autocratic government because they gave the illusion that the people were participating in the government, whereas in fact the ultimate decision-making was in the hands of the appointed governors. Implying that the elected assemblies were only a smoke screen for autocratic government, he wrote: "Sage kings in the past benefited the public through personal rule, and the state enjoyed great peace. Hegemons profit by instituting public systems, and the state still can be peaceful. The system of assemblies is a hegemon's method."[56]

As Huang admitted in later years, he changed his views of the People's Rights movement and Western-style democracy more than once. For this reason, there are some conflicting statements on these subjects in different sections of the *Treatises on Japan*. The "Treatise on Scholarship" contains a very negative opinion of the principle of democracy. Here Huang attacked the concept of the natural rights of individuals and egalitarianism as anathema to the Confucian social order:

> Discussing righteousness [*i*] and principles [*li*], they [advocates for the People's Rights] say that men have received a mandate from heaven and earth to live free and independent lives. Discussing rights [of individuals], they say that ruler and subjects, father and son, and man and woman are entitled to equal rights. Those whose scholarship is shallow stretch this theory as they please. They even regard the Three Bonds and the Five Cardinal Virtues as fetters.[57]

Huang later explained to Liang Ch'i-ch'ao that his negative views in the "Treatise on Scholarship" had resulted from his experience in the United States, where he stayed from 1882 to 1885 as Chinese Consul General at San Francisco. "In the United States I witnessed the dishonesty and greed of officials, dirty politics, selfish labor unions, and the violence in election campaigns that resulted in riotings and even assassinations. I thought that, if a great country of advanced civilization was like this, it was impossible [to adopt democracy] in a country where the people were insufficiently educated. Therefore I stated my opinions in my discussion of Mo-tzu in the 'Treatise on Scholarship.'"[58]

In fact, Huang's denouncement of egalitarianism was based on the same idea that he had conveyed to his conservative friends in Japan. He maintained the immutability of the Confucian social order and insisted on the primary importance of Confucian learning for all, including those studying Western subjects.[59]

As to the question of whether Japan would adopt a constitutional monarchy or even a democratic system, Huang thought the question was still open at the time he completed the *Treatises on Japan*. He wrote in the "Treatise on Royal Succession" that, "whether or not this country, which has had a sovereign for 2,500 years, would ever change into a country of constitutional monarchism or democracy, no one can tell. It will be determined by the spirit of the times. [*shih-shih*]"[60] His comments on the parliamentary system were quite open-minded, and he did not discuss the relationship between the system and its philosophical and ethical foundations. When the National Diet finally opened in 1890, Huang was serving at the Chinese Legation in London. Commenting on the event, he expressed his admiration of the speed of Japanese accomplishment.[61]

In 1898 when a reprint edition of the *Treatises on Japan* was published in Shanghai, Huang added some comments on the People's Rights movement. He interpreted the movement as a product of the interaction between the inexorable forces of history (heavenly timing) and human actions. In the feudal era, he stated, the best way to rule a country was by dividing the feudal lords, which Tokugawa Ieyasu well understood. In the modern world, however, no nation could afford divisive elements within itself because the struggle for survival among nations was too intense. For this reason, the new government of Japan must win over the hearts of the people so as to achieve national unity. For this purpose, Huang noted, the Five-Article Oath issued at the restoration included a declaration that all governmental affairs would be decided by public discussion. Thereupon, samurai and commoners alike demanded a greater share of political power and an expansion of civil rights. Since the imperial court and the bureaucracy could no longer maintain a power monopoly, parliamentarianism was inevitable. Evidently, Huang concluded, the trend of time had been heading toward the gradual adoption of a system in which the sovereignty of the Emperor and that of the people would harmoniously coexist (*chün-min kung-chu*). Summarizing the achievements of Meiji Japan, he stated that "the rise of Japan began with the overthrow of the Tokugawa and was completed with the establishment of the parliament." He praised the heroic efforts of the government leaders who had guided the nation to Meiji constitutionalism.[62]

In the notes to the 1898 edition, Huang also mentioned the popular uprisings of the late 1870s in protest against tyrannical local officials in Sakata and Yokohama. Although the uprisings mentioned by Huang were only precursors of the peasant uprisings in Fukushima, Gumma, Kabasan, Chichibu, Iida, Nagoya, and Osaka that occurred between 1882 and 1887, it is significant that Huang sensed that the mass disturbances were an important element of the People's Rights movement. Indeed, the frustrated populace, whose hopes after the Restoration had been betrayed by the new government, poured tremendous energy into the People's Rights movement. The radical movement of those peasants, which culminated in the Chichibu uprising in 1884, marked the final phase of the movement.[63]

The People's Rights movement had many facets, and Huang reacted specifically to each. He did not approve of the movement's opposition to the oligarchy from Satsuma and Chōshū. He supported the leadership of the Meiji Government on the grounds that they deserved their positions because of their contribution to the establishment of the nation-state. Furthermore, Huang responded negatively to the liberal thought of the movement. With respect to it as a movement to establish parliamentarianism as a new form of government, Huang reserved judgment until 1890, saying that time would determine the outcome. Finally, insofar as the movement encouraged popular protest against autocracy, Huang was sympathetic. However, even when he expressed concern over the plight of the masses, he never criticized individual leaders of the government. He consistently praised the "two or three great heroes" who had led the restoration movement and had taken the initiative in laying the foundation for the new nation. Undoubtedly, his emphasis on the importance of heroic leaders reflected his hope that similar leadership would arise to bring about reform in China.

THE CULTURAL IDENTITY OF MODERN JAPAN

How to plane a piece of wood and fly it like a bird?
How to build a fortress and ladder to scale its walls?
This "Western" learning they prefer to our Confucian lore
Is from the Mohist canon and of Eastern origin.[64]

Huang Tsun-hsien approved Japan's adoption of Western technology and institutions for their practical value, but he questioned
the wisdom of adopting the Western dress and lifestyle. In Confucian culture, one's costume and hairdo were important because
they expressed respect for propriety (*li*), a basic Confucian virtue.
Traditionally, the adoption of Chinese costume by non-Chinese
ethnic groups had been regarded as a sign of their advance toward
civilization; conversely, its neglect was interpreted as abandon-
ment of civilization. Naturally, therefore, the Japanese adoption
of Western clothes was detested by many Chinese observers.
Huang disapproved, not only from the Sinocentric point of view
but for practical reasons. He contended that Westernization of
costume and lifestyle was wasteful, even ruinous, to Japan's
economy because it necessitated excessive imports of foreign
goods. Japan's adoption of the Gregorian calendar was another
offense in the eyes of many Chinese. The calendar was regarded
as the key instrument for regulating the social order in harmony
with the cosmic order, and the Chinese calendar symbolized the
acceptance of universal order under the Son of Heaven. The
Taipings, who rebelled against dynastic rule and adopted their
own calendar system, upset the social-cosmic harmony. Although
Huang did not denounce Japan's adoption of the Western calendar
on traditional grounds, he seriously doubted its usefulness. The
old Chinese lunar calendar was arranged to guide the work schedule in an agrarian economy; hence Huang wondered what would
be gained by switching to a calendar that did not indicate the
change of seasons.[65]

What truly disturbed Huang was the Japanese neglect of Confucian studies that followed upon their enthusiasm for Western
learning. Most of the Confucian temples that had been maintained
by the *han* during the Tokugawa period were either converted to
government offices or abandoned to decay; only the one at
Shyōheizaka in Tokyo was kept up. It was a pity, Huang thought,
to see Confucian scholars neglected and living precariously.[66] He
was indignant that many Japanese regarded Chinese learning as
useless in the modern era. In his opinion, Western learning

could not take the place of Chinese (that is, Confucian) learning.

In defense of Confucian learning, Huang maintained that learning in the West was no more than an outgrowth of a marginal part of China's tradition. As he put it, "In my opinion, Western learning is none other than the teachings of Mo-ti." The principal elements of Western learning were, in his view, science, technology, and Christianity. The roots of all of these were present in the teachings of Master Mo (c. 479–372 B.C.). In the *ching* (canons) and *ching-shuo* (expositions on canons) of the *Mo-tzu*, Huang argued, rudimentary concepts of dynamics, chemistry, optics, biology, and other branches of science were explained, transmitted to the West, and developed into modern science. To bolster his argument, he quoted from the chapters on canons and the explanations of canons, which were a confusing mixture of moralistic, political, and legal, as well as scientific, terms. Huang's argument was as difficult to follow as the fragmentary and obscure original:

> *Hua* [transformation] means *i* [alteration] of *cheng* [appearance] as [a tadpole changes into] a frog, and [an egg changes into] a quail; water, fire, earth of the five elements burn when each touches the other and melts the metal; *t'ung* [sameness] means the sameness of the weight, physical entity, consistency and the species . . . These are the origins of chemistry. ([Huang's] note: By comparing the weights of things, [Mo-ti] classified things into various categories. The Westerners' theory concerning nitrogen, hydrogen, carbon, oxygen, and so forth, is an imitation of this idea. *Chün* [balance] can be explained from a stretched hair with weight on both ends; if the hair splits, the weight was not balanced; if the hair does not split, the weight was balanced. This is the origin of *chung-hsueh* [physics; lit. "study of weight"].)[67]

Joseph Needham has acknowledged that there were some promising scientific observations in the *Mo-tzu*, for example, on the problems of strains and stresses, which he assumes were not examined theoretically in the West until the Renaissance. Mohist optics was free from the erroneous theory of visual ray emissions from the eyes, which dominated ancient and medieval optics in the West. He suggests that the later Mohists were pushing their investigations toward the establishment of a thought system on which to base experimental science. Needham, however, refused to entertain the idea of Chinese influence on the development of Western science, stating that Chinese science and Western science had little in common for two millennia before the coming of the Jesuits.[68]

Huang asserted that Christianity too was of Mohist origin. He identified Christian doctrines with Mohist messages such as *shang-t'ung* (egalitarianism), *chien-ai* (universal love), and *shih-t'ien* (worship of heaven). Biblical teachings such as "Worship God" and "Love your neighbor as yourself" were to be found in the *Mo-tzu*.[69] Huang objected to the egalitarianism of the *Mo-tzu* because it conflicted with the Confucian human relationship of the Three Bonds, which rested on filial piety, loyalty, and obedience. In Huang's view, it was unfilial to regard one's father as an equal and treat him no differently than a stranger would be treated. Indeed, for this very reason, Mohism had been refuted as dangerous by the Confucian philosopher Mencius in the third century B.C.

Huang was not alone among the late Ch'ing intellectuals in associating the *Mo-tzu* with Western science and technology. Shimada Kenji has suggested that there was a trend among the late Ch'ing intellectuals to re-examine the *Mo-tzu* and other non-Confucian writings which had been ignored for centuries. As an early example of the *Mo-tzu* study in the nineteenth century, he mentioned the *Hsueh-chi i-te* (Record of learning, 1844) by Tsou Po-ch'i, a scholar from the Nan-hai district of Kwangtung. In his discussion of optical science, Tsou frequently quoted from the *Mo-tzu*.[70] Joseph Levenson pointed out that Sun I-jang (1848–1908), author of the most comprehensive commentary on the *Mo-tzu*, and Wo-jen (d. 1871), the die-hard conservative who opposed the study of Western science, also believed that the *Mo-tzu's* ideas were close to the modern conception of physics.[71] Onogawa Hidemi has suggested that the writings of Chang Tzu-mu and Wang Chih-ch'un were early examples of relating Western technology to the Chinese classics. In fact, discussions on modern science in Chang's *Ying-hai lun* (A discourse on the sea powers, c. 1884) and Wang's *Ying-hai chih-yen* (Miscellaneous talks on the sea powers, c. 1884) are almost identical with Huang's writings on the *Mo-tzu* in *Miscellaneous Poems on Japan*. Ch'en Chih also expressed an opinion similar to Huang's concerning the origins of Christianity in his *Yung-shu* (Utilitarian discourse, c. 1893). He wrote that in the Old and New Testaments one could find that Western religion originated in the *Mo-tzu*, that Moses was a transliteration of Mo-ti, and that the biblical Exodus was Mo-ti's escape from the Ch'in ruler. He asserted that, when Mo-ti went to the Western Regions, the classical canons were transmitted to the West.[72]

The purpose of Huang's assertion that the principal elements of Western learning had originated in the Chinese Classics was to counter the Japanese belief that Western learning must replace Chinese learning in the modern era. In Confucian tradition, learning was essential for the cultivation of a moral personality. How could Western "learning," derived from some marginal elements in Chinese tradition, replace the essential core of Chinese learning? Explaining why he discussed the *Mo-tzu* at such length (his commentary on Western learning in *Miscellaneous Poems* is longer than any of his other comments), he wrote:

> We cannot say that all the superior technologies of the Westerners were derived from the Chinese classics. But the Chinese made the beginnings, and the Westerners elaborated on them. Therefore we must learn their superior technologies. In these days, however, those who blindly admire Western learning are inclined to discard their own [way] and follow the Westerners. There are even those who say that the study of the Chinese classics is of no use. Therefore I have quoted from the *Mo-tzu* in detail in order to silence such foolish arguments.[73]

Huang was especially bitter about the popularity of the "American theory of freedom," because it led people to neglect cardinal human relationships.[74]

One reason why the Japanese rushed to embrace Western learning, Huang pointed out, was their national tradition of borrowing foreign culture and worshiping foreign goods:

In olden times, the Japanese looked up to China [as their teacher]. From the calendar, bureaucratic and military systems, court decorum, writing system, to the details of daily life such as food and toys, there was nothing in Japan that had not been adopted from the great T'ang. In modern times, ever since Japan concluded the treaties with the Western countries, there is nothing in Japan that has not been adopted from the West . . . Enchanted by foreign goods, they buy imports from afar, spending all their money; they discard like trash the things they had in their own country. It is quite amazing![75]

It is a fact that the Japanese cherished imported goods. The term *hakurai* (lit., "goods coming on a ship") was a synonym for exquisite goods; it meant imports from China during the Tokugawa era and, later, imports from the West. However, it was not easy for the Japanese to adapt certain elements of foreign culture to their own. During the early Meiji period, the problem of Japan's cultural identity in the era of Westernization was seriously debated.

The most popularized discussion was contained in the *Tōkyō shin hanjōki* by Hattori Bushō. Three students—one of Western learning, one of Chinese learning, and the third a devotee of national learning—met at a new-style restaurant where beef dishes were served. They began to converse. The student of Western learning said: "Considering the trend of the world today, we should have no other learning but that from the West. Its breadth encompasses all aspects of world affairs—economy, natural resources, politics, military forces. There is nothing that is not dealt with in Western learning . . . The teachings of Confucius have fallen to the ground along with the privileges of the samurai class; these things have so little value that they are no better than junk in an antique shop. To rely on education in Chinese learning and to expect to climb the ladder of officialdom is like sitting on bean curd: such people will sooner or later disgrace themselves and will eventually rot with the bean curd (lit., "rotten beans") and will literally become 'rotten Confucians.'" Upon hearing this, the young man sitting next to him said with irritation: "I am a student of Chinese learning. The *tao* of Confucius is the most broad and righteous. How could it be even mentioned in the same breath with the way of the barbarians? . . . First of all, what is scholarship? Isn't it for the cultivation of humanity? . . . Without humanity and righteousness under heaven, subjects commit regicide, sons kill fathers, government officials become corrupt, and merchants monopolize profits. Look at the peoples in the West. They forget about human ethics in their pursuit of profit." The student of Western learning retorted: "So-called Confucianists have classical principles on their lips but not in their conduct . . . Look at present-day China. There is nothing worth adopting from that country. The despotic ruler restricts the freedom of his subjects and arrogantly calls the country the Middle Kingdom. The Chinese do not know how to communicate with other countries. It would be rather appropriate to call them the barbarians and the Westerners' country the Middle Kingdom." Then the student of national learning broke into the conversation and attacked the other two for their admiration of foreign countries. He reminded them that Japan was a divine country possessing an imperial house whose line of succession was unbroken. At the point when the argument became very heated, an old man who had been listening to them intervened: "For performing a *kyōgen* [comic drama], it is necessary to have an orchestra, a singer, and a dancer. If any one of these is lacking, *kyōgen* cannot be performed." He suggested that a great scholar of the divine country should combine the disciplines of Western, Chinese, and national learning. Upon hearing the old man's speech, the students fell silent and each returned to his dormitory.[76]

The trichotomy of Western, Chinese, and national values was a favorite topic of discussion among the Japanese throughout the Meiji era. In his famous treatise, *San suijin keirin mondō*, (Debates of three scholars over wine, 1888), Nakae Chōmin took up that very issue. A matter of deep concern for the Japanese in the Meiji era was how to combine Western values with a Japanese tradition that had been heavily influenced by Confucian values. On various levels of sophistication, the Japanese sought a new identity in the modern world.

It appears that Huang did not acknowledge Japanese efforts to find a new cultural identity. To him, those who had adopted the

Western style appeared to have discarded their own culture and were blindly imitating the Westerners. As Huang confessed later, he was not sympathetic to the followers of Western learning primarily because his friends were mostly traditional literati. However, there was at least one outstanding scholar of Western learning among those with whom Huang associated. Nakamura Masanao (Keiu, 1832–1891) was well known as the translator of works by Samuel Smiles and John Stuart Mill and was a member of the celebrated Meiroku Society that had been organized by the advocates of Westernization of Japanese culture. An examination of the relationship between Huang and Nakamura sheds light on Huang's attitude toward modern Japanese intellectuals.

Nakamura Keiu had a distinguished career as a scholar of traditional Chinese learning before he became famous as a pioneer of Western learning. He gained the prestigious position as the Confucian instructor (*jusha*) at the Shōheikō at the unusually young age of thirty-one. Four years later, in 1866, when the *bakufu* sent twelve students to England, Nakamura volunteered to accompany them as supervisor. He had been secretly studying English since his student days at the Shōheikō. In his petition to the *bakufu*, he expressed the wish to investigate the spiritual rather than the material aspects of Western culture. He explained that Western scholarship could be divided into two fields: spiritual learning (*seirei no gaku* or *keijijō no gaku*), which covered language, logic, ethics, government, law, literature, and fine arts; and material learning (*busshitsu no gaku* or *keijika no gaku*), which consisted of physics, engineering, chemistry, geography, astronomy, medicine, and biology. Since Western learning in Japan up to that time had been limited to the material, Nakamura now volunteered to study the spiritual aspect of Western learning, a difficult field for the young because to judge between good and evil required maturity. His petition was approved, and he lived in London from 1866 to 1868. There he observed Victorian society, which was vigorously expounding a puritan ethic, and came to understand that the moral principles of the British people were rooted in Christianity.[77]

Nakamura characterized Victorian moral principles as embodying faith, hope, and charity, and he believed that the prosperity of English society was buoyed up by its benevolent and courageous people. At the time Nakamura was in England, various new religious sects were springing up. Despite sectarian differences among the groups led by Arnold, Newman, and the Evangelicals, all of them attacked what they called "nominal" Christianity and the lax or feeble conception of morality that went with it. This creed of earnestness in religious life was combined with the secular ethic glorifying work. The moral qualities of hard work and persistence were exalted as a supreme virtue, while idleness was scorned. These ideas were illustrated in the popular treatise by Samuel Smiles, entitled *Self-Help* (1859), written in anecdotal style and intended to guide young men on the road to success.[78] When Nakamura and the students were about to return home because of the restoration, an English friend gave him a copy of *Self-Help* as a parting gift. He was so impressed by the book that, soon after returning to Japan, he translated and published it in 1871 under the title *Saikoku risshihen* (Stories of self-made men in the west). Many schools in Japan adopted it as a textbook, and it is said that the wood-block print of the first edition sold several hundred thousand copies and was one of the three best sellers in the Meiji era, the other two being *Seiyō jijō* (Things in the West) by Fukuzawa Yukichi, and *Yochi shiryaku* (Outline of world geography) by Uchida Masao.

Nakamura's immediate purpose in translating and publishing *Self-Help* was to present a new philosophy of life for himself and his fellow men, particularly former retainers of the Tokugawa who had retired to Shizuoka with a small pension. Nakamura himself followed the Tokugawas to Shizuoka and taught at a Confucian school. His concern was to survive in a rapidly changing world while maintaining his moral integrity as a man who had received a Confucian education. In his commentaries on *Self-Help*, Nakamura urged his readers to maintain a positive attitude toward life, to nurture willpower, to set up a goal of life, and to pursue that goal with diligence, patience, honesty, and frugality. In the preface, he wrote: "Reading the biographies of the distinguished Western men of the past and present, I found that all of them possessed an

independent spirit and the courage to overcome difficulties. These
men revered heaven and loved their fellow man with great earnestness. Their great accomplishments benefited their countries. The
prosperity of Western countries is founded on the diligence and
endurance of these men."[79]

After the fall of the old regime, feudal ethics were denounced
as evil, but no alternative had been offered, except for some vague
ideas expressed in the slogan *bummei kaika* (Civilization and Enlightenment). Under these circumstances, Nakamura's translation
and commentaries provided much-needed moral guidance to help
his contemporaries find a new framework for morale. Many successful self-made men of the Meiji and Taishō periods claimed that
they were inspired by reading Nakamura's work in adolescence.
In 1872, Nakamura published his translation of John Stuart Mill's
On Liberty under the title of *Jiyū no ri*. Nakamura's commentaries
emphasized that in the Christian ethic lay the secret of the wealth
and power of the West. Because of his nationalist preoccupations,
Nakamura ignored Mill's warning against the danger to individual
liberty posed by a tyrannical government. Although this translation
attracted fewer readers than *Self-Help*, it did inspire the leaders
of the People's Rights movement during the second decade of the
Meiji.[80]

Nakamura's understanding of Christian doctrine was colored by
the Confucian ethic and his nationalist orientation. His work on
Christianity, "Treatise on Reverence to Heaven and Love of Men"
("Keiten aijin setsu," 1868) used Confucian terminology exclusively; not a single Christian term was employed to express God or
creation. He stated that the only meaning of the command to revere heaven was to have *jen* (benevolence) of mind, and that all
men inherently received the capacity to follow the way of heaven.
Sin and salvation were equated with calamity and good fortune,
which would be bestowed by heaven in response to man's good or
evil conduct.[81]

Out of his conviction that the Christian ethic was the foundation
of the West's vitality, Nakamura addressed an open memorial to the
Emperor, recommending not only that the ban on Christianity

be lifted but that Christianity be adopted as the national religion. The memorial, consisting of some 1,900 words, was in English, and published in an English-language newspaper in Yokohama. To conceal his identity, Nakamura pretended to be a Westerner. According to the pseudo-Westerner, the Japanese had concentrated on the material achievements of the West while neglecting the spiritual basis upon which they were founded:

> In general, we may say that the condition of Western countries is but the outward leaf and blossom of their religion, and religion is the root and foundation on which their prosperity depends. Now Your Majesty's subjects, pleased with the branches and foliage, wish to make them all their own, and they try to imitate them. This is more ridiculous than the mimicry of apes, and it seems to me a delusion to reject the very cause of the prosperity of those nations.[82]

He urged the Emperor to transplant the good tree—that is, Christian religion—to Japanese soil rather than merely picking its fruits. If the Emperor wished to establish Christianity in Japan, he himself should be baptized first in order to become the head of the Christian Church in Japan.[83] When the memorial was published in Japanese in *Shimbun zasshi* (News magazine) in August 1872, furious refutations were made against the anonymous author. Nakamura was forced to publish an erratum deleting the sentence in which he recommended baptism for the Emperor. Although Nakamura himself became a Christian, he confessed in later years that he never lost his respect for Confucius. [84]

Nakamura moved to Tokyo in 1872 and opened a private school, Dōjinsha, in Edogawa district the following year. The major subjects taught were English, mathematics, and the Chinese Classics. Foreigners were invited to teach not only English grammar and composition but geography, history, economics, science, and ethics.[85] The fine arts and religion were also important because they were regarded as useful moral subjects that would help build a strong personality. *Risshi* (Set high purposes) was the motto of the school. Nakamura valued the spirit of independence, which had some affinity with the Neo-Confucian tenet of self-cultivation. Like Keiō Gijuku founded by Fukuzawa Yukichi, Dōjinsha enjoyed the reputation of a prestigious private school, though it did not survive as long. A noteworthy feature of Dōjinsha was that it admitted women and eventually established a separate school for them. Since Nakamura recognized the weight of a mother's influence on her children, he regarded the education of women as crucial for building a strong nation. He published his opinions on female education and was known as a major advocate for its advancement. For this reason, when the Tokyo Normal School for Women (presently Ochanomizu University) was founded by the government, Nakamura became its president, serving from 1875 to 1880 while also president of Dōjinsha. It was during this period that Huang Tsun-hsien met Nakamura.[86]

Huang came into contact with Nakamura through his friends in literary circles, and their association followed the same pattern as that between Huang and the traditional literati. Huang participated in the activities of the literary group organized at Dōjinsha and contributed to its journal. Nakamura admired Huang as a scholar and solicited Huang's comments on his own writings in classical Chinese.[87] A poem Nakamura dedicated to Huang shortly before his departure from Japan expressed respect for Huang as a scholar and promising statesman. The poem reveals that Huang had discussed Christianity and Western learning with Nakamura:

Master Kung-tu*, you are inspiring, buoyant, bright.
Your company releases me from life's anxieties,
One evening with you far exceeds ten years of reading books,
Each encounter like discovering a jewel in the sea.
Your thesis that our Mo-tzu and Western scholarship
Are one is a unique thought, never before conceived.
. . . .

With all this, you are most concerned with able government.
Your writing, now in draft, will soon be ready for the world.
While I, a wandering sheep, trying path after path,
Have achieved nothing; what is more, my hair is turning white.
I envision you as one day ruling millions with grand sway,

Your mighty wings stretched over thousands of square miles.
Oh, when that happens, please protect this little island realm![88]

*Huang's *tzu*

The last stanza of the poem was more than an expression of courtesy to the Chinese guest. Nakamura believed that China was truly
a great country and the Chinese were a great people, and he was
seriously concerned about the growing tendency among the Japanese to slight China. His article "China Should Not Be Despised,"
written for *Meiroku zasshi* (Journal of the Meiroku Society), was a
reminder to the Japanese of China's formidable potential despite
her temporary weakness. He wrote that, from antiquity to the
present, China had produced great men—countless sages, wise
rulers, heroes, and men of extraordinary ability. He maintained
that it was because of their own great culture that the Chinese did
not rush to learn from the West. However, once Chinese students
were sent abroad, they would quickly attain high standards in
Western scholarship. China's present weakness was attributable to
the Manchu rulers; the Chinese people were unable to realize their
potential, being paralyzed by the narcotic of the Tartars. However,
once they awoke from their induced sleep, Nakamura predicted,
a hero would emerge, and under his aegis China would become a
powerful state.[89] He repeatedly warned against the Japanese tendency to neglect classical Chinese learning, the basis of moral
education. At his school, Chinese classics were taught as an important subject side by side with the new subjects in Western learning.[90]
He decried the expedition to Korea and the annexation of Ryukyu
on grounds that the ancient sages deplored taking advantage of
neighboring countries. Small countries were always vulnerable;
Ryukyu might be a small country in Japanese eyes, but Japan was
a small country in the eyes of the Chinese.[91] Because of his Confucian outlook, Nakamura was called the "saint of Edogawa" by
his contemporaries.

In view of Nakamura's background and accomplishments as an
advocate of Western ethical values, he could have been a good

source of information for Huang on Western learning in Japan, particularly from the spiritual standpoint. However, Huang was obviously not interested in Japanese efforts to assimilate the Western ethic. He saw little point in Nakamura's efforts to integrate Christian moral values into the Confucian framework. In Huang's eyes, Nakamura's theory of Christianity was harmful; it could mislead naive people to think that the Confucian principles of human relations could be replaced. Indirectly criticizing Nakamura's explanation of Christian faith in terms of the Confucian ethic, Huang wrote;

> Thus the prosperity of Western learning [in Japan] is like the rising sun. Once Western learning became popular, those who followed its teachings increased, and many others were influenced by it. In their discussion of religion, they say that serving God is the same as the Confucian idea of *ching-t'ien* [Revere heaven] and that "Love others as you love yourself" is the same as *jen-min* [Benevolence to the populace], and that "Save your soul" is the same as *ming-te* [Illuminate virtue] in Confucian teaching.[92]

Aside from this passage, Huang made no direct reference to Nakamura in his writing. Perhaps it was owing to his confidence in the universality of Confucian values that Huang did not recognize the inevitability of moral reorientation of a society in the process of modernization. He lamented the Japanese infatuation with the West and their neglect of Confucian studies, which he believed to have fostered their disrespect for China. He also believed that their contempt for China lay at the root of Japanese aggression in areas peripheral to China.

FOUR

Japan's Aggression on China's Periphery

Although the Chinese delegation were surrounded by friendly Japanese at social gatherings, they had to confront officials who were discourteous over diplomatic issues. Japanese officials were well educated in the Chinese classics; some of them even joined the social groups of Huang's literati friends. Where official business was concerned, however, they did not share the Confucian values of the Chinese diplomats. They turned a deaf ear to moral suasion concerning Japan's aggression in China's borderlands. The Japanese officials not only dressed like Westerners; they justified Japan's actions with Western logic. The Japanese intentionally ignored China's traditional ties with her tributaries, maintaining that only modern international law was a valid standard. Of course, the real problem for China was that Japan itself did not live up to the spirit of international law. No sooner did the Japanese learn the idealized pronouncements of modern international relations than they began to copy the imperialistic expansion the Westerners were practicing in Asia.[1]

The sense of crisis generated by the Western advance in Asia prompted the Japanese to take action on China's periphery. In the meantime, Japan prematurely attempted to adopt the pattern of Sino-Western relationships in dealing with China. At the negotiations for the Sino-Japanese Friendship Treaty of 1871, the Japanese demanded the insertion of a most-favored-nation clause, which would allow Japan the same privileges that the Western Powers had gained from China, particularly the freedom to travel and trade in the interior.[2] Japan could not achieve this aim in 1871 but expected to find an opportunity to revise the treaty with China. The Ryukyu Incident provided that opportunity. The controversy over Ryukyu was the major diplomatic issue between China and Japan during the period when Huang was in Japan.

THE RYUKYU INCIDENT

The diplomatic expertise of the Chinese delegates was not as brilliant as their adeptness in cultural and social activities. Their role in Tokyo was limited, since the Japanese government, following Western practice, negotiated major issues with the government in Peking through Japan's resident minister. Moreover, the Chinese minister's inexperience in modern diplomacy was taken advantage of by the Japanese, who were unwilling to negotiate the Ryukyu problem. From the Japanese point of view, Japan's annexation of Ryukyu had been an accomplished fact by the time the Chinese delegation arrived.

The kingdom of Ryukyu, comprising a chain of islands stretching between Kyushu and Taiwan, had long been a tributary state of both China and the Satsuma *han* of Japan. Despite the Satsuma rulers' tight control over the government of Ryukyu, the Ryukyuans were allowed to continue their tributary relationship with China, primarily because Satsuma could thus indirectly engage in the China trade.[3] After the Meiji Restoration, however, the central government did not tolerate the dual suzerainty of Ryukyu. As its first task in foreign relations, the Meiji Government clarified the lines of demarcation. On the north the Kurile Islands were secured as Japanese territory in exchange for Sakhalin by the terms of the treaty with Russia (1874). Japanese sovereignty over the Bonin Islands off the Pacific coast was not contested (1876). On the southeastern border, Ryukyu was declared an integral part of Japan. In 1872, the Japanese government informed the Ryukyuans of its plan to make Ryukyu a *han*, to appoint the King *han-ō* (king of the *han*) and raise him to the peerage. The management of Ryukyu's foreign affairs would be taken over by the Foreign Ministry of Japan, and the Ryukyuans were forbidden to send tributary missions to China or to receive investiture from the Chinese Emperor.

To obtain China's consent to the Japanese jurisdiction over Ryukyu, the Japanese government had resorted to a tactical maneuver. Under the pretext of punishing the aborigines who had killed some fifty shipwrecked Ryukyuans in 1871, the Japanese sent an expeditionary force to Taiwan in 1874. This action led to negotiations between China and Japan. By the Peking Agreement of October 1874, the Chinese agreed to compensate the families of the murdered Ryukyuans as a condition for Japanese withdrawal from Taiwan. By agreeing to these terms the Chinese government unwittingly acknowledged the Japanese claim that the Ryukyuans were Japanese subjects. At this point, however, the Chinese leaders, including Li Hung-chang, did not realize that such an agreement would give legality to Japan's claim over Ryukyu; their sole concern at the moment was Japan's military presence in Taiwan.[4]

Hyman Kublin has pointed out that the Chinese became alarmed over the situation in Ryukyu only when the tributary mission failed to arrive. In other words, so long as the missions continued to come, the Chinese paid little attention to the change in legal status of Ryukyu, not realizing that China's suzerainty over Ryukyu was being challenged by the Western concept of the nation-state.[5] For their part, the Ryukyuans took their tributary obligation to China seriously. Despite the Japanese government's prohibition, the King of Ryukyu sent a mission to China when the Kuang-hsu Emperor ascended the throne in 1875. The presence of the mission was detected by the Japanese Acting Minister in Peking; his attempt to reprimand the Ryukyuans was obstructed by Chinese officials. After this incident, the Japanese government dispatched an official from the Ministry of Home Affairs to Ryukyu to enforce the order against sending tributary missions to China. At the same time, the government ordered the Ryukyuans to use the reign title of the Japanese Emperor for their calendar, to observe Japanese laws, and to pattern their bureaucracy on the Japanese model. The Ryukyuans continued to protest strongly against the order to discontinue tributary relations with China.

In 1877, the year when the regular tributary mission was due, the King of Ryukyu secretly sent a court noble to Foochow to appeal for support from China. The King's letter, submitted to Governor General Ho Ching and Governor Ting Jih-ch'ang of Fukien, was essentially an apology for not being able to send the tributary goods and a plea for help in removing the obstacle posed by the Japanese, which hindered the fulfillment of his tributary obligation. The letter did not mention the other measures taken by the Japanese.[6] Ho Ching and Ting Jih-ch'ang recommended that the government instruct Ho Ju-chang, the recently appointed Chinese minister to Japan, to straighten out the matter in Tokyo. They stated that, although Ryukyu was a small, poor country without much economic value and of little strategic importance, nevertheless, if China rejected Ryukyu's appeal, the Western nations would interpret it as weakness on the part of China and would instigate trouble in other peripheral areas. Ho Ju-chang was to persuade the Japanese to withdraw from Ryukyu and at the same time invite the intervention of Western diplomats in Tokyo. Their recommendation was accepted and Ho Ju-chang was ordered to pursue the matter in Tokyo.[7]

Upon his arrival in Tokyo, Ho Ju-chang's first step in regard to the Ryukyu Incident was to recommend a practical approach. In May 1878, he advised the Tsungli Yamen and Li Hung-chang to take strong action at once. The letters, undoubtedly drafted by Huang Tsun-hsien,[8] stated that, if China supinely allowed Japan to take over Ryukyu, then China's loss would not be limited to Ryukyu; Korea, Taiwan, and the Pescadores would be threatened within a few years. On the basis of this reasoning, the letters proposed three alternative actions. The first was to send warships to compel Ryukyu to send a tributary mission to China while the negotiations with the Japanese government were continuing. Presumably the Japanese would feel threatened and would yield to China's demand. The second was to have the Ryukyuans declare war against Japan and then to help them defeat the Japanese. The third was to invite the diplomatic corps in Tokyo to discuss the matter in the light of international law. To do nothing would be folly. These three procedures were based on Huang's judgment that Japan's national strength was not yet consolidated, that its army was still below full strength, and that China could defeat Japan. Huang predicted that Japan would not dare to fight: the government could not finance a war; its military forces—especially the navy—were inferior to China's; and there was dangerous social discontent in Japan caused by heavy taxation and the introduction of conscription. Huang thought a rebellion was likely if the government demanded more sacrifices from the people. The letters also urged the need for immediate action. "If we allow the tiger to grow bigger, we will never be able to control it in the future."[9]

It is significant that Huang recommended the use of military force to protect the kingdom of Ryukyu. He obviously began to see that the issue was larger than one of tributary relationship: the Ryukyuans had been foolish to inform China only of Japan's intervention in the matter of the mission and not to have reported the incorporation of Ryukyu as a *han* and the other actions taken by the Japanese.[10]

Despite the recommendations from the legation in Tokyo, the Chinese government took no action. Li Hung-chang explained that Ryukyu was not worth a war, and he instructed Ho Ju-chang to try to solve the issue through negotiation. Thereupon Ho attempted moral suasion. On September 3, 1878, Ho visited Foreign Minister Terashima Munenori. The meeting was a disaster, as the following excerpt from their conversation shows:[11]

[Ho:] The reason why I visited you today is because I have some questions about Ryukyu. I have heard that it has recently become a dependency of your country. Your government must know that it has also been sending tribute to our country. Nevertheless, I hear that you

strictly ordered the Ryukyuans not to send tribute to our country. Because this is very inconvenient for the Ryukyuans, we wish you to leave the matter of tribute as it traditionally has been.
[Terashima:] There were precedents in the past that small countries became the tributary of a large country; however, in recent years, small countries incapable of being independent have been threatened with absorption into other countries. In the past we let Ryukyu have its own diplomatic relations with other countries; however, because of the above-mentioned danger we took over its foreign relations. Therefore Ryukyu no longer has to deal with foreign countries.
[Ho:] Then is Ryukyu part of Japanese territory?
[Terashima:] Yes.
[Ho:] Do the Ryukyuans say that they are Japanese?
[Terashima:] If I do not like Japan, I can go to another person and say that I am not a Japanese. Some Ryukyuans who do not like their own country may say that they are not Japanese.
[Ho:] From the standpoint of geography, Ryukyu belongs to our country.
[Terashima:] That is another question.

Clearly, when Ho began to contest Japanese sovereignty over Ryukyu, Terashima took the stance that there was no need for discussion; the Japanese regarded the annexation of Ryukyu as a domestic affair and not subject to interference by another power. Ho assumed that China's suzerainty over Ryukyu would be honored by the international community; for him the continuation of the tribute was of primary concern.

To reiterate his position, Ho Ju-chang sent a note to Terashima on October 7. He decried the interruption of Sino-Ryukyu relations and reproached Japan for its unjust oppression of a small and weak country. After recounting the historical and cultural evidence in favor of the status quo, Ho continued:

Suddenly we heard that your country prohibited Liu-ch'iu [Ryukyu] from sending tribute to our country. Upon hearing this, our government regarded the act as insincere, unrighteous, cruel, and unreasonable on the part of Japan, a respectable great country, to betray its neighbor and bully the weak country . . . The first article of the Sino-Japanese Friendship Treaty states that each country shall treat the other with courtesy [*li*] and shall not infringe upon the other's territory. . . . Now if you oppress Liu-ch'iu and arbitrarily change its traditional establishment, how can you say that Japan has a relationship based on trust [*yueh*, lit., "pledge" or "tie," also means "treaty"] with our country or with Liu-ch'iu? Although Liu-ch'iu is a small country, its loyalty to our court is deep and would not easily yield to oppression. Today, all the countries in the world communicate with each other and courtesy is of primary importance in international relations. To judge from human feelings and international law, all the countries in the world would disapprove the action of your country in oppressing a small state. . .

We hope your country will treat Liu-ch'iu with courtesy, will let it maintain its traditional government and state, and will not prohibit its sending tribute to China. Then we shall be able to maintain friendly relations, consolidate our ties as neighbors, and avoid the derision of all the nations in the world.[12]

The Japanese read Ho's note as hostile, and inquired whether the Chinese government intended to break off diplomatic relations. Thereafter, the Japanese refused to negotiate any further unless Ho's note was withdrawn with an apology.[13]

Ho's note might have been accepted as diplomatic rhetoric in China during the Warring States period, but he was mistaken in expecting the Japanese to respond to his reprimand. The Japanese interpreted the note as implying hostility, according to the practice of diplomacy among Western nations. The outspoken note earned Ho the reputation of being unqualified as a diplomat. Also, he was criticized for confiding diplomatic secrets to the entire diplomatic corps in Tokyo. The Japanese government was always aware of Chinese plans in advance because of Ho's indiscreet remarks to Western diplomats.[14] Undoubtedly, Ho's purpose was to mobilize world opinion in China's favor, but he did not succeed.

Shortly after the exchange of notes, the Japanese government announced the abolition of the Ryukyu *han* and designated the territory as an Okinawa prefecture. On December 27, 1878, Matsuda Michiyuki of the Ministry of Home Affairs was dispatched to Shuri, the Ryukyu capital. He completed the military takeover of the capital on March 31, 1879. The King and court were moved to Tokyo, and the newly appointed prefect arrived in Ryukyu in early April. To Huang's regret, the Chinese government was unwilling to act to defend Ryukyu.

In the meantime, the Ryukyuans resisted Japan's direct rule and continued their appeals to China for intervention. One after another, Ryukyu officials visited the Tsungli Yamen in Peking, Li Huang-chang in Tientsin, and the Chinese Legation in Tokyo. They threw themselves on the ground and literally cried for China's help.[15] Although Li Hung-chang was moved by their desperation, he was still unwilling to risk war with Japan. Instead, he took advantage of the timely visit to China of the former United States President, General Ulysses S. Grant. When Grant arrived in Tientsin in June 1879, Li asked for his good offices in solving the dispute over Ryukyu. Grant agreed to take up the matter in an unofficial capacity. The Japanese took Grant's mediation very seriously. They were eager to gain the support of such a celebrity as Grant to aid their efforts for treaty revision with the Western nations. Grant simply recommended a peaceful settlement of the matter in a spirit of compromise, warning that hostilities between the two countries could be used to advantage by an aggressive European nation.

In accordance with Grant's suggestion, Ho Ju-chang withdrew his note of October 7, 1878, and negotiations were opened in Peking in August 1880 between the ministers of the Tsungli Yamen and the Japanese minister in Peking. The Japanese used the opportunity to attempt to revise the Sino-Japanese Treaty of 1871. They proposed that the islands of Ryukyu be divided into two parts, with the southern island group of Miyako and Yaeyama to be retained by China. In return, Japan demanded that a most-favored-nation clause be added to the treaty. The Chinese initially refused to accept such a condition on the ground that the Sino-Japanese Treaty was based on the principle of equality and friendship and was different from China's treaties with the Western powers, which had been concluded under duress. After three months of negotiation, however, the Chinese yielded and agreement based on Japan's proposals was reached on October 21, 1880. The Chinese were anxious to reach a quick settlement with

Japan, primarily because China was threatened by war with Russia over the Ili crisis. Then, to the outrage of the Japanese, the Chinese government did not sign the treaty, on the grounds that strong objections were being raised by high officials. Li Huang-chang was of the opinion that it was a mistake to grant Japan such a major concession as the most-favored-nation treatment in exchange for the barren islands of southern Ryukyu. The Chinese government proposed to reopen the negotiations in early 1881, shortly after the conclusion of the Treaty of St. Petersburg with Russia, but the Japanese government did not respond. Ryukyu was then abandoned by China without any legal settlement.[16]

Huang Tsun-hsien grieved bitterly over China's failure to help Ryukyu. He narrated the history of the kingdom in a poem, emphasizing its loyalty to China. He described the moving scene of his first encounter with a Ryukyu official, which took place when he first arrived in Japan. The ship that carried the Chinese delegation had arrived in Kobe. Late that night, an old Ryukyu official stealthily came aboard:

> *White-haired minister bathed in tears,*
> *Topknot disheveled, dark green robes,*
> *Has come distraught across the sea*
> *To tell us the fate of his country.*

Unfortunately, no one could understand his dialect. Then he presented a secret letter from the King of Ryukyu, begging the Chinese to rescue his kingdom from the Japanese. Huang sympathized with the Ryukyuans and was deeply moved by their loyalty to their King. He lamented the fate of their hapless country and regretted the Chinese government's lack of action. Strongly criticizing his own government, Huang wrote that "from China merely benevolent words of consolation were bestowed on the despairing Ryukyuans."[17]

THE KOREAN COMMISSIONER KIM HONG-JIP

Korea was another tributary state of China's that Japan eventually annexed. No sooner was the Meiji Government established than the Japanese challenged the traditional pattern of diplomacy between Japan and Korea which had been regulated within the framework of the Sinocentric world order. In late 1868, the Meiji Government sent a note to Korea concerning the restoration of the imperial rule and expressing its wish to establish diplomatic relations with Korea. The Korean officials rejected the note, which ignored the traditional formalities. The Japanese use of the term "emperor" was especially offensive, since that title was reserved for the Emperor of China. Contrary to Japan's desire to establish modern diplomatic relations, the Koreans demonstrated their determination to maintain the traditional relationship.[18] In Japan, an argument over the question of sending an expeditionary force to Korea resulted in a serious split within the top government leadership. After consolidating its power base, the oligarchic leadership resorted to sending gunboats to Korea to force the unwilling Koreans to comply with Japan's demands. As a result, the Treaty of Kanghwa, Korea's first treaty with a foreign power, was concluded in February 1876. Its terms were modeled after the treaties between Western powers and Japan; Korea was obliged to open Pusan and two other ports for trade with Japan and to recognize the extraterritoriality of Japanese residents in Korea. In addition, Japan secured tariff exemptions on Japanese goods and the right to use Japanese currency in Korea.

When the ports of Pusan, Wonsan, and Inchon were opened— in 1876, 1880, and 1881 respectively—Japanese merchants, mainly from the Kyushu and Osaka areas, rushed to engage in a lucrative export-import business in Korea. They imported coarse cotton fabrics made in Britain, which they purchased at Nagasaki or Shanghai, and exported rice, soybeans and other foodstuffs and gold. Their use of Japanese currency and the large amounts of grain that they obtained very cheaply disrupted the local economy and caused food shortages when the crops failed. Naturally, anti-Japanese feelings among the populace were generated.[19]

As a means of nurturing pro-Japanese sentiment in Korea, the

Japanese government invited a friendship mission to Tokyo immediately after the treaty was concluded. The mission, headed by Kim Ki-su, arrived in May 1876 and stayed in Japan for about twenty days. The Koreans were lavishly entertained and, to impress them with Japan's superiority, were taken on tours to army and navy drilling fields and arsenals, shipyards, museums, factories, prisons, hospitals, courts, schools, libraries, and so on. Upon returning to Korea, Kim Ki-su reported favorably on Japan, which relaxed the suspicions of the King and officials.[20]

Huang Tsun-hsien was deeply concerned about the future of Korea. His sense of history reminded him of Japan's earlier attempts to conquer Korea: first by the legendary Empress Jingū, whom he identified with the Himiko described in Chinese dynastic history; then by Toyotomi Hideyoshi, whose notorious invasion was recorded by Chinese historians. Most recently, the Meiji Government had seriously debated the possibility of dispatching a military expedition to Korea.[21] Huang had no doubt that Japan was a serious threat to Korea. In the immediate future, however, Russia appeared to be the greater menace because of its powerful military force and its policy of expansion to the east. In Huang's perception of the contemporary world situation, which he compared to the period of the Warring States in ancient China, Russia resembled the wolflike Ch'in which overpowered the other states. Korea's position, threatened by the great power on the north and by her eastern neighbor, was comparable to Turkey's position in Europe.[22]

The lesson of Ryukyu taught Huang that the tragedy of the small country stemmed from its ambiguous legal status. One way to protect Korea, he thought, was to make it an integral part of China. In 1880, he recommended to the Tsungli Yamen that China annex Korea in order to prevent foreign intervention, but his proposal was ignored. Then he proposed sending a resident commissioner to Korea to take charge of its foreign affairs as a demonstration to the world that Korea rightfully belonged to China. To Huang's regret, the court rejected this proposal too, saying that political affairs in Korea had always been left to the autonomous decisions of the Koreans.[23] Thereupon, Huang presented a personal recommendation to the Koreans when the second mission from that country visited Japan in the summer of 1880.

The second mission, headed by Kim Hong-jip, arrived in Tokyo on August 11, 1880, and stayed for about a month. Despite the Japanese government's displeasure over Chinese contacts with the mission, Huang visited the Koreans on August 20 and welcomed them on behalf of the Chinese government. On the following day, Kim visited the Chinese legation and discussed Korea's problems. The Koreans had belatedly realized the disadvantages of their tariff agreements with Japan and were attempting to have the treaty revised.[24] On this and subsequent occasions, Kim and the Chinese conversed in writing. Huang's far-sighted views on the world situation and on Korea's position in Asia impressed Kim. Huang emphasized the significance of the changes in the world and the need to react to them without delay. At their first meeting, Huang told Kim: "Changes happening in the world today are unprecedented in the past four thousand years and were never dreamed of by Yao, Shun, Yü, or T'ang. It is impossible to cure the illness of today by following the prescriptions given by those ancient sages."

When Kim responded by saying that a small country like Korea looked to China for protection, Huang sharply retorted: "Your words express loyalty and love [toward China]. However, what is urgent today is to strengthen your own country." In saying this, Huang undoubtedly had in mind the fate of Ryukyu. He told Kim that it was anachronistic to refuse to trade with Western countries; the tide of the world had changed, and Korea must respond to the new reality. Huang emphasized that the traditional ties between China and her tributaries no longer guaranteed the security of those states; thus Koreans should conclude friendship treaties with Western powers. Otherwise, he warned, the Westerners would come with expeditionary forces and would extract humiliating treaties at gunpoint.[25] It was an eye-opening experience for Kim to hear such words from an official of Korea's suzerain. Confucian scholars in Korea had stubbornly opposed opening the country to the West because they were committed to the doctrine of the Sinocentric world order. In conversing with Huang, Kim gained significant insight into Korea's position in international politics. He confessed to Ho Ju-chang that, during his visit to Japan, which was his first trip abroad, he had learned much about the outside world and had found that the greatest problem for Korea was the fact that its scholars and officials were as ignorant of foreign affairs as Chinese scholars had been thirty years before.[26]

On September 6, two days before the Korean mission departed, Huang presented Kim with a booklet entitled "Ch'ao-hsien ts'e-lueh" (Korean strategy), saying that a brief conversation had not been enough to explain his ideas about Korean relations with other countries. Huang signed the manuscript as a private individual from Kwangtung. In this handwritten booklet, Huang pointed out that Russia, the most ambitious expansionist power in the world, was the greatest menace to Korea and that nothing was more vital for Korea than to defend itself from the Russian threat. Thus, he recommended that Korea keep close ties with China and establish alliances with Japan and the United States. At the same time, he urged the Koreans to strengthen their country; Huang believed that China was Korea's most valuable ally because of her wealth and loving concern. Also, China shared a long borderline with Russia and was the only country in Asia capable of stopping the Russian advance. Aside from China, Japan was Korea's next closest neighbor, geographically speaking, and Japan's own security depended on defending Korea from Russian aggression. Although Japan was not an entirely reliable ally, there was no danger that Japan would attack Korea for the moment because Japan was almost bankrupt and was threatened by internal rebellion. He felt, too, that the Japanese were not as shameless as Koreans believed from their experiences with Japanese merchants in Pusan. As for the United States, Huang described it as a nation of idealists who had been willing to fight a war to achieve independence and who were therefore sympathetic to oppressed small countries.

Huang urged the Koreans to open their country to foreign trade by establishing a treaty relationship with the United States. He gave various reasons why such treaties would benefit Korea, emphasizing that foreign trade was the basis of the wealth and power of a state. As for the negative effects of foreign trade, Huang pointed out that China suffered from the importing of opium and that Japan was driven to bankruptcy by importing foreign luxury goods. If the Koreans would eschew foreign opium and luxuries, they would suffer no harm from foreign trade. Further, the Koreans should not fear the advent of missionaries. There were different sects in Christianity, just as there were the Chu Hsi school and the Wang Yang-ming school in Neo-Confucianism. The Protestants, for example did not interfere in the domestic affairs of foreign countries and, because of their modesty, no Protestant had been killed in China for his missionary activities. Since the teaching of the Duke of Chou and Confucius was superior to Western religion, and the Koreans were deeply versed in this superior teaching, there need be no worry that Koreans would be attracted to the foreign religion. He also recommended sending students to China, Japan, and the West.[27]

Huang's recommendation for opening Korea was basically in line with the policy of the Chinese government. In August 1879, the government adopted a decision to encourage Korea to conclude treaties with Western nations for the purpose of offsetting the Japanese advance. Ting Jih-ch'ang, who proposed the policy, stated that Japan had forced a treaty on Korea and had made evident its ambition to absorb Korean territory. The most effective way to curb Japan was to invite the intervention of those Western powers to which Japan was most vulnerable.[28] The Ch'ing court ordered Li Hung-chang to convey its wish to Korea, it being deemed inappropriate to make an official recommendation concerning the foreign policy of a tributary state. Thereupon Li wrote to Yi Yu-wŏn, a high official who had stayed in Peking as an envoy of the Korean King and had had personal contact with Li.[29] Yi's response was negative. Li reported to the Tsungli Yamen in late 1879 that the Koreans were determined not to open trade relations with the West; hence, China could not coerce them into concluding treaties with Westerners. Again, in March 1880, Li reported that he had failed to convince Yi, despite repeated efforts. To his despair, Li found it impossible to enlighten the Koreans about the world situation: Koreans had been isolated so long and hated foreigners so deeply that their attitudes could not be changed overnight.[30]

Although the Ch'ing Government, primarily concerned with the prospect of a Japanese advance into Korea, regarded Russia as only a secondary menace, Huang underscored Russian aggression as the greater danger to Korea and all East Asia, including China. To explain Huang's emphasis on Russia, Hō Takushū has suggested that Huang might have been influenced by the Japanese, who were alarmed by Russia's southward expansion.[31] This may have been the case; however, Huang was also aware of Japan's ambitions in Korea. His main point was to advise the Koreans to establish diplomatic ties with the West and to adopt positive policies for modernizing their own country instead of relying on China's protection.

In contrast to Li Hung-chang's frustrated efforts to persuade the Koreans, Huang's booklet had an earth-shaking impact on the Korean government. King Kojong circulated copies of the booklet among the court officials, who were favorably impressed by it. Kim Hong-jip wrote to Ho Ju-chang, praising Huang's far-sighted views; he said that, although official opinion had not reached a consensus on the issue of opening the country, the overall opinion at court was changing.[32] Yi Tong-in, who was sent to Japan in the fall of 1880, also confirmed to Ho that the tone of official opinion had been dramatically reversed after Kim Hong-jip returned, and that the King was inclined to institute negotiations with the United States.[33] In late 1880, the Korean government began to reform the bureaucracy and the army. A new government bureau, which combined the functions of the Grand Council and the Tsungli Yamen of the Chinese government, was set up. The bureau was subdivided into departments responsible for foreign affairs, military affairs, border defense, foreign trade, shipbuilding, and training in foreign languages. In February 1881, the King sent a group of 62 officials to Japan to study government and military institutions, and in April he invited Japanese army officers to train Korea's newly organized troops. These sweeping changes reflected the reorientation of Korean foreign policy. Students of the modern history of Korea agree that Huang's booklet played a decisive role in bringing about these changes.[34]

While Huang's booklet gave momentum to court-initiated reforms, it also provoked stormy controversy among Confucian scholars and conservative officials inside and outside the capital. They were outraged by his suggestion to open the country to foreign trade and to make alliances with Japan and the United States. Their memorials denouncing Huang's proposals flooded the court; some were written by scholars of national reputation who influenced many younger scholars. Yi Man-son's fiery memorial—representing 10,000 scholars from the southeastern provinces—began with this statement: "Respectfully, it makes our hair stand on end and our blood boil to read the booklet which was privately presented by Huang Tsun-hsien and brought back by Kim Hong-jip." He condemned the idea of an alliance with Japan and the United States on the grounds that the Japanese and Americans, like the Russians, were barbarians, and that all barbarians were to be rejected. He denounced Huang's encouraging Koreans to learn Western science and technology; Korea already had good institutions. He accused Huang of being an agent of the Japanese and of the Christian missionaries who were trying to subvert the Koreans. He wanted Huang's booklet burnt and Kim Hong-jip punished. Another memorial, presented by Hong Jae-hak, had been drafted by the well-known Confucian Kim P'yong-muk. It not only condemned Huang's proposals but insinuated that the booklet attributed to Huang was probably the work of a traitor among the court ministers. For this daring attack on the government and the powerful Min family, Hong Jae-hak was executed, thereby becoming a martyr in the eyes of those who shared his opinions. Yi Man-son and other memorialists were banished.[35]

The Korean scholars' protest against the adoption of Huang's proposals was the culmination of their movement to "Guard orthodoxy and repel heresy" (*wijŏng ch'ŏksa*); in other words, to uphold Neo-Confucian orthodoxy and repel Western influences. The movement had begun in the late 1860s when foreign vessels anchored offshore to demand trade relations. At that time, the scholars supported the anti-foreign policy of the regent Taewŏn'gun (in power from 1864–1873). After the Min family ousted Taewŏn'gun, the Korean government yielded to Japan and concluded the Treaty of Kanghwa in 1876, despite the protests of the Confucian scholars. One of their number, Ch'oe Ik-hyŏn, carried an ax to the court and begged to be beheaded with it if his remonstrances against the treaty were not heeded. His basic objection to the treaty was that the Japanese were now no different from the Western barbarians, having adopted Western customs and dress. Ch'oe Ik-hyŏn was banished to an island and the protest movement was suppressed.[36]

The impact of Huang's booklet on the development of political events in Korea increased as the Confucian protest became entangled with factional politics. At the height of the scholars' movement in the summer of 1881, Taewŏn'gun attempted a coup d'état to overthrow the Min family, but the plot was discovered in time. In the summer of 1882, the former regent seized another opportunity for a coup. The soldiers stationed in Seoul mutinied when their salary rice failed to arrive. In addition, there were bad feelings among the soldiers whose positions were threatened by the reorganization of the army, which was part of the modernization program. The soldiers were joined by an angry populace whose lives had been severely affected by the rising price of rice and the food shortage, a result of opening Korea to Japanese traders. The mob not only destroyed some government buildings and houses of officials who belonged to the Min faction but also attacked the Japanese Legation and killed the Japanese officer the Korean government had hired to train the newly organized army. The Japanese Resident Minister barely escaped; he fled to Nagasaki on the British gunboat. The uprising was suppressed by the Ch'ing army, and Taewŏn'gun was taken to Tientsin as a prisoner.[37]

The Seoul uprising of 1882 marked a turning point in Sino-Korean,

Korean-Japanese, and Sino-Japanese relations. The Ch'ing Government departed from its traditional practice of noninterference in Korea's domestic and foreign affairs by sending troops to put down the uprising, and thereafter exerted great influence over the Korean government. For the Japanese, the incident was a shock. The advocates of brotherly cooperation with Asian neighbors retreated, and the Japanese were inclined to adopt Western-like arrogance and ruthlessness in dealing with Asian countries. By 1885, the national consensus on Asian policy was formulated in the term *datsu A* (departure from Asia). The rivalry between China and Japan over Korea became overt, with Korea as the major source of conflict.

Huang Tsun-hsien left Japan a few months prior to the rebellion of 1882. His stay in Japan had coincided with the period when the Japanese attitude toward its Asian neighbors was in a state of flux, a period of transition that now hardened into an imperialist policy modeled after the West's. During this brief transition period, there had been hope for a genuine cooperation between Japan and other Asian nations that would put an end to Western domination. For this reason, Huang had had some optimistic expectations for the future of Sino-Japanese cooperation.

COGWHEELS IN ASIA?

Huang often used the term "Asia" (Ya-hsi-ya) in his writings during and after his stay in Japan. It was a new term the Japanese had adopted from the Western vocabulary. Although the Chinese also used the term, it did not become as popular in China as in Japan. For both Japanese and Chinese, the concept of Asia became possible only after their contact with the Western world in the mid-nineteenth century. In the traditional Sinocentric world, there was little sense of community among the countries that maintained diplomatic and/or trade relations with China. Each tributary state individually established its own tie with China by accepting a vassal's status. The Chinese policy of preventing alliances among vassal states and of keeping them submissive to China severely

restricted contact among these states and inhibited the development of a sense of community in Asia.[38]

The Japanese proposal to establish treaty relations with China
in 1871 was a challenge to China's traditional position in East
Asia. A conservative governor of Anhui who regarded Japan's
demand as improper stated that, if China should grant a treaty to
Japan, a vassal state of China, then the rest of the tributary states
would follow suit and the entire tributary system would collapse.
Although he was mistaken in stating that Japan had always been a
tributary of China, his argument was consistent with the logic of
the Sinocentric world.[39] The advocates of the treaty based their
arguments on another traditional concept, that of controlling barbarians with a loose rein. In recommending a treaty with Japan,
Li Hung-chang emphasized the advantage of treating Japan with
generosity in order to prevent it from making alliances with the
Western powers against China. Should China reject Japan's request, he cautioned, Japan would enlist assistance from the West
to force China's compliance. He regarded Japan as a potential
threat to China's security because of its geographical proximity
and ties with the West; hence, he recommended concluding a treaty
with Japan for strategic reasons. He did not subscribe to the
Japanese assertion that Western aggression could be staved off by
mutual assistance. According to Li's report, "Each time Yanagiwara
Sakimitsu and other [negotiators] came to see me they said that
the Westerners had forced Japan into treaty relations [with them],
that the Japanese were dissatisfied, and that it was difficult for
them to resist [the Westerners] by themselves. Therefore, they
said, they sincerely wished to establish friendship ties with China
and to cooperate [with China] for common goals." Li's reaction
was cynical: "Of course, it is not what they really think."[40] Nevertheless, concealing his belief in Japan's duplicity under the cloak
of diplomacy, Li proposed to attach to the treaty an article pledg-
ing mutual good offices should either nation become involved in a
conflict with a third power. Although the Japanese objected,
fearing the article would be misinterpreted by the Western powers,
Li had his way. Obviously, he had no faith in Japan's sincerity.

At the least, he hoped to prevent Japan from becoming an out-station (*wai-fu*) of the Western powers; but his larger purpose was to make Japan a defensive wall (*fan-p'ing*) between China and the West.[41]

In contrast to Li Hung-chang, Huang Tsun-hsien genuinely supported the ideal of cooperation between China and Japan to bring peace and prestige to Asia. He believed that all Asian peoples suffered from the aggression of the Westerners and that strengthening the brotherly ties between Asian nations would eliminate future humiliation. He exalted the idea of "Raise Asia" (*kō A*) which was gaining popularity in Japan. His poem dedicated to Prince Arisugawa Taruhito at an anniversary of the opening of the army officers school expressed gratitude for Japan's modernized army and hope for the prosperity of Asia:

> *Asian neighbors since ancient times,*
> *China and Japan should cooperate*
> *Like two cogwheels that interlock*
> *Or two hunters who make themselves a team,*
> *One seizing the deer's horns,*
> *The other the hind legs.*
> *Each of us should grow in wealth, in power*
> *And, as we rise together, all the scorn*
> *Of outsiders will fade and disappear.*
> *Then we shall throw off our armor and rejoice*
> *In a Grand Peace to last thousands of years.*[42]

Huang was proud of Japan's progress in modernization and praised its accomplishments in strengthening its military power; he was sympathetic toward the small country he regarded as China's little brother. At the same time, he hoped Japan's success would help raise the status of Asia as a whole.

While Huang was in Japan, one of the earliest pan-Asianist associations, Kōakai (Raise Asia Society), was organized to promote cooperation between China and Japan, based on the recognition that the two countries shared the same culture and were geographically positioned so as to be cogwheels, dependent on each other. The society's principal organizer, Sone Toshitora, espoused this idea after observing the Western presence in China. Sone was an ex-samurai from Yonezawa who became a naval officer. He traveled to China in 1873 as an escort of Foreign Minister Soejima Taneomi, whose mission was to exchange copies of the ratified Sino-Japanese Friendship Treaty. Sone made several other trips to China to collect intelligence information for the navy. His realization of how Western influence had penetrated China's coastal areas led him to believe that Japan should train experts who were fluent in the Chinese language. Upon returning to Japan in 1877, he organized the Shin-A sha (Revive Asia Society) with a few friends. He was introduced into the social life of the Chinese legation through Soejima Taneomi, and demonstrated his capacity to compose classical-style poems. He soon found that Ho Ju-chang and the late Ōkubo Toshimichi wanted to organize a language-training program for Japanese and Chinese students to learn each other's language. With the help of Miyajima Seiichirō, a senior government official from Yonezawa closely associated with Ōkubo, Sone canvassed government officials and literary circles for support in establishing a Chinese-language school in Tokyo. Thus the Kōakai was organized in March 1880 with Nagaoka Moriyoshi as president; its language school was quartered in the building of a Buddhist temple.[43]

The Kōakai had 153 members at its inception. The majority were government officials, especially China specialists in the Foreign Ministry, members of the peerage, military officers, and scholars in the Chinese classics. At the Kōakai's inauguration on March 10, 1880, Yanagiwara Sakimitsu, Shigeno Yasutsugu, Sone Toshitora, and Miyajima Seiichirō delivered addresses; Nakamura Masanao (Keiu) recited his poem of congratulation; and Chang Tz'u-fang, a language teacher in the school, gave a talk in Chinese. Ho Ju-chang was absent, but Sone assured the gathering that the Chinese Minister supported the society.[44] The speakers emphasized the need for cooperation between China and Japan and warned of the danger inherent in rivalry between the two nations. At the same time, they dwelt on the greatness of China and on

Japan's need for help from China in fending off Western aggression. Their emphasis on the greatness of China was not simply diplomatic phraseology. In the early 1880s, the Japanese still held their traditional inferiority complex toward China. Moreover, they were acutely aware that Japan's military strength, especially the navy, and its economic resources were not equal to China's. During the early 1880s, the Japanese who expressed pan-Asianist views, including the romantics and liberals, proposed brotherly cooperation with China based on egalitarian principles. Only after the Sino-Japanese War of 1894–1895 did the idea of Japan's mission as the leader of Asia become firmly established in Japan.[45]

The organizers of the Kōakai aimed at extending its membership to include Koreans, Vietnamese, Cambodians, Indians, Persians, and all other Asians. In the beginning, the Chinese minister and the staff of the Chinese legation were the only non-Japanese members. During the 1880s, a Korean monk, Yi Tong-in, joined and played an important role as a mediator for the exchange of personnel between Korea and Japan. In the meantime, the membership expanded to include some Chinese and Korean residents in the Tokyo area. Sone Toshitora attempted to recruit members in China when he traveled to Shanghai and Hong Kong.[46] It is doubtful, however, that the society acquired any significant number of members outside Japan.

The Japanese membership of the Kōakai included some liberal intellectuals. For example, Ueki Emori, a leader of the People's Rights movement, participated in its meeting at Osaka. But the majority of the members were the old literati from the literary circles surrounding the Chinese diplomats. Thus, the monthly meetings of the society were very little different from other social gatherings of the literati, in other words, replete with the cordial atmosphere induced by wine, poems, and optimistic speeches on the future of Asia. When the Korean government dispatched missions to observe the progress of Japanese modernization in 1880 and 1881, the Kōakai held large receptions to welcome them. The Koreans were impressed by their friendly reception and were optimistic in their belief that a tripartite alliance was in the offing.[47]

Huang Tsun-hsien attended a party given by the Kōakai on May 26, 1881, in honor of the Korean mission. It is unclear how often Huang participated in the Kōakai's activities or to what extent he associated with Sone Toshitora. Since Sone frequented the legation, he was mentioned in the conversations recorded by Ōkōchi Teruna, although Ōkōchi did not think highly of Sone and disapproved of his association with the Chinese diplomats. Ōkōchi appears to have assessed the Kōakai as a kind of literary society and to have regarded Sone's socializing with the Chinese literati as a pretension. For this reason, the Chinese friends of Ōkōchi were unwilling to discuss their association with the Kōakai.[48] Huang referred to the society in his poem written in 1890 as part of his reminiscences of Japan, but he did not reveal his opinion of the organization.[49]

The unity of the Kōakai, based on romantic idealism, could not endure. After the anti-Japanese rebellion in Seoul in 1882, the Japanese became disillusioned with their hope for brotherly relations with their Asian neighbors. Furthermore, the rivalry between Japan and China over Korea that surfaced after 1882 affected the Kōakai. At the January 1883 meeting, the Chinese members raised an objection to the name of the society, saying that it was pretentious. As a result, the society was renamed the Ajia Kyōkai (Asia Society). Thereafter, attendance of the Chinese at the meetings fell off and the organization gradually became exclusively Japanese. Eventually it was absorbed into the Tōa Dōbunkai (East Asian Common Culture Society, 1900–1945), the major channel for Japan's cultural imperialism in China.[50]

Huang supported the idea of "Raise Asia" and wished the Japanese would live up to the ideal of cooperation in Asia. However, the Japanese actions in Ryukyu and Korea indicated that they were not practicing what they advocated. Commenting on Japan's aggression on China's periphery in an official report to his government, Huang wrote: "In Asia, China and Japan should unite their strengths and cooperate as one; however, the Japanese slighted us once we had yielded to them." He warned that, not only was Japan unreliable in an emergency, but was becoming more and more greedy and belligerent toward China. In order to establish a desirable relationship based on mutual support and cooperation, he recommended crushing Japan's arrogance before its national strength was consolidated. He felt that the Japanese invaded Ryukyu not only out of greed for gain, however small, but, more important, because, in slighting China, they were expressing admiration for the West.[51] Indeed, admiration for the West and condescension toward China—two sides of the same coin—shaped the course of Japanese actions up to 1945. Huang's observation of Japan's growing scorn for China was acute, as was his insight in pointing out that Japan's overbearing posture was a result of its cultural reorientation toward the West. Japan's loss of respect for China made it impossible to realize the ideal of cogwheels in Asia.

FIVE

California, 1882–1885:
Confrontation with Racial Antagonism *

Underlying the concept of the Middle Kingdom lay an optimistic assumption that all peoples under heaven belonged to a universal human community and that, potentially, they could live in harmony. Behind this assumption was a belief in the universality of Confucian humanism and in a universal empire as a normative goal of human history.[1] Even before he first left China, Huang Tsun-hsien had criticized the supercilious attitude of the Chinese toward foreigners and denounced the arrogance of their Sinocentric view of the world. However, he did not question the basic assumptions underlying the concept of the Middle Kingdom and optimistically believed that East and West were one family. The framework of Huang's world view did not substantially change while he was in Japan; on the contrary, his observations of Japan confirmed his belief in the universality of Confucian culture. Only after his shocking experiences in the United States clearly demonstrated the futility of his Confucian precepts did Huang adopt a Darwinian view: the world was essentially an arena of strife among nations. This realization, in turn, became the core of his reform thought and prompted him to urge the creation of a powerful state in China.

The United States, the first modern Western country that Huang observed, was greatly admired by the Japanese for its wealth and power and its science and technology. While in Japan, Huang had

shared the same high opinion of the United States. His views on
the subject were explicitly stated in his booklet written for Kim
Hong-jip, the Korean commissioner who visited Japan in 1880:

> The country was originally a dependency of England. However, about
> one hundred years ago, there was a man called Washington who refused
> to submit to the harsh rule by the Europeans; his courageous determi-
> nation made the country independent. Ever since, the people of the
> country, following the moral teaching of the great founder, have
> governed the country in accordance with propriety and righteousness;
> they do not infringe upon other lands or other people, and they do
> not interfere with other governments. For over ten years since the
> country concluded treaties with China, it has never caused China the
> slightest trouble. As to its relations with Japan, it guided Japan into
> international trade, advised her in building a modern military system,
> and assisted in the revision of treaties. These facts are well known to
> the whole world.
>
> It is a democratic country; the government is based on republican-
> ism . . . Since the founding of the country was brought about by in-
> dignation over the tyrannical rule of England, it has always been
> friendly to Asia and has treated Europe with reserve. Although the
> people belong to the same race as the Europeans, the strength and
> wealth of the country are much greater than that of European coun-
> tries. It is located between the Eastern and Western oceans; it always
> helps the weak, supports universal righteousness, and thus prohibits
> the Europeans from doing evil.[2]

The United States, in Huang's mind, was not only powerful,
prosperous, and the possessor of strong moral principles, but
also sympathetic toward Asians who had been oppressed by
Europeans.

Huang's idealized view of the United States was also expressed
in his long poem, "The Closure of the Educational Mission in
America," written in late 1881 when about a hundred Chinese students were recalled from the United States. In 1872, the students
had been sent to Hartford, Connecticut, as China's first educational
mission, but the project was abruptly discontinued because of
objections from conservative officials in the Chinese government.
It appears that Huang saw some of these students when they
passed through Japan on their way home. He greatly regretted

the termination of the "magnificent and far-sighted" project,[3] but this incident opened a way for Huang to visit the country he admired. Ch'en Lan-pin and Jung Hung, who had taken the students to the United States and had subsequently been appointed Ministers to Washington, were recalled when the educational mission closed. In early 1882, the new Chinese Minister to the United States, Cheng Tsao-ju, appointed Huang the Consul General in San Francisco. Huang left Japan on March 7 and arrived in San Francisco on March 30.[4]

The milieu that awaited Huang in San Francisco was radically different from that of Tokyo, and the reality of the United States was not like the image he had nurtured. In California in the 1880s, the rule of law was not yet well established, and violence and abuses abounded. The conflict between Chinese immigrants and American laborers was harsh, even bloody. Because of the place and the time, Huang was faced with an ugly, lawless aspect of America.

The position of the Chinese in California was so humiliating that Huang's pride was terribly injured. By 1873, there were about 62,500 Chinese in California, many of them laborers. Despite their great contribution to the development of the West, Chinese laborers were the most unfairly treated group of newcomers.[5] During the 1870s, anti-Chinese sentiment was heightened in California by the militant labor unions which had been bolstered by the economic recession in the state during the decade. As Alexander Saxton has demonstrated, the Chinese issue was exploited as an "indispensable ' organizing tool by labor leaders in California who played a major role in state politics.[6] Chinese laborers were accused of working hard for cheap wages and of being willing to accept substandard living conditions. Moreover, they were suspected and feared as a culturally unintegrated group which persisted in its own way of life. Stuart C. Miller suggests that the Chinese were rejected primarily because they were alleged to be unassimilable immigrants.[7]

The anti-Chinese passion, openly expressed in arson, robbery, murder, and rioting during the 1870s, led to the Chinese Exclusion

Act of 1882. Earlier, the Burlingame Treaty of 1868 had given the Chinese the right of unrestricted immigration to the United States. In 1879, pressured by the demands of the Californians, whose votes were very important in national politics, Congress passed a bill restricting the entry of Chinese laborers for ten years. President Rutherford B. Hayes vetoed the bill on the grounds that it contravened the Burlingame Treaty. In 1880, the government sent negotiators headed by James B. Angell, then president of the University of Michigan, to China for the purpose of modifying the treaty provisions. In November 1880, an agreement was reached between the two governments in which China conceded the right of the United States to restrict Chinese immigration.[8] Thus, the Chinese government itself cleared the way for the introduction of the Chinese Exclusion Act.

Even though the declared purpose of the Exclusion Act was to halt the influx of Chinese "laborers," its terms were so vague that almost any Chinese could be affected. Only diplomats and other government officials were specifically exempted. "Chinese laborer" was defined broadly "to mean both skilled and unskilled laborers and Chinese employed in mining."[9] The law indicated a turning point in the immigration history of America, for it marked the end of an open policy toward immigration and led the way to even more rigid restrictions.

The Chinese Exclusion Act became law soon after Huang arrived in San Francisco. The long poem "Expulsion of the Immigrants" expressed his great disappointment that the Chinese laborers who had endured so many hardships in the new country were now insulted and persecuted by the bigoted Americans.[10] He lamented the fate of these fellow countrymen without means of livelihood in China, who were now threatened with expulsion from their new country. Most of the Chinese laborers in California came from the southeastern coast of China where the population pressure was high and land scarce. Unable to support themselves, they had left their homes to seek new lives in a foreign land. Not all the immigrants were law-abiding, Huang admitted. The lawless individuals, he believed, were former followers of the

Taipings who had been exiled from China as criminals. In fact, far from being a homogeneous group, the Chinese in San Francisco were so diverse that armed warfare often broke out between different groups.[11]

Huang regretted the Americans' betrayal of the ideal of George Washington, who had declared less than a hundred years earlier that "American land is vast and its people few; anyone who comes to this land shall be treated equally, regardless [of whether he is] yellow, white, red, or black."[12] Huang praised Washington as a symbol of American ideals, describing him as a man of supreme virtue, who raised the banner of independence from oppression, the equality of all races, and the freedom of mankind. To Huang, Washington, the founding father of his country, was comparable to the legendary "sage kings" in early Chinese history.

Only after coming to San Francisco did Huang awaken to the grim reality that a Chinese person in the United States was an object of contempt, and that the concept of "Great China" or "Middle Kingdom" was a laughingstock. Indeed, the term "celestials" was frequently used as an expression of contempt. It would be easier to be a black slave who cared nothing about his origin, observed Huang, than to be a Mandarin in California.[13]

Though disappointed with the United States, Huang believed the Chinese government had to share responsibility for the Exclusion Act. He blamed the officials in Peking for readily consenting to the fateful agreement with the United States without considering its grave consequences. Any protests against the exclusion of a Chinese person were doomed to fail, though Huang tried desperately to prevent the implementation of the Exclusion Act.[14] Although he was the accredited envoy of a great empire, he had no authority to negotiate with American officials. "Even with all the water of the four great oceans," he lamented, "my suffering from this disgrace cannot be washed away."[15]

Huang was correct in his contention that the Chinese in the United States received no protection from their own government. The decline of China's prestige as a great empire, he believed, was the ultimate cause of the humiliation of the Chinese overseas.

"Five thousand years have passed since the reign of the Yellow Emperor," he wrote. "Now the country has become extremely weakened. It is difficult to fathom the minds of goblins and vipers [foreigners] and to tame monsters [foreigners]. How could we ever have imagined that we would be treated as subhuman by these foreigners?"[16]

Huang's experiences in California awakened him to the reality of a Darwinian world. "On the five continents," he noted "each and every race thinks only of its own: they mutually exclude each other, hate each other, and curse each other. The world today is not a world of grand harmony; only one's own wit and might can be relied on for defense against others."[17] This conviction became the source of Huang's nationalism and reform ideas for the rest of his life. All his suggestions for reform, which were spelled out in his later years, were directed toward building up a powerful and efficient government in China so that China could survive the greatest changes in its history.

While in San Francisco, Huang did his best to protect the legal rights of Chinese residents in the United States and Canada.[18] Immediately upon assuming his post, he openly objected to assaults on Chinese in California. On May 29, 1882, the Chargé d'Affaires of the Chinese Legation in Washington, D.C., sent a note conveying Huang's protests to the State Department:

> Sir: I have the honor to inform you that I have received a communication from Mr. Wong [Huang], Chinese Consul General at San Francisco, in which he complains that some Chinese fish-dealers in the town of Martinez, about 35 miles south of San Francisco, were on the night of the 6th of April maliciously attacked by a mob, who, surrounding the houses of the Chinese, forced their way in, breaking open the doors, and proceeding to destroy the property of the occupants. The Chinese occupants were flung from the windows of the upper stairs; eight of them received injuries and one has since died of wounds.
>
> The Consul General therefore requests me to lay these facts before you, and to ask that you will be pleased to communicate with the authorities of California and instruct them to give proper protection to the Chinese residents of the state, with the view of preventing the recurrence of such outrages.[19]

Huang was also alert in defending the rights and privileges of Chinese under the law, particularly the right of laborers to return to the United States after traveling to China or other countries. The Exclusion Act recognized the right of Chinese laborers to reenter the United States, provided their earlier residence could be verified. However, the procedure for gaining reentry was complicated. It required the Collector of Customs or his deputy to board every ship leaving the United States with Chinese and to record their names, ages, occupations, last places of residence, physical marks or peculiarities, and all facts necessary for identification. The Chinese laborers were entitled, upon application, to receive certificates of registration from the Collector. The role of the Chinese Consulate was not mentioned.[20]

In order to facilitate reentry of the laborers, Huang proposed that the Chinese Consul General issue certificates of identification and passports to all Chinese when they left the United States. Since most of them did not understand English, Huang stated, it was difficult for them to apply for certificates of registration without assistance from the Consulate. Also, certificates of identification by the Consul would help the Collector in obtaining the information for the certificates of registration. The United States government agreed that certificates could be issued at the Chinese Consulate on condition that they be free of charge, issued in the name of Consul General Huang, and countersigned by the Collector of Customs.[21] This system worked satisfactorily for more than a year.

The system was eventually undermined by illegal entries, which caused ever-increasing tension between Californians and the Chinese communities. Many Californians believed there were loopholes in the Exclusion Act and that the federal government made little effort to prevent the smuggling in of Chinese laborers. Various cases of fraud were reported: some Chinese falsely claimed United States citizenship by birth in the United States or by having been born of United States citizens abroad; some laborers pretended to be students or traders; some came with certificates purchased in Hong Kong from the rightful owners, who had decided to remain in China. Such practices encouraged rigidity on the part of immigration officers; in their zeal to apprehend illegal entrants, they often violated the rights of Chinese who sought entry legally.[22]

In February 1884, the special Deputy Collector of Customs at San Fransicso abruptly announced that, henceforth he would issue certificates to Chinese merchants departing from the United States and that certificates issued by the Chinese Consul General would not be honored. Huang persuaded the Chinese Minister in Washington to protest to the State Department. If the Consul's certificates were ignored, he explained, then Chinese merchants would have great difficulty in exercising the privileges guaranteed by the Treaty of 1880, which permitted them "to go and come of their own free will and accord" and to enjoy the same "rights, privileges, immunities, and exemptions as are enjoyed by the citizens or subjects of the most favored nation." Since most of the Chinese merchants in the United States did not understand English, they would encounter difficulties in applying for certificates at the Collector's office. The case was referred to the Secretary of the Treasury, who informed the Collector of Customs at San Francisco that his announcement had violated the Act of 1882 as well as the Treaty of 1880. Certificates issued by the Consul General should be regarded as issued by the Chinese government and were therefore prima facie evidence of the holder's right to enter the United States.[23]

Because of the increasing pressure from Californians who demanded tighter restrictions on Chinese immigration, the Exclusion Act was amended in July 1884. The amended act's definition of "merchant" excluded hucksters, peddlers, and fishermen who dried and exported seafood. The new measure also required more detailed information; for example, the individual, family, and "tribal" name in full for certificates of identification.[24] Soon after the amended act passed, twenty-four Chinese merchants bearing passports and certificates issued by the Chinese Consul were denied permission to land in San Francisco on the grounds that the new law excluded them. Technically, their certificates did not conform to the specifications of the amended act. Huang immediately telegraphed Washington, pointing out that their ship had left China before the passage of the new law and that the merchants could not have complied with its provisions. He succeeded in obtaining permission for the merchants to reenter the United States.[25]

In view of the fundamental differences between the Chinese and Western concepts of law, it is remarkable that Huang was able to win these legal battles against the Collector of Customs. In China, individual rights were not recognized by law; the primary purpose of law was to maintain peace and harmony in the society as a whole, not to defend an individual's rights against state authority. Moreover, in legal cases, judgments were rendered according to the Confucian moral code, and the distinction between legal and moral values was not sharp. Moral persuasion had greater weight than legalistic arguments, and the former was more often used by officials and commoners to advance their cause. For this reason, it is noteworthy that Huang's arguments were free of the moralistic approach and that he took full advantage of the provisions of the existing treaties to defend the interests of Chinese in the United States. He was particularly interested in defending the rights of Chinese merchants and demonstrated his determination to fight for Chinese commercial interests in the United States when the case of the *City of Peking* arose.

In October 1884, some Chinese merchants and their families aboard the *City of Peking* were refused landing rights by the Collector of Customs in San Francisco, who insisted that the amended act required certificates of identification issued in China by the government. In his opinion, Chinese merchants who traveled outside the United States or lived in foreign countries must return to China to obtain certificates before coming to the United States. Huang complained that, if the Collector's decision was enforced, it would result in great hardships for Chinese merchants and would impair their rights under the treaty. Many Chinese merchants in the United States had large commercial interests in Victoria (British Columbia), the Sandwich Islands, Cuba, and Panama. If these merchants could not be readmitted to the United States without returning to China it would virtually destroy their trade. Huang's arguments proved persuasive. The Treasury Department overrode the Collector and declared that certificates issued by Chinese consular officials stationed in the United States or in other countries were to be honored.[26]

Huang also confronted the problem faced by Chinese laborers who had to pass through the United States en route to Canada or to South American countries. In July 1884, the *Rio de Janeiro* arrived at San Francisco with Chinese laborers bound for British Columbia. They were denied permission to land temporarily. Since there was no direct transportation between China and British Columbia or between Panama and other South American ports, travelers from China had to transfer at San Francisco or New York. Prior to this incident, Chinese laborers who were passing through the United States had been allowed to land temporarily with transit certificates issued by the Chinese Consul General.[27] When the *Rio de Janeiro* arrived however, the Collector adopted a strict interpretation of a Treasury Department regulation concerning Chinese laborers in transit. The regulation, he argued, referred only to Chinese laborers entering the United States at one port and leaving the country from a different port. Chinese laborers arriving at and departing from the same port were not entitled to land and should be kept on board until transferred to another vessel. Huang complained sharply to Washington, pointing out the great inconvenience to the passengers, who were required to wait on board for some ten to twenty days. The Secretary of State admitted that the Collector of Customs had too rigidly interpreted the letter of the law and confirmed that Chinese laborers who were compelled to touch at United States ports in transit to foreign countries could land under the regulation.[28]

Huang's adversaries were not limited to the immigration authorities. He also had to fight San Francisco's city officials, who shared the popular antagonism against the Chinese. One of the bases of the anti-Chinese feeling was the public image of China-town as an overcrowded, filthy ghetto. To control sanitary conditions in the Chinese section, the city authorities issued regulations concerning housing in residential areas and allowed city officials to resort to high-handed treatment of the Chinese to enforce the regulations. Such measures were supported by the American public, which had become sensitive to the relationship between filth and disease by 1870 and feared that the Chinese were a threat to the nation's health. There was a widespread belief that the Chinese would afflict the nation with syphilis, cholera, leprosy, and, worse, "nameless contagions spawned in the flesh-pots of Oriental lechery."[29] One incident regarding hygiene in San Francisco's Chinatown will demonstrate Huang's skill in handling the problems between Chinese residents and city author-ities. Charged with violating a housing ordinance requiring a certain number of cubic feet per individual, some Chinese resi-dents were arrested and jammed into prison. Huang immediately sent a subordinate to measure the cells. Then he protested the arrest, accusing the city government of violating its own ordi-nance. Unable to refute Huang's charge, the officials apologized and released the prisoners. An account of this episode was re-corded in his biography in the official history of the Ch'ing dynasty.[30]

Despite the hostility Huang generally received from govern-ment authorities, one American did support his efforts to protect Chinese immigrants. Colonel Frederic A. Bee, the Chinese govern-ment's Consul at San Francisco and an attorney of the Chinese Six Companies, had actively assisted the Chinese in San Francisco and was appointed Consul some time before Huang's arrival. Huang reminisced about Colonel Bee in his poem on unforgettable persons. On one occasion at the customs office, the two men were surrounded by a group of American laborers, one of whom pointed a pistol at them and announced that, if they brought in any more Chinese workers, they would be shot. Bee smiled, took his pistol out of his boot, and said, "Do you dare to?"[31]

Huang's devotion to the welfare of the Chinese in the United

States can be explained by his sense of responsibility as the "father and mother official" or local magistrate for the Chinese abroad. Also, perhaps it compensated him for his injured national pride. In any case, his energetic activities in San Francisco were motivated by his nationalism and his positive evaluation of overseas emigration.

In the early years, the Ch'ing Government strictly prohibited emigration because of the military need to suppress Cheng Ch'eng-kung, the last opponent of Manchu rule, who was based on Taiwan. Even after the suppression of Cheng, overseas emigration was forbidden (disobedience carried the death penalty), and the prohibition was repeatedly confirmed by decrees of the K'ang-hsi and Yung-cheng Emperors.[32]

In reality, however, the Ch'ing Government was unable to prevent its subjects from migrating to Southeast Asia and later to America and Australia. It not only tacitly permitted the emigration of those whom economic necessity compelled to seek a living abroad but also consented to the Western Powers' recruitment of Chinese laborers. Agreements on the emigration of laborers were made in treaties between China and Great Britain (1860), China and France (1860), and China and Spain (1864), although the dynastic law prohibiting overseas emigration remained technically in effect. This was a practical response on the part of the Ch'ing Government and perhaps exemplified what Thomas A. Metzger has described as the parallel existence of fixed order and administrative flexibility in the law-making practices of the Ch'ing Government.[33]

The attitude of the Ch'ing Government toward the Chinese overseas was one of indifference. From the government's point of view, those who drifted to foreign lands were not worth looking after, and the wealth they acquired in foreign countries was of no concern to the imperial government. This point was made graphically to W. A. P. Martin, who was present at the negotiation of the Treaty of Tientsin in 1858. When the American delegates suggested that China send a consul to look after her people in the United States, the Viceroy of Chihli responded: "The Emperor's wealth is beyond computation; why should he care for those of his subjects who have left their home or for the sands they have scraped together?"[34]

But in 1874, when the abuses of the notorious coolie trade had become serious, the government took the posture of protector of its nationals. It was partly for this reason that the first Chinese legations were opened in the United States, Europe, and Japan during the late 1870s. But even this change in policy did not mean that the government recognized the economic value of overseas emigration or considered the emigrants a matter of national concern. Consequently, little effort was made by the Ch'ing Government to defend China's treaty rights of unrestricted immigration to the United States. In 1880, when the United States commissioners, headed by James B. Angell, arrived in Peking to negotiate the revision of the Burlingame Treaty, they had no difficulty in achieving their objectives. Only at the beginning of the conference were they challenged by the Chinese negotiators, who questioned the rationale for the restrictions.[35] Summarizing his experiences in Peking, Angell wrote in his diary: "We signed treaties in 48 days from our first business meeting. Such expedition in dealing with the Chinese save at the cannon's mouth has rarely or never been known. The Foreign Ministers here are surprised."[36]

Records of the negotiations confirm that it was not ignorance of the treaty rights that prompted Chinese officials to agree to the restriction on Chinese immigration; rather, it was lack of political interest in overseas immigration.[37] Official attention was limited to humanitarian concern for Chinese subjects abroad, a concern that was in line with the primary duty of Confucian officials to protect the public welfare. This point was demonstrated in the memorial of the officials who conducted the negotiations. In asking for imperial sanction of the revised treaty, they emphasized that, if unlimited emigration continued, there would be increased agony among Chinese in California, thus leading to a situation contrary to the will of the Emperor, whose greatest concern was the well-being of his subjects.[38]

Huang's view of the overseas Chinese was one step ahead of the thinking of officials in the central government. He recognized the need to promote the welfare of his countrymen abroad, not only for humanitarian reasons but also out of concern for the national interest, that is, the economic value of the overseas Chinese. While in San Francisco, he investigated the banks in the city and discovered that the total sum of money per year that the Chinese sent to Canton was at most $1,600,000 and at least $1,000,000— an annual average of about $1,200,000 during the previous four years. These figures were only for remittances from San Francisco; those from Cuba, Peru, Saigon, Singapore, and other larger centers of Overseas Chinese were several times greater. The total yearly remittances from overseas Chinese, Huang concluded, would equal the amount of silver that flowed out of China every year.[39] Huang believed the most important means of increasing the total wealth of a nation was through foreign trade and remittances from abroad. From this rather mercantilist point of view, the overseas Chinese were a valuable resource for the national economy; moreover, increasing emigration would solve the population problem at home.

Despite his bitter experiences in California, Huang maintained his high opinion of the United States as the most advanced nation on earth. He was particularly impressed by the institutions for management of a complex society, such as the specialized and precise legal codes and the administration of justice.[40] While he admired the administrative institutions of the United States, he held a negative view of democracy, particularly of election campaigns. He witnessed the presidential campaign of 1884 in which Grover Cleveland was elected. One of Huang's two poems on the United States dealt with this subject. He compared the campaigns of the two parties, each of which resorted to underhanded tactics and violence, to the bloody fighting and political maneuvering among the warring states in ancient China. He also commented on the assassination in 1881 of President James A. Garfield by a disappointed office-seeker. Election campaigns, believed Huang, were nothing but greedy power struggles for high office.[41]

Though Huang's viewpoint differed sharply from that of Alexis de Tocqueville, he too presented valuable insights into democracy in America. The pursuit of egalitarian principles would ultimately lead to the breakdown of the social order, he predicted. Uncontrolled individual freedom would promote self-love and selfishness among the people. So long as the country enjoyed prosperity and the public morale remained healthy, the system could be maintained; however, once the country suffered from economic difficulties and the people grew restless, there would follow ruthless fighting among self-seeking individuals.[42] De Tocqueville had criticized the trait of selfishness: "Each of them, standing aloof, thinks that he is reduced to care for himself alone."[43] While de Tocqueville was concerned with the fate of liberal values under the democratic system, Huang was primarily concerned with maintaining Confucian human relationships, which he regarded as essential for the survival of a society.

In September 1885, Huang asked to be released from his post in San Francisco.[44] His resignation was approved and he was about to leave for China when the infamous massacre of the Chinese at Rock Springs, Wyoming, occurred. Huang cabled the Minister in Washington to ask for an investigation. Many Chinese had been wounded or killed and a large amount of property belonging to the Chinese residents had been stolen or destroyed. Minister Cheng at once dispatched Colonel Bee and Huang Sih Chuen (Hsi-ch'üan), who had been serving at the Consulate in New York, to Wyoming.[45] The massacre at Rock Springs proved to be the most violent anti-Chinese demonstration during Huang's stay in the United States. This incident had important repercussions in China. K. C. Liu has suggested that evidence shows the report of the United States government's initial refusal to indemnify the victims of the massacre, publicized in the Chinese newspapers at the treaty ports, contributed to an anti-missionary riot in a Yangtze port in 1886.[46] From that time on, in the Yangtze area, including Szechwan, incidents of violence against missionaries occurred frequently. Later, in 1895, Huang was commissioned to settle these cases, some of which had been left undisposed of for ten years.

Huang departed from the United States around September 23, 1885. His task as Consul General in San Francisco had been

onerous. It had been a traumatic experience to witness the humiliation of his countrymen in a foreign country. Undoubtedly the most
significant insight he had gained was a new image of a world in
which peoples of different races and cultures competed for survival
and prosperity. Such an image was antithetical to the Confucian
view of a potentially harmonious world. Huang expressed his feelings about these matters in a poem composed in the mid-Pacific on
the night of the full moon of the eighth month. The night of the
Mid-Autumn Festival was celebrated throughout China, but Huang
noted that the Westerners on board did not share his sentiment
over the moon. Crowded onto the lower deck, the Chinese coolies
were in deep sleep. Alone, Huang watched the moon and reminisced
about the years he had spent abroad:

> *Although the whole world shares this moon*
> *All do not share our Festival*
> *Of Mid-Autumn. In the West*
> *They count the waxing, waning moons,*
> *Have reached about two thousand years.*
> *The pilot stands in the compass room.*
> *The ship sails westward with the stars.*
> *Red-beard sings loudly, blue eyes are drunk.*
> *And the foreign tune depresses me.*
> *Those voyagers below our decks*
> *Only in sleep are free from toil,*
> *Packed like ants across the floor,*
> *A sprawl of weary arms and legs.*[47]

Huang thought of the 400 million Chinese people; each family in
China must be celebrating the festival either in the happiness of
being together or in the sorrow of separation. In "Impressions
When Passing Japan on My Way Home," Huang reminisced about
Ho Ju-chang, banished to Sinkiang after the Foochow shipyard of
which he was the manager was destroyed during the Sino-French
War of 1884.[48] There is no indication that Huang landed in Japan
to see his old friends.

After his encounters with racial antagonism in California, Huang's world view changed substantially. He began to see the world as an arena in which nation vied with nation for power. The white race, having enslaved the blacks, was now determined to conquer the whole world, it seemed to Huang. India fell, Egypt was subjugated, Turkey was turned upside down, and all Asia was threatened; undeniably, the white race was gradually encroaching upon the entire world. During and after his stay in the United States, Huang repeatedly used the phrase "The weak become the prey of the strong" to describe the international situation and with special reference to the yellow race.[49] In a poem grieving over the loss of Vietnam to France in 1885, he wrote, "The weak become the prey of the strong by the slash of a carving knife." In the same poem, he wrote that China was exposed to danger after losing its peripheral areas: "They licked off the husk but have not yet reached the grain; / Once they peel off the skin they will eventually get to the bone."[50] A long narrative poem on the history of Ceylon, composed on a visit to that island in 1890, ended with indignation over the humiliation of the Asians and lamentation over the powerlessness of the Middle Kingdom to protect that small Asian country.[51] In a poem presented to a friend in 1900, he exalted the yellow race: "Precious are the 400 million of the yellow race!"[52] A song written to encourage children to attend school said: "Why is the yellow race not the only race in the world? Why is not the globe square? I asked these questions of my mother, but she could not answer them. Go to school; don't remain frustrated!"[53] He aggressively expressed his pride in the yellow race in a stanza for a military march: "Harmony among the five continents cannot yet be realized. Blacks and reds were humiliated by the whites. Now the whites are afraid of the 'yellow peril.' What is the yellow peril? It is we, we Asians! We! We! We!"[54]

Huang thought the Darwinian theory of natural selection explained the racial conflict in the world very adequately. The belief in the correlation between the laws of nature and the human world was the basis of cosmology in China. In a poem on gardening written in 1899, he stated that, by grafting a peach onto a plum, he was able to produce wonderful fruit. "No wonder the white men throve in the new world onto which they grafted themselves by expelling the native red men."[55]

Huang accepted the fact that progress was an inexorable element in human history and that competition and struggle encouraged progress. In order to survive the strife that accompanied progress, every nation must constantly reform its institutions. No nation could afford to preserve outdated systems in the modern world. He believed that autocratic monarchism was the greatest obstacle to China's progress. In the poem written on his deathbed, Huang stated that the four-thousand-year-old despotic system must go and that twentieth-century China must have a parliamentary system because the world was gradually progressing toward a grand harmony.[56]

Although Huang saw the world as an arena for strife, he also believed that the normative goal of human history was the realization of "grand harmony" (*ta-t'ung*), a universal human community. The term *ta-t'ung* began to appear in his poems simultaneously with the notion of racial conflict. Universal peace between the peoples in the East and the West was the ultimate goal of progress, even though it was accompanied by the brutal process of competition and natural selection. He noted that many flowers and fruits in China had come from overseas and that there were no national boundaries in the world of flora; therefore the world of flora foreshadowed the future of mankind.[57]

The concept of *ta-t'ung*, of an ideal human community, was expounded by K'ang Yu-wei in his *Ta-t'ung shu* (Book of universal commonwealth), written during the 1880s and posthumously published in 1935. K'ang proposed to achieve a utopia by eliminating national boundaries and racial differences through interracial marriage.[58] For both Huang and K'ang, their acute awareness of and despair over the world of strife made them yearn for the realization of a harmonious world.

SIX

Reform Proposals for China:
Completion of Treatises on Japan

The experience of living in a foreign country, especially in a country much more powerful and prosperous than one's own, often arouses strong sentiments of patriotism even in the most self-seeking, apolitical mind. Even while being dazzled by the higher living standards of an advanced society, one cannot but think of one's own family and wonder why one's own people should remain in poverty. Moreover, in many cases, prolonged stay in a foreign country is accompanied by more or less humiliating experiences, primarily resulting from a limitation of command over customs and systems in an alien land. Frustration and injured pride sharpen one's sense of national identity. For many leaders of the nationalist movements in Asia, their experiences while studying abroad motivated or strengthened their commitment to the nationalist cause.

Huang Tsun-hsien's bitter experiences in the United States not only deepened his patriotic sentiment but spurred him to ponder what should be done to save China from humiliation. Growing up during the dawn of nationalism in China, Huang had been awakened to patriotism. He articulated this sentiment in a poem written on his first visit to Hong Kong, the British colony on Chinese soil. Not until his stay in the United States, however, did he clarify his understanding of the nature of struggle among nations and develop his ideas on the prerequisites for building a strong state in China.

Fully accepting the ideas current in the age of nationalism, Huang believed the highest fulfillment of life could be attained through devotion to his country. His heroes were Cavour and Mazzini in Italy and Saigō, Kido, Ōkubo, and other leaders of the Meiji Restoration. He had very positive expectations for China's future and his role in it. At a time when an old establishment was about to give way to a state of flux anticipating the birth throes of a new nation-state, a man's active contribution to the nationalist cause could be channeled into a rewarding career. Huang presented his proposals for reform as an integral part of his efforts toward his career development. His resignation as Consul General at San Francisco put him in the category of tentative retirement from government service; therefore, he had to seek another appointment in the bureaucracy in order to reactivate his official career. He naturally aimed at gaining a higher position and hoped he could eventually obtain a position influential enough to promote reform. Hoping that his views and ideas would receive recognition, he worked on *Treatises on Japan* for ten years. Although the *Treatises* began as a compendium of information on Japan, in the final drafts Huang presented his recommendations for reform to the Chinese government, to whose officials he submitted copies.

Upon returning from the United States, Huang went to Wu-chou in Kwangsi province, where his father served in the local tax bureau. His mother had died while Huang was in San Francisco, and his duties there had not permitted him to go home. His short poem "Painful sorrow at arriving at Wu-chou" expressed the grief of a child who could not find his mother when he returned home. Following tradition, Huang performed a ceremony of formal burial at Chia-ying and wrote a tomb inscription.[1]

Huang's father had ordered a local publisher to reprint *Miscellaneous Poems on Japan,* and the printing was just completed at the time Huang arrived. He wrote a preface to the reprint edition, explaining the circumstances of its publication:

My book has been widely circulated, because the Japanese appreciated poems by the Chinese and also because the Chinese could acquire knowledge of Japan from the book. Because I spent nine years abroad, I have received many letters from friends inquiring about foreign countries. Since it is troublesome to answer every letter, I sent a copy of my book instead. Also, many colleagues of my father at the local government office in Kwangsi have asked him for a copy; however, the copies were out of stock at the bookstores. Therefore he had the book reprinted in the spring of 1885. It is based on the T'ung-wen-kuan edition.[2]

For about three years, from 1885 to 1888, Huang lived quietly in Chia-ying. When Chang Yin-huan, who was appointed Minister to Washington, asked him to return to San Francisco as Consul General, Huang refused, saying that the problems of the Chinese immigrants there were too formidable for him to face again. He also declined Chang Chih-tung's invitation to travel about Nanyang for investigation, on the ground that he wanted to complete the manuscript of *Treatises on Japan,* which had been suspended while he was in the United States.[3]

Huang enjoyed both the reunion with his family after the eight years' separation and the peaceful life in the countryside surrounded by old friends. His poems during this period reflect the joys of life at home. A lovely poem about his nine-year-old daughter who begged him for a story every evening illustrates a scene from his family life:

> *My family gathers around an oil lamp,*
> *The bamboo curtains drawn, the doors left open.*
> *My little daughter pulls my beard and asks*
> *"Over there was the sun close above your head?"*
> *Or "Can I measure the ocean with my hands?"*
> *Her mother watches, listens.*
> *I spread out a map of all the world.*
> *A windblown insect falls beside the lamp.*[4]

To make up for the disruption in his family life during his absence, Huang took care of important family affairs. He married his eldest son, who was seventeen. The bride had been selected many years before and came from the family of Huang's great-grandmother. One year after his return, Huang's wife gave birth to their third son, and, in the following year, the fourth. His wife, née Yeh (biographers do not give her full name), had to spend most of the prime years of her womanhood separated from her husband and caring for his household. Although Huang was sympathetic to these hardships, social custom and his domestic situation did not allow him to take her overseas with him.

An important event in the family during Huang's stay at home was a visit to the tomb of his great-grandmother. He commemorated the occasion in "Visit to the grave of my great-grandmother, née Li," often regarded as one of Huang's best poems.[5] It is an autobiographical narrative of his childhood centered around the memory of his great-grandmother. At the Ch'ing-ming festival in early spring, the entire family, including Huang's seventy-nine-year-old grandfather, two brothers and their wives and children, Huang's wife, the eldest son and his wife, and the younger sons and daughters, went together to the graveyard on a hill thickly covered with pines. Everyone was dressed formally. Huang wore a brilliantly embroidered official gown he had recently purchased in Kwangsi. One of the necklaces he wore, made of rhinoceros horn with blue grain, was a gift from his mother. His brothers wore black silk gowns, which represented their status as degree-holders who had passed the first examination. They spread a large red carpet before the tomb and arranged offerings on the altar: on the top level, they placed red incense sticks; in the middle, rice wine; and, below, rice cake with meat filling wrapped in green bamboo leaves, and lotus root decorated with purple strings. When the gong for the invocation sounded, everyone prostrated himself on the carpet. In the forefront knelt Huang's grandfather, behind him Huang and his brothers, and behind them their children. Like bamboo shoots, as Huang described it, they lined up in order, taking turns offering wine to the altar, according to precedence. Tomb visits were a ritualistic reunion of family members, both living and deceased. On this occasion, Huang regretted that his beloved mother was not among the living. He wished she had lived to the age of his great-grandmother so that he could have attended her in her old age, and he pitied his children who were deprived of their grandmother's loving care.

Huang's neighbors and old acquaintances in the village rushed to welcome him home. They were enthusiastic about having him back and were eager to hear about his travels. One spring evening, at Huang's invitation, the villagers came to his house. Dispensing with formality, they indulged in lively conversation until late at night. With great curiosity, the villagers pressed question after question on Huang and eagerly debated what he told them. He spoke of Japan, the history of America, the Pacific Ocean and the adventures of a voyage on a huge ship, and the scenery and people of the United States. Describing banquets in the United States, he said that Western food tasted strange, and perhaps the villagers would never like it. Commenting on the Western custom of growing a beard before reaching old age, he said he could not recommend it. (In China a beard was the privilege of old age.) Pouring out his indignation at American chauvinism, Huang said that, if the Americans assumed that they could dominate the world, they were greatly mistaken; looking at a map of the globe made it apparent that all countries were as small as insects in contrast to the greatness of the universe. Everyone joined the chorus in support of Huang's point. The more they drank, the more uninhibited they became, and their bursts of laughter seemed strong enough to blow off the roof tiles.[6] Huang's talk with his fellow villagers revealed his pride in China and his vexation over Western arrogance. In such unsophisticated company, Huang could speak freely; but for the literati audience, most of whom were dogmatic Sinocentrists, his sentiments had to be expressed differently. Thus *Treatises on Japan* emphasized the need to learn from the West. His deep-seated confidence in China and his national pride should not be confused with the xenophobia of Confucian scholars.

In the early summer of 1887, Huang completed the *Treatises.* Although he had written much of the manuscript while in Japan, he now spent a great deal of time incorporating into it the source materials he had gathered in Japan. Upon completing the manuscript, he wrote a poem in which he said that he dared to compare his work with the *Huang-shu* (Yellow book) by Wang Fu-chih (1619–1692), a Ming loyalist.[7] (Wang's book, a discourse on government, was filled with fundamental criticisms of the Ch'ing rule.) Huang also expressed his critical view of the institutions of China. However, the *Treatises* primarily contained concrete proposals for reform rather than criticism of the government. In substance, it was a report on Meiji Japan, which Huang thought would be useful as a reference for reform in China. As he stated in the preface, "My reports on Japan are detailed on the present and brief on the past. In other words, I reported in detail on things that are close [to us], and briefly about things that are distant. Among other matters, I investigated Western methods most thoroughly, with the intention of paving the way for their adoption in China."[8]

Huang's reform proposals in the *Treatises* encompassed government bureaucracy, the financial system, military organization, the judiciary, agriculture, industry, trade, education, and language and literature. As an essential prerequisite for successful reform, he emphasized the importance of national cohesion. To that end, a central government that could gain the positive support of the people was crucial. He advocated the rationalization of institutions for the purpose of establishing a powerful central government capable of promoting national interests. He supported the Legalist idea of government by law; however, he condemned the autocratic monarchism in which the ancient Legalists believed. Since mutual trust between the government and the people was the most important foundation for national unity, he emphasized the need to generate new public morale to support the national government.

Huang felt the immediate obstacle to reform was the conservatism and xenophobia of the elites. He repeatedly criticized Confucian scholars for their Sinocentric arrogance: "Chinese scholars indulge in discussions of [China's] antiquity. They are content to be secluded in their studies and to pay not the slightest attention to the outside world." For example, "They regard Japan as three

mysterious islands which could be seen but not reached."[9] He had
lamented over China's ignorance of Japan in 1879 when he wrote
Miscellaneous Poems. At that time, he explained that it was partly
due to the ban on overseas trade. But in the *Treatises* he severely
blamed Chinese scholars for their arrogant indifference toward foreign countries, particularly Japan, as well as their habit of seeking
knowledge exclusively from the classics, which kept them from acquiring up-to-date information about the outside world. He accused
them of discussing world affairs without going beyond the fences
that enclosed their property and of expecting to cure today's ills
by following ancient prescriptions.[10] Huang not only criticized the
false pride of Sinocentrism and xenophobia but emphasized the
benefit of contact with other cultures. Western countries had become strong through competition in military strength and by developing technology. Even in China during the Warring States
period, competition among the states stimulated progress in useful
arts and skills.[11]

To persuade the Chinese to adopt the superior technology of
the Westerners, Huang argued that Western scholarship and technology had their origins in ancient China. He asserted that the
basic principles of Western methods were to be found in the Chinese classics, especially in the *Chou Rites,* which described the institutions of the early Chou dynasty. Among the best legacies of
the Chou, which had been lost in China and found in the West,
was the concept of government based on a mutual trust between
people and government. As Huang put it, before the imperial bureaucracy had been established under the Ch'in and Han, the
relationship between ruler and ruled had been close and warm.
Thereafter, the ruler became more and more remote from the
people. At the same time, the people became indifferent to the
government and lost their sense of obligation to support it. It
was China's greatest weakness, Huang observed, in comparison
with the Western countries, which possessed national cohesion and
the united strength of their people.[12]

Another lost asset of ancient China was the tradition of practical learning. Huang pointed out that practical arts and skills were

once a respected field of learning, and he deplored the fact that "the practical learning [*shih-hsueh*] of the ancients has been neglected." Ancient scholarship had been destroyed, first by the book-burning under the Ch'in, then in the vogue of the Pure Talk during the Six Dynasties, and for the third time by the domination of Neo-Confucian metaphysics during the Sung and Ming. As a result, the orientation of intellectual activity was dramatically changed from ancient times, and practical arts and skills were no longer respected by scholars. "Every Westerner says that China is conservative and incapable of change. In my view, however, China has been changed too radically from ancient times," Huang concluded.[13]

Huang argued that China's adoption of Western methods was nothing but the recovery of its own legacy. He recalled the old saying, "When rites are lost [in the capital], search for them in the countryside."[14] To justify adopting Western methods, Huang used an analogy: There was a family who lost their precious prescription handed down from the ancestors and discovered it after a long while in a neighbor's house. They would, of course, be willing to pay a thousand (units of gold) to recover it.[15]

Huang criticized those who feared that adoption of Western technology and institutions would result in the Westernization of dress and customs in China, as had happened in Japan. The ready acceptance of Westernization in Japan, he explained, was a product of the national character of the Japanese, who worshiped foreign culture. Such a worry was unnecessary for China; the benefits of Western methods should not be rejected because of such groundless fears. The essential ingredient of Chinese culture (namely, the Confucian ethic) could not be affected by the introduction of Western technology. "The teachings of sages permeate the people's minds so deeply and the benevolence of the present dynasty touches their hearts so deeply that the people know that *tao* [the Way] is immutable just as heaven is eternal."[16]

Huang urged that the adoption of Western methods was necessary to defend the *tao*. "It is undeniable that the Westerners' capacity in agricultural production, industry, and military science is so great that no one else under heaven can match them. Moreover, they are daily humiliating us and pressing us, taking advantage of their superior skills and technology. Under these circumstances, we cannot afford to continue sitting with writing brushes and contemplating the *tao*. Those who wish to protect the *tao* cannot but borrow the Westerners' methods [*fa*] in order to do so. If we supplement Western methods with Chinese talent and wisdom, we shall surpass them in a few years; then, at home we shall restore the glory of the Three Dynasties, and in the world China shall rank at the head of the nations." It was only a temporary humiliation to borrow superior skills and technology, and it would be against the teachings of the ancients to adhere to the letter of the Classics and refuse to adopt the advanced technology and institutions of others.[17]

Huang maintained that, in a sense, reform was a restoration of the vitality that had existed in China's past. He was convinced that the secret of China's strength was to be found in its own tradition.[18] He argued that the basic principles of Western-style government, characterized by systematization and specialization of official functions, were to be found in the official system described in the *Chou Rites*:

> Although not all the government systems in the West during the past two thousand years since the unification under Rome are the same as the systems described in the *Chou Rites,* there are elements in common between the two. For example, the Western system makes no distinctions between officials who were recruited through regular and irregular routes, between inner-court officials and government officials, and between civil and military officials. The responsibilities and functions of the officials are clearly defined as to minute details. These features existed in the Chou official system, in which there were officials in charge of gold and tin, forest officials in charge of timber, and judges versed in the law and who promulgated the royal will. None of these offices have existed since the Ch'in and Han.[19]

Huang's use of the *Chou Rites* as a basis for reform was not unprecedented. It was a common practice among the late Ch'ing reform advocates to justify their proposals by referring to the

Classics, especially the Chou Rites.[20] In an early example, Prince Kung quoted the "K'ao-kung chi" (Treatise on works) in the Chou Rites in his memorial of 1866 requesting the court to establish a school of astronomy and mathematics in the Translators' College in Peking. He argued that Western astronomy and mathematics originated in China and developed in the West, and that work that had been frowned upon by Confucian scholars was given respectability in the Chou Rites.[21] Prince Kung's discussion, however, was limited to Western science and technology. On the subject of the association between Western political institutions and the Chinese Classics, Onogawa Hidemi has pointed out that there is a record of a conversation between Tseng Ch'i-tse and his son-in-law Ch'en Sung-sheng in 1879 in London.[22] Ch'en Sung-sheng said that the government and teaching (cheng-chiao) of the Westerners reflected much that corresponded to the Chou Rites, that Lao-tzu was a Chou official and was banished to the Western desert bearing some writings on the constitutions and laws of the Chou, but that the problem with this theory lay in proving it. Tseng thought it a new and interesting idea; he wrote in his diary that ancient Europe was uncivilized, that literature and the arts of government were gradually transmitted from the East, and hence Western customs and civilization resembled ancient China's. He also wrote that all kinds of Western machines originated in ancient China.[23]

The Chou Rites had been used by controversial reformers throughout Chinese history, beginning with Wang Mang, the usurper of the Former Han dynasty, Wang An-shih of the Northern Sung, and most recently by the Taipings. Since the Chou Rites were considered a delusion,[24] Huang began his discussion of Western-style bureaucracy by vindicating them. It was not the fault of this canon that Wang Mang forged the classics and that Wang An-shih misled the Northern Sung; rather, these men were to blame for misusing the canon. Then he refuted the charge of Ou-yang Hsiu against the Chou Rites. Ou-yang Hsiu contended that the bureaucratic system of the Chou Rites required more than 50,000 officials, exluding minor officials in the local government and the army; hence the total tax receipts from the entire Chou territory would not have sufficed to support such a huge bureaucracy. Refuting Ou-yang Hsiu, Huang wrote that the King of Chou monopolized the profit from the resources in mountains, woods, rivers, and marshlands and collected large amounts of taxes from marketplaces and city gates; thus the King had the means to support the bureaucracy, and the people would have benefited from the civil service employment opportunities. Moreover, the bureaucracy under the Chou court was specialized and systematized, and, consequently, a large number of officials were required. Huang pointed out that one of the most important features of Western-style government was a specialized bureaucratic organization supported by ample finances.[25]

As a part of institutional reform, Huang advocated the modernization of the legal system. Western legal codes were more advanced and comprehensive than Chinese codes, and in the West the criminal codes received the same respect as the canons or the words of the sages. But in China, moral codes were exalted and criminal codes were looked down upon as unworthy to be discussed by scholars. He was impressed by the fact that, in the West, legal codes functioned as the major tools of government, not as supplements to the moral code.[26] He confessed that, before he left China, he had thought the Westerners' laws must be as unsophisticated as those of primitive tribes in the western regions or of the barbarians in the north. Only after he witnessed the Japanese efforts to study Western law and then observed the function of law in the United States did he realize the superiority of the Western legal system. He understood that, because of the development of legal institutions, Western laws were a hundred times more complex than Chinese laws. He was especially impressed by the existence of detailed rules for every step of litigation in the United States, whereas in China legal procedures had never been fully codified. The purpose of the detailed rules for litigation was, Huang explained, to minimize the possibility of punishing the innocent and to avoid abuse of authority by officials. He was impressed by the fact that, in the Western system, all citizens were equal before the law, regardless of social status, and that all countries in Europe and America were governed by laws, no matter what their size or political system.[27]

Huang interpreted the differences between the concept of law in China and that in the West as differences in the degree of progress of the two societies. He maintained that, the more advanced a society, the more complex and precise its codified laws. In general, ancient criminal codes were simple because the laws were supplementary to the moral code; but modern criminal codes had become more refined because they had gained equal status with the moral code. He realized that the criminal codes of the Wei and Chin dynasties were more comprehensive than those of the Han dynasty, and that the T'ang codes were more comprehensive than those of the Wei and Chin dynasties. By the same token, the criminal code of the Ch'ing was more comprehensive than that of the Ming. He pointed out that the laws became more and more complex with time, and that the wisdom of the sages could not equal the richness of knowledge of later generations. The body of Western law represented the accumulated experience and knowledge gained over hundreds of years, and the precision of Western laws had now reached a height undreamed of by the sage kings or Legalist ministers in ancient China.[28] In this regard, Huang saw the history of mankind as one of linear progress and challenged the belief in the absolute wisdom of the sages, favoring instead, empirical knowledge. Men were able to create better legal institutions by learning from experience, and the legacy of history was much richer than the teachings of the ancients. This point was consistent with his earlier doubts of the sanctity of antiquity and was supported by the Darwinian theory of evolution he accepted after his sojourn in the United States.

Among his various reform proposals in the *Treatises,* Huang paid great attention to state finance, writing more commentaries on this subject than on any other. Pointing out the importance of economics, he wrote, "In the West there is a saying that to be defeated in nine out of ten wars is not as great a worry as the loss of resources and the decline in production." Westerners were dedicated to increasing the wealth of their nations because they knew that economic power was the secret of national strength. Huang understood that the economic activities of the Western countries were greatly motivated by nationalist considerations; thus in the West, he believed, the citizens of each nation were devoted to increasing the wealth of their own country.[29] Perhaps his interpretation of the ethic of capitalism in the West was influenced by the Japanese attitude toward industrialization, which they regarded primarily as a means of enriching the state.

Huang emphasized the importance of the roles of national government in the modern economy and pointed out that there were six essentials to which Westerners paid attention in order to increase national wealth: conducting an accurate population census; collecting sufficient taxes; setting up an annual budget and publishing the balance sheet; buying government bonds; regulating the currency; and promoting overseas trade. He argued that rudimentary ideas about these measures could be found in the *Chou Rites* and the *Kuan-tzu* (a book on statecraft by Kuan Chung), and pointed out that people's trust in their government was the prerequisite for implementing these measures.[30]

In his discussion of population, Huang felt that the traditional preference for a large population was a detriment in the modern world. In ancient times when productivity depended on a large human labor force, rulers feared the loss of manpower in their territory. But, in the modern era, overpopulation caused serious problems; the number of people engaged in unproductive and even harmful occupations increased, and there was the constant danger of rebellion. He noted that the Europeans dealt with overpopulation by using the unemployed for mining or for opening up new territories. The Japanese government solved the problem by cultivating the wasteland in Hokkaidō and by encouraging new industries. Stating that only those who were ignorant of the problem clung to the outworn philosophy of cherishing a large population, he criticized the Ch'ing government for not paying heed to the unemployment problem.[31]

Concerning taxation, Huang criticized the ideal of Confucian government, which favored leaving the maximum surplus production in the hands of the people. This practice led to the corollary that the government should reduce expenditures to a minimum. Huang disagreed with such thinking and proposed to increase state revenues by adopting the Western concept of taxation. He deplored Chinese indifference to the financial responsibilities of the state and to the people's obligation to support their government:

> The Chinese people look only at the steamboats possessed by the British, Russian, French, and Americans and envy their wealth, but are not aware that the annual tax revenue of these governments amounts to as much as seventy million pounds. For China to raise this amount of revenue, taxation would have to be increased by five or six times.
>
> Only by doing so would it become possible to get steamships and all the other means of wealth and power. Precisely because of the shortage of annual revenue, the Chinese government has no choice but to temporize with both foreign and domestic problems. It can stand still but cannot take any action. Is this not a result of light taxation?[32]

He regretted that far-sighted officials like T'ao Shu (1779–1839), who improved the system of grain transport, and Hu Lin-i (1812–1861), who raised funds through the collection of likin (transit tax), suffered from public resentment and accusation. It was unreasonable, he declared, that these men were stigmatized as harsh officials.

Huang noted that, in Japan, the government's revenue was great despite the smallness of the country. The annual revenue amounted to 50 or 60 million yen, the equivalent of 35 or 42 million taels.[33] Huang thought it was no wonder the Japanese government had to impose taxes on all kinds of commodities, as well as on arts and skills that rendered income. If taxes like these were collected in China, the scholars would severely criticize the government for its harsh exactions. He noted that governments in the West were like Japan's: they collected heavy taxes and in return used them for the people's benefit, as well as for national defense. This argument was similar to that of the Legalist statesmen in the famous discourse on salt and iron at the Han court in 81 B.C. The Confucian argued for the abolition of the state monopoly on salt and iron and favored lighter taxation; the Legalists maintained that heavy taxation on the produce of mountains and marshes (that is, produce aside from regular agriculture) was essential for the maintenance of state finances. The Legalists argued that heavy taxes would eventually benefit the people, since they would enable the state to defend the people effectively from foreign invasion.[34]

Huang's recommendation for a tax increase was unique among the late Ch'ing reform proposals. The majority of the reform advocates discussed the reduction of miscellaneous taxes and the abolition of the transit tax, or likin. For example, Hsueh Fu-ch'eng advised the eventual abolition of the likin in his memorial of 1875.[35] Cheng Kuan-ying, reflecting his occupational interest as a comprador, criticized the Ch'ing government's taxation on commerce, particularly the levy of the likin. He recommended its abolition and an increase in the rate of duties on importation of foreign merchandise.[36] Wang T'ao, a treaty-port intellectual, also argued that the likin should be eliminated, since it had been intended as a temporary emergency measure during the Taiping Rebellion, and the complex system of collecting it plagued the merchants.[37] Huang's assertion that the government should have ample tax funds was revolutionary according to Chao Feng-t'ien, who made a comprehensive survey of economic thought in the late Ch'ing period.[38] He stated that Huang's advocacy of ample taxation was not seconded by any other reform advocate until Ho Kai (Ch'i) and Hu Li-yuan wrote *Hsin-cheng lun-i* (Discussions on the reform of government; first publication 1895). Ho Kai was an English-educated physician in Hong Kong who founded the Alice Memorial Hospital where Sun Yat-sen studied from 1887 to 1892. He wrote the book in collaboration with Hu Li-yuan, who had better command of literary Chinese. They asserted that a considerable amount of taxation was necessary in order to finance state expenditures.[39] In the late 1890s, Yen Fu's view on taxation in his translation (1897–1900) of the *Wealth of Nations* was almost identical to Huang's.[40]

In connection with taxation, Huang discussed the need for eliminating corruption in the bureaucracy. He pointed out that taxation was extremely light under the Ch'ing government and that low taxes meant underpayment of government officials. Officials were forced to collect customary fees from the people to support themselves and their staff. Such a practice plagued the people. Huang proposed to collect all the necessary expenses to maintain the bureaucracy in the form of taxes.[41] His concern over the morale of officials was shared by other reform advocates in the late 1870s and the 1880s who proposed to revitalize the bureaucracy through improvement in the civil service examination system and the elimination of corruption. They agreed that corruption among the officials was not just their personal failure but stemmed from the built-in faults of the system, which forced them to depend on bribes. Feng Kuei-fen and Cheng Kuan-ying urged paying substantial salaries to officials in order to eliminate the evils of bribery and the overwhelming corruption of the government.[42] During the 1890s, Ch'en Chih discussed the problem of official salaries from the viewpoint of the morale of officials. He argued that increased salaries would encourage men of ability to devote themselves to their official duties, and at the same time strict punishment of negligence and corruption would become possible.[43] Ho Kai and Hu Li-yuan discussed the problem of bribes, stating that, in any discussion of the Chinese economy, the salaries of officials should take precedence.[44] Unlike these reform advocates, however, Huang never mentioned the improvement of the examination system, since he saw little hope for it. Instead, he dwelt on the creation of a new education system modeled after the Western pattern.

Huang paid close attention to the creation of modern budgetary, currency, and banking systems in Meiji Japan. The establishment of these systems was a major goal in the financial administration of the Meiji Government during its first decade. He discussed the principles of a Western-style budget system, emphasizing the fact that it was made public, that it was based on trust between the people and the government, and that extensive taxation was possible because the people knew for what purpose their taxes were used.[45] He argued that such trust between the government and the people had existed in China in the past. The description of official systems in the *Chou Rites* revealed that the Chou Court reported to the public its revenue and expenditures at the end of every year, so that everyone knew that the money was properly expended and that nothing was kept by the court. "Trust and harmony between the ruler and the populace were the reasons for the prosperity of the Chou." Of course, the expenses of a modern government were much greater, and more funds were needed for military defense of the country. Therefore, it was even more necessary to administer government finance with public spirit.[46] Chao Feng-t'ien pointed out that Huang was the earliest among the late Ch'ing intellectuals to pay attention to the Western budget system. After Huang, Cheng Kuan-ying, Ho Kai and Hu Li-yuan, and Chang Chien recommended the adoption of such a system.[47]

On the subject of government loans, Huang emphasized again the importance of the people's trust in the government. National loans should be made for government enterprises, since he felt that foreign loans were helpful only in the short run and benefited foreigners in the long run. He deplored the Chinese ignorance of government bonds, and recounted the anecdote about King Nan of Eastern Chou who was made a laughingstock by building fortresses on borrowed money.[48] According to Chao Feng-t'ien, Huang's discussion of national bonds preceded those of T'ang Shou-ch'ien, Cheng Kuan-ying, and Ho Kai, who discussed the subject during the 1890s. Chao also suggested that discussions of a standard currency and national banking system began to appear in the late 1870s, and that Huang's was one of the earliest fairly detailed expositions.[49]

Speaking of overseas trade, Huang pointed out the differences between the traditional concept of trade in agrarian societies in Asia and the modern Western concept. Asian countries were agriculturally oriented and did not regard trade as important. Asian rulers were reluctant to export goods for fear it would cause shortages of commodities and thereby increase prices. In the modern West, Huang noted, trade competition between countries for profit was intense.[50] In essence, the Western nations were fighting an economic war, which demonstrated one aspect of the Darwinian struggle for survival.

Huang recognized the importance of trade, especially export, as a means of increasing the wealth of a nation, and he realized that Westerners were serious about improving and increasing their export trade. He commended Japanese efforts: "Since the restoration, the Japanese have wholeheartedly intensified their efforts to increase export commodities, such as silk to England, tea to the United States, and seafood to China. We must say that they know what is the most important."[51] Because Westerners were aware of the importance of trade, Huang noted, they were united as a whole nation to do their best to promote it: "They station consuls and dispatch commissioners to other countries to survey the customs and tastes of the people there so that they can suit their export merchandise to the customers' tastes. Sometimes they make imitations. When they cannot compete with others in trade, they resort to war, destroy the other party's merchant marine, and attempt to monopolize the profit of trade."[52]

Huang also cautioned against the negative effect of foreign trade, having witnessed the financial problem in Japan caused by a trade deficit. However, he noted that it was mainly the Japanese adoption of Western clothes and lifestyle that necessitated the importing of luxury merchandise. Although he thought that, in Japan, the harm caused by trade was greater than the benefit, he admitted that trade raised the production of tea, silk, and other goods.[53]

Huang's belief in the importance of trade was shared by his contemporaries. About 1860, Feng Kuei-fen wrote that, for China, exporting tea and silk was the best means of gaining wealth. At the same time, he believed that national wealth could be increased by opening new mines.[54] Hsueh Fu-ch'eng emphasized the importance of exporting tea and silk in his memorial of 1875. In connection with the proposal to encourage exports, Hsueh advocated the naval protection of merchant ships. He wrote that the wealth gained from the merchant marine would help to build and maintain warships. Cheng Kuan-ying saw the world as a world of commercial rivalry because of his experiences as a comprador in Shanghai and Hong Kong and ardently advocated promoting export trade and state protection for the commercial activities of Chinese merchants. In his view as a merchant, advancement of the interests of the merchant class would contribute to the strengthening of the nation, since the prosperity of commerce and industry was the foundation of a strong state.[55]

To build a strong army and navy had been the major target of reform efforts in China from the 1860s. In discussing military reform, Huang pointed out that the Chinese must first change their view of military forces. China did not have a well-trained army because, as Huang explained, "China regards the army as something like medicine, to be used only when the body is sick, while Westerners regard military forces as something like the four limbs of a body, to be kept healthy and fit all the time."[56] China's antimilitarist society was a natural consequence of the long years of peace under a unified empire, he reasoned. "In general, at the time of the founding of a country, the military is honored but, after consolidation of the regime, civilian culture prevails." It was always true from ancient times, Huang reminded his readers, that those who relax their defenses are bound to become weak. Particularly in a world where the Powers kept a covetous watch on the weak, seeking for their prey, every Western country had been competing with every other in building military strength. Even in peacetime, Huang continued, they built fortresses and giant warships, cast cannons and drilled soldiers every day because they knew that peace would not last and that war could be prevented only by preparing for it. This point had been made by the Duke of Chou in his admonishment to King Ch'eng.[57]

Huang commended the conscription system developed in the West and adopted by Japan. The advantage of the system was that it allowed the state to draft men between certain ages and enlist them for a specific, limited period of time. In contrast, under the Chinese system after the T'ang, the government was obliged to feed its recruits for life. Thus, China had many old and disabled soldiers in the ranks. Such an army not only cost the state a great deal but proved to be useless when the Taiping Rebellion erupted. While criticizing the contemporary military system in China, Huang also disagreed with the Confucian scholars who believed in the idealized militia system of ancient China, in which all soldiers were normally engaged in agriculture and rendered military service only when it was required. He pointed out that, in ancient times, the need for military service was small, but increased mobilization in later times made it impractical to continue the militia system.[58]

As for the navy, Huang emphasized the importance of a unified command in order to end the rivalry between the Northern and the Southern Fleet. The problem of naval disunity had been discussed and several proposals were made in the early 1880s; however, no admiralty was established before the Sino-Japanese War of 1894–1895. In Huang's opinion, the British navy's strength was primarily owing to its unified command under one admiral, whose efficient communication system enabled him to direct all parts of the fleet. Second, British naval officers came from the educated classes—even princes and aristocrats received military training—and the public regarded military service as an honor. Third, naval shipyards were amply supplied with shipbuilding materials as well as skilled shipwrights.[59]

As for technology, Huang called for a revolutionary change in the Chinese attitude toward manual work. As a major reason why China lagged behind in developing a modern technology, Huang blamed the scholars' neglect of practical learning:

> In my view, in the beginning of Chinese history what was called sacred wisdom was nothing but pharmacology, architecture, dressmaking and toolmaking. Although these arts have been demeaned as manual skills [*kung-i*] in recent times, those who invented them were regarded as sages by the ancients. Out of the six major positions in the Chou bureaucracy, one position was allocated for the official in charge of manual work. . . . This indicates that the ancients greatly respected work and skills. Scholars in later times cherished empty talk and regarded work and skills as too base to mention. Thereupon, the task of making tools gradually fell into the hands of petty craftsmen. Since scholars never personally attended to it, the practical learning of the ancients was neglected.[60]

In contrast to the situation in China, Huang stated, Westerners respected practical skills and established specialized training for each branch of technology. Consequently, Westerners had made marvelous achievements in medicine, agriculture, military equipment, transportation, and communications.[61] Concerning the social status of technologists, the same observations had been made by Huang's contemporaries. In his famous letter to the Tsungli Yamen reporting on the superiority of Western firearms (1864), Li Hung-chang criticized Chinese literati for their indulgence in the impractical art of literature and their scornful attitude toward craftsmanship. Hsueh Fu-ch'eng stated in his memorial of 1875 that China's technological backwardness was a result of the intellectuals' neglect.[62]

In his treatise on the writing system in Japan, Huang discussed the problems arising from the discrepancy between the spoken and the written language in China and suggested the need for reform. Modern Chinese people were content to read and write in the ancient language simply because they were accustomed to doing so. Huang believed the Chinese writing system had originally derived from the spoken language, and that, although the spoken language altered over time, the written language remained little changed. In the Japanese language, the discrepancy between the spoken and the written word was greater than in any other language because the Japanese had borrowed their writing system from a country whose spoken language was totally different from their own. "Since the Japanese did not have a writing system, they forcibly made Chinese characters represent Japanese words, and they read the Chinese characters with a Japanese pronunciation." To overcome these inconveniences, he explained, the Japanese invented phonetic symbols, *kana*, or the Japanese syllabary system, to enable them to transcribe their language. He commended *kana* as a great innovation, saying that even the legendary divine creator of the writing system of China had not thought of the need for such symbols.[63]

Huang acknowledged the positive role *kana* played in promoting literacy in Japan, noting the presence of books written entirely in *kana* and circulated among commoners and women. He compared the contribution of *kana* to the European languages which had supplanted Latin and given rise to national literatures. "It is natural," he wrote, "that the greater the gap between the spoken and written languages, the fewer the literate people; the narrower the gap, the greater the number of literate people."[64] If the Japanese did not have *kana,* the majority of the nation would have remained illiterate. In this connection, he criticized Ogyū Sorai, the Confucian scholar of Tokugawa Japan who had been famous for being an extreme Sinophile. Sorai denounced the Japanese method of reading Chinese and advocated the use of spoken Chinese.[65]

In connection with the language situation in Japan, Huang discussed the problems of China's writing system and predicted the need for simplified characters. Although it had been said that the Chinese writing system was the oldest in the world, Huang argued, it originated from picture writing and had been changed many times. Noting that modern characters had been simplified over the centuries, he advocated still further simplification in order to make them available to everyone—peasants, artisans, merchants, women, and children:

> Since the Chou and Ch'in dynasties, the style of writing has often been changed. The style of memorials, circulars, edicts, and verdicts of judgment in the modern era is plain and direct, and priority is given to conveying the message. This kind of style cannot be found in the writings of the ancients. [At present] novelists write in the vernacular, and their writing is almost identical with the spoken language. I would not preclude the possibility that the style of the popular novelist may become the standard for writing in the future.[66]

Huang had expressed concern over the alienation of the written from the spoken language when he was about twenty years old; he sensed that the future direction of the evolution in the writing system was toward unification of the spoken and written languages. It is noteworthy that he highly esteemed *Hung-lou-meng* (*The Dream of the Red Chamber*) and recommended this vernacular novel to his Japanese friends as the best literary work in China. He even stated that it could be considered the equal of such classics as the *Tso chuan* (Tso commentary of Spring and autumn annals), *Kuo-yü* (Conversations of the states), and the *Han shu* (History of the Han dynasty).[67]

Through his experiences in Japan and the United States, one of Huang's greatest discoveries was the dynamics emanating from groups of people who formed political parties and various voluntary associations, which he called *she-hui* (associations). The Chinese term originally meant religious organizations and then guilds or other professional associations.[68] He was amazed to find in Japan that various kinds of associations provided the basis for cohesion among people and generated tremendous energy. He wrote that associations were organized for the purpose of uniting the people's abilities and resources for the accomplishment of common goals. In Japan, there were many political parties—Jiyūtō, Kyōwatō, Rikkentō, Kaishintō, and Zenshintō. In the academic field, there were societies of astronomers; geographers; scholars of Chinese classics, of Dutch studies, of English; poetry associations, bar associations; religious organizations; associations of doctors, agronomists, biologists, businessmen, and administrators; associations of people who shared the same hobbies; mutual-aid associations; and various organizations for the improvement of agriculture and handicrafts. He noted that there was probably no Japanese who did not belong to one of these associations and that they were utilized by the government to mobilize people toward creating a prosperous nation.[69]

Huang pointed out that associations were well developed in Western countries and that Westerners always carried out their objectives through the cooperation of individuals united in a group. He was struck by the fact that, through the united strength of individuals, Westerners achieved such tremendous tasks as the miracle of steamship and cable communication, and expansion in the world by overcoming the barriers of mountains and oceans. They had developed the techniques and group ethic to organize individuals and to maintain group solidarity. He emphasized that nothing could be more powerful than the united strength (*lien-ho li*) of the people.

Citing Hsun-tzu, he stated that mankind could become master of the natural world, thanks to its ability to work together:

> Heaven created men without the ability to fly like birds or run as fast as beasts. Nonetheless, men are superior in the world. The reason is that men can pool their strength, which beasts cannot do. In the world nothing is stronger than the power of unified force. It is like burning coal: if the pieces are scattered, even a child can kick and extinguish them; if they are put together in a stove, the heat is so intense that no one can even approach it.[70]

Huang added the words of precaution that group power could become so strong that competition among different groups would tend to be very violent, as in the case of the presidential election campaign he witnessed in the United States. He wrote that the disaster caused by a struggle between opposing groups would be many times more devastating than the harm caused by the factional strife in China during the Han, T'ang, Sung, and Ming times. He was aware that modern voluntary associations could unite people on a broader basis and could exert much more power than political factions in a traditional society.[71]

Hsueh Fu-ch'eng shared Huang's opinion on the advantages of voluntary associations. In his essay written in London between 1890 and 1894, Hsueh commended the advantages of the joint-stock corporations as an aggregate form of wisdom, ability, and financial resources for many people, and attributed the secret of Western expansion to the corporations organized for various enterprises. At the same time, he pointed out that failure to develop the business corporation was one reason for weakness in China's industries and commerce.[72]

By 1897, Huang developed his concept of "association" into a more general notion of "grouping" (*ch'ün*). In a speech in Huan in 1897, he emphasized the idea that the strength of men rested on their ability to unite, and asserted that the collective strength of the people was the basis of a strong nation.[73] This same idea was developed by Huang's younger friend Liang Ch'i-ch'ao, who regarded grouping as the "basic principle for giving order to the world" and presented the concept of "new citizenship" as the central theme of his reform proposals.[74]

In summary, the main theme of Huang's proposal was that China needed to make practical adjustments to the demands of the modern world in which nations struggled for survival. The most urgent task was to enrich and strengthen the country through institutional reform. For concrete reform, he pointed out, the Chinese must change their traditional attitude toward basic government institutions. Contradicting traditional Confucian ideas, he proposed that bureaucracy should be organized for functional purposes and should be staffed by specialists in each field; the government should collect enough taxes to ensure the adequate financing of national defense and state enterprises; the government should actively promote industries and trade; the status of the military should be upgraded; the judiciary should be based on a comprehensive legal code rather than dominated by an unwritten moral code; the skills and crafts of manual workers should receive the respect accorded scholarly knowledge; the writing system should be simplified to make it viable for the masses; and literature should be written in the vernacular.

Although Huang pointed out some undesirable features of the Westernization of Japan, his reform proposals as a whole were oriented toward the creation of a powerful state after the model of Meiji Japan. He believed the leaders of the Meiji Government were doing the right kinds of things to provide for the foundation of a powerful nation. The most crucial factors of Japan's successful start as a modern state were, as Huang observed, strong leadership of the central government, administrative efficiency, especially in the area of control over the human and economic resources of the country, and mobilization of popular enthusiasm for achievement of the national goals, as well as government initiative in application of modern science and technology in agriculture, industry, transportation, and communication systems. Huang recommended that China follow the Japanese example in these areas. To provide practical information on how the Japanese organized modern institutions, he included in his *Treatises* numerous statistical tables, regulations, and by-laws of government institutions, as well as detailed accounts of the development of new systems. In this respect, his book was distinguished from the writings of his contemporaries, who expressed their reform ideas abstractly. He hoped his concrete and detailed information would be utilized by government leaders for the purpose of planning for reform in China. Therefore, he prepared the *Treatises* for submission to the Tsungli Yamen for publication.

Upon completion of the *Treatises*, Huang sent a copy of the manuscript to Li Hung-chang, seeking his support for publication. Li sent it to the Tsungli Yamen, complying with Huang's request. In his letter of recommendation for the manuscript, Li wrote that it was a comprehensive and insightful account of the reform in Japan, which was modeled after the Western systems, and that the author's intention was to offer a useful reference for coping with the problems of the time. In comparison with famous *Ch'ao-hsien-kuo chi* (Chronicle of Korea) by Huang Hung-hsien, an imperial commissioner to Korea during the Ming, Li stated that *Treatises on Japan* contained much more substantial and detailed information. Huang made another copy to send to Chang Chih-tung, Governor General of Kwangtung and Kwangsi, seeking his recommendation. Chang endorsed Huang's statement that, since all of the basic institutions in Japan, such as bureaucracy, state finance, the military system, and the judicial system, were modeled after Western institutions, Huang was able to introduce Western-style institutions by describing the new institutions in Japan. He highly recommended Huang's work. Comparing it with Yao Wen-tung's *Jih-pen ti-li ping-yao* (Japanese geography and military forces), which had been published by the Tsungli Yamen in 1884, Chang stated that Huang's book was far more comprehensive and profound, and that it was an indispensable reference book for diplomats assigned to Japan. Besides submitting copies through these influential officials, Huang decided to take a copy personally to Peking to ensure that it reached the Tsungli Yamen. Since it had to be handwritten, reproducing a copy of such a huge volume, which contained more than 560,000 characters, was an onerous task.[75]

In late 1888, Huang traveled to Peking with a copy of the manuscript, optimistically expecting that the government would publish it and that he would subsequently obtain a higher diplomatic position, perhaps a ministership. Contrary to his expectation, however, the Tsungli Yamen was not interested in the manuscript. It was a great disappointment to Huang, and he remained embittered about it for many years. Not until around 1895 did he finally manage to have it published by a private press in Canton. By that time, the Sino-Japanese War had changed the political and intellectual situation dramatically. After the war, it became obvious to all that the Japanese efforts for modernization after the Western model were fruitful, and advocating reforms after the Japanese model became commonplace. For Huang, the most regrettable consequence of the delay in publication was that the leaders of China, especially those who were in favor of war with Japan, had been uninformed about Japan due to lack of first-hand information. He told a friend in 1897 that, if his book had been published in time, Chang Chien and Wen T'ing-shih would not have advocated the war so strongly.[76] At any event, the fact that the *Treatises* was not published in the late 1880s reflected a lack of interest among government leaders in the developments in Meiji Japan. Consequently, Huang's reform proposals were not taken seriously, and his outcry remained a voice in the wilderness.

SEVEN

The Other Half of the Globe:
Reflections in London and Singapore

In this planet's vast sea of people
I am but one lonely water drop.
And, as I feel the weight of middle age,
I sense the lack of lustre in my life.
Manager of a ten-thousand house domain?
Victorious general, medals on his chest?
Capable minister?—those glories won't be mine.
Even so, why should I worry and feel sad?[1]

In Confucian culture, and perhaps in any culture, reaching the age of forty reminds one to stop to think how much one has accomplished and what to pursue for the rest of his lifetime. Huang had ample time for reflection in his early forties, especially when he lived in London and Singapore. During this period, he began to advocate the need of revolution in poetry. His "declaration of independence" from ancient literary conventions made him famous as a precursor of the vernacular literature movement. Through his observation of European countries, he deepened his understanding of the nature of progress in the modern world and the significance of the Japanese efforts.

Huang was forty-one when he traveled to Peking with his manuscript of the *Treatises*. He was disappointed that the government would not publish it, not only because his effort to contribute to reform in China was not appreciated, but also because he had hoped the book would facilitate an official appointment at higher rank. For about a year, he stayed in Peking awaiting an official assignment. He was willing to serve at an overseas post again, especially in Europe, because he was anxious to see the other half of the globe where he had not yet been.[2] While in Peking, he cultivated friendships with metropolitan officials who were sympathetic to his reform ideas. Most of them were junior officials who later emerged as the promoters of the Reform Movement. Among them was Ch'en Chih, author of the famous reform tract *Yung-shu*, and also Wen T'ing-shih (Yun-ko, 1856–1904), a Hanlin compiler, later active as the organizer of a discussion group of reform officials. Others were Yuan Ch'ang (Shuang-ch'iu, 1846–1900), Secretary of the Tsungli Yamen; Ch'iu Feng-chia (Chung-yen, 1864–1912), a Hakka from Taiwan who would lead the movement for an independent Taiwan in 1895; Hsu Ching-ch'eng (Chu-yun, 1845–1900), Chinese Minister to Japan in 1880, then to Germany and France from 1885 to 1888; and Liang Ting-fen (Hsing-hai, 1859–1919) from Canton, a close associate of Chang Chih-tung.[3] These men were concerned about China's foreign affairs and were critical of the conservatism of those in power. Huang's association with them brought him into contact with K'ang Yu-wei, who was to be the central figure of the Reform of 1898 ten years later. Huang had especially close ties with Yuan Ch'ang, who recognized the value of *Treatises on Japan* earlier than anyone else. In fact, he was so impressed by the work that he called Huang a treasure of the state. When China was defeated by Japan in 1895, Yuan told Chang Chih-tung that, if the *Treatises* had been published earlier, China would have been spared the payment of the 200 million taels indemnity.[4]

While Huang was in Peking, a tragic incident occurred at home. Huang's reaction to it reflected his attitude toward religion and the superstitious beliefs prevalent in his time. In the 5th lunar month of 1889, his younger brother Tsun-lu (Kung-wang, 1855–1889) died mysteriously. He had suffered from a mental disorder for three years but had gradually recovered. Then he had another attack; this time he refused medicine, saying his illness could not be cured by medicine. He confided to a friend that, from the time he first became sick, he often saw a vision of a white-haired old man who appeared like a god or demon and numbed his senses. Recently, a vision of a beautiful girl of seventeen or eighteen had disturbed him. He asked his friend not to mention these visions, since they might be interpreted as symptoms of evil conduct. Previously, there had been roses growing by the house of a clan member who lived next to Huang. Because someone had seen one of the rose bushes changing into a human figure, and there was subsequently a mental case in the family, they transplanted the bush to the eastern corner of the lot, which happened to be close to Huang Tsun-lu's room. It was shortly after this occurrence that he became ill. Huang's family suspected that the rose had magical power and decided to destroy it. On the 17th day of the month, they cut down the bush and dug out the roots. Tsun-lu did not know about it; however, at the same moment, he stabbed his abdomen and collapsed with a terrible scream. Although the wound was shallow, he died the following day.[5]

Huang's grief was deep; he loved this brother, seven years younger, who was close to him during their boyhood.[6] Huang refused to accept the superstitious explanation of his death that his family and other relatives believed. Contemplating the meaning of death and fate, he wrote the tomb inscription for his brother. Expressing his basic rationalism, he wrote: "Man absolutely cannot escape death. However, we should not be awed by death either. We can only be mindful of it and let things take their own course." He wondered whether his brother killed himself as a result of illness or madness. Whatever the case, it made little difference, he thought. More disturbing was whether the incident was the work of a dead spirit. After debating the question with himself, he decided it was no use to continue. Nevertheless, his mind was unsettled about the meaning of death and fate and he concluded the inscription in these words:

I asked the question of Buddha; Buddha had many words to evade an answer. I asked Confucius; he says that he does not know the answer.

> Even if I could raise the Yellow Emperor from his tomb and ask him
> to be the judge to settle this issue, I would be unable to get a clear
> answer. . . . So I composed this piece to express my grief. I still pose
> a question to the sage who made the wanton statement that he knew
> the mandate of Heaven, and ask who is responsible for this tragedy.[7]

Huang's stand against superstition had been enunciated in his comment in the *Treatises* on the domination of astrology in the court politics in early Chinese history. He decried the belief that the movements of heavenly bodies and human affairs were linked; after all, the view of the stars in the sky had been shared by all people, past and present, throughout the world. How could the constellations reflect the moment-by-moment affairs of each individual?[8]

In view of the fact that the belief in correlation between the cosmic and human worlds was the basis of Chinese cosmology incorporated into the Confucian orthodoxy, and that it provided the theoretical foundation to the concept of the mandate of heaven, Huang's statement was astonishingly bold. Of course he did not mean to challenge the Confucian myth as a whole. His criticisms were limited to astrology in the narrow sense. Nevertheless, his rejection of superstition and criticism of religion foreshadowed the anti-religion movement of the May Fourth intellectuals who were to come after Huang's generation.

In late 1889, Huang was assigned to the position of 2nd Class Counselor at the Chinese Legation in England, to accompany Hsueh Fu-ch'eng (1838–1894), who was appointed Minister to England, France, Belgium, and Italy. Huang's appointment was obtained through the good offices of Yuan Ch'ang, just promoted to Senior Secretary of the Tsungli Yamen. Huang accepted the position gratefully but with a heavy heart because his rank did not increase. Hsueh departed from Shanghai on a French liner on January 31, 1890. Huang returned home to Chia-ying and joined Hsueh's party at Hong Kong. With him was his second son, Ting-ch'ung, and a servant. On their way, they stopped over at Saigon, Singapore, and Ceylon.

In Ceylon, they visited an impressive Buddhist temple which

held a giant statue of a reclining Buddha. Huang wrote a poem of over three hundred verses on the history of Buddhism and the colonization of South Asia by the Westerners. He asked why, with all the magical power attributed to them, the Buddhist deities failed to protect the land of Buddha from British invasion. Along with the fate of Buddhism in India, he gave thought to the rise and fall of ancient civilizations: Greece and Rome fell and only the Middle Kingdom in Asia survived with its 4,000-year history. Pondering this, Huang wondered, "Who are those who insult the yellow race?" He concluded the poem: "The weaker ones have to serve other nations; if a country is well governed, it can attain a powerful position in the world. China has not had a great ruler for a long time; looking in all four directions, I feel uneasy."[9]

Passing through the Suez Canal, they landed at Marseilles on March 1, 1890. They proceeded to Paris by train, where they were met by former Minister Liu Hsi-hung. After about two weeks in Paris, they crossed the Straits of Dover. On May 5, Huang accompanied Hsueh to Windsor Castle to present their credentials to Queen Victoria. Sir Halliday Macartney (Ma Ko-li), the 1st class Counselor at the Chinese Legation, accompanied them and served as interpreter.[10] The magnificent castle, especially because of its tall pillars, reminded Huang of the palace said to have been built in the ancient capital of China by order of Empress Wu (624–705) in commemoration of her glory. Impressed by England under the Queen's rule, he stated that fifty years' prosperity under a woman ruler had had no counterpart in history since that of the legendary sovereign Nü Kua.[11]

In London, Huang's duties were light. Hsueh Fu-ch'eng himself drafted the memorials to the throne and letters to superior officials; Hsu Chueh (Ching-shan) drafted the letters to the Tsungli Yamen, governors of the coastal provinces, and all other officials of equal rank. Huang's duty was to draft letters to officials of lower rank and answer routine correspondence. In overseas legations, these kinds of letters were few. Besides, in England there were no Chinese immigrants, nor was there a throng of literary hosts eager to entertain the Chinese literati. Except for diplomatic exchanges, the life

of the Chinese representatives in London was isolated and mono-
tonous. Moreover, Hsueh's diary reveals that, except on formal
occasions, Hsueh did not take Huang when he visited British officials or other foreign representatives.

During the period when Huang stayed in London, there were
few diplomatic issues between China and England. The major ones
during this period were: (1) negotiations for establishing a Chinese
consulate in Hong Kong and major trading centers within British
territories in Southeast Asia; (2) a Sino-Burmese border dispute
that became a diplomatic issue from around May 1892 and resulted
in the Anglo-Chinese Convention of 1894; (3) missionary cases in
the Yangtze areas for which Hsueh was merely consulted by the
Tsungli Yamen while not involved in the negotiations. Hsueh himself had plenty of time to study while in England; his diary is filled
with notes from his reading. In the first two years, he studied the
legation archives and the writings of the former Ministers to England, Tseng Ch'i-tse and Kuo Sung-t'ao, which had been kept in
the legation. He expressed great admiration for Tseng Ch'i-tse as
the best diplomat and for Kuo Sung-t'ao as the second best. Besides studying legation archives, he investigated the political, economic, and social institutions of European countries and recorded
his impressions in his diary. During 1892 and 1893, he recorded
much of his reading about Japan. Obviously Hsueh was most interested in the economic aspects, particularly overseas trade among
the Western countries. He wrote: "The European countries have
commerce as the foundation of the country; the wealth of their
nations and the strength of their military force are actually based
on this foundation."[12] Hsueh was concerned about the under-
development of trade in China. Huang Tsun-hsien shared Hsueh's
concern and discussed the issue with him.

London's foggy, gloomy weather kept Huang inside the legation. "Heavy fog" reflects Huang's melancholy:

> *These weary, indoor days!*
> *What shall I do?*
> *If only I had a ship I'd sail for home.*

Thoughts crowd my head.
Sometimes I make calligraphy in air.
Fog darkens the city; the damp cold
Tamps down the fireplace to a pallid glow.
Just as I look up a yellow crane
Flies up, away from here on a high wind.[13]

In another poem on the dense fog, he wrote that he had heard that the territories of the British empire spread all over the globe and that the sun never set on the empire; however, he had never imagined that the sun could not be seen in its own capital city.[14] Gloomy weather made him homesick. He wrote a poem on his wife, "Now, in Separation," an imaginary description of her life, longing for him and wishing to be able to fly in a balloon to him on the other side of the globe. He deplored that, in the modern world, faster ships could carry people farther apart, which made separation more harsh.[15] He had plenty of time to recollect the past. A result was "Reminiscence of Old Friends at the End of the Year," a poem of reminiscence about people he had met in China, Japan, and the United States.[16]

While in London, Huang reviewed all his past poems. By the summer of 1890, he had revised the *Miscellaneous Poems on Japan*. He added new poems and commentaries to give more detailed descriptions of Japan; some poems he rewrote. In the preface to the revised edition, he expressed admiration for the modernization in Japan, reflecting new insights he had gained after his observation of England:

> [When I stayed in Japan] it was just the beginning of the Meiji reform; various renovations were made and yet they did not have a steady direction. Some people argued that Japan was strong outside but hollow inside; like the horse of the Kingdom of Cheng, its blood vessels were hard-pressed; the others said that, even though its size was small, Japan would eventually put all-under-heaven under her sway like the eagle of the Sung which was born of a sparrow. There were many opinions about Japan, but no single opinion was accepted by everyone.[17]

Japan's accomplishment within less than ten years after Huang's departure was indeed impressive. He wrote in the same preface: "This year, they have already opened a parliament. The speed of their progress is not rivaled by that of any other country in the East or West, past and present."

In the same year, Huang began to compile a new collection of his older poems as a basis for his collected poems to be completed toward the end of his life. He named the collection *Jen-ching-lu shih-ts'ao* (Poems of the Master of the Jen-ching-lu studio), which was published after his death.[18] The work gave him an opportunity to reflect on the nature of his poems and to clarify his attitude toward literature. When he wrote the preface for the collection in the 6th month of 1891, he included his views on poetry: his poems expressed his personal feelings and thoughts, rather than slavishly adhering to ancient conventions. Criticizing the contemporary practice of modeling one's poems after the style of some poet in the past, Huang wrote: "The present day is different from the past. Why should today's people imitate the ancients?" He was willing to learn from great poets, but he would not attempt to imitate the style of any particular poet. He also declared that he would not hesitate to include in his poems unconventional material, such as information on official reports, gazetteers, popular sayings, or everything that he saw or heard.[19] On the opening page, he placed "Kan-huai" (Impressions), composed when he was about seventeen. It was, in essence, a declaration of revolt against literary and scholarly conventions. Another early poem he selected for the first volume of the collection was "Tsa-kan" (Impromptu), in which he questioned the authority of antiquity and proposed to write in the vernacular (see Chapter 1).

Huang stated his view of poetry clearly in a letter to a friend. The central idea was that he, a poet, was unique and was worthy of existence in his own right, not just in the shadow of an ancient poet. "In my poem I will write what I personally experience, what my eyes see, what my ears hear. Why should I pretend to be an ancient man?" He criticized his contemporaries: "They discard themselves and follow others. Some of them claim to style their poems after the Han; some the Wei; some the Six Dynasties;

some the T'ang; and some the Sung. Of course, they are mistaken. They are superficially imitative, and by imitating they lose themselves. Once one loses oneself, and one's voice is no longer his own, where can poetry exist?'' In opposition to the practices of the contemporary poets, he declared that he would write his own poems: "The time in which I happen to live, events I happen to encounter, people I think of, and the ideas I embrace have never existed in the past, nor will they exist in the future. They exist only within me. Therefore, neither the ancients nor those who will live in the future can replace me."[20] He had been aware of the uniqueness of individuals since he had been very young. He contemplated the meaning of his own existence in the incessant stream of time when he began to write poems. The concept of passing time was an important theme in his poems. The earliest of his poems that he remembered had a verse: "Where does spring come from, and where does it go? Even the birds cry for it." It had been presented to his teacher when Huang was ten, and had won him a reputation as a genius.[21] In later years, his conscious revolt against the myth of antiquity strengthened his belief in the uniqueness of individuality. Also there are strong suggestions of Buddhist influence on his notion of the transitory nature of existence.[22] Although he denounced Buddhism as a religion, especially as a state-sponsored religion, he was attracted to Buddhist philosophy and attentively read the sutras.

In the summer of 1891, Huang wrote "Mountain Songs", a series of short vernacular poems based on Hakka folk songs. He sent the fifteen pieces to an old friend, Hu Hsi (1844–1907), a Hakka from Chia-ying, and expressed his interest in writing a book on the Hakka dialect. He wished to clarify the origins of Hakka and its relation to the ancient form of the spoken language. He had already collected a hundred or so notes for the book. Although the book never materialized, Huang maintained that the classic form of the language had been the spoken language in ancient times and that the Hakka dialect still preserved the ancient language spoken in the Central Plain. In a note attached to the end of the "Mountain Songs," he wrote:

These fifteen local ballads are excellent
And have no match in the past and present.
They were composed incidentally in the mouths
Of women and young girls.
Even if erudite scholars try to compose them with their
writing brushes,
It would be rather impossible.[23]

Huang's pride as a Hakka and his anti-scholasticism were behind this statement.

In retrospect, Huang was successful in putting his own theories of poetry into practice insofar as topics for his poems were concerned. He wrote a friend that he would not be restricted to conventional subjects: "When our voices become sentences, they become poems. All the things between heaven and earth contain poetry, whether or not they make noise: even quarrels on the streets, children playing, or fights between the housewife and her mother-in-law."[24] His poems expressed his thoughts on modern institutions, racism, colonialism, and wars, and narrated historical events in quite unconventional terms, because he meant to make poetry a vehicle for meaningful communication, especially to advocate new ideas.

As to the style of his poetry, however, he used classical language and remained within traditional patterns, except for some poems written in the style of folk songs, such as those written for military marching or as songs for children.[25] Mostly he composed classical-style poems on modern topics to express his new ideas. Commenting on Huang's style, Chou Tso-jen wrote that Huang put new wine into old leather bottles.[26] Huang himself admitted that he could not practice everything he proposed for the creation of a new world of poetry; however, he believed that he would have followers. In a letter written in 1902, he confessed to a friend that he felt like an isolated Puritan marching through the wilderness of the New World, and hoped that those who followed his trail would accomplish a poetic revolution, just as Washington, Jefferson, and Franklin had followed the Pilgrim Fathers. He recognized that his own ability was limited; however, he was convinced that the power of literature was mighty. "Although the path of poetry is narrow, poets in Europe who wrote on behalf of the progress of civilization were, after all, powerful enough to change the world."[27] This statement of Huang's on the power of literature in bringing about revolution foreshadowed the words of young Lu Hsun (1881–1936), who made up his mind to become a writer and discontinued his training as a medical student when he realized he could use the power of literature to save his country and his people.[28]

Huang was right to recognize himself as an isolated precursor of literary revolution. It was not until the early Republican period that Huang's assertions found many sympathizers, enough to make a revolution in literature. Hu Shih (1891–1962), leader of the vernacular literature movement of the May Fourth era, acknowledged that Huang had proclaimed the "Declaration of Revolution in Poetry."[29] In fact, Huang's proposals were identical with five of Hu Shih's famous Eight Principles of Literature published in 1916: (1) Avoid the use of classical allusions. (2) Discard stale, time-worn literary phrases. (3) Do not avoid vernacular words and speech. (4) Do not imitate the ancients; what you write should reflect your own personality. (5) What you write should have meaning or substance.[30] In many respects, Huang foreshadowed the May Fourth generation, and his proposal for vernacular literature was the best known.

While in London, although Huang had limited opportunities to meet people, he gathered information about the English parliamentary system and thought it should eventually be adopted in China. England appeared to him to have an ideal society. When he was received in audience by the Kuang-hsu Emperor in 1896, he told the Emperor that he had heard from the elders in London that, one hundred years earlier, England had not been as advanced as present-day China, and that the superiority of the West was brought about by reform. The Emperor was taken by surprise but, when he understood, he smiled.[31]

After Huang had been in London for about seven months, the negotiations for opening the Chinese Consulate General in Singapore began. The Singapore Chinese Consulate had been established in 1877 on the initiative of Kuo Sung-t'ao, the first Chinese Minister to London. For the first Consul, Kuo chose Hu Hsuan-tse (Hoo Ah Kay, known as Whampoa), a Chinese merchant who had settled there. Hoo's successor was Tso Ping-lung, Tseng's staff member at the Chinese Legation in London. By 1890, Tso had held the position in Singapore for nine years. In September 1890, the Tsungli Yamen asked Hsueh's opinion about a memorial from the Admiral of the Northern Fleet, Ting Ju-ch'ang, who proposed to station a consul general in Singapore and consuls in the major trade centers in British territories in Nan-yang (South Seas, that is, the Malay Peninsula and the Straits areas which were reached by ocean from China), such as Penang, Malacca, Johore, Selangor, Seremban, and Perak.[32] Hsueh supported Ting's proposal and, with Huang's assistance, actively promoted the issue. Their action was based on their recognition of the importance of overseas trade for the national economy. In his long memorial recommending the establishment of consulates in the major cities in Nan-yang, Hong Kong, and Australia, Hsueh wrote that, in the West, there was no country that did not regard trade as the basis of wealth and strength of the nation and that every country had a consulate at every trading port to protect its merchants. He quoted Huang's account of the significance of the remittance from overseas Chinese communities, and emphasized the importance of protecting Chinese merchants abroad. He stated that it would not only benefit the merchants but, in the long run, contribute to the prestige of the country.[33]

In the ensuing negotiations, the British did not assent to the Chinese proposal to open a consulate in Hong Kong but did approve establishment of Chinese consulates in British territories in the Straits Settlements and the promotion of the status of the Chinese Consulate in Singapore to Consulate General. On December 1, 1890, Hsueh received a note from Foreign Minister Shaftesbury informing him of the British government's decision. In his reply, Hsueh said that Huang Tsun-hsien would be nominated Consul General in Singapore and would be concurrently in charge of Penang, Malacca, and other places in the Straits.[34]

Huang's appointment as Consul General in Singapore was confirmed during the summer of 1891, and he left London in late September. When he arrived in Paris, he visited the Eiffel Tower. He was struck by this achievement of modern technology and praised the tower as a milestone in the progress of man's liberation from dependency on nature. "Although man cannot fly, he can come up to this height. Great are men; relying on their own capacity, they cease their state of dependency." From the tower, large things looked very small, which made him wonder how the world would look from heaven. Viewing the land stretched below, he mused over the Hundred Years' War which had been fought there, Naopleon who had risen and fallen there, and the contemporary great powers in Europe which still engaged in struggle for hegemony. He stretched his imagination to the future and wondered if he could someday travel by air riding in a balloon:

> *When can I lift off from the ground*
> *And sail my balloon wherever I wish?*
> *Floating on air for ninety-thousand miles!*
> *Oh, what a mad dream!*[35]

On October 13, Huang passed through the Suez Canal, another great achievement of modern technology. He stated that the canal was even greater than the work of the legendary sage Yü, and that, at the moment the canal was built, the earth shrank; heaven was humbled by the sight of the ships that passed through the canal.[36]

Huang arrived in Singapore in late October 1891, accompanied by Na San from Kwangtung, who had served as an interpreter at the Chinese Legation in London. The Consulate General in Singapore was under the supervision of the Minister in London, and Huang maintained close contact with Hsueh. The formal reason for establishing overseas consulates was to protect Chinese subjects abroad; more important, however, the Consulate in Singapore was to cultivate good relations with overseas Chinese and gain their loyalty to Imperial China. This point was demonstrated by Wen Chung-chi in his careful study based on local documents and the reports of the Straits government.[37]

In achieving the purpose of extending cultural influence over the Chinese communities, the Chinese Consul at the same time undermined the influence of British authority. This naturally resulted in conflict with the Straits government. While Tso Ping-lung was Consul at Singapore, there was not much conflict with the British. Tso was fluent in English and his approach was flexible. In contrast to Tso, Huang took aggressive stances which were bound to cause friction. He was motivated by an urgent sense of crisis that Chinese influence in the South Seas area was receding because of the challenge from Western colonial powers. He was aware that China and Britain were engaged in keen competition in Southeast Asia, not only in terms of political influence but also for control over economic resources. "Miscellaneous Poems on Singapore" reveals his patriotic indignation over the British advancement in the South Seas between the lines describing beautiful oceanic scenes, rich products from woods and mines, tropical fruits with heavenly taste, and the lives of natives and their superstitious beliefs. He was aggravated by the arrogance of white men in Singapore, especially government officials. Their haughty manner reminded him of the customs officers in California; however, the only difference between Singapore and California was, he said, that there were no customs collectors in the free port of Singapore. Huang had to deal with the Protector of Chinese, G. T. Hare, whom he noted as a most greedy and arrogant man.[38]

Huang reported on the life and customs of the Chinese residents in Singapore in a picturesque poem describing a wedding banquet at the magnificent family compound of a rich merchant. The wedding ceremony, feast, and the entertainment following, which included an opera, acrobats, gambling, and opium smoking were typically Chinese. Among the guests were a ship magnate who had started as a poor fisherman, a successful copper mine owner who had begun as a penniless laborer, and rich farmers whose profitable acres produced fruits and vegetables the year round. In the crowd were gamblers, opium pushers, and litigation tricksters. Huang emphasized that Chinese migrants were loyal to China even while living in foreign lands. They observed the Chinese calendar, performed the proper rituals at births, deaths, and weddings, and maintained the Manchu hair style and clothing. Moreover, after achieving wealth, they were eager to obtain official titles and ranks from the Chinese government and gladly contributed to relief funds for the recurring famines in China. Most of the Chinese were illiterate and few could read Chinese, but many of them had learned English. In order to retain the loyalty of the 3 million Chinese in the South Seas, he argued, the Chinese government must provide schools and take more positive measures to protect them from the encroachment of Western colonizers.[39]

Huang traveled in the major commercial centers in the Straits Settlements and cultivated ties with leaders of Chinese communities. In his report to Hsueh Fu-ch'eng, he proposed to establish a consulate in Penang and recommended Chang Pi-shih (1840–1916), a multimillionaire and the most prosperous Chinese person in Southeast Asia, for the post. Hsueh was pleased with Huang's report, stating that it was comprehensive and clear and demonstrated well the spirit of practical learning. Hsueh also consented to the appointment of Chang Pi-shih.[40] The appointment was an important step in extending the influence of the imperial government to the Chinese community in the Malay Peninsula.

In June 1892, Huang requested the Tsungli Yamen to take steps to control the Chinese ships which formed squadrons and engaged in piracy against merchant ships. Huang attempted to register all ships that belonged to the Chinese merchants in the Straits Settlements. This action met with protest from the Governor of the Straits.[41] Furthermore, when Huang issued passports to the Chinese residents who were returning to China, serious friction arose between Huang and the Protector of Chinese, G. T. Hare. Hare denounced Huang's action as ultra vires and posted a proclamation in Chinese to explain that the Consul General had no authority to issue passports to Chinese who were living under British rule.[42]

More serious friction arose between Huang and the Straits government when Huang organized an efficient fund-raising campaign for famine relief in north China. The Straits government, seriously concerned about the tax payments of Chinese who had British nationality, was alarmed when there arose a suspicion of "exaction" by the Chinese authority. Huang raised funds through sales of official titles and ranks to the Chinese residents, using the Chinese newspaper *Lat pau* to appeal to the Chinese for relief funds for China. He also announced the names of the purchasers of the titles and ranks in the newspaper. The network of Huang's fundraising activity was extended outside Malay through business connections. Perhaps subscriptions to the relief funds were not always voluntary, especially in the cases of those whose contributions were small. A letter of Hsueh Fu-ch'eng to Li Hung-chang in 1893 indicates that Hsueh was encouraging Huang to raise more and more relief funds for the Famine Relief Office (Ch'ou-chang chü) in Tientsin. It also reveals that Hsueh sent a letter thanking the Governor of the Straits for his cooperation in the fund-raising in Singapore.[43] Hsueh's letter suggests that the Chinese government tried to secure the cooperation of British authorities concerning the collection of relief funds in British territory. Nevertheless, Huang was criticized by the British for his fund-raising activities. We do not know the amount of the funds raised by Huang; but his contribution was acknowledged by the Kuang-hsu Emperor.[44] As a result of his fund-raising activities and conflicts with the British, Huang was later accused of corruption after he returned to China, which caused him serious disgrace. Wen Chung-chi suggests that Huang did engage in embezzlement related to opium-smuggling from Singapore to China.[45]

While in Singapore, Huang seems to have laid the foundation for his family fortune. For generations, his family had engaged in moneylending and, when Huang was in Singapore, he started a new pawnshop in partnership. This fact was not divulged in official or private biographies of Huang, but his grandson, Huang Yen-yü, contributed the following account. Huang realized that his integrity required financial security; income from a government job was not secure because the appointment depended on political favor and the superior's pleasure. Because of his family background, he knew that business provided a more reliable income. In Singapore there were two of his friends, Chung Kuei-t'ien and Ho Shun-yang, Hakka from Ta-p'u, who shared his views. Huang entered into partnership with them and started the Heng Fa Tang (Forever prosperous) pawnshop. Huang Yen-yü was not sure if the store was opened while Huang was in Singapore but, whatever the case, it was managed by his partners and turned out to be profitable. It provided financial support to the Huang family for many years to come.[46] In later years, Huang was well known as a proud man who refused to show subservience to his superiors, even to the degree ordinarily expected in officialdom. This attitude, primarily a matter of personality and self-confidence, was reinforced by the financial independence he acquired while in Singapore.

In Singapore, Huang not only efficiently collected funds from the Chinese immigrants but took positive actions for their benefit. On the whole, overseas Chinese were badly treated when they returned to China, partly because the government ban on overseas emigration was in effect, despite the fact that millions of Chinese had emigrated to Southeast Asia, California, and South America by the end of the nineteenth century. They were treated as outlaws and persecuted by their neighbors and relatives when they returned home, as illustrated in Huang's poem:

> *An overseas Chinese coming back home*
> *Is preyed upon by fellow villagers*
> *Who rifle his baggage. Neighbors*
> *On one side scold him angrily;*
> *Neighbors on the other side censure him;*
> *Even ancestral ghosts join the attack.*
> *One man returned from a Dutch territory*
> *Carrying one hundred pieces of luggage.*
> *The eyes around him watched with envious greed.*
> *And, when they could not grab his property,*
> *People accused him as a criminal*
> *And charged him publicly with felonies.*[47]

Huang reported to Hsueh Fu-ch'eng about the treatment directed against the returned overseas Chinese by jealous and suspicious neighbors. He expressed anxiety that, if these attitudes were not changed, the wealthy merchants overseas would rather identify with the British or Dutch and would ignore their mother country. Huang stated that, among the residents in the Nan-yang area, one-tenth were Arabs and seven-tenths were Chinese; among the Chinese two-sevenths came from Ch'ao-chou in Kwangtung province and five-sevenths were from Chang-chou in Fukien province. These places were not far from Huang's home, and he was familiar with the stories about returned overseas Chinese. To change the attitude toward the overseas immigrants, Huang proposed lifting the imperial ban on emigration and publicizing the fact that emigration was no longer illegal. Based on Huang's recommendation, Hsueh memorialized the throne, asking for removal of the ban. As a result, the edict of September 13, 1893, legalized emigration.[48]

In the same year, Admiral Ting Ju-ch'ang led his fleet on a world tour, stopping over in Singapore at Huang's request. Huang reported to Hsueh that the Chinese fleet was received with great enthusiasm and pride by their compatriots. Soon afterwards, Hsueh memorialized the throne, asking for permission to use warships to protect merchants in overseas ports in case of emergency. The proposal received imperial endorsement.[49] For more than half a century, the Chinese had seen the Western gunboats that were sent to protect Western merchants in China. Now, for the first time, Chinese merchants were entitled to the protection of their own warships.

In March 1894, Hsueh Fu-ch'eng resigned as Minister to England, France, Belgium, and Italy. While he was in Paris on his way home, he received a copy of the manuscript of Huang's *Treatises on Japan* and wrote a long preface for it. He praised the work, saying that few books of this kind had been written in the past several hundred years.[50] Hsueh stopped at Singapore for one day. Then, arriving at Shanghai in July, he suddenly died at the age of fifty-six.[51] Thus, this outstanding man who shared Huang's reform ideas did not have the chance to participate in the Reform Movement in China following the Sino-Japanese War of 1894–1895. And Huang had lost a senior colleague who would have been his supporter in promoting his position in the bureaucracy.

Despite Huang's activity in Singapore, he had ample time for reflection, especially when he was recuperating from malaria during his second year in Singapore. Rest was prescribed, and Huang was invited by Chinese merchants to use their resort houses at various scenic locations in the Malay Peninsula. His wife arrived to nurse him. When she heard of a man in the village who healed illness by prayer and heard that the power of the angels was greater than Buddha's, she urged Huang to recite the Koran. Of course Huang refused to countenance religious beliefs. A humorous poem demonstrates his stand on the supernatural:

> *Soft moonlight shining on the ocean waves*
> *And something squatting on a seaside rock.*
> *My strong conviction that there are no ghosts*
> *Was fading nervously that eerie night.*
> *The shape took clearer shape, turned out to be*
> *A black native crouching near the sea.*[52]

A poem on the flowers in a vase reflected his thoughts on the coexistence of different races of the world and a grand harmony in the future of mankind. When he put lotuses, chrysanthemums, peach blooms, and other flowers in a vase, he thought it was like putting yellow, white, and black races together to make a country. He imagined that the principle of struggle in the Darwinian concept was at work among the flowers, but thought they were all one family after all. He entertained the idea of creating a new breed of flower by grafting or cross-fertilizing. To him, everything seemed possible by modern technology. "Who knows but that some day it may be possible to change lotus into peach, and peach into chrysanthemum, and eventually to amalgamate tens of thousands of kinds of flowers into one." He expanded his imagination further, using the Buddhist concept of reincarnation. In the poem, he spoke to the flowers:

The life of everything alive is rooted
In a past life. You flowers may not have been flowers then.
Plants, animals travel through birth and death cycles.
In his next life, this man may be a flower,
This flower may be born as a man.
Depending on what the "sixty-four matters" means,
My decomposing body could become
Anything at all. Matter decays; the spirit endures forever.
If some spirit has lasted for thousands of years
It can trace how a flower and I are reincarnated,
Changing places with each other in our lives.
You flowers, if you come again as persons,
Put me in a vase and water me.
And please recite this poem so I can hear it![53]

This poem indicates a universalist orientation in Huang's vision of the future world. Although he was very nationalistic in his view of the present world, he looked forward to a world in which universal harmony would prevail. The fantasy of blending different races— yellow and white in particular—was entertained by K'ang Yu-wei and other reformers as a means of creating a harmonious world. Huang not only imagined such a possibility but noted the presence of mixed-blood residents in Singapore and recorded his curiosity about mixed-blood singing girls in his poem.[54] The more he observed the domination of the white race over others, the more he yearned for the realization of a utopian world of harmony. The concept of grand peace (*t'ai-p'ing*) and grand harmony (*ta-t'ung*) became increasingly important in his future image of the world.

EIGHT

The Sino-Japanese War and the Post-War Reform Movement

Liang Ch'i-ch'ao wrote that the Sino-Japanese War of 1894–1895 shook the Chinese out of their four thousand years' dream.[1] The whole of China was shaken by its humiliating defeat by the small island country the Chinese had looked down on for centuries. Out of shock and indignation at defeat and the severe peace terms, the Reform Movement emerged as a political movement. Up until that time, those isolated voices calling for reform of traditional institutions had remained merely cries in the wilderness. Huang's *Treatises on Japan* was one of these isolated efforts during the 1880s, and it did not get even enough attention to be printed. After the defeat by Japan, however, Huang's work suddenly became famous, and his services were sought after by powerful political figures. In the three-year period after the war, Huang came to be known as a prominent figure in the Reform Movement.

ON THE STAFF OF CHANG CHIH-TUNG AT NANKING

The outbreak of the Sino-Japanese War brought Huang back to China. In early November 1894, Chang Chih-tung, the wartime Acting Governor General of Liang Kiang (Kiangsu, Anhwei, and Kiangsi) provinces requested of the throne that Huang be recalled from Singapore, since Chang badly needed capable assistants. Chang recommended Huang for his wide knowledge of foreign countries, especially Japan.² Chang's request was granted, and Huang returned to China.

When Huang arrived in China in late 1894, China's defeat was imminent, and the court was preparing for peace negotiations. Huang's old friend Chang Yin-huan was appointed to negotiate. He sought Huang's advice before leaving for Japan. After arriving at Hiroshima, Chang was rejected by the Japanese on the grounds that his credentials were not satisfactory. To meet the Japanese demand, the seventy-two-year-old Li Hung-chang was appointed.

Huang was not surprised by the military defeat; however, he was distressed by the manner of the defeat. Although he had been aware of the low morale of the Chinese military and its lack of unified command, the situation turned out to be worse than he had expected. Chinese troops retreated in crucial battles on land and sea. In his war poems, Huang pointed out that Chinese weakness lay not in equipment but in lack of morale and unity of purpose between commanders and soldiers. These symbolized the weakness of China itself. Huang maintained that creating a feeling of national cohesion was the most essential task for strengthening the country. "Sorrow over Pyongyang" depicted the battle at the old capital of Korea which took place in September 1894. The Chinese forces dispatched for defense of the city were plagued by discord among the generals. When the Japanese attacked the city, the Chinese general who led the major force from Seoul was quick to flee. Pyongyang fell; pursuing the demoralized Chinese troops, the Japanese crossed the Yalu in late September. Huang stamped with vexation over the cowardice and stupidity of the generals.³

China's naval defeat was even more depressing. The Northern Fleet, supposedly superior to the Japanese navy, lost the command of the Yellow Sea after a single battle off the Yalu on September 17. Huang depicted the spectacular scene of the battle in "Poem on the Yellow Sea," and wrote that, thereafter, the Chinese ships hid and never fought again. "We have been told that we had a superior fleet and not to worry; actually, we had the ships but not the men to fight in them."⁴

The fall of Port Arthur dramatically demonstrated the uselessness of strong forts without manpower. The fort was regarded as impregnable, for reasons of both geographical advantage and military equipment. Nevertheless, the Chinese commanders did not use their advantage and were ready to flee when the Japanese landed at Dairen on November 21. The Japanese attacked the fortress from the rear, and this strong fortress fell in one day. The city of Port Arthur was looted, and the citizens massacred. In his "Lament for Port Arthur," Huang highlighted the greatness of the fortifications, China's pride in them, and the despair when they fell to the enemy.[5]

In late January 1895, the Japanese navy attacked Weihaiwei. In a week, this strategic point in Shantung was occupied. The Governor of Shantung fled with the best part of the army division under his command. Although one commander was determined to fight to the death, his soldiers deserted him, forcing him to commit suicide. Huang wrote "Weep over Weihaiwei" in an unusual form to express his extreme distress. Each verse consists of three words, which produces a dismal tone. As a conclusion, he wrote: "Alas, navy and army! The enemy's forces were united; ours were divided. Like an insect which can only shrink, we could not stretch our might. Like fighting cocks, we were incapable of uniting ourselves."[6]

In his "Song of the Surrendered General," Huang presented the tragedy of Admiral Ting Ju-ch'ang as a symbol of the tragic war. At the final sea battle in defense of Weihaiwei, China's seamen refused to fight and begged Ting for their lives for the sake of their families. The Western advisers aboard the ship thought it was impossible to persuade the demoralized men to fight. Thereupon Ting ordered the captains to sink all the ships simultaneously; however, the captains refused. Ting was forced to surrender his entire fleet on February 12. During the night, when the seamen were rejoicing over the end of fighting, Ting silently committed suicide. His tragedy was that, although he had well-equipped gunboats, he did not have men willing to fight for him.[7]

On April 17, the peace treaty was concluded in Shimonoseki. The treaty stipulated that China pay 200 million taels indemnity, cede Taiwan and Liao-tung Peninsula, and acknowledge the Japanese right to establish settlements in newly opened ports and to construct factories in China. A few days after the conclusion of the treaty, Russia, France, and Germany intervened to force Japan to give up Liao-tung. In his "Event in Shimonoseki," Huang expressed his indignation over the national humiliation, symbolized in the personal humiliation of Li Hung-chang, who had been injured by a Japanese assassin. Huang was greatly worried about the huge indemnity, which would have a devastating effect on China's economy. Expressing his despair over the treaty, Huang wrote to a friend: "The new treaty is already concluded. Heaven is overturned, and the earth is upset. The southern provinces remained idle spectators when Taiwan, which they relied on as the frontier guard for two hundred years, was given up to the foreigners. To chew our bones and suck our marrow, the foreigners extract a huge sum of indemnity from us. To deprive our people of their livelihood, foreign manufacturers are coming to build factories on our land."[8] He was most concerned over the Western Powers' encroachment on Chinese territory, especially the hidden motivation of Russia, which led the tripartite intervention. He called Japan a brother country even immediately after the war, and warned that brothers should defend each other from external threats instead of quarreling within the family.[9]

Of the losses of the war, the ceding of Taiwan caused the greatest emotional pain for Huang as for many others. He placed some hope on the resistance of the people in Taiwan against Japan. When the leaders of the movement for an independent Taiwan proclaimed the Republic of Taiwan on May 25, 1895, it created a legal basis for asserting the island's independence from the Ch'ing Empire. The Republic, however, did not last long. In a few days the Japanese army began to land, and in early June the President-elect left for the mainland. When the news came that Taiwan had finally fallen to the Japanese, Huang was visiting the famous scenic spot, Yellow Crane Pavilion on the Yangtze bank in Hupei. He suddenly lost all interest in the beauty of the landscape and turned back.[10] In his "Poem on Taiwan" he wrote:

Blue sky! Blue sky! My tears fall like rain.
The Japanese have torn away Taiwan.

He narrated the history of the Taiwanese people's resistance movement against the Japanese takeover and the about face of the local gentry who welcomed the Japanese army. He concluded the poem:

Sad, sad Taiwan, so loyal yesterday
And so brave, yet today so cowardly!
Everything changes in these changing times.
Without a standing army for defense
How can loyalty, honor be sustained?[11]

This pragmatic point of view had been expressed in his poem on Ryukyu, in which he stated that loyalty without adequate defense forces was not enough to save the state.

As a practical man, Huang devoted his efforts in his official capacity to minimizing the disaster of China. His appointment by Chang Chih-tung was that of Director of the Office of Foreign Affairs (Yang-wu chü) in Nanking. This office, one of the new establishments created by the provincial governors after the Taiping Rebellion, was charged with matters related to diplomatic negotiations and the adoption of Western technology within its jurisdiction. As a general tendency after the Taiping Rebellion, the central government's control over the provincial government was weakened, and the provincial governors gained increasing autonomy. This tendency had grown conspicuously in the area of the lower Yangtze, which was under the jurisdiction of the Governor General in Nanking. The area had been governed by extraordinarily powerful men in succession: Tseng Kuo-fan (1860–1865, 1866–1868, and 1870–1872), Li Hung-chang (1865–1866), Liu K'un-i (1875, 1880–1881, 1891–1894), Tso Tsung-t'ang (1881–1884) and Tseng Kuo-ch'üan (1884–1890).[12] Foreign diplomats were aware that diplomatic negotiations relating to provincial interests could not become effective without the cooperation of the Governor General of the area. As a result, de facto diplomatic negotiations often took place at the Governor General's office.

The Office of Foreign Affairs under a Governor General was a part of his private staff (*mu-fu*). Its members were privately engaged and were not a formal part of the imperial bureaucracy. The system of a private staff was traditional in provincial and district governments, because the officials always needed assistance from experts in legal, fiscal, or other matters that required highly specialized knowledge. During the eighteenth and nineteenth centuries, when administrative burdens increased as a result of population growth, the size of the bureaucracy remained the same but the number of privately engaged staff members increased at all levels. In the areas related to foreign affairs and modernization projects, a new type of expert was in demand. This situation created opportunities in the sub-bureaucracy for capable men who were qualified but had not received official positions. After the Taiping Rebellion, increasing numbers of qualified scholars took such positions. Since the provincial officials had the privilege of recommending men of talent for official positions, the staff members of prominent officials could expect their recommendations to be a quick route to official appointment. Not a few outstanding statesmen in the late nineteenth century began their careers via this route, including Li Hung-chang, who had served on the staff of Tseng Kuo-fan. Only a fraction of the official candidates, however, made their careers in government service through recommendation. According to K. C. Liu's assessment, only about 4 percent of the local officials in the empire between the 4th and 7th ranks were recommended by provincial authorities as of 1870, and the percentage dropped to 1.5 in 1895. Nevertheless, the clear-cut demarcation between the bureaucracy and the private staff became less and less distinct with the increase in administrative functions carried out by private staff members.[13]

As Director of the Office of Foreign Affairs, Huang demonstrated his ability in diplomatic negotiations and established his reputation as an expert in foreign affairs. His first assignment was to negotiate with the French authorities on missionary cases. From the 1880s on, the Catholic churches and some Protestant missionaries in the Yangtze area, from Nanking to Hupei and Szechwan, were frequently attacked by the antagonistic local populace. The anti-missionary rioting in the area culminated in 1891 when Catholic churches were attacked. The Chinese government paid indemnity for the damages and executed some suspected agitators. The cases seemed to be settled for the moment; however, local antagonism against the missionaries persisted, and the uneasy tension between the Catholics and the local community was not eased. In the summer of 1894, the French government put strong pressure on Chang Chih-tung to negotiate the unsettled issues concerning missionary cases in the five Yangtze provinces. Chang chose Huang as his agent for the negotiation.[14]

Upon receipt of Chang's order, Huang traveled to Hupei to investigate the local situation relating to the missionary cases and to conduct negotiations with the French Consul General in Shanghai. Huang was successful; the French authority and the Catholic fathers were pleased with the solution, which did not offend the local communities either.[15] Chang Chih-tung was impressed with Huang's capability and memorialized the throne, recommending him as a man of unusual talent who would be a good choice for Supervisor of Maritime Customs.[16] When Chang returned to his pre-war post of Governor General of Hupei and Hunan in March 1896, he wished to take Huang to Wuhan and requested Huang's transfer. As an excuse, Chang stated that the convenience of the river transportation between Wuhan and Shanghai would allow Huang to continue to conduct diplomatic negotiations in Shanghai. About the same time, Huang's service was solicited by Wang Wen-shao, the Governor General of Chih-li. Chang was strongly opposed to transferring Huang to the north, since it would disrupt the diplomatic negotiations in the Yangtze area. Meantime, Liu K'un-i, who had resumed his position as the Governor General in Nanking, would not release Huang. He telegraphed Peking asking for the Emperor's endorsement to keep Huang in Nanking. As a result, Huang stayed in Nanking, traveling frequently to Shanghai, where the major diplomatic negotiations took place.[17]

Huang brilliantly demonstrated his skill as a diplomat in negotiations with the Japanese over their settlement in Soochow. The

Shimonoseki Treaty had stipulated Japanese rights to establish a settlement in Soochow, but the exact site and details of the administration of the settlement had not been worked out. The negotiation began in October 1895 at the Office of Foreign Affairs in Soochow. For the site of the settlement, the Chinese proposed an area far from the city of Soochow, which was not acceptable to the Japanese. After frustrating sessions, the Japanese team headed by Chinda Sutemi, Consul General at Shanghai, left Soochow in mid-November. Huang was absent from the talks in Soochow because he was engaged in negotiations with the French Consul in Shanghai. The negotiations were reopened in early April 1896 between Arakawa Motoji, Japanese Consul at Soochow, and Huang, Director of both Offices of Foreign Affairs in Soochow and Nanking. Huang was delegated by Liu K'un-i, the Governor General of Liang Kiang and the Superintendent of Trade for the Southern Port, to conduct the negotiation.[18] Among the members of the Japanese team was Narahara Nobumasa, who had studied Chinese under Huang at the Chinese Legation in Tokyo.

Huang took advantage of Narahara's presence to confide his personal views to him. The Japanese were eager to hear Huang's opinion because they believed Huang exerted great influence on China's policy-making. Huang's informal talk with Narahara was immediately reported to Tokyo as an important piece of information. Huang's message was clear and straightforward. He stated that discussions over the site of the settlement could not yield fruitful results unless the administrative status of the settlement was clarified beforehand. In the Treaty of Shimonoseki, it had been stipulated that Japan could establish settlements in newly opened ports and that the administration of settlements should be in accordance with the regulations governing the existing treaty ports. As a matter of fact, Huang pointed out, there were various types of foreign settlements in China, which could be classified into three categories—the Shanghai type, the Shameen type, and the Ningpo type. Characterizing the Shanghai type settlement, Huang said:

In Shanghai, each foreign country has its own settlement, and the construction and maintenance of the roads, piers, bridges, and the like have been controlled by the country which occupies the settlement. Police and civil administration are also under the control of that country. The Chinese merchants who live within the settlement are under the jurisdiction of foreign officials in the same way as the foreign merchants. If a Chinese criminal flees to the settlement, the Chinese authority cannot arrest the criminal without notifying the foreign authority. This is nothing more than partitioning a part of the country and giving it to a foreign country.

He further commented that the arrangement in Shanghai developed because, during the Taiping disturbance, defense of the city was left to the foreign residents, due to the incapability of the Chinese government to defend the city. Thereafter the government entrusted an essential part of the administration and police functions to the foreigners. It was, then, because of historical events that foreigners in Shanghai had gained such extraordinary privileges. Huang pointed out that their privileges were not stipulated in any treaty, and argued that the Shanghai-type arrangement was a stretched application of the extraterritoriality and over-enforcement of the rights of Treaty Powers. The second category, the Shameen-type settlement, was exclusively for foreign residents, and no Chinese were allowed to live within it. Administrative rights within the settlement belonged to the foreign authority. The third category, the Ningpo type, was a mixed settlement where Chinese merchants lived and engaged in business side by side with foreigners. The maintenance of roads, bridges, and other buildings, as well as the police, were under the jurisdiction of the Chinese government. Huang pointed out that this third category was the arrangement of foreign settlements in Japan.

The Treaty of Shimonoseki did not specify which of the existing models for settlements should be used for Soochow and Hangchow, which were to be newly opened for foreign trade. Huang emphatically stated that the Shanghai-type settlement was not acceptable to China, first, because it conceded sovereign rights of China in excess of treaty obligations and, second, because Soochow and Hangchow were located in densely populated inland areas, whereas all previous treaty ports and attached foreign settlements had been built on unused land in the coastal areas. It was unbearable for China to give up jurisdiction of any part of the inland territory. Moreover, he reasoned, lands were not available in the crowded inland areas in case each of the Treaty Powers demanded a Shanghai-type settlement.

As a practical solution, Huang proposed to build a mixed settlement near Soochow for the convenience of foreign and Chinese merchants engaging in business. The construction and maintenance of roads, bridges, piers, and the like, as well as police rights, were to be retained by the Chinese government. Although the Chinese government did not have the right to control the foreigners in China, it had the right to control the land within the foreign settlements. In case the Japanese government insisted on building a settlement after the Shanghai model, Huang warned, the Chinese government would choose an area for the settlement at a remote place from the city of Soochow and would prohibit Chinese subjects from living in it. In such a settlement, the Japanese might be able to build factories, but trade would not prosper cut off from the Chinese community. Huang reminded the Japanese of the evils of extraterritoriality from which Japan itself had suffered until recent times. If Japan would give consideration to China's position, China would cooperate with the Japanese toward commercial prosperity. Huang also recommended that the Japanese continue the negotiations with the provincial authority instead of taking the case to Peking. So long as the authority to negotiate remained in the hands of the governor general at Nanking, Huang could serve as the chief negotiator and would solve the issue for the benefit of both parties.[19]

Huang and Arakawa began negotiations on April 8. On April 13, they signed an agreement over the site and the provisions for the regulation of the settlement. The designated site was the area near Soochow, and the provisions followed the line of Huang's preference as expressed to Narahara. It was made clear that construction and maintenance of the roads, bridges, and piers were under the control of the Chinese government, and that, so long as Chinese subjects lived within the settlement, the authority of administration, including the police, was reserved to the Chinese government.[20] The government in Tokyo was displeased with the agreement and sent strongly worded instructions to Arakawa that the settlement should be exclusively Japanese, and that the authority of administration, including the police, should belong to the Japanese. If the negotiations with the Chinese local authority could not produce the desired agreement, the Japanese government would shift the negotiations to Peking.[21]

In accordance with his instructions, Arakawa resumed talks with Huang on July 2. On July 4, Huang sent a memorandum to Arakawa, firmly stating that there was no stipulation in the Treaty of Shimonoseki that the settlements in new ports be exclusively Japanese, and that the Chinese government had never agreed that the settlement in Soochow be exclusively Japanese. The negotiations broke down immediately, and Huang left Soochow. Arakawa, reporting on Huang's memorandum, advised the Foreign Minister to make concessions to the Chinese and do what was best for the development of commerce.[22] Huang had obviously overwhelmed Arakawa, who now shared Huang's opinions and was trying to persuade his government to adopt Huang's proposal. However, the Japanese government dismissed Arakawa and shifted the negotiations to Peking. In the final agreement, signed on October 19, the Chinese government granted Japan exclusive settlement in Soochow with control over the police and the roads.[23] Consequently, Huang's efforts came to nothing.

Huang was unhappy in Nanking; he thought the position given him by Chang Chih-tung was not commensurate with his ability. He compared himself to a bored sea gull and accused Chang of keeping him idle after having urgently called him back from Singapore.[24] Personally, Huang did not get along well with Chang and adopted an arrogant attitude from their first meeting, a fact K'ang Yu-wei reported with great astonishment: Huang sat with his legs crossed and kept his head upright, refusing to assume the humble posture normally expected in the presence of a high-ranking official.

As a result, Chang was offended and gave him unimportant assignments.[25] A story handed down in Huang's family illustrates Huang's
relations with Chang. Chang used to stay up late and often sent a
sedan chair to Huang's residence after midnight whenever he had
some matter for consultation. Because he was an early riser, Huang
declined to go out at such an hour.[26] Contrary to Huang's com-
plaint, we have observed that Chang gave him at least two important assignments and recommended him to the throne. For Chang,
Huang's service was valuable. Perhaps it was because Huang did
not want to be identified as a personal protégé of Chang that he
emphasized the negative aspects of his experience with him. After
leaving Nanking, Huang expressed his dissatisfaction with the bureaucracy there to Weng T'ung-ho, a rival of Chang's.[27]

The post-war Reform Movement in China reflected not only the
intellectual trend of China's elite but also the power struggle within
the bureaucracy, which developed as a political movement. Although Huang was not primarily concerned with factional politics,
his political affiliation largely determined the scope of his participation in the movement. The Reform Movement among officials
evolved during the Sino-Japanese War as a criticism of the compromising policy toward Japan Li Hung-chang was believed to favor.
Those who opposed the humiliating peace and were identified as
the "war party" constituted the reformist group in post-war China.
This group, led by Chang Chien and Wen T'ing-shih, and patronized
by Weng T'ung-ho and Chang Chih-tung, emerged as the opposition against officials in the government, particularly Li Hung-chang.
The criticism against Li was locked into the factional strife between
the Empress Dowager's faction and Emperor's faction in the court.
The Empress Dowager Tz'u-hsi had consolidated her powerful
position as the regent and maintained her control over the imperial
government by strictly checking the power of the young Kuang-hsu
Emperor, who had assumed the imperial function in 1889. Court
officials were manipulated by the bureaucratic machine of the
Empress Dowager. Her protégés and the supporters of the young
Emperor engaged in exhausting factional strife. Li was the most
powerful official among the protégés of the Empress Dowager.

John Schrecker has suggested that the Reform Movement was an outburst of an unbroken trend among junior government officials who called for renovation from around the 1870s, and that the trend is identifiable as a *ch'ing-i* (Pure Talk) movement.[28] It is not clear to what extent they were identified or active as a group until around 1894; however, there was a group of officials who often held discussions when the peace treaty with Japan became the major political issue. The leader of the discussion meetings was Wen T'ing-shih. Perhaps it was not only coincidence that most of the metropolitan officials with whom Huang was associated in the late 1880s when he visited Peking with his manuscript of *Treatises on Japan* were prominent members of this group, namely, Wen T'ing-shih, Ch'en Chih, Shen Tseng-chih, Shen Tseng-t'ung, Chang Yuan-chi, Liang Ting-fen, and Huang Shao-chi. They were advocates for moderate reform within the imperial establishment. When K'ang Yu-wei came to Peking as a candidate for the metropolitan examination and began his campaign to organize the Reform Movement in 1895, he was successful in gaining the support of this group of officials. It was primarily because of their support that K'ang was able to organize the first political association for reform, the Strength Study Society (Ch'iang-hsueh hui). It was this group of officials who became the key members of the society and gave it political significance. Because the society was recognized as a viable political force, Chang Chih-tung and Liu K'un-i responded to its appeal and made financial contributions. Li Hung-chang also wished to be listed as its supporter and offered a contribution, but he was flatly rejected. British and American diplomats and a Protestant missionary, Timothy Richard, supported the society. It reflected the reformist group's pro-Anglo-American outlook as opposed to the pro-Russian stand of Li Hung-chang. Huang shared the gradualist ideas of reform with metropolitan officialdom, especially insofar as many of his own reform proposals were in agreement with the viewpoints of Ch'en Chih published in his *Yung-shu* (Utilitarian discourse). As Hsiao Kung-ch'üan has pointed out, this group of officials represented the major trend of the Reform Movement in the 1890s. (K'ang Yu-wei's radical reform program was a departure from the trend, despite the great publicity he received as the organizer of the post-war Reform Movement.[29]) Huang maintained personal contact with the mainstream group. When Wen T'ing-shih came to Nanking in July 1895 on his way home to Kiangsi, Huang and Liang Ting-fen, an associate of Chang Chih-tung, held a banquet on the boat. On this occasion, Huang exchanged poems with Wen condemning the ceding of Taiwan.[30]

Huang continued his personal ties with Li Hung-chang. As we have noted, he had admired Li as a great statesman in his youth and was proud of receiving complimentary words from him. He sympathized with Li over the humiliating role Li was forced to play at the peace negotiations with the Japanese. Li's only grave mistake was, Huang noted, his pro-Russian policy, in particular the Sino-Russian secret Treaty of Alliance of 1896. Huang privately saw Li in Shanghai when he returned from his trip to Russia and other countries. Li told Huang that he hoped the treaty would guarantee peace for twenty years. Contrary to his hope, however, the Powers launched a scramble for concessions within a year. Huang attributed this mistake of Li's to old age. At Li's death in 1901, Huang wrote a eulogistic poem evaluating his statesmanship. Perhaps Li was one of few outstanding figures Huang admired.[31]

Huang's association with K'ang Yu-wei was brief. He met K'ang in late October 1895, when K'ang came to Shanghai to establish a branch organization of the Strength Study Society. Huang visited K'ang in company with Wu Te-hsiao, a *chin-shih* from Kwangtung province. K'ang reported his impression of Huang at their first meeting, stating that he had extraordinary talent. K'ang was struck by Huang's self-confidence: with his head held upright and his legs crossed, Huang talked about international affairs, while Wu was taken by surprise and listened to him mute as a stone. When K'ang stayed in Shanghai for a few weeks, they visited each other almost every day.[32]

Although Huang shared reform ideas with K'ang, he did not subscribe to K'ang's interpretation of Confucianism. K'ang asserted that Confucius founded the Confucian school in the same sense that other philosophers founded their schools of philosophy during the last years of the Chou dynasty and decried the belief that Confucius was a historical transmitter of the tradition handed down from the Three Dynasties. Furthermore, he claimed that the sage kings, Yao, Shun, and Wen, who were supposed to have created the ideal institutions in the Three Dynasties, were the intellectual creations of Confucius. K'ang also asserted that the true teachings of Confucius were revealed not in the orthodox Old Text version of the Classics but in the New Text which had been long neglected. To support this point, K'ang published a controversial book, *Hsin-hsueh wei-ching k'ao* (An inquiry into the Classics forged during the Hsin period, 1891), demonstrating that the Old Text Classics, notably the *Chou Rites*, the Tso Commentary on the *Spring and Autumn Annals*, and the Mao version of the *Book of Odes*, were forged by Liu Hsin, the scholar who served Wang Mang, the usurper of the Former Han Dynasty. By denouncing the Old Texts, K'ang opened a way to reexamination of the authenticity of the whole Confucian canon. K'ang presented a new interpretation of the Confucian Classics for the *Spring and Autumn Annals*, *Analects*, *Mencius*, and part of the *Book of Rites*. His interpretation of the *Spring and Autumn Annals*, based on the Kung-yang commentary (New Text) supplemented by Buddhist and Western literature, served as vehicles for his political philosophy. Huang rejected K'ang's assertion that the ancient sages and the institutions of the Three Dynasties were not historical; in fact, he often referred to the *Chou Rites*, discredited by K'ang as a forgery, to explain the ideal government he was advocating.[33]

Huang maintained a limited association with K'ang as a colleague in the Reform Movement. When K'ang organized the Shanghai branch of the Strength Study Society, Huang became one of its sixteen members. However, he did not attend the inaugural meeting, and let Liang Ting-fen sign his name.[34] The political style of K'ang was not congenial to Huang, although they stood basically on the same ground in terms of their career objectives. Both of them had been disappointed with the established system for official recruitment, which had little room for new-type intellectuals versed in modern world affairs. They wished that the imperial bureaucracy would recruit a new type of talent and give them important roles in the government. It would not only help the government cope with new problems but would help ameliorate unemployment among the degree-holders. In the late nineteenth century, the saturated bureaucracy could not absorb a great portion of the successful candidates of the examinations, and the restlessness of degree-holders without employment was increasing. Huang himself was a product of the dismal situation: because of the uncertainty of securing a regular appointment with a *chü-jen* degree, he had purchased an official title and volunteered to serve as a staff member at one of the newly opened overseas legations. It was a gamble at the time because diplomatic service was not a promising route to success in the bureaucracy. At least one successful example around Huang was Chang Yin-huan, who had started his official career as a provincial authority's assistant as an expert in foreign affairs, served as the Minister to the United States, and finally attained a high position as a Vice-President of the Board of Revenue and a member of the Tsungli Yamen. Around 1895, he enjoyed tremendous imperial favor and was frequently summoned for a private audience. While Huang aimed at achieving his long-range career goals by accumulating merit as an expert in foreign service, K'ang was eager to attain prominence in more aggressive and political ways. K'ang was ready to be a full-time reform advocate. Their strategies for reform were also different. While Huang supported a gradualist approach, K'ang advocated quick reform, which he formulated in the phrase, "The Japanese did in thirty years what the Europeans had done in three hundred years. China should be able to accomplish it within three years."[35]

Despite his distance from K'ang, Huang established a very close and a long-lasting friendship with Liang Ch'i-ch'ao, K'ang's most famous disciple. It was through the publication of *Shih-wu pao* (*Journal of Curent Affairs*, the original English subtitle was *Chinese Progress*) that Huang came into contact with him. When the Strength Study Society was banned in early January 1896, and its Shanghai branch was closed, Huang was indignant and proposed to continue advocating reform by publishing a magazine; he donated another 1,000 yuan to the balance of 700 yuan the society already had. He invited Wang K'ang-nien, a disciple of Chang Chih-tung who had been teaching at the Self-Strengthening Academy in Wu-ch'ang, to become the business manager. For the chief editor, he chose Liang Ch'i-ch'ao. By this time, Liang had established his fame as an excellent journalist by writing editorials for the publications of the Strength Study Society in Peking. In the beginning, Chang Ping-lin had been recommended; however, Huang decided that his highly classical style was unsuitable for a magazine.[36] Cheng Hsien (pseudonym), a grandson of Huang, provides a vivid account of Huang's encounter with Liang. When Liang came to Shanghai to meet Huang, Huang talked about world affairs, the progress of reform in Japan, China's position in the modern world, and his resolution to publish a journal to propagate new ideas. To test Liang's ability as a writer, Huang told him to summarize their talk. Liang left Huang's house around ten o'clock in the evening, and early the following day he returned with a manuscript of 40,000 or 50,000 words. Huang, astonished, asked, "Why did you come so early?" Liang replied: "I am at an early stage of life; my knowledge is shallow; I have never been abroad, and my experiences are very limited. After hearing your talk last night, I felt as if bushes impeding my sight were suddenly cleared, and I realized that what I had previously learned had been superficial. I could not sleep because I was so excited." Huang was pleased with the manuscript and told himself that Liang was an ideal editor for the magazine.[37] At the time, Huang was forty-eight and Liang was twenty-three. Liang respected Huang as his mentor. Their intimate relationship lasted for the rest of Huang's life. Huang wrote to Liang one year before his death: "In the whole country, no one knows you as well as I do, and no one knows me as well as you do."[38]

The first issue of the *Journal of Current Affairs* appeared on August 9, 1896. It was published every tenth day in about thirty double pages. Its major contents were imperial edicts, memorials, editorials, and articles mostly written by Liang Ch'i-ch'ao, although some were by Wang K'ang-nien and others. Translations from Japanese, English, French, and Russian newspapers were also regular features. The controversial subject of the interpretation of the Confucian Classics was avoided. Huang refused Wang K'ang-nien's suggestion, advocated by K'ang, to use the calendar system based on the birth date of Confucius. It was a significant way of demonstrating that the journal did not support the philosophy of K'ang Yu-wei.[39] This journal was indeed the first modern magazine in China, and its influence was enormous. The 4,000 copies originally planned were not sufficient to meet the demand and over 10,000 copies were printed. As the editor of this journal, Liang Ch'i-ch'ao established himself as the most influential journalist in late Ch'ing China.

In November 1896, Huang was summoned to Peking for an imperial audience, a promising sign for his official career. It was a practice of the Ch'ing government that officials who were due for promotion or new appointment were presented to the Emperor by the Board of Civil Appointment. Shortly before this, the Minister to England, Kung Chao-yuan, had memorialized, recommending Huang.[40] However, when the imperial order was sent to the Board of Civil Appointment to escort Huang for a regular audience (*yin-chien*), the board rejected Huang. Thereupon, the Emperor sent a special order summoning Huang for a private audience (*chao-chien*); Huang was received by the Emperor on November 20.[41] During the audience, the Emperor asked Huang why the governments in the Western countries were superior to China's. Huang answered that the strength of the Western countries resulted from reform and told the story, which he had heard in London, that England had been very backward a hundred years before. The Emperor expressed surprise but soon understood what Huang meant and smiled. Shortly after the audience, the Emperor requested a copy of *Miscellaneous Poems on Japan*, which was presented by Chang Yin-huan, then Senior Vice-President of the Board of Revenue.[42]

On November 23, Huang was appointed Minister to Germany, a newly created position. He received another imperial audience on November 26, together with Lo Feng-lu and Wu T'ing-fang, who

were appointed Ministers to England and the United States, respectively.[43] Huang was delighted with this appointment, but an
unexpected obstacle arose. When Huang's appointment was announced, the German Minister in Peking, Baron Edmund Von
Heyking, objected strongly. At that time, Kaiser Wilhelm II was
trying to obtain concessions in Shantung. Having been frustrated
by the firm rejection of the Chinese government, the German government sought an opportunity to create a diplomatic issue. Various incidents were used by German diplomats for the purpose, of
which the Tsungli Yamen was aware.[44] The German Minister regarded Huang's appointment as an excellent chance to cause
trouble, since he had obtained information that the Chinese government had originally intended to assign Huang to England but
changed its plan because of British objections. On November 29,
Von Heyking telegraphed the German government advising it to
reject Huang because of unfavorable rumors concerning him.[45]
According to rumor, Huang had engaged in corruption in Singapore by seizing large amounts of money from Chinese merchants.
As the Tsungli Yamen denied the charge that Huang had been rejected by the British government, Von Heyking personally visited
the Tsungli Yamen to protest Huang's appointment. He made a
furious speech in front of Li Hung-chang, Chang Yin-huan, Weng
T'ung-ho, and others who received him. He denounced the "anti-
German" attitudes of the Chinese government. Among all the indiscreet actions of the Chinese government, the worst was appoint-
ing as the minister to Germany a man who had been rejected by
the British. He took up a wine glass from the table and said, "Is
it your friendship to offer us a glass of stale wine which has been
rejected by someone else?" Li Hung-chang insisted that Huang was
never rejected by the British government, and showed a letter
from Minister Claude M. MacDonald which certified that the British government had never rejected Huang. Von Heyking argued
that MacDonald had told him that Huang engaged in corruption in
Singapore. After arguing for one and a half hours, Von Heyking,
still hurling threats, departed, saying: "We Germans are fond of
music. But we have various kinds of music. One kind could be the

gentle, friendly melody to which China has been listening until now. We also have sharp, noisy music—such as the military march. We hope China will not cause us to play this kind of music."[46] After several unsuccessful attempts to persuade the German Minister to accept Huang's appointment, the Chinese government gave up and appointed Hsu Ching-ch'eng instead.[47]

The German rejection of Huang's appointment was not only a disappointment but a disgrace, because some people suspected that Huang had indeed attempted to embezzle a large sum of money in Singapore. Weng T'ung-ho wrote in his diary that he heard from the British Minister MacDonald that Huang had seized $40,000 from merchants in Singapore and intended to appropriate it for himself.[48] To calm suspicion, Huang wrote an open letter addressed to the former Governor of the Straits Settlements, Sir Cecil C. Smith, for publication in an English newspaper in Shanghai. It was published on February 12, 1897, and its Chinese version appeared in a Singapore newspaper. Huang stated that the scandalous charge originated from a distorted report by G. T. Hare, the Protector of Chinese, with whom he had not been on good terms. An incident occurred in May 1893, when the Inspector General of the Imperial Maritime Customs sent a messenger to Governor Smith requesting his assistance in enforcing new regulations concerning duty on opium imports via Singapore, which required opium traders to sign a duty certificate. The Governor reluctantly agreed to implement the regulations on a tentative basis. At the news, demand for opium increased, and the shippers, all of them Chinese, attempted to rush a large amount of opium. In Singapore, 800 or 900 chests of opium were gathered on 50 or 60 junks. Each junk had about 30 men aboard, a total of about 1,500 men. To their great inconvenience, they were not permitted to leave the port because the shippers refused to comply with the new regulations, which required a payment of $80 per chest. After stormy negotiations between the Chinese merchants on the one hand and the Chinese Consul General and Protector of the Chinese on the other, the merchants petitioned Huang, volunteering to deposit $40 per chest (totaling $40,000) and requesting permission to leave the port without delay. (Together with the open letter, Huang published translations of the petitions from the Chinese merchants and his reply to them.) After obtaining Governor Smith's consent, Huang arranged to let them leave and promised to explain their hardships to the Chinese government. He ordered them to place the deposit in the custody of the merchant Tsai Mun-pow (Ts'ai Wen-pao) until instructions from the Tsungli Yamen were received. Soon afterward, Cecil Smith resigned. The Protector of Chinese told the new governor that the money was a compulsory fee from the merchants and that Huang intended to appropriate it for himself. The Protector took the money away from the merchants and deposited it with the Colonial Treasury. Huang expressed his indignation in the open letter over the accusation that he seized the money which had never been under his charge.[49] This issue subsided soon; however, the rumor against Huang was used by anti-reformist censors who attempted to impeach him in 1898.

REFORM IN HUNAN

Huang remained in Peking after his appointment to Germany was canceled. He enjoyed the patronage of Weng T'ung-ho, who was at the peak of his political influence as President of the Board of Revenue, Grand Councilor, member of the Tsungli Yamen, Associate Grand Secretary and, most important, as the former Imperial Tutor. As soon as he arrived in Peking, Huang visited him and presented a copy of *Treatises on Japan*. Thereafter they frequently visited each other.[50]

Owing to Weng's patronage, Huang received an appointment as the Salt Intendant of Hunan province. It was his first appointment to an official post in China. He left for Changsha on July 15 to take up his new position.[51] Upon his arrival in Hunan, he was concurrently appointed the Acting Judicial Commissioner of the province during the absence of the Judicial Commissioner, Li Ching-hsi, who had been summoned to Peking. In his official capacity, Huang promoted the Reform Movement in the province which had been started by the Governor and Provincial Director of Education with the enthusiastic participation of the local gentry.

After the Sino-Japanese War, the Hunanese, who had been famous for their anti-foreignism and conservatism, now enthusiastically embarked on new enterprises using modern Western technology. Their efforts to build modern industries could be interpreted as a new form of resistance against foreign invasion. They sensed that, unless they started new enterprises, foreigners would come in to exploit the resources of Hunan.[52] The Hunanese took the national crisis more seriously than any other provincials, partly because they were shocked when Hunan soldiers led by Governor Wu Ta-ch'eng volunteered to fight against the Japanese in the north and were miserably defeated. Those soldiers were sons of warriors of the famous Hunan army who had crushed the Taipings. Besides their awareness of the national crisis, the strength of the leadership of Hunanese gentry and the timely appointment of the reform-minded officials in the provincial government, as well as encouragement from Governor General Chang Chih-tung, created conditions favorable to the promotion of reform activities in Hunan.[53]

The Governor of Hunan, Ch'en Pao-chen, a Hakka from Kiangsi province, was determined to make Hunan the center for strengthening China when he was appointed to the position in the fall of 1895. He had especially close feelings for Hunan because he had served as a staff member of Tseng Kuo-fan during his campaign against the Taipings and had become familiar with the local customs and sentiments of the Hunanese.[54]

His son, Ch'en San-li, a *chin-shih* of 1889 and a highly esteemed poet, followed him to Hunan and ably assisted him. He was a close friend of Huang and respected him as a poet. He persuaded Huang to take the position in Hunan when Huang received the offer.[55] The Provincial Director of Education of Hunan, Chiang Piao, was also an enthusiastic promotor of reform. When he took the post in late 1894, he found the Hunan gentry extremely xenophobic and hostile to modern innovations. Thereupon he resolved to change the attitude of the scholars in his capacity as the supervisor of education. He introduced a new type of essay question on current affairs in the annual examinations, which all the government students (*sheng yuan*) were obliged to take, and made the study of new subjects, such as mathematics, world geography, and English, available at Chiao-ching Academy. He published a tri-monthly journal *Hsiang-hsueh pao* (Hunan reform news) to popularize the new topics in the examination essays and promote interest in new learning.[56] The appointment of Huang Tsun-hsien as the Acting Judicial Commissioner strengthened the team of reform-minded officials in Hunan.

By the time Huang arrived in Hunan, the reform program was well under way. It included new industrial enterprises. By the summer of 1897 a group of 6 gentry founded a match factory, the first modern manufacturing company in Hunan; it employed 700 workers of whom 600 were women. Other industries were the Pao-shan Production Company for manufacturing electric bulbs, rickshaws, gunpowder, textiles, and for husking rice and pressing oil; and a steamship service to connect Hunan and Hupei through Lake T'ung-t'ing. The leader of the group was Wang Hsien-ch'ien (1842–1917), a renowned classicist, a former Libationer of the Imperial Academy of Learning, and currently the Director of the Yueh-lu Academy in Changsha. He was an old friend of Ch'en Pao-chen. Undoubtedly his personal trust in Ch'en greatly contributed to the favorable environment for reform programs. In the group was Hsiung Hsi-ling (1870–1942), a *chin-shih* of 1895, who later became Prime Minister of the Republic. He was a younger member of the gentry and participated in the activities of young intellectuals.[57] They embarked on these new enterprises after extensive discussions with Governor Ch'en on how to strengthen the Hunan economy.[58] The moving force behind these enterprises was the growing interest of the gentry in industrial investment and their anxiety over the foreign intrusion and the future of the Chinese empire. The governor's encouragement and guidance were crucial, however, in motivating them to action. The governor himself took the initiative in starting mining industries to exploit the mineral resources in Hunan and to bolster the economy of the province.

The same group who started the new enterprises proposed to open a modern school in Changsha and donated money for school buildings. It was named the School of Current Affairs (Shih-wu hsueh-t'ang). According to the announcement of Governor Ch'en inviting students to the entrance examination, the best students were to be sent, upon graduation, to the newly established university in Peking or to study abroad; the second best were to be recommended as staff members of Chinese overseas legations, the navy, army, shipyards, or other, new government institutions. Furthermore, for students who wished to make careers as officials through the regular route, the Governor would allow them to take the provincial examination together with those who had passed the district-level examinations. Ch'en's policy implied a significant step toward modification of the official recruitment system, but it received imperial endorsement without raising controversy. Ch'en stated that such an arrangement not only would contribute to strengthening China but also would give an opportunity to students anxious for careers.[59] When the first entrance examination was given on September 24, 1897, in order to select 40 students, more than 4,000 candidates gathered.[60] In selecting faculty members, Huang recommended Liang Ch'i-ch'ao to be Dean of Chinese Studies, and Li Wei-ko, the English translator of the *Journal of Current Affairs,* to be Dean of Western Studies. The gentry leaders, as well as Ch'en Pao-chen and Chiang Piao, endorsed these appointments. Liang accepted the position on condition that the choice of instructors of Chinese Studies be left to him. He invited two of his classmates at K'ang Yu-wei's school in Canton. As a result, the school became the discussion center of K'ang's political ideas such as "people's rights" and "equality."[61]

Huang inspired young intellectuals in Hunan through his writing, public speeches, and informal personal contact with them. For the Chinese intellectuals after the Sino-Japanese War, the most crucial question was the secret of Japan's success in building a strong nation in a short period of time. They sought answers in Huang's *Treatises on Japan.* Although the book had been written about ten years before and its information did not go beyond 1882, it was the most comprehensive account of the institution and culture of Meiji Japan written in Chinese. Its first edition came out about 1895; in 1898 it was reprinted by two publishers in the Shanghai area.[62] In the same year, the revised edition of *Miscellaneous Poems on Japan* was published in Changsha. Huang wrote a new preface for the edition reflecting his new perspective of the reform efforts in Meiji Japan. Hsu Jen-chu, the new Director of Education in Hunan, who arrived in September 1897, contributed his calligraphy for the title on the book's cover.[63]

Huang's account of the Meiji Restoration, especially his appraisal of the spirit of self-sacrifice among the loyalists, appealed to the ideals of the young Hunanese. They aspired to make Hunan China's Satsuma and Chōshū, which had provided the greatest leaders of the Meiji Restoration. Huang emphasized the role of the loyalists (*shishi*) in explaining the Meiji Restoration. K'ang Yu-wei and Liang Ch'i-ch'ao accepted the view and attributed Japan's success to the spirit of determined individuals. K'ang's comments on Takayama Hikokurō and other loyalist heroes strongly suggest that his source of information was Huang's writings. Liang Ch'i-ch'ao told his students at the School of Current Affairs that Japan emerged as a strong nation as a result of the Meiji Restoration and that the movement had been started by a group of courageous men motivated by righteous indignation. Liang deplored China's lack of men willing to sacrifice their lives for a patriotic cause.[64] Their students, especially T'ang Ts'ai-ch'ang (1867–1900) and T'an Ssu-t'ung (1865–1898), were determined to be among the first to shed their blood for the cause of reform in China, following the examples of the heroes of the Meiji Restoration. T'ang Ts'ai-ch'ang, a teaching assistant at the School of Current Affairs, wrote: "Japan and China belong to the same part of the world, share the same writing system, and suffered from the same kind of oppression from the Western countries. . . . Japan has achieved today's position thanks to the two or three heroes who dared to speak out." He felt that the temperament of the Japanese loyalists resembled that of the Hunanese.[65] (He carefully avoided saying that the Hunanese resembled the Japanese. Probably it was unacceptable to propose that any respectable Chinese resembled the Japanese.) T'an and T'ang died as martyrs in 1898 and 1900.

Huang's book did not fully explain how Japan became strong after the restoration, or how the new regime survived the initial difficulties, or how the Japanese built modern industries. After all, the book was written when Meiji Japan had been in existence for only ten years. Nevertheless, it gave young intellectuals an optimistic hope that, once a new regime committed to reform was established, and dedicated individuals took leadership roles, all problems could be overcome. While such an optimistic interpretation prevailed among the young activists, a careful scholar like P'i Hsi-jui (1850–1908) raised a question after reading the *Treatises*: Who were really responsible for making Japan strong after the restoration? "Huang's *Treatises* never mentioned that the Emperor was wise or was a good military leader. It seems that Japan does not owe its strength to its Emperor. Those who initiated the reform, such as Saigō and Ōkubo, were killed. Who were responsible for making Japan rich and strong in such a short time? Did it rest on the leadership of Inoue Kaoru and Itō Hirobumi?"[66] He asked *who* rather than *what* made Japan powerful because he shared with young activists the assumption that efforts of dedicated leaders were essential for transforming a weak country into a powerful one.

The Hunanese elite strengthened their resolution to make their province a stronghold of resistance against foreign domination when the Germans occupied Kiaochow in the Shantung peninsula in November 1897. The German action and the ensuing scramble for concessions created a sense of crisis throughout China because it appeared that China faced the imminent danger of being sliced up by the Powers. To promote the self-government of their province to the extent that it could exist independently of the central government in case China was ruled by foreigners, the Hunanese leaders were aroused to make preparations. Their motivation was nationalistic. They regarded the independence of their province as the last bastion for resisting foreign domination so as to preserve China at least in part as a basis for the revival of all China in the future. The concept of self-determination, which the term "independence" implies, was alien to them.[67] In preparing for self-government, T'an Ssu-t'ung and T'ang Ts'ai-ch'ang proposed to organize a Southern Study Society (Nan-hsueh hui) in December 1897, which received support from Governor Ch'en. It was primarily an institution for public education, but at the same time was expected to function as the prototype of a local assembly. Its core members were chosen by Governor Ch'en from among gentry leaders, who were responsible for recruiting members from each district. Anyone with distinction in "virtue, talent, or skills" could be a member with the recommendation of three members, regardless of his occupation. One of the objectives of the society was to break down the barriers between classes for the purpose of creating a sense of community, or cohesion (*ho-ch'ün*), on the principle of equality as a basis for national strength. Branch chapters were to be set up in prefects and districts outside Changsha. P'i Hsi-jui was elected president of the society.[68]

Huang was chosen as one of the four lecturers of the society and was in charge of lecturing on government and religion. The weekly public lectures constituted the major activities of the society. At the inauguration meeting on February 21, 1898, Huang gave his first lecture, together with Governor Ch'en, P'i Hsi-jui, and T'an Ssu-t'ung. There was an audience of 200. P'i was impressed by the style of Huang's lecture which was clear and persuasive. He assumed Huang had learned the style in Western countries. Many people considered Huang as eloquent as a missionary preacher.[69]

In his lecture, Huang discussed the ideal relationship between the government and local community, and encouraged local leaders to partake in the responsibility of government for the purpose of creating a cohesive community, which would be the foundation of national strength. Repeating his statements in *Treatises on Japan,* he pointed out that the strength of the Western countries and Japan lay in their ability to achieve national cohesion based on mutual trust between the people and the government. In China such an ideal relationship existed in ancient times, but after the Ch'in unification autocratic principles prevailed. He especially criticized the rules concerning the appointment of officials in the local government under the Ming and Ch'ing, where the chief concern was to maintain maximum security for the central authority and to minimize the danger of development of regional power. He pointed out that, because their terms of office were short, local officials were not interested in local welfare in the long run, and thus mutual trust between official and local community could not be fostered:

> Gentlemen, gentlemen: [an adaptation of Western-style opening; obviously there were no ladies in the audience] Many of you must have read the Twenty-four Dynastic Histories. In the histories there are numerous examples of famous ministers, talented generals, able officials, and meritorious subjects. When you come to the section of biographies of upright officials, however, you find only half a volume, a few dozen chapters, or twenty to thirty examples of upright officials. Throughout history, there was no time without officials, no place without officials. The Han, T'ang, Sung, and Ming dynasties lasted for several hundred years, and yet the number of what can be called "upright officials" was very small. Isn't it surprising? . . . One reason for this is that local officials are not familiar with local dialects, geography, customs, and practices among the local people. I once met a Grain Intendant in Canton. I asked him if he had accustomed himself to the place. He said that everything, including food and clothes, was different, the language was incomprehensible, and that, after leaving Peking, everything changed like a descent from heaven to earth; his wife and all his servants complained every day and looked forward only to returning to the north. How could we expect a good local government under this kind of official? . . . They are not much different from strangers at a banquet.[70]

Unless the relationship between the government and the people was improved, he maintained, it would be impossible to advance overseas trade, agriculture, and industries or to promote education and achieve peace and stability of the society. As a remedy, he proposed to expand the rights of the local people to participate in government.

Huang suggested that an ideal relationship between the government and people existed in China's past. Paradoxically, he pointed out, the feudal rule under the Chou showed much more concern for the people than the centralized government under the Ch'in after the unification. Under the Chou rule, there was a sense of community because of the benevolent nature of the government. Although, under the Chou system, he argued, the land and the people were owned by feudal lords, the feudal rulers maintained close ties with the people and made no decisions without consulting with the elders among the people in their territories; in this sense the nature of government was truly "public" even though territory was private. In the centralized system after the Ch'in, the officials were very carefully selected to serve the people as public servants; but, in reality, once an official assumed his position, he paid little attention to the welfare of people, leaving them to live or die alone. In addition, unworthy officials took advantage of their authority and exploited the people by manipulating the provisions of the law; since the local officials did not care for the people's well-being and were simply interested in promoting their own interests, the officials were a source of trouble, and the people wished there were no officials in their locality. For this reason, the centralized bureaucratic system was very "public" in principle but very "private" in practice. Huang suggested that, in order to remove this defect of the centralized system, local people must participate in local government to cooperate with the officials who were appointed by the central government.[71]

It was a recurrent theme in Huang's reform proposals that the healthy spirit of ancient China had degenerated in the course of history, and that China must revive that spirit in order to build a powerful nation-state that could withstand the struggle for survival. The most conspicuous symbol of the degeneration of Chinese culture was the custom of foot-binding. Huang condemned it not only as an inhumane practice which infringed upon the "human rights" (*jen-ch'üan*) of women but also as a great handicap for the state because it crippled one half of China's 400 million human resources. He also pointed out that the grotesque custom was a laughingstock in foreign countries and that it added one more source of humiliation for China. In his capacity as the Acting

Judicial Commissioner, he issued a public announcement to persuade people not to practice foot-binding, and promoted an anti-foot-binding movement in the province. By November 1897, the Hunan Anti-Foot-Binding Association was organized in Changsha. Such an association had been organized in Canton and Shanghai by K'ang Yu-wei in 1894. Their practical purpose was to protect women with normal feet from discrimination in marriage by obliging their members to arrange marriage for their sons with girls whose feet were unbound.[72] In late Imperial China, when so much value was placed on "lily-feet," women whose feet were normal suffered a tremendous stigma. Even for Hakka women, who did not share the custom as a group, ethnic jokes about their "big feet" were sources of humiliation. Being a Hakka, Huang proudly denounced the custom and, at the same time, expressed sympathy for his daughter who had had to suffer humiliation.[73]

While in Hunan, Huang made his greatest efforts toward the establishment of a Police Bureau (Pao-wei chü), which proved to be the most long-lasting institution created during the reform in Hunan.[74] It was a modern police system in the city of Changsha. For cities in prefectures and districts outside Changsha, a new network of the militia system was to be organized under the command of the Police Bureau in Changsha.[75] When Governor Ch'en discussed with him the problems in maintaining security in Changsha, Huang proposed establishing the Police Bureau. The modern police system was one of the institutions Huang had regarded as the best among those the Japanese had adopted from the West. In China, the system operated in the foreign concessions in treaty ports. After studying the police systems in Shanghai and other treaty-port cities, he drafted bylaws for the Police Bureau. In fact, however, the Police Bureau was more than an institution for police service. Huang expected to make it the basis of local self-government and the foundation of all the new institutions in the province. It was to be jointly managed by local government officials, gentry, and merchants in the city of Changsha. The officials were in charge of arresting criminals and handling legal disputes, and the gentry and merchants were responsible for financing the system and providing street-cleaning services, a special emphasis because of a passion for clean streets among the Hunanese. Many visitors to Shanghai and Hong Kong were struck by the clean streets in foreign concessions and regarded them as a symbol of the prosperity and orderliness of the Westerners' community.[76]

As spelled out by Huang in the bylaws, the head office of the Police Bureau was to be built in the center of the city. Under its command were 4 police stations in the east, west, south, and north sections of the city and one outside the city wall. The director of the head office was to be assisted by a committee of gentry and merchant representatives. Each police station was to be headed by a local government official of the rank of assistant magistrate, who was to be assisted by a committee of gentry and merchant representatives. Under the jurisdiction of each police station, 6 branch stations were to be created, each headed by local government officials of the lowest rank and staffed by a police chief, 2 police officers, and 14 policemen. Since there were about 30,000 households in the city, each branch station was in charge of about 1,000 households. From among them, 5 representatives were to be chosen to serve on the committee at the branch station of their district. Altogether, 420 policemen were required for the entire system. The policemen were paid and provided with meals, a uniform, and a police club.

Huang made meticulous stipulations concerning discipline to make it clear that the policemen were different from the runners in the local government who had performed police duties and had been notoriously corrupt. Policemen were not allowed to accept fees or bribes, smoke opium, drink as a group in public places, or fight or play with people on the streets. The qualifications for becoming a policeman were good health, age between twenty and thirty, some knowledge of reading and writing, and no criminal record. Policemen's duties included assistance to sick or lost persons, keeping records of the residents on each street and watching out for strangers, preventing the gathering of mobs, and arresting criminals. These provisions were taken from the regulations of the Japanese police as recorded in *Treatises on Japan*. The Japanese had the same problem concerning discipline, because policemen at the end of the Tokugawa era were notorious for their corruption.[77] As a part of the police system, Huang proposed to institute five rehabilitation centers (*ch'ien-shan-so*) and to offer at each vocational training for forty unemployed who had committed crimes.[78]

Huang initially had difficulty in mobilizing adequate support for the police system from gentry and merchants in the city. Antagonistic rumors were spread that the Police Bureau was for the protection of Westerners and missionaries and that heavy taxation would be imposed on owners of houses or stores in order to finance the system. Huang enlisted the help of Tso Hsiao-t'ung, a son of the famous general Tso Tsung-t'ang, to canvass the gentry. Huang himself spent much time at the office of the old local security unit to explain the new institution to the gentry. T'an Ssu-t'ung and T'ang Ts'ai-ch'ang enthusiastically supported Huang's efforts because they were hopeful that the Police Bureau would be the foundation of self-government in Hunan. The gentry who had been suspicious began to cooperate with Huang as soon as he announced the names of the nominated committee members to serve at the head office of the Police Bureau.[79]

The bureau was inaugurated in late July 1898, with Huang as the director of the head office. Prior to its opening, Huang hired six former policemen (Chinese) who had served at the foreign settlement in Hankow to train the policemen in Changsha. When the policemen made their first appearance on the streets, the residents of the city were suspicious because their uniforms, which consisted of short jackets with tight sleeves and pants, looked like Western clothes. After the policemen made some arrests of thieves and returned stolen goods, suspicious merchants were convinced of the benefits of police protection. Those few cases of violence perpetrated against police stations were by drunken sailors or gamblers, and local residents were not involved. The police system turned out to be successful. It survived the conservative reaction against reform. When the Empress Dowager Tz'u-hsi ordered reformist institutions closed down, Chang Chih-tung circumvented her order by reorganizing the Police Bureau as the Local Security Bureau (Pao-chia chü).[80]

There were good reasons why the Police Bureau was welcomed by the residents of Changsha. As a petition from a merchant requesting early opening of the bureau describes, there was growing social unrest in the city. "Vagabonds wander about the streets in broad daylight and create disturbances. They come around asking for money or rice and, if refused, they smash everything in the building and disappear into the crowd on the streets." Gangs of wanderers often entered stores and disrupted business. There were racketeers who spread malicious rumors about commercial establishments, sometimes driving them into bankruptcy. Exactions by runners of local government (there were about 1,000 of them in the city) were becoming increasingly avaricious.[81] Governor Ch'en himself pointed out that, as a result of the expansion of population in the city, thieves, bandits, and vagrants had increased dramatically. In one year, more than one hundred robberies had occurred, but culprits were arrested in only a few cases. The local security units, *pao-chia* or *t'uan-fang chü,* had been incapable of preventing these crimes.[82] Although there was a traditional militia organization in Changsha,[83] it obviously did not fill the police needs of the city. Merchants and rich gentry members who took residence in the city especially needed protection as the crime rate went up, a symptom of social crisis. Huang and his colleagues were primarily concerned with protecting the urban elite from the crimes of the unemployed. Those who drifted into the city and became beggars or robbers were destitute peasants. It was beyond the scope of reform efforts during the 1890s to face the real question—how to deal with the source of banditry, the crisis in the countryside.

Huang was charged with organizing the Learning Center for Officials (K'o-li-kuan, or K'o-li-t'ang). It was for the reeducation of official candidates and local officials, including low-ranking assistants in prefectural and district governments. Its primary purpose was to give them professional training, since the civil service examination centered on literary achievement and did not prepare administrators. According to the bylaws, the Learning Center was to offer the opportunity to study subjects in education, agriculture and industry, civil engineering, judicial administration, police administration, and foreign relations. Foreign relations included overseas trade, diplomatic negotiations, and the protection of missionaries. Huang believed that many of the anti-foreign riots were due to the negligence and xenophobia of local officials, and that it was essential to educate the officials in order to prevent attacks on missionaries. He planned to station those trained in diplomatic negotiations in the neighborhood of Christian churches for the purpose of preventing minor incidents from becoming serious conflicts. He told a friend that the cost for protection of missionaries would be much less than the amount of indemnity required to pay for damages against them.[84]

Periodic examinations were to be given at the Learning Center with rewards for those who passed with high grades. No lectures were to be given, but there was a library equipped with books on new subjects, and the students were offered the opportunity to communicate with instructors by writing in specified notebooks. They were given two notebooks in which they wrote essays and questions and received comments and answers from the instructor. This method had been used at the School of Current Affairs. By early June 1898, Huang had completed preparations for the opening. However, he had difficulty in persuading officials to attend. It was also difficult to secure instructors. P'i Hsi-jui was one of those asked to teach, but he was reluctant because he thought it inappropriate for local people to teach local officials who were supposed to be the fathers and mothers of the people.[85] It is not clear to what extent the Learning Center functioned, because, from the time it opened, the entire reform program was under attack.

Among Huang's greatest concerns after his return to China were anti-foreign violence and popular disturbances. He confided his anxieties to Weng T'ung-ho when he visited him the night before he left Peking. He said that the greatest sources of trouble for China were anti-missionary violence, banditry, and a possible war among European nations, any of which, he thought, could bring about the partition of China.[86] In his thinking, the most urgent task at the moment was to avoid inciting further foreign aggression, which would result in more concessions and eventual loss of territory. To prevent foreign interference, it was essential to maintain internal peace and to secure the safety of foreigners in China. His basic stand on the foreign presence in China was that the Chinese had better accept the fact that China had concluded treaties with foreign Powers agreeing to exchange diplomats and let traders and missionaries come into China. It was prudent to protect them within the scope of treaty obligations in order to prevent their taking advantage of disorder in China. But it was a mistake, Huang pointed out, to yield to unreasonable pressure from missionaries. In his capacity as the Acting Judicial Commissioner, he warned local magistrates not to be intimidated by letters from missionaries who often interfered with judicial administration. He made a strong statement on this point in his official comment on a legal case involving a Chinese Christian who committed suicide. A man who had no relationship with the suicide victim reported to a Chinese priest that death was caused by a beating the deceased had received from his relatives because of his religion. The priest sent a letter to the district magistrate intimating that the case would become international. Commenting on the report from the magistrate, Huang stated that the priest was a Chinese and therefore should be punished by Chinese law. "There is no need to be shaken up at the sight of a letter from a missionary or priest. On the other hand, a magistrate should not be disgusted with a case simply because a missionary is involved. Hereafter, whenever a magistrate encounters such a case, he should not entertain any bias and should investigate the facts and deliberate the circumstances."[87]

Huang believed that the unequal treaties had to be abrogated eventually, as in the Japanese case, by consolidating China's national strength through reform. Since it was unavoidable that China was going to be involved more and more in international trade and politics, it was better to learn the game and win the competition. From his experience in San Francisco, he had found that, by mastering the Westerners' law and practices, he could use them to restrict Western excesses and protect China's rights. As practical tactics, he approved the Japanese approach in abolishing unequal treaties by modernizing their own penal code and judicial administration, and establishing an efficient police system to secure domestic peace and order.

Huang's gradualist, internationalist approach was shared by his colleagues in the Reform Movement in Hunan; however, it was not accepted by all the Hunanese. In fact there was tension between the officials and reform-minded gentry on the one hand, and the masses and traditional literati—whose sentiment was represented by Chou Han, the anti-missionary propagandist—on the other. The traditionalists rejected the admitting of foreigners to the province and called for resistance to the bitter end. The tension heightened during the year 1897 because the opening of Yueh-chou, the first treaty port in Hunan, was scheduled for the spring of 1898. As soon as Governor Ch'en posted his announcement appealing to the Hunanese for the need to protect foreigners and warning against anti-foreign behavior, an anti-foreign wall poster appeared alongside offering a reward of two hundred yuan for killing a foreigner. An abundance of pamphlets and posters denouncing the official reform programs appeared. The traditionalists attacked the Police Bureau as a device for protecting foreigners and the *Hunan Reform News* as a propaganda organ for the Christian religion against Confucianism.[88]

From the traditionalist view, it was unforgivable that officials would accommodate and protect foreign intruders. In an underground resistance effort against official policies, traditionalists spread malicious rumors against missionaries. To counter their propaganda, Huang and Governor Ch'en had to give public lectures to refute the rumors that missionaries cut out human hearts and eyes, or the like.[89] Governor Ch'en stated that Chou Han had brought shame on China because his abusive pamphlets crudely slandering Christianity convinced the Westerners that even literate Chinese were absurdly ignorant, and therefore that China was only semi-civilized. Huang had told Ch'en that in San Francisco the story of Chou Han was a constant source of embarrassment for him.[90]

There was a struggle between two lines in coping with the advancement of Western imperialism. The officials, who were obliged to implement China's treaty agreements with the Powers, tried to find a realistic compromise. The traditionalist literati, however, called for all-out resistance and persistantly attacked the official line by encouraging the xenophobic populace. Governor Ch'en finally ordered the arrest of Chou Han, who was imprisoned until 1910. At heart, the Governor was sympathetic to the popular indignation against Western advancement accompanied by gunboats. In his public notice, he explained that the court decision to admit Westerners was a strategy not unlike the policy of the Emperor Wen of the Han dynasty who had adopted an appeasement policy toward the aggressive nomads on the northern borders. He warned against disobedience to the government order forbidding anti-foreign violence on the ground that any country that failed to control its own people was vulnerable to foreign intervention.[91] The gentry who supported Governor Ch'en's position were also sympathetic to the popular sentiment against foreigners, but they were opposed to self-destructive resistance. Chiang Ping-k'un contributed an article to the *Hsiang pao* (Hunan newspaper) on this point: "Some say that, if Westerners come to Hunan, we should fight against them to the end, saying: 'If we win, our purpose will be accomplished. If we do not win, we are prepared to die. Since no one can avoid death, why should we be afraid of it, if it could contribute to eradicating the humiliation of the court and prevent suffering of the people.' I am afraid that if we fight with bare hands without the necessary preparations, we will simply invoke the further aggression of the enemies and, even before the corpses of the courageous fighters are cold, our land will be occupied by them."[92]

For historians of modern China, evaluating the reformists' efforts and the traditionalist resistance against them poses not only intellectual but also ideological questions, because the history of modern China has been a constant struggle between two lines:

the idealist-nationalist line versus the pragmatist-internationalist line.

The idealist-nationalist line took a traditionalist-conservative outlook in the late nineteenth century. In the twentieth century, however, it became the mainstream of the revolutionary movement which was bolstered by an anti-imperialist movement. The Communists who successfully mobilized the masses against the Japanese imperialists won the victory over the Nationalists who had inherited the internationalist-gradualist line. In Japan, on the other hand, the pragmatist-internationalist line which had been adopted by the Meiji Government continued to prevail, despite the disruption caused by the upsurge of the nativist reaction during the 1930s and 1940s and constant criticism from the right and the left. In China, the reformist strategy for following the path of Meiji Japan did not succeed. Historians in China today declare that the reformist path was a blind alley, that it could have led nowhere. In Japan, too, historians' judgments on the Chinese reformist approach to the problems of imperialism tend to be harsh. On the one hand, the purist aspect of the traditionalists' resistance and the popular uprisings against foreign domination have been greatly appreciated. On the other hand, the limitations of the reformers stemming from their social background as ruling elite have been emphasized. In fact, the reformers consented to suppress the dare-to-die resistance of the masses not only because they feared the foreign aggression, but also because they feared popular uprisings as a grave threat to established order. Around this time in Hunan, there was growing economic unrest because of drought. In 1898, the price of rice inflated and riots broke out in the populace against the rice merchants in Hsiang-t'an. Local leaders in other districts were worried that rioting might spread to their localities. It was reported that the agitators of the rice riots admitted that they were members of the secret society Ko-lao hui.[93]

By the summer of 1898, the Reform Movement in Hunan had disintegrated into ideological strife between, on the one hand, the young activists who were supported by the reform-minded officials and, on the other, the gentry leaders who attacked reformist thought as a threat to the established order. Wang Hsien-ch'ien mobilized his students at the Yueh-lu Academy to counter the reformers. Slanderous rumors against the instructors of the School of Current Affairs were circulated. In the late spring, several of Wang's students petitioned Wang to request the Governor to dismiss Liang Ch'i-ch'ao from the School of Current Affairs. They leveled accusations against Huang, together with Provincial Director of Education Hsu Jen-chu and Hsiung Hsi-ling, who was in charge of the administration of the school. They stated that "ever since Commissioner Huang Kung-tu (Tsun-hsien) came, the theory of people's rights was asserted."[94] Thereupon, Wang Hsien-ch'ien and several gentry members wrote a letter to Governor Ch'en accusing Liang Ch'i-ch'ao and asking for reorganization of the School of Current Affairs. To counteract Wang's move, Hsiung Hsi-ling, in his capacity as a gentry member of Hunan, wrote to Governor Ch'en asking for a reorganization of all the schools in the province. The letter was jointly signed by several gentry. Then wall posters appeared abusing the School of Current Affairs in insulting words. Posters and rumors were both powerful political weapons in Hunan.

A young scholar-gentry, Yeh Te-hui, was in the forefront of the attack against the reformers, especially their writings in the *Hunan Newspaper*. Among others, he attacked a poem by P'i Hsi-jui's son: "If one takes a look at the globe, one finds that China is not in its center. The globe is round. How is it possible to say who is in the center and who are at the four corners?" Apparently these were offensive remarks against the concept of the Middle Kingdom. When I Nai published his article, "China should change from the weak to strong," in the *Hunan Newspaper* in April, it caused a great uproar. He advocated merging Chinese and Western institutions and social ethics, equalizing the people's rights and sovereign rights, and intermarrying with the white race. Yeh Te-hui violently attacked I Nai's writing as abhorrent.[95] Huang himself was not involved in ideological controversies. Although he was sympathetic to the young activists, he discouraged radicalism out of strategic considerations.

Commenting on I Nai's article, he told P'i Hsi-jui that in Japan there had been two types of reformers, those who desired radical reform and those who were gradualists, and that, after realizing the difficulty of quick change, the Japanese chose the gradualist path. Referring to the press law in Japan, he asked rhetorically, If the Japanese government was not immune to the fear of radicalism, how could the Chinese government be?[96]

Governor General Chang Chih-tung strongly reacted to I Nai's article. He telegraphed Ch'en Pao-chen and Huang Tsun-hsien, warning against extremism, stating: "If these kinds of ideas spread, outlaws and evil elements will use them to instigate rebellion." In reply, Ch'en regretted the publication of the article and promised that Huang would censor major articles in the Hunan journals.[97] Around the same time, Wang Hsien-ch'ien, Yeh Te-hui, and other gentry in Hunan sent letters to Hunanese officials in Peking appealing for help in getting rid of the provincial officials who had caused trouble in their province. In response, Censors Hsu Shu-ming and Huang Chün-lung presented memorials to the throne asking for the impeachment of Ch'en Pao-chen and Huang Tsun-hsien.[98] The Emperor did not respond.

By late spring, the conservative campaign had gained ground in Hunan, and the major figures among the reformists were driven out of the province. P'i Hsi-jui resigned the presidency of the Southern Study Society on May 30 and left for Kiangsi, where he had been teaching until the previous summer. Hsiung Hsi-ling resigned from the School of Current Affairs at about the same time. The instructors from Canton also left, exasperated by the malicious rumors against them. Liang Ch'i-ch'ao had become seriously ill in the early spring and went to Shanghai for treatment; when he recovered, he left for Peking to join K'ang Yu-wei. While the Reform Movement was ebbing in Hunan, it was gaining momentum in Peking, which mounted the One-Hundred-Day Reform.

K'ang Yu-wei reactivated his campaign for radical reform in Peking, seizing the moment of national crisis caused by the German occupation of Kiaochow in late 1897. He sent his fifth memorial to the throne, describing the grave situation and urging the Emperor to start reform without delay. It failed to reach the throne, but copies were circulated and had considerable impact on officials who had been advocating gradual reform within the imperial establishment. On January 24, 1898, K'ang was summoned to the Tsungli Yamen to be questioned by the ministers about his reform proposals.

He answered all their questions brilliantly and confidently. In his discussion, he pointed out that Japan had adopted Western institutions and successfully modernized the country, and that it would be easy for China to emulate Japan's efforts because China and Japan were so close to each other. He also told the ministers that he had written two books, *Jih-pen Ming-chih pien-cheng chi* (A record of Meiji Restoration in Japan) and *O ta Pi-te pien-fa chi* (A record of the political reform by Peter the Great of Russia), which could serve as reference works. On the next day, Weng T'ung-ho reported on the interview to the Emperor, who ordered that K'ang submit the details of his proposals together with his books. In response, K'ang sent a memorial on January 28 in which he outlined the reform measures taken at the Meiji Restoration. Among them, the most important was, K'ang stated, the establishment of a state bureaucracy administered by the Emperor's top advisors. To start reform in China, he recommended establishing a Bureau of Institutions staffed by knowledgeable and capable young men. As to the book on the Meiji Restoration, he took time to transcribe it, and presented a copy in mid-April.[99]

In his writings, K'ang attempted to create an image of the Meiji Emperor as the key figure in the restoration. Perhaps he thought it was not convincing enough to the Kuang-hsu Emperor because, in fact, the role of the fifteen-year-old Emperor was not essential to the restoration. Probably it was for this reason that K'ang offered the story of Peter the Great simultaneously in order to present an image of a powerful monarch as the leader of reform. Obviously, K'ang's presentation had a strong effect on the Kuang-hsu Emperor, who had been attempting to increase imperial power against the dominant faction of the Empress Dowager.

Shortly after K'ang's interview at the Tsungli Yamen, Huang's

Treatises on Japan reached the Emperor by his earnest request. The Emperor had been familiar with Huang's work after he had acquired a copy of *Miscellaneous Poems on Japan* in late 1896. Probably being inspired again by K'ang's proposal to emulate the reform in Japan, the Emperor ordered Weng T'ung-ho to present Huang's *Treatises.* Weng did not comply immediately, however. On February 13, the Emperor chided Weng for his delay and prodded him on. Weng presented two copies on the following day. Hsiao Kung-ch'üan suggests that Weng was reluctant to present *Treatises on Japan* because, by that time, Weng had begun to withdraw his support of K'ang after K'ang received the unexpectedly overwhelming confidence of the Emperor. Moreover, he disapproved of K'ang's idea of following Japan's example, which implied Westernization and institutional reform beyond the scope that Weng would welcome.[100]

In the spring, K'ang Yu-wei organized the Protect-the-Nation Society (Pao-kuo hui) in Peking. It was a continuation of his efforts to recruit the support of metropolitan officials, which he'd begun in 1895 by organizing the Strength Study Society.[101] Zeal for reform inside and outside the imperial court was heightened as spring progressed. Finally, on June 11, the Emperor issued a decree declaring the beginning of reform. On June 13, Hsu Chih-ching, a Hanlin academician and the father of Hsu Jen-chu, recommended Huang for imperial consideration for appointment to an important position, along with K'ang Yu-wei, Chang Yuan-chi, T'an Ssu-t'ung, and Liang Ch'i-ch'ao. In the memorial, Hsu stated that Huang had served for twenty [*sic*] years as Counselor at the Legations in Japan, England, and the United States and was well acquainted with the principles of government in these countries; he was knowledgeable and far-sighted; his handling of government affairs was precise and accurate; and he was reliable and effective.[102] On the same day, an imperial edict was issued summoning K'ang and Chang to an imperial audience, ordering Governor General Chang Chih-tung to escort Huang and T'an, and ordering the Tsungli Yamen to investigate Liang.[103] K'ang Yu-wei was finally received in imperial audience on June 16 and was given a position in the Tsungli Yamen and the special privilege of directly memorializing the throne. Thereafter, K'ang acted as the chief architect of reform by writing numerous memorials for reform proposals.

Huang did not promptly respond to the imperial order to come to Peking. According to the observations of the local leaders, Governor Ch'en did not let him hurry to Peking because Huang was indispensable for the reform programs in Hunan which had barely begun. P'i Hsi-jui wrote to Huang, congratulating him on the honorable recommendation and, at the same time, begging him to consider what would happen to reform in Hunan if he should leave.[104] On July 30, the Emperor again ordered the Governor to let Huang proceed to Peking without delay. Huang still remained in Hunan. In the meantime, he became ill. On August 11, the court appointed him Minister to Japan and ordered him to hurry to Peking. The court's decision to appoint him to the post was made to comply with the Japanese government's wish, informally expressed when Minister Yü-keng resigned.[105]

On August 24, Huang finally left Changsha for Peking via Shanghai. His pace was slow, however, because of his illness.[106] Undoubtedly another factor was his reluctance to reach Peking with its unstable political situation caused by the sudden rise of K'ang's group in the imperial government. By the time Huang departed from Hunan, attacks on the reformers' group were mounting, and the danger of getting involved in the politics in Peking was obvious. At Huang's departure, Ch'en Pao-chen saw him off to the ship and bade farewell in tears, fearing they would never see each other again.[107]

When Huang arrived in Shanghai in mid-September, his condition was serious; he was suffering from dysentery. Being unable to continue on his trip to Peking, he requested sick leave and was granted two months' leave. Shortly after his arrival in Shanghai, the Empress Dowager carried out her coup d'état. While suffering from a high fever, Huang read the news of the arrest of the Kuanghsu Emperor and the Empress Dowager's declaration of the resumption of her regency on September 23. Five days afterwards, T'an Ssu-t'ung and five other reformers were executed. Huang was in danger too; on September 26, and October 1 and 6, the Censors Huang Kuei-yun, Chang Chung-hsin, and Huang Chün-lung requested that Huang be punished on the charge of his association with K'ang Yu-wei's group, his suspicious collaboration with Englishmen in Hankow, his corruption in Singapore and Hunan, and his close association with Chang Yin-huan. Chang had received a death sentence, later reduced to banishment. Huang begged to be released from his appointment as Minister to Japan on the grounds of illness; his resignation was accepted on October 3.[108] The Empress Dowager was not satisfied with removing Huang from office; on October 9 she secretly ordered Governor General Liu K'un-i to arrest him. Huang was staying with his own son in the Office of Foreign Affairs, a building located near the foreign settlements. The Intendant of Shanghai asked Huang to move into the Chinese city and, when Huang refused, sent 200 or more soldiers to surround the building.[109]

The foreign observers in Shanghai were alarmed by the siege against Huang. At the time, the former Prime Minister of Japan, Itō Hirobumi, was visiting Shanghai with Narahara Nobumasa, once Huang's student. Itō ordered the Japanese Minister in Peking to inform the Ch'ing Court that excessive punishment of Huang, who had been designated as Minister to Japan, would affect the friendly relations between the two countries.[110] The Western community was aroused by the terror against the reformers. The *North China Herald & S. C. & C. Gazette* wrote that Huang's life was in danger: "It is to be hoped that steps will be taken to at least save this well-educated and liberal-minded official's life."[111] Alarmed by the strong reaction of the foreign community against Huang's arrest, Liu K'un-i recommended leniency and the postponement of disciplinary measures. In the Tsungli Yamen, Yuan Ch'ang made efforts on Huang's behalf. As a result, Huang was released after a two-day siege and ordered to return to his original domicile.[112]

Huang left Shanghai on October 15 by sea. "Like a wounded solitary goose returning to the south," he sailed along the lonely sea coast. His illness, the frightening moments under siege, and the catastrophic end of the Reform Movement distressed him deeply.

Most of the colleagues with whom he had shared hopes for reform were executed, banished, removed from office, or had become refugees in foreign lands. He felt that the chance for reform was gone and that China's future was dismal.[113]

And so the Hundred-Day Reform of 1898 marked the zenith and, at the same time, the nadir of Huang's official career. He received the honor of being summoned by the Emperor for a special audience and was appointed an Imperial Commissioner to represent China in Japan. Such a position was his long-cherished dream. However, the appointment was made under the most strained political circumstances, and he was forced to resign it. Despite his cautious avoidance of too close association with K'ang Yu-wei, he was accused of having participated in K'ang's alleged scheme to take over the government. Undoubtedly the fact that he was recommended, together with K'ang, Liang and T'an Ssu-t'ung, at the very beginning of the official reform created an image of Huang as a close associate of K'ang. As a result, Huang became a national figure. It was ironic that the very events that brought him fame destroyed his lifelong efforts to further his career as a bureaucrat.

NINE

Master of the Jen-ching-lu: Hope for a New China

After returning home to Chia-ying, Kwangtung, Huang Tsun-hsien lived the rest of his life in retirement. The name of his studio, Jen-ching-lu, was taken from a famous poem by T'ao Ch'ien (365–427):

> *I built my house near where others dwell [jen-ching],*
> *And yet there is no clamor of carriages and horses.*[1]

He had adopted this style, of being Master of the Jen-ching-lu, for a long time before the Jen-ching-lu had even existed. Soon after he was settled at home, he purchased a piece of land adjacent to his house and had the Jen-ching-lu built. He made sure the building had large windows with glass panes. He had dreamed of sitting in a studio with sunlight flooding through bright window panes, as he had written in a poem when he was twenty. In the sunny living room, he kept exotic plants brought from Singapore, and he furnished his study with Victorian furniture. The calligraphy for the tablet on the front door, saying Jen-ching-lu, was contributed by a Japanese calligrapher friend in Tokyo. In the garden, he planted various fruit trees and flowers—orchids, bananas, bamboo, plums and peaches. There were roses from London, and chrysanthemums from Germany. He introduced papaya to Chia-ying, and it became a profitable local product. He took pleasure in working in the garden or walking around the countryside clad in a short jacket.[2]

While he lived abroad, he had become accustomed to Western

food. He especially liked beef soup, despite the Buddhist prohibition and the Chinese avoidance of eating beef.[3] After retiring, in addition to bread, he continued to use butter and milk,
which he imported from Switzerland through a Swiss mission
which ran a hospital and a high school in Chia-ying for the study
of German. It was not simply that he enjoyed Western food; he
believed in its nutritive value. Because he was very careful of his
health, he observed a fixed schedule to an almost obsessive extent.
He believed in Western medicine. Whenever he became sick, he
visited the Swiss hospital or sent for a doctor from the hospital;
he never trusted a Chinese herbalist.[4] This was evidence of his
faith in modern Western science.

During this time, he composed more poems than at any other
period of his life, except for the 150 poems composed in less than
a year for *Miscellaneous Poems on Japan*. His friend Ch'iu Feng-
chia, a Hakka poet with whom he exchanged poems, often visited
him at Jen-ching-lu. After the attempt to create the Taiwan Republic failed, Ch'iu had returned to his home, which was not far
from Huang's home.[5]

As the master of Jen-ching-lu, whose ideal was to live as a rec-
luse, Huang declined all invitations to government service. In 1899,
he was invited by Li Hung-chang to join his staff in Canton. Having been dismissed from the Tsungli Yamen during the Reform of
1898, Li served as Governor General of Kwangtung and Kwangsi
from 1899 until he was recalled to negotiate the settlement of
the Boxer Incident in 1900. Li asked Huang's opinion on how to
govern the province of Kwangtung. Huang recommended setting
up a modern police system and abolishing the transit tax on rice.
Then Li wanted to commission Huang to organize a police system
and to open mines in Kwangtung. Having received several pleading
letters from Li, Huang paid him a visit. After a conversation about
mines and railways, Huang respectfully declined Li's offer and
returned home. He refused all other invitations, including those
from Chang Chih-tung and Liu K'un-i.[6] His real reason was dis-
trust of the government which was dominated by the Empress
Dowager and the Manchu princes. His loyalty remained with the

Kuang-hsu Emperor. When the announcement was made on January 24, 1900, that a son of Prince Tuan was to be the heir apparent to the late T'ung-chih Emperor, he bitterly expressed his indignation and deplored this injustice to the Kuang-hsu Emperor.[7] The announcement was taken as the Empress Dowager's first step toward deposing the Kuang-hsu Emperor. Moreover, most of the reform-minded officials who had recommended Huang or were associated with him in Hunan had been purged. Because of the severe suppression of the reformist faction, panic seized the officials, who became very cautious in expressing themselves. Huang thought the unfavorable atmosphere for reform would last for a while. He decided that, for the time being, it was best to nurture his physical vitality, cultivate high spirits, and broaden his knowledge through reading at home. If opportunity arose, he would again devote himself to the cause of reform, whether or not it proved personally successful.[8]

The political situation in the Imperial Court led to gloomy premonitions at the dawn of the year 1900. Huang's poem commemorating the beginning of the twentieth century expressed his anxieties over China's survival as a nation; he was especially worried that the rulers were ignorant of international politics and that the government officials feared to speak out.[9] The year was marked by the Boxer Rebellion, the largest popular uprising against foreigners in the modern history of China. This kind of event was one that Huang had dreaded most. It appeared to him that violent xenophobia would draw catastrophe down upon China. He was alarmed when the Empress Dowager invited the Boxers to Peking in the spring. He condemned the Empress Dowager and the court officials who encouraged the ignorant masses to reckless action. In the summer, at the news of the advance of foreign troops into the capital, he trembled in fear. When the Boxers were finally suppressed by the Allied Forces, he pitied their ignorance in believing in supernatural forces and their fanaticism in trying, with little more than bare hands, to prevail over foreign troops.[10]

In the turmoil caused by the Boxers, Huang lost his closest friends. Yuan Ch'ang, a member of the Tsungli Yamen, was accused by pro-Boxer officials and was given the death penalty for opposing the court's encouragement of the Boxers. Yuan had twice warned the court that the Boxers followed a heterodox sect related to the White Lotus, and he had pointed out the need to protect the foreign legations. Wu Te-hsiao, as magistrate of Hsi-an district in Chekiang province, attempted to curb the violence against the Catholic Church. The excited masses killed him and his whole family, together with the Westerners. Chang Yin-huan, who had been banished to Sinkiang after 1898, was executed without warning during the Boxer upheaval. In the same year, T'ang Ts'ai-ch'ang of Hunan was put to death when the uprising of his Independent Army was suppressed by Chang Chih-tung. Huang bitterly mourned the death of these friends and dedicated a eulogistic poem to each of them.[11] Huang's bitter feelings deepened against the Empress Dowager and the Manchu princes who had invited the fiasco.

Huang devoted most of his time to the education of his sons, younger cousins, and nephews. At his family school, he had five students and taught five subjects: ancient institutions, history, classics, mathematics, and physiology. Each student was responsible for reporting on a subject at every class session. Besides teaching, Huang helped organize the Tung-shan Elementary Normal School in Chia-ying.[12] After the Boxer affair, the Ch'ing Government launched a program for institutional reform, one of the reform programs being to encourage local officials and gentry to build schools for the teaching of modern subjects. Huang was critical of the Ch'ing Government's new educational policy because the government emphasized higher education; he personally believed in the importance of popularizing elementary education. Besides, the government encouraged the immediate opening of schools without building normal schools to educate teachers and without providing sufficient textbooks. The government emphasized education in the Classics, while he thought that it was enough to teach only relevant parts of the Classics as supplementary texts for the study of current affairs. The government disregarded the importance of modern sciences in education and tried to retain the traditional subjects to prepare students for civil service examinations.[13] Huang was convinced that the traditional scholarship should be replaced by the new learning. After many years' residence in the Western world, he realized that classical studies had no practical value. Commenting on the scholarship of Tseng Kuo-fan, he wrote: "He was a first-rate Confucian scholar of the Ch'ing dynasty who ably combined the superior elements of the scholarship of textual criticism, art of writing, and discussion of principles. All these were, however, stale and barren enterprises and were of no use in today's world. They were the products of the time when no one dreamed of modern Western science and philosophy."[14]

Huang encouraged his own students to study in Japan. In 1904 he sent a son, a grandson, a cousin, a nephew, and a disciple to study in Japan. Around this time, the number of Chinese students in Japan reached its height, and short-term normal schools were built in Tokyo for them. Huang's son and students were sent to this kind of school as preparation for teaching at Tung-shan Normal School.[15]

In the spring of 1902, Huang made contact with Liang Ch'i-ch'ao, who had been exiled to Japan since late 1898. Liang began to publish the *Ch'ing-i pao* (The pure criticism journal) as soon as he arrived in Japan, supported by the Overseas Chinese community in Yokohama. He had published its 100th issue by late 1901, when the publication was discontinued because of fire. In early 1902, he started to publish the *Hsin-min ts'ung-pao* (The new citizen journal), a very popular journal that continued until 1907. Copies were smuggled into China, and Huang obtained them through the Office of Foreign Affairs at Swatow. He could receive a copy in about twenty days.[16] After he received the second issue of the *New Citizen Journal* in the spring of 1902, Huang began to write to Liang. He wrote at least seven letters during 1902, one in 1904, and one on February 21, 1905, about a month before his death. (During 1903, Liang was traveling in the United

States.) Liang published six of Huang's letters in the journal under the various pseudonyms with which Huang signed them.[17]

Huang had great hopes that Liang's journalism would advance the cause of nationalism and reform. After the failure of the Reform of 1898, he strongly felt the need of public political education to raise national consciousness and to enlist support for reform. Huang put much faith in journalism as a means of educating the people. He believed that the might of the pen could gradually transform the passive masses into responsible citizens. When Liang published the *New Citizen Journal*, Huang enthusiastically wrote:

> The *Pure Criticism Journal* far excelled the *Journal of Current Affairs*. Now the *New Citizen Journal* surpasses the *Pure Criticism Journal* a hundred times. Its contents alert people's minds and arouse their feelings. . . . It cannot fail to move the people, even those whose minds are like stone or iron. From antiquity to the present, there has been no example that has demonstrated the might of the pen so powerfully as this journal.[18]

From the time he entrusted Liang with the editorship of the *Journal of Current Affairs* in 1896, Huang had admired his talent as a journalist. Looking at the *New Citizen Journal*, he noted that Liang had attained mastery in writing journal articles. He expressed unreserved admiration for Liang, admitting that Liang deserved to be respected as his superior. He compared Liang to the legendary monkey king who transformed himself into a great master of martial and magic arts after many years' discipline, and compared himself to the boar who became the disciple of the monkey and followed him on the journey to escort the Buddhist monk to India.[19] In a letter written after he became seriously ill, Huang encouraged Liang to continue his efforts until their original goals of publishing journals were achieved:

> Ever since the *Journal of Current Affairs* turned out to be successful, I decided to entrust the responsibility of publication to you. We have not yet attained our goals, but I hope you will continue your devotion to this task. The eventual harvest will be enormous.[20]

With the humility of an experienced old man advising a young talent, Huang sincerely and earnestly expressed his thoughts to Liang on vital issues concerning China's future. First, he took up the nature of Confucianism and the question of what to do with it while making reform efforts toward progress in the modern world. In response to Liang's article, "'To Preserve Confucianism' does not imply respect for Confucius," published in the second issue of the *New Citizen Journal*, Huang expressed the thoughts on Confucianism he had been writing down and discussing at his family school.[21] He intended to publish a book entitled *Yen K'ung* (Discourse on Confucius). In his letter to Liang, Huang pointed out the rational and universal nature of Confucianism and its compatibility with modern developments. In his view, Confucius was a great teacher of humanism: he taught humanism by commenting on matters of everyday life, such as eating and drinking, and did not resort to empty talk (*k'ung-t'an*) about ghosts, spirits, or other supernatural beings. Huang believed that, in this respect, Confucianism was superior to the major religions of the world. Each of the founders of Christianity, Islam, and Buddhism claimed that he was the son of God, the messenger of God, or the most superior one. They all preached heaven and hell and told people that they could enter heaven only by following their doctrines. In ancient times, Huang explained, men were ignorant and needed the encouragement provided by the story of heaven and hell. After human knowledge expanded as the result of development of science and advancement of education, everyone knew that such things as heaven and hell never existed. In the modern age, human reason prevailed. Eventually, Huang predicted, people would discard all superstitious beliefs and myths. At that time, the teachings of Confucius would be recognized as superior because they were concerned with questions of how to do one's best to achieve humanity (*jen-tao*) and the ideal way to participate in the process of the universe (*ts'an-tsan*).[22] This point had been expressed in his speech at the Southern Study Society in Hunan in 1898. At that time, Liang was propagating K'ang Yu-wei's philosophy of

Confucianism and supported K'ang's movement for the promotion of Confucianism as a religion.

Commenting on K'ang Yu-wei's theory of Confucianism, Huang made it clear that he had never accepted K'ang's ideas that Confucius was the founder of Confucianism as a religion, that the Six Classics were written by Confucius, and that the sages Yao and Shun were the intellectual creation of Confucius. He rejected K'ang's idea of "protecting Confucianism," saying that, while other religions had exclusive doctrines and jealously forbade their followers to worship other gods, Confucius never forced anyone to follow his teaching. In Huang's view, Confucianism was a universal teaching of humanism and therefore had no need to be defended or preserved:

> Great was Confucius. His teaching does not even have a name. How should it be protected? It has no enemy and it has no religious dogma. Where does one start to preserve it? The truth of the teaching of Confucius will be accepted by the people for thousands of generations; as long as mankind exists, this teaching will prevail. Why should it be preserved? Those who were worried that our teaching would perish and who urge us to preserve it are like those who are worried that the heavens will fall and the earth crumble.[23]

Huang understood that K'ang Yu-wei's call to "Preserve Confucianism" was based on his anxiety that Western religion was about to encroach on Chinese minds, just as the Western Powers were encroaching on Chinese lands. On this point, Huang was much more optimistic than K'ang. He was confident of the superiority of Confucianism and its compatibility with the progress of the modern world. He even stated that Confucius had noted in his commentary on the *I Ching* the truth of evolution and the principle of the survival of the fittest which Darwin discovered only after ten thousand things had evolved.[24]

To Huang's delighted surprise, Liang's ideas in the article in the *New Citizen Journal* were almost identical with his. Liang declared that Confucianism need not be "preserved" because its superiority enabled it to withstand the development of science and the expansion of freedom of thought. He denounced K'ang's plan to "Preserve

Confucianism" by making it a state religion, on the grounds that such a movement would create a sect within Confucianism and that it would restrict freedom of thought. Furthermore, by declaring Confucianism to be the greatest teaching that ever existed in the world, and one that was capable of encompassing all mankind in the twentieth century, Liang denied K'ang's effort to identify Confucianism with the Chinese culture and race.[25] In other words, Liang regarded Confucianism as the universally valid teaching of a great philosopher-educator. For this reason, he declared that *chiao* (teaching) and *kuo* (country) were not the same, and that what ought to be preserved was the country, not the teaching.

This article indicated that Liang had turned away from his previous views of Confucianism. It marked the first step in Liang's split from his teacher, K'ang Yu-wei.[26] It has been pointed out that Huang's opinions exerted decisive effects on Liang during the years between 1902 and 1904 when Liang experienced crucial changes in his thinking. His drawing away from his mentor over the issue of the preservation of Confucianism was one of the most crucial of these changes. Although Huang's opinion was not the single cause for the changes in Liang, it has been regarded as a powerful influence.[27]

Huang applauded Liang's brilliant argument against "preserving Confucianism"; however, he objected to Liang's statement that Confucianism was one of the nine schools of teaching in ancient China. Huang argued that Ju (Confucianism is referred to as Ju-chiao) was certainly one of the nine streams of teaching, but that the teaching of Confucius was not limited to Ju because Confucius combined all the nine streams of teaching. Huang stated that Ju, which originally meant "softness" or "docility," was the teaching of the Duke of Chou, who taught the people how to be obedient.[28] Huang indicated that he had his own view of Confucius which was different from either that of the scholars of the Han School or the Sung School. Unfortunately, he did not complete the proposed book on Confucius.

Huang was confident not only of the universality of Confucian teaching but also of the greatness of China's heritage. When Liang Ch'i-ch'ao consulted him about his plan to publish a journal for the promotion of national learning (*kuo-hsueh*), Huang endorsed the idea; however, he disagreed with Liang's idea of preserving a national essence (*kuo-ts'ui*). Obviously, Liang's notion of nurturing the national essence was influenced by such a movement in Japan. It was a nativist reaction against Westernization during the first two decades of the Meiji era. The journal *The Nippon* had been published in 1889 by nativist Kuga Katsunan, who stated the purpose of its publication:

> Japan in modern times has lost its original identity. After discarding everything they had, all the people in the country are about to turn to the West. As a result, "Nippon" is going to be reduced merely to a name for this island on the map. . . . *The Nippon* aims at reviving and upholding the national spirit.[29]

Huang was against Liang's proposal to campaign for the preservation of China's national essence. He maintained that there was no such need in the case of China and that the more urgent task for China at the moment was to be more receptive to new ideas from outside. Emphasizing the difference between China and Japan, he stated:

> The Japanese do not have Japanese learning. In ancient times, the Japanese adored Sui and T'ang China, and the whole nation was focused upon the East; in modern times, when they admired Europe and America, the whole nation turned toward the West. Their craziness in rushing from East to West was like racing with their own shadow. They were in the state of being drunk or in a dream. When they calmed down a little, they found themselves lost, and began to wonder where had they originally come from. Thereupon, they began to assert their national essence. In the case of China, we have a great tradition. Our trouble lies not in our inability to preserve it but in our arrogance and obstinacy.[30]

China should, he thought, be more daring in opening itself to the New Learning or Western Learning, which was the foundation of modern science, technology, and the institutions of the modern Western society:

Now let us throw open the gates to welcome the New Learning. After the study of New Learning prospers, let us compare it with the traditional Chinese learning, and let them compete with each other. Then the real spirit of the traditional learning will become clear, and its true value will become obvious. As to what to do with the New Learning, we can either take or discard it, welcome or reject it, or harmonize it with our traditional learning and let them coexist; it is our choice and not anyone else's.

Since the country has been weakened to this extent, I am not without anxiety that it may be taken over by the others. Nevertheless, I am convinced that we can count on our four thousand years' history, our four hundred million people who have their own language and customs, and our great sage and at least a dozen enlightened scholars.[31]

His advocating an open-minded attitude toward new ideas was supported not only by his deep-rooted confidence in China's tradition but also by his belief in the validity of the ancient ideals revealed in the Classics. For him, the ultimate goal of human society was to realize the ancient and universal ideals of the ancestors who had established the glorious tradition of China in the Central Plain. After all, adoption of Western technology, science, and institutions was nothing but the means to achieve ancient Chinese ideals. In this respect, Huang and his fellow countrymen were vastly different from the contemporary Japanese who identified their ideals with those of the modern West. In pursuing the goals of "Civilization and Enlightenment," the Japanese wholeheartedly believed in the universal nature of modern Western ideals and earnestly desired to realize them in Japan. Huang was right to state that the Japanese did not have "Japanese learning," in the sense that there was no ancient Japanese ideal comparable to the Confucian utopia.

The most immediate and urgent goal of reform was to preserve China's integrity as a nation and to establish a strong state capable of competing in the struggle for survival in the modern world. For this reason, Huang's reform proposals were focused on how to build a strong Chinese state. In his letters to Liang, he talked about the best form of government for twentieth-century China. One letter written in the summer of 1902 confided his belief that the most adequate government for twentieth-century China was a constitutional monarchy after the English model. He had held this idea for over a decade, but he had not dared to reveal it even to Liang, his closest friend. He was afraid Liang might not understand. Any discussion of an alternate form of government was dangerously subversive. Huang noted that, when he had mentioned this idea to the Japanese Minister, Yano Fumio, on July 5, 1897, Yano sternly warned him not to mention it to anyone else. Huang went on to confess further about how he had gotten into touch with modern Western ideas of democracy and constitutional monarchism and how he had changed his ideas concerning an ideal polity for China in the modern age: he had read the works of Rousseau and Montesquieu in 1880 or 1881 in Japan and was greatly excited by the thought that the utopian world must be democracy. While staying in the United States, however, he witnessed the corruption of bureaucrats, dirty politics, and the arbitrariness of political parties, and realized that actualization of the ideals of democracy was difficult, even in a country that had advanced institutions and a high level of education. He decided that China was far from ready to adopt democracy or republicanism. Thereafter, while he was in London, he came to think that China should model its government after the constitutional monarchy of England. From that time on, he stated, he maintained that idea and had never changed his mind.[32] Huang repeated the account of his previous infatuation with the ideal of democracy in a letter to Liang in the summer of 1904, stating that it was fortunate he had never publicly announced it because now he believed in a gradual transition to constitutional monarchy.[33]

Huang discredited autocracy as outdated in the twentieth century. The primary reason was that, under such a system, it was impossible to enlist the people's support and, consequently, there was no hope of realizing a powerful state. At the same time, however, Huang opposed a revolutionary movement to overthrow the monarchical system in China. It has been pointed out that Liang Ch'i-ch'ao advocated revolution around 1901 and 1902. In his novel "Hsian Chung-kuo wei-lai chi" (The future image of China), serially published in *Hsin hsiao-shuo pao* (New novel, a new literary journal which Liang published from late 1902), he alluded to the fall of the Ch'ing dynasty and the rise of a Republic within ten years. Also, in his article "Hsin-min shuo" (On the new people), serially published in the *New Citizen Journal* from early 1902, he spoke of the need for destruction as a preliminary to progress.[34] Huang admonished Liang for his reckless ideas. In a long letter of late 1902, he told Liang that his recommendation of destruction for people who had no idea of civil rights, political principles, or the state was like giving a dagger to an eight-year-old child.[35]

Huang pointed out to Liang that Chinese monarchy was not the same as the despotic regimes in Europe that had been overthrown by revolution. In his understanding, the despotic monarchs in Europe had oppressed the people in a manner beyond comparison with any harsh ruler in Chinese history. Despotism in early modern Europe was so harsh that, once Rousseau's *Social Contract* appeared, its message penetrated into people's minds, and at an opportune moment popular wrath exploded with enough force to overthrow the monarchy. Comparing Chinese despotism with its Western counterpart, Huang wrote that Chinese ingenuity had no match. Chinese despots skillfully tamed scholars and made them docile slaves; as a result the population became numb and unable to feel pain or itch; they knew only how to lower their heads and quietly endure their sufferings. To such a people, it was impossible to propose the concept of people's rights, even if tens of hundreds of Rousseaus would shout until they wore out their vocal cords. Therefore, Huang admonished Liang not to instigate the people to destruction but rather to prepare them gradually for constitutionalism.[36]

Another reason Huang opposed Liang's suggestion for racial (that is, anti-Manchu) revolution was that he felt it was imperative to support the existing regime in view of the foreign threat to China. In a world where struggle for survival was increasingly intense, the ruled and the rulers must cooperate to face foreign pressure. The foreigners were behaving like masters of China, and foreign governments were treating the Ch'ing Government like slaves.

Although the Chinese people were unwilling to remain the slaves of slaves, he stated, they were not yet prepared to be their own masters. He believed the important task of the Chinese for the moment was to help the "slave" of the foreign powers, that is, the Ch'ing Government, to resist foreign domination.[37]

As another practical reason why he opposed an anti-Manchu revolution, Huang reminded Liang of the rebellion of Saigō Takamori of Japan in 1877. Saigō had thousands of followers armed with sickles and spades and sticks. "How could a rebellion participated in by 20 or 30 percent of the population of the country and supported by 70 or 80 percent fail?" The answer was that the government had steamships, railroads, and guns. Huang added that, even though the Ch'ing Government was weak, it still had more than enough power to suppress internal rebellions and that he did not want to see the blood of patriots soaking the ground and their skulls piled up in the wilderness.[38]

Shortly afterwards, Liang stopped promoting an anti-Manchu revolution. In the final part of "On the New People," published in June 1904, he even denounced an anti-Manchu revolution, stating that "some extreme anti-Manchu revolutionaries say that, even if the Ch'ing Government were to grant them English- or Japanese-style parliamentarianism, they would not accept it; they would rather perish as Han Chinese than survive under the Manchus. This kind of statement is overly emotional. Advocates of true patriotism and revolution cannot accept such an idea."[39] Chang P'eng-yuan suggested that it was partly because of Huang's admonition that Liang dropped his radicalism and began to oppose revolution, although he admitted that Liang's trip to the United States in 1903 as a guest of the Association to Preserve the Emperor (Pao-huang hui), also exerted a decisive impact.[40]

Except for Liang's advocacy of revolution, Huang fully endorsed the assertions of his "On the New People." Liang emphasized the importance of public morality (*kung-te*) and the cohesion of people (*ho-ch'ün*), along with other ideas such as freedom, natural rights, progress, self-government, and the nation-state.[41] Huang especially supported Liang's emphasis on the need for national cohesion and public morality to unite the people beyond the family and clan. Liang's article had amplified the same ideas as Huang's, expressed in *Treatises on Japan* and in his speeches in Hunan. Huang noted as early as 1887 that one essential factor that made Japan strong was the ability to unite the people as a nation. The notion of the need for national cohesion was widely accepted by Chinese intellectuals after the Sino-Japanese War, together with the concept of Social Darwinism. Yen Fu's translations of Huxley's *Evolution and Ethics* had a profound influence on these ideas. Benjamin I. Schwartz has demonstrated that one of Yen Fu's major discoveries concerning the vigor of English society was that the people's energies were united into a collective force which made the whole society enormously powerful.[42]

Huang admired Yen Fu but criticized him for the style of his writing, which was like the "writing of a man who lived during the Six Dynasties." In fact, Yen Fu chose to write in a highly elegant style to attract readers among the elite. Because of his enormous influence, Huang persuaded Yen that he should consider creating a new style to express new ideas in plain language:

> You think there is no revolution in the world of literature. I think there is no revolution, but there is reform. For example, the forty-two-chapter sutra, the earliest Chinese translation of a Buddhist sutra in the Later Han period, was in the old style; only after Kumarajiva created a new style of translation did Buddhism become popular in this country. Moreover, the ancient style is no longer used in official documents in the present dynasty nor in the popular stories narrated by the storytellers ever since the Yuan and Ming dynasties. Only when the people respect it and feel at ease with it is a language well established.[43]

Writing to Liang, to congratulate him on the publication of "On the New People," Huang discussed how to create cohesion among the Chinese. He wrote that, in China, the clan system functioned as a means of uniting people up to a point. However, in a village where people belonged to different clans, there were perpetual feuds; clan organization was no longer adequate as a unit of modern society. Other kinds of traditional organizations, such as provincial associations or groups of those who passed their examinations in the same year, were not strong enough. Merchants' associations or guilds were organized on a voluntary basis but were not powerful enough to exist independently. The most cohesive groups that existed in Chinese society were secret societies. The Five-Peck-Rice Sect instigated rebellion and finally toppled the Han dynasty; the Fang La Rebellion in the Sung, Hsu Hung-ju's rebellion in the Ming, and the recent rebellion of the Taipings threatened the dynasty. All these rebellions were organized by secret societies which attracted a great mass of followers by their principle of egalitarianism and their spirit of mutual help. Huang suggested that the principles of clan organization, supplemented with the techniques of the secret societies and Western social sciences, might offer a means to create cohesion among the people. He wished Liang to propagate the need for cohesion in his journals for two or three years so that people would become educated and be prepared for parliamentarianism. Otherwise, Huang wrote, people would not be ready for self-government even if they were granted it.[44] Liang did not betray Huang's expectation and energetically carried out the task of publishing journals for the political education of the public.

Huang himself made some efforts to use his literary talent for the purpose of promoting a nationalist spirit among the populace. He composed military marches to whip up patriotic sentiment among soldiers. With his letter of late 1902 he sent a copy of his songs to Liang, who published some of them in his journal.[45] One march begins with the stanza:

> Our country has been here four thousand years
> And all of this land is our own land.
> In the twentieth century, who will its masters be?
> We are in armor now to settle this.
> Behold the waving yellow-dragon flags.
> Drum! Drum! Drum![46]

The first stanza of "A Song in the Military Camps" goes:

To be great, to be great, you nice young men,
The best death is death on the battlefield.
Since death must come to everyone,
Don't waste your chance to make death count.
Die! Die! Die![47]

Each stanza of his march songs had refrains such as "Fight! Fight! Fight!," "Must! Must! Must!," "Win! Win! Win!," "Forward! Forward! Forward!," or "Brave! Brave! Brave!" The creation of national cohesion and the cultivation of patriotism among the populace were the two most important steps in making a country strong, he wrote to Liang in August 1904, noting the Japanese victories over the Russians in the battles in Manchuria.[48]

Huang placed his hope in the younger generation and paid more and more attention to primary education. In his final letter, he asked Liang to compile textbooks for primary school students.[49] He himself composed a song for young children, persuading them to go to school. The refrain was "Go to school, don't be late/Go to school, don't stay ignorant/Go to school, don't be lazy."[50] "A Chorus for Primary School Students" in nineteen stanzas summarized his messages to the younger generation; the need for national cohesion, the spirit of independence and self-reliance, rationalism (anti-religion), obligations to the state, and the national humiliations which needed to be wiped out. In essence it was a condensation of his assertions during his final years, expressed in short, plain verses suitable for chanting. The first stanza begins:

Come now, little students,
Look into your mirrors.
Remember what your race is.
Remember all the races
Of the five continents.
Red Indians hid, lay low.
Blacks were brutalized.
The red-haired and blue-eyed
Dominate the world.

Now they're getting ready
To jump in and trample us.
Listen, little students,
One half the world is yellow,
So how can we save face
If we let ourselves be trampled.[51]

From the spring of 1904 on, Huang suffered from a disease of the lungs that caused him difficulty in breathing. By the winter of that year, he was bedridden and knew that his illness was incurable. In the midst of the Russo-Japanese War, Huang lay on his death-bed. He had a nightmare about the assassination of Liang, and composed a poem on Liang, his last. In his dream, a gust of damp wind blew in; then he saw Liang enter, holding his own skull. Liang told him he had been assassinated by radicals who attacked his idea of moderate constitutional monarchism. The disembodied spirits of T'an Ssu-t'ung and T'ang Ts'ai-ch'ang accompanied Liang's ghost. When Huang tried to hear more of Liang's words, the cock crowed. In the dim light, he saw Liang's head hanging on the wall and the wall covered with blood; wiping his eyes to see better, he saw on the wall a map of China which had been divided by the Powers. In the second stanza of the poem, he narrated briefly the major events of his life and wished he could live to witness the inauguration of a parliament in China. He regretted that he was already old when the country was about to be reborn. In the last stanza, he wondered where the sleeping lion would go after being awakened by foreign gunfire. He reminded Liang that they had always shared the same dream, and that he had once aspired to be Cavour (1810–1860), an able diplomat, liberal, a patriot and the first prime minister of Italy, while Liang admired Mazzini (1805–1872).[52] Although Huang's ambition to be a prime minister was not fulfilled, he was hopeful that constitutional government would be realized in China in the near future. He placed his hope in Liang to carry out the task of promoting constitutionalism.

On March 28, 1905, Huang Tsun-hsien died, aged fifty-seven. His eldest son Mien (Po-yuan), then serving at the Chinese Consulate in Kobe, rushed to the deathbed of his father. Overwhelmed by grief, the son died soon after arriving home.[53]

TEN

Conclusion

The preceding pages have attempted to reconstruct the world of Huang Tsun-hsien. Growing up in the turmoil of the Taiping Rebellion, aroused at an early age by scenes of foreign domination in Hong Kong and Canton, he continuously voiced his patriotic concern for China's future, until his death in the midst of the Russo-Japanese War. A gifted poet, he eloquently expressed his indignation, frustration, and sorrow over the events that brought humiliation to China. His lamentation over the declining prestige of the Chinese empire was a recurrent theme. In his active life, he identified his personal ambitions with his patriotic sentiment. He was inspired by the realization that a new type of statesman had emerged in the creation of the new nation-states of Italy, Germany, and Japan. He aspired to be the Camillo Benso di Cavour of China. He wanted to attain high position through recognition of his merit as a professional bureaucrat and his knowledge of the modern world. The manner in which he developed his official career reflected a new trend in the bureaucracy which Kenneth Folsom has characterized as a development "from an elite of the scholar to an elite of the professional."[1]

One of the major issues reflected in Huang's life is the development of nationalism among the Chinese intellectuals in the nineteenth century. China in the nineteenth century was an empire which in theory potentially extended to all-under-heaven.

China's transition from an empire to a nation involved a transformation of the traditional concept of the universe and a corresponding transformation of basic Chinese assumptions about the source of political authority and the ethical goal of government, since the assumptions underlying China's self-image as the Middle Kingdom were interlocked with the organizing principles of Confucian society. Nevertheless when a man accepted the modern concept of nation-state as a "terminal unit"[2] he did not necessarily disavow the whole set of traditional assumptions. As Benjamin Schwartz has suggested, it was a matter of priority in commitment—authentic commitment to traditional values or the commitment to "the preservation and advancement of the social entity known as the nation"—and, where the latter takes priority over the former, "nationalism in a precise sense is already on the scene."[3]

Huang's primary commitment was certainly not to traditional values, but he always maintained at least one of the basic Confucian assumptions: that the ultimate goal of human society was the realization of a harmonious community embracing all-under-heaven. This assumption was expressed in different ways at different stages in his life. Before he left China, Huang demonstrated an open-minded attitude toward the outside world. He protested against the strong tendency toward xenophobia among conservative literati. Criticizing their hostility toward foreigners and foreign culture, Huang denounced their Sinocentric notions as arrogant. He declared that, in the modern world, East and West were one family. At that time Huang optimistically assumed that East and West would eventually and naturally compose one harmonious world community. Undoubtedly, such optimism stemmed from his confidence in the superiority of Chinese civilization. With a touch of the superior's generosity, he maintained that foreigners who came to China should not be disdained. This kind of optimism about China's relationship with the rest of the world was expressed by other early reform advocates, Wang T'ao and Cheng Kuan-ying. They believed that the *tao,* or the Confucian Way, would prevail throughout the world as a result of the opening up of the communication between China and the West.[4] We might call this kind of open-mindedness to the outside world "Confucian cosmopolitanism."

The outlook of Huang's world view did not change substantially during his stay in Japan. Despite its adoption of Western institutions, Huang regarded Japan basically as a cultural province of China. He recognized Japan's aggressions in Ryukyu and Korea as disturbing signs of Japan's inclination to shift its cultural identity to the West. He was indignant that the Japanese seemed to forget their cultural debt to China and seemed to slight China as a consequence of their infatuation with Western culture. Nevertheless, Japan's action did not shake his basic assumptions about the world order. It was not until his humiliating experiences in the United States that his optimistic view of the world was shattered. With great pain he realized that the world was an arena of strife among nations, that nations were exclusive units which engaged in a relentless struggle for survival, and, worst of all, that the Chinese were being humiliated as an inferior race by the "barbarians." The more deeply he realized the harshness of the struggle among nations, however, the more dearly he cherished the utopian ideal of universal peace and harmony. Increasingly he expressed in his poems a yearning for the ideal world of universal peace and harmony. At the same time, as a practical adjustment to the present situation, he proposed reform following the example of Meiji Japan.

As early as the 1880s, Huang commended Japan's accomplishment as a successful pattern of reform to meet the Western challenge. In its basic orientation, Japan's response to the challenge was a positive adoption of the "Western method" and a pragmatic adjustment to the modern world system built on Western concepts of diplomacy and trade. Huang had little doubt that the Japanese had made a wise decision in following this line. Being a small and poor country and much more vulnerable to foreign aggression than China, Japan was sensible in endeavoring to strengthen itself through the adoption of advanced Western technology and institutions. But in the early 1880s when Huang left Japan, the prospects for its success in modernization were not yet certain. Financial crises and popular discontent reflected the strain caused by ambitious efforts at nation-building. There were conflicts between old and new attitudes. Huang was often confused by the conflicting opinions of radical social changes taking place in Japan under the slogan of "Civilization and Enlightenment," chiefly because he was surrounded by those who resented the changes. Nevertheless, he was convinced that the policies promoted by the Meiji leaders for the creation of a prosperous and powerful state after the model of the West were essentially right. This conviction was confirmed when he traveled to the United States. After seeing an advanced Western country with his own eyes, Huang had a better perspective on Japan's efforts.

In his accounts of the reform in Meiji Japan, Huang underscored the importance of centralized efforts in Japan's successful start as a modern state. He observed how the Meiji Government played an active role in introducing new technology in agriculture and industry, developing transportation and communication systems, establishing modern financial systems, and promoting universal education, while creating a powerful military force. Since the realization of a prosperous and powerful state was such an enormous task, Huang believed that the first priority in reform was to create a powerful central government.

Huang singled out the Meiji Restoration as the most important event contributing to Japan's national solidarity. In the wake of the national crisis caused by Western pressure, the restoration of the imperial government provided the ground for the creation of a national leadership. Of all his accounts of Japan, the account of the heroes of the Meiji Restoration is the most moving. It is based on the theme of loyalism and the spirit of martyrdom of those who devoted their lives for the patriotic cause. This account of the restoration contributed to the creation of the cult of martyrdom among the Chinese intellectuals who advocated reform in the late 1890s. It also bred the hope that, once a national leadership was formed by dedicated and far-sighted individuals, reform of the entire system could be successfully accomplished. Undoubtedly, the Hundred-Day Reform of 1898 was inspired by such optimism.

Although Huang emphasized the leadership role of government, his concept of government was quite different from the Confucian concept of "rule by men." Unlike most of his contemporaries who proposed reform, Huang did *not* call for the recruitment of moral men or men of talent (*jen-ts'ai*) as the fundamental solution to problems. Instead of relying on the moral influence of virtuous men as a means of winning the hearts of the people, Huang proposed to create objective mechanisms to enlist popular support for the government.

Huang was enthusiastic about modern science and technology. He hailed technological accomplishments as symbols of the advancement of man's ability to control the natural world. He was excited about the greater possibilities that the advancement of science and technology would bring in the future. His faith in science reflected the rationalist inclination he had demonstrated in his rejection of superstitious beliefs in ghosts and disembodied spirits, commonly accepted even by the Confucian scholars of his day. Related to his rationalist outlook, he had, from an early age, a positive notion of progress in human society. His youthful rebellion against the myth of antiquity and his determination not to imitate the style of the ancients in writing poems were rooted in that notion.

In his optimistic faith in science and progress, Huang's intellectual outlook foreshadowed that of the May Fourth generation of the early Republican period. But, unlike the May Fourth intellectuals, who challenged Confucianism itself, Huang maintained that the philosophy of Confucius, because of its rationalist nature, was compatible with developments in the modern age. He was confident that Confucianism had universal validity as a philosophy of life and was much more acceptable to men in the modern world than any of the great religions of the East and West.

In his advocacy of reform along Western lines, Huang fully admitted that Western societies were a few steps ahead of China in the path of progress toward affluence and freedom. He regarded the struggle for survival among nations as an inevitable step toward progress. Therefore reform was not only for the sake of survival in the struggle but also to catch up with currents in the modern world. In his view, however, the advanced West represented only one step of the progress whose ultimate goal was the realization of the world of universal peace and harmony. Thus, he identified the ultimate goal of human society with the ancient Chinese ideal of realizing the Confucian utopia. This meant that the universal norm was to be found in China's own past.

It was partly because of his confidence in the universality of ancient Chinese ideals that Huang was so amazingly open-minded to Western learning. He did not regard science and modern institutions as being "theirs," as opposed to China's own. In his view, scientific development was a part of universal progress. He even argued that the primordial concepts of various branches of science had existed in ancient China but that the Chinese themselves had not been able to develop them into modern science because of their loss of the spirit of practical learning necessary for the development of science and technology.

In these arguments, Huang was, in fact, idealizing the past. He believed that the ancients had practical minds and the pristine virtue of hard work, and that the ancients were more progressive and open-minded than his contemporaries. It was in this sense that he called for a return to ancient virtue. In his belief, reform could be achieved through restoring the vitality China had possessed in the ancient past. Underlying this assertion was his vehement pride as a Hakka, a stigmatized minority group, who believed themselves to be the true heirs of the legacies of those who had lived in the Three Dynasties. From a Hakka point of view, he subtly criticized the majority culture of Ch'ing China in his description of Japanese society, where he found reminders of ancient China.

While Huang's rationalism, scientism, and faith in progress were impressive, his persistence in the universality of the ancient Chinese ideal was even more impressive. Perhaps one of the most basic differences between the Chinese and Japanese in their responses to the West lay in their perception of ultimate goals. For both China and Japan, the advancement of the Western Powers was an unprecedented threat, militarily, economically, and ideologically, and it was apparent that the challenge could be met only through the adoption of the superior weapons of the Westerners. The two countries shared the immediate target of enriching and strengthening the state to defend themselves from imperialist aggression. The Japanese, however, aimed at more than a practical adjustment and earnestly pursued the ideals of the West. Huang's contemporaries in Japan were not only fascinated by what Benjamin Schwartz called "the Faustian-Promethean" aspect of the modern West but also identified their own ideals with various idealist principles of the West in their socio-political, ethical-religious, and even aesthetic life. Because of their search for ideals in the Western ideals, the intellectual history of Japan since the late nineteenth century has been characterized by the tension between indigenous and Western values. In this regard, Huang's indifference to the efforts of Nakamura Keiu is most revealing. Huang attributed such efforts on the part of the Japanese to their lack of an ideal comparable to the Confucian utopia. In retrospect, the Japanese today have obtained what they set out to gain in the late nineteenth century. Theirs was a possible target because the ideals they pursued had already been realized in the West in one form or other. By contrast, the Chinese have continued to search for a formula to realize their ancient ideals in the modern or post-modern world.

Huang did not speculate about what form the Confucian utopia would take in the future, and he thought there was an unfathomable distance between the existing world and the world of universal peace and harmony. But he had hope for twentieth-century China and great expectations of the new generation. He was confident that the Chinese people in the twentieth century would no longer live under an autocratic government and that China would be reborn as a new nation. He imagined that the development of science and technology would change the entire world. For Chinese intellectuals, the late nineteenth century was not only a time of crisis and despair but also a time of great excitement over the broadening horizons of China's future.

Appendixes

Notes

Glossary

Bibliography

Index

Appendix A

Simplified Chart of the Genealogy of Huang Tsun-hsien

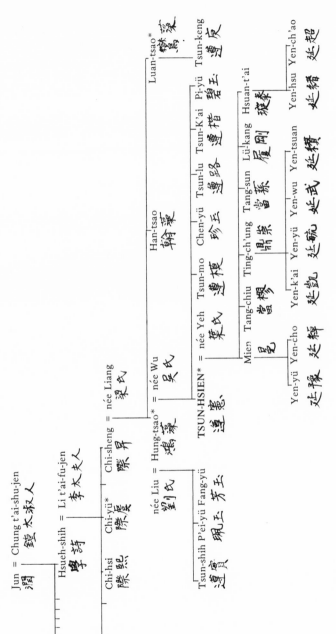

* Holder of *chü-jen* degree.

Appendix B

*A List of the Staff Members of the Chinese Diplomatic Mission
in Japan, 1877–1882*

Legation in Tokyo

Ch'in-ch'ai ta-ch'en (Imperial Commissioner)	Ho Ju-chang (Tzu-o)*	何 如 璋 (子 莪)	Kwangtung
Ch'in-ch'ai fu ta-ch'en (Associate Commissioner)	Chang Ssu-kuei (Lu-sheng)*	張 斯 桂 (魯 生)	Chekiang
Ts'an-tsan (Counselor)	Huang Tsun-hsien (Kung-tu)*	黃 遵 憲 (公 度)	Kwangtung
Sui-yuan (Attendants)	Shen Wen-ying (Mei-shih)*	沈 文 熒 (梅 史)	Chekiang
	Yang Shou-ching (Hsing-wu)	楊 守 敬 (惺 悟)	Kiangsu
	Ch'en Wen-chung	陳 文 忠 (史)*	
	Chang Hung-ch'i* (Son of Chang Ssu-kuei)	張 鴻 淇	Chekiang
	Ch'en Yen-fan	陳 衍 蕃 (範)*	
	P'an Jen-pang (Mien-ch'ien)	潘 任 邦 (勉 騫)	
	Ho Ting-ch'iu* (Younger brother of Ho Ju-chang)	何 定 求	Kwangtung
	Wang Chih-pen (Ch'i-yuan) (temporary appointment)	王 治 本 (漆 圓)	Chekiang

	Wang Fan-ch'ing** (Ch'in-hsien)	王藩青 (琴仙)	
	Li Yü-chieh	李郁階	
	Huang Hsi-ch'üan**	黄錫銓	Kwangtung
Hsi fan-i (Translator of Western languages)	Yang Shu (Hsing-yuan)	楊樞 (星垣)	Kwangtung
Tung fan-i (Translator of Japanese language)	Shen Ting-chung* Feng Chao-wei*	沈鼎鐘 馮昭煒	
Yang-yuan (Foreign staff)	Mai Chia-ti (D. B. McCartee)*	麥嘉締	United States
Family members	Ho Ch'i-i* Chang Tzu-ching* Shih Chi-hsing* Chang Te-yao* Lo Chen-i*	何其毅 張子菁 施積型 張德耀 羅貞意	

Consulate in Yokohama

Cheng li-shi kuan (Consul)	Fan Hsi-ming*	范錫明	Kwangtung
Sui-yuan	Liu K'un (Ching-ch'en)*	劉坤 (靜臣)	
Hsi fan-i	Ts'ai Kuo-chao	蔡國昭	Kwangtung
Tung t'ung-shih (Interpreter of Japanese language)	Lo Keng-ling	羅庚齡	

Consulate in Kobe

Cheng li-shih kuan	Liu Shou-k'eng (Hsiao-p'eng)	劉壽鏗 (小彭)	
	Liao Hsi-en (Shu-hsien)*	廖錫恩 (樞仙)	Kwangtung
Sui-yuan	Wu Kuang-p'ei (Han-t'ao)*	吳廣霈 (瀚濤)	Anhwei
Hsi fan-i	Chang Tsung-liang (Chih-hsuan)*	張宗良 (芝軒)	Kwangtung
Tung t'ung-shih	Yang Chin-t'ing	楊錦庭	

Consulate in Nagasaki

Cheng li-shih kuan	Yü Keng (Yuan-mei)*	余瑧 (元眉)	Kwangtung
Sui-yuan	Jen Ching-ho* (Tzu-lun)	任敬和 (子綸)	
Hsi fan-i	Liang Tien-hsun (Chin-t'ang)	梁殿勲 (縉堂)	
Tung t'ung-shih	Ts'ai Lin	蔡霖	Kwangtung

Note: The list is based on Fu Yun-lung, *Yu-li Jih-pen t'u-ching,* chüan 18, pp. 70–70b, "Chung-kuo shih-ch'en piao" (List of members of the Chinese mission). The names marked * were reported to the Japanese authority on their arrival on December 1877 and recorded in *Nihon gaikō bunsho,* 10: 188–189, no. 86. The names marked ** are added from Li Yü-shu, "Shou-jen chu-Jih kung-shih Ho Ju-chang," in *Pai-nien lai Chung-Jih kuang-hsi lun-wen-chi,* pp. 1043–1045.

Abbreviations

HPLT	*Hsiang-pao lei-tsuan* 湘報類纂 (Classified articles in *Hsiang-pao*). Comp., Chueh-shui-chai chu-jen 覺睡齋主人 . Shanghai Chung-hua pien-i Press, 1902. Reprint, Taipei Ta-t'ung shu-chü, 1969.
JCLST	Huang Tsun-hsien 黃遵憲 , *Jen-ching-lu shih-ts'ao chien-chu* 人境廬詩草箋注 (Collection of poems by Huang Tsun-hsien, annotated). Annotation by Ch'ien O-sun 錢萼孫 , Shanghai, Ku-tien wen-hsueh Press, 1957.
JPTSS (1880)	Huang Tsun-hsien, *Jih-pen tsa-shih shih* 日本雜事詩 (Miscellaneous poems on Japan). Punctuated by Iijima Yūnen 飯島有年 . Tokyo, 1880.
JPTSS (1898)	Ibid. Changsha, Fu-wen-t'ang, 1898.
JPKC	Huang Tsun-hsien, *Jih-pen-kuo chih* 日本國志 (Treatises on Japan). Canton, Fu-wen-chai, 1890.
JPKC (1898)	Ibid. Shanghai, T'u-shu chi-ch'eng i-shu-chü, 1898. Reprint, Taipei, Wen-hai Press, 1968.
Liang nien-p'u	Ting Wen-chiang 丁文江 , *Liang Jen-kung hsien-sheng nien-p'u ch'ang-pien ch'u-kao* 梁任公先生年譜長編初稿 (The first draft of the chronological biography of Liang Ch'i-chao). Taipei, Shih-chieh shu-chü, 1962.
"Nien-p'u"	Ch'ien O-sun, "Huang Kung-tu hsien-sheng nien-p'u" 黃公度先生年譜 (Chronological biography of Huang Tsun-hsien) in *JCLST*.
PTIK	Cheng Tzu-yü 鄭子瑜 and Sanetō Keishū 實藤惠秀, comps. *Huang Tsun-hsien yü Jih-pen yu-jen pi-t'an i-kao* 黃遵憲與日本友人筆談遺稿 (Records of conversations in writing between Huang Tsun-hsien and

his Japanese friends). Tokyo, Waseda University, Tōyō Bungaku Kenkyūkai, 1968.

WHPF   *Wu-hsu pien-fa* 戊戌變法   (The reform of 1898), in Chien Po-tsan 翦伯贊 et al., eds., *Chung-kuo chin-tai shih tzu-liao ts'ung-k'an* 中國近代史資料叢刊 (A collection of materials on the history of modern China). 4 vols. Shanghai, 1953.

WHPFTS   *Wu-hsu pien-fa tang-an shih-liao* 戊戌變法檔案史料 (Archival materials on the Reform of 1898). Comp. Kuo-chia tang-an-chü Ming Ch'ing tang-an-kuan 國家檔案局明清檔案館. Peking, Chung-hua shu-chü, 1958.

Notes

NOTES TO PREFACE

1. Marius B. Jansen, *Japan and China: From War to Peace 1894–1975* (Chicago, 1975).
2. Joseph R. Levenson, *Confucian China and Its Modern Fate, A Trilogy* (Berkeley and Los Angeles, 1968), 1, 103.
3. Paul A. Cohen, *Between Tradition and Modernity: Wang T'ao and Reform in Late Ch'ing China* (Cambridge, Mass., 1974), p. 5. The most comprehensive studies of the traditional Chinese concept of the world are in John K. Fairbank, ed., *The Chinese World Order: Traditional China's Foreign Relations* (Cambridge, Mass., 1968).
4. Mary C. Wright, *The Last Stand of Chinese Conservatism: The T'ung-chih Restoration, 1862–1874* (Stanford, 1957).
5. K. C. Liu, "Nineteenth century China: The Disintegration of the Old Order and the Impact of the West," in Ping-ti Ho and Tang Tsou, eds., *China in Crisis,* vol. 1, book 1 (Chicago, 1968); "Cheng Kuan-ying, *I-yen*: Kuang-hsu ch'u-nien chih pien-fa ssu-hsiang," in *Ch'ing-hua hsueh-pao,* new series, 8.1–2:373–425 (August 1970); "The Confucian as Patriot and Pragmatist: Li Hung-chang's Formative Years, 1823–1866," *Harvard Journal of Asiatic Studies* 30: 5–47 (1970); "The Ch'ing Restoration," in John K. Fairbank, ed., *The Cambridge History of China,* vol. 10 (Cambridge, 1978), pp. 409–490.
6. John E. Schrecker, *Imperialism and Chinese Nationalism: Germany in Shantung* (Cambridge, Mass., 1971).
7. Benjamin Schwartz, *In Search of Wealth and Power: Yen Fu and the West* (Cambridge, Mass., 1964).
8. Hao Chang, *Liang Ch'i-ch'ao and Intellectual Transition in China, 1890–1907* (Cambridge, Mass., 1971), pp. 297–298.
9. Daniel H. Bays, *China Enters the Twentieth Century: Chang Chih-tung*

and the Issues of a New Age, 1895–1909 (Ann Arbor, 1978); Yen-p'ing Hao, "Cheng Kuan-ying: The Comprador as Reformer," *Journal of Asian Studies* 29.1: 15–22 (November 1969).

10. Kung-ch'üan Hsiao, *A Modern China and a New World: K'ang Yu-wei, Reformer and Utopian, 1858–1927* (Seattle, 1975), pp. 409–437.

11. P'eng Tse-chou (Hō Takushū), *Chūgoku no kindaika to Meiji ishin* (Kyoto, 1976).

12. Don Price, *Russia and the Roots of the Chinese Revolution* (Cambridge, Mass., 1974), pp. 213, 219.

13. Paul Cohen, *Between Tradition and Modernity*, Chapter 9.

14. On the unemployment of intellectuals, see K. C. Liu, "Nineteenth Century China."

1: HUANG TSUN-HSIEN'S NATIVE HOME

1. Huang Tsun-hsien, "Wu-ch'ing tao-chung tso" (Poem composed when traveling through Wu-ch'ing), *JCLST*, p. 46.

2. Mantaro J. Hashimoto, *The Hakka Dialect: A Linguistic Study of Its Phonology, Syntax, and Lexicon* (Cambridge, 1973). For studies of the history of the Hakka, see Lo Hsiang-lin, *K'o-chia yen-chiu tao-lun* (Kwangtung, 1933); Lin Ch'uan-fang, "Hakka to Chūgoku no kindai," *Ryūkoku shidan* 71: 1–23 (September 1973). Myron Cohen, "The Hakka or 'Guest People': Dialect as a Sociocultural Variable in Southeastern China," *Ethnology* 15.3: 237–292 (summer 1968).

3. For studies of the conflicts between the Hakka and Cantonese speaking groups, see Myron Cohen, "The Hakka or 'Guest People'"; Philip A. Kuhn, "Origins of the Taiping Vision: Cross-Cultural Dimensions of Chinese Rebellion," *Comparative Studies in Society and History* 19.3:350–366 (July 1977).

4. Chia-ying department had 5 constituent districts, of which Chia-ying district was located in the center and was the seat of the *chou* (department) government. It was renamed Mei-hsien in the early Republican era. Huang's home was in Chia-ying district, later Mei-hsien.

    For a history of Chia-ying, see Wen Chung-ho et. al., comp., *Kuang-hsu Chia-ying-chou chih* (1898). For the origins of the Huang family, see Huang Tsun-k'ai, "Hsien-hsiung Kung-tu hsien-sheng shih-shih shu-lueh," in Huang Tsun-hsien, *Jen-ching-lu chi-wai shih chi* (Peking, 1960) p. 119; Wu T'ien-jen, *Huang Kung-tu hsien-sheng chuan kao* (Hong Kong, 1972), pp. 13–14. Wu T'ien-jen bases his accounts on Huang Tsun-hsien, comp., "P'an-kuei-fang Huang-shih chia-p'u" (Genealogy of the Huang family in P'an-kuei-fang), which I have not seen.

5. "Kao-tsu P'u-ch'üan fu-chün shu-lueh" (A brief biography of great-great-grandfather Huang P'u-ch'üan) *JCLST* p. 10.

6. "Kao-tsu-pi Chung t'ai-shu-jen shu-lueh" (A brief biography of great-great-grandmother, née Chung) *JCLST* p. 11.

7. Mai Jo-p'eng, *Huang Tsun-hsien chuan* (Shanghai, 1957), pp. 2–3. Huang Jun was posthumously granted an honorary title because of the merit of his grandson, Huang Tsun-hsien, who served as an official. See *Kuang-hsu Chia-ying-chou chih,* chüan 22, "feng-tseng." The compiler, Wen Chung-ho, was personally acquainted with Huang. See ibid., 32:4b.

8. Huang, "Pai tsung-tsu-mu Li t'ai-fu-jen mu" (Visit to the grave of my great-grandmother, née Li), *JCLST*, pp. 153–157.

9. "Nien-p'u" p. 26, 32. *Kuang-hsu Chia-ying-chou chih,* 23:83b. Huang I-nung, *I-nung pi-chi* (Essays by Huang I-nung), *Ssu-en tsa-chu* (Miscellaneous essays by Huang I-nung), and *T'ui-ssu-wu shih-wen-chi* (Poems and essays by Huang I-nung); these are quoted in *Kuang-hsu Chia-ying-chou chih,* 32:25, 32; 29:33, 54, and in Mai Jo-p'eng, *Huang Tsun-hsien chuan,* p. 3.

10. Y. Y. Huang, "Whether Huang Tsun-hsien engaged a concubine or not while in Japan," a note to the author, 1973.

11. Remarks by Ch'en San-li quoted in Liang Ch'i-ch'ao, *Yin-ping-shih shih-hua* (Shanghai, 1910), 1, 19b–20.

12. Huang, "Pai tsung-tsu-mu Li t'ai-fu-jen mu." Hu Shih stated that this poem was the best in *JCLST.* See Hu Shih, *Wu-shih nien lai Chung-kuo chih wen-hsueh* (1929), p. 48. Huang, "Sung nü-ti" (Farewell to a sister), *JCLST* pp. 10–12.

13. Huang, "Hsin-chia niang shih" (On a new bride), in *Jen-ching-lu chi-wai shih chi* (Peking, 1960), pp. 8–13.

14. Huang, "Shan-ko," in ibid., pp. 16–17.

15. Huang, "Ku-hsiang-ko shih-chi hsu" (Preface to the collection of poems by Yeh Pi-hua, 1900). Printed in Cheng Tzu-yü, ed., *Jen-ching-lu ts'ung k'ao* (Singapore, 1959), pp. 174–175. Yeh Pi-hua was a Hakka woman poet.

16. *Kuang-hsu Chia-ying-chou chih* 31:31–37. Hsieh Kuo-chen, *Chia-ying p'ing-k'ou chih-lueh,* prefaced 1879.

17. Tso Tsung-t'ang, *Tso Wen-hsiang kung ch'üan-chi* (1890), "tsou-kao" 16:49.

18. Huang, "I-ch'ou shih-i yueh pi luan Ta-p'u San-ho hsu" (11th month, 1865, taking refuge at San-ho village of Ta-p'u district), *JCLST,* pp. 4–6.

19. Huang, "Ch'ao-chou hsing" (Going to Ch'ao-chou), *JCLST,* p. 7.

20. Huang, "Pa tzu tsei chung shu so wen" (Extracts of what I overheard from the bandits' conversations), *JCLST,* p. 6.

21. Huang, Letter to Liang Ch'i-ch'ao (10th month 1902), published in *Hsin-min ts'ung-pao* 24:33–35 (January 1903).

22. Huang, "Luan-hou kuei-chia" (Coming home after the turmoil), *JCLST* pp. 8–10.

23. Huang, "Sung nü-ti," *JCLST*, pp. 10–12.

24. Ibid.

25. Lo Hsiang-lin, *K'o-chia yen-chiu tao-lun*, p. 4.

26. Ibid., pp. 5, 27n19.

27. Lin Ta-ch'üan, "K'o-shuo," in Wen T'ing-ching, comp., *Ch'a-yang san-chia wen-ch'ao*; Wen Chung-ho, comp., *Kuang-hsu Chia-ying chou-chih* 7, 84–91, "fang-yen" (dialect).

28. Lo Hsiang-lin, *K'o-chia yen-chiu tao-lun*, pp. 2, 25. In 1900, Chung Yung-ho, a man from Chia-ying, wrote an article "T'u-k'o yuan-liu-k'ao" (Origins of the Punti and Hakka) for a newspaper in Hong Kong in order to refute the author of *Ssu-hui hsien-chih* for his prejudiced treatment of the Hakka. In 1905, two study groups on the origins of Hakka, K'o-chia yuan-liu yen-chiu-hui, and K'o-chia yuan-liu tiao-ch'a-hui, were organized by the Hakka from Chia-ying department.

29. Huang, "Chi-hai tsa-shih" (Miscellaneous poems of 1899), *JCLST*, p. 294.

30. K'ang Yu-wei, preface to *JCLST*, 1910, *JCLST* pp. 2–3. Huang, Letter to Liang, (4th month 1902) printed in Wu T'ien-jen, *Huang Kung-tu hsien-sheng chuan kao* (Hong Kong, 1972), p. 59.

31. Huang, "Mai-shu" (Purchase of books), in *Jen-ching-lu chi-wai-shih chi*, p. 22, describes how difficult it was to pay for books.

32. Huang, "Erh-shih ch'u-tu" (On my twentieth birthday) in ibid., p. 6.

33. Huang took *yuan-shih* (the circuit examination) and became a department student; "Nien-p'u," p. 20. Shang Yen-liu, *Ch'ing tai k'o-chü k'ao-shih shu-lu* (Peking, 1958), p. 4, notes that there was a special quota for Hakka students called *k'o-t'ung* as part of a special quota for ethnic minorities. There is no information about whether or not Huang benefited from this special quota.

34. Huang, "Yu Feng-hu" (My Trip to Lake Feng), *JCLST*, pp. 12–14.

35. K. C. Liu, "Nineteenth Century China" vol. 1, book 1, p. 114.

36. "Nien-p'u," pp. 21–22. Shang Yen-liu, *Ch'ing-tai k'o-chü*, pp. 20, 28–30. Each independent department (*chih-li chou*), of which Chia-ying was one, had a quota of 30 salaried students.

37. Huang, "Chiang ying t'ing-shih kan-huai" (Now I am about to take the court examination), *JCLST*, pp. 43–44.

38. Huang Tsun-hsien, "Keng-wu chung-ch'iu yeh shih-shih Lo Shao-shan yü ai-wu chung, sui chieh Shih-wu kung teng ming-yuan-lou k'an yueh, Shao-shan yu shih tso tz'u chui-ho, shih Kui-yu meng-ch'iu yeh" (On the night of the full-moon of the 8th month of 1870, I met Lo Shao-

shan in the examination hall. In company with Chü-shih, we went up to the top of the tower in front of the examination hall to see the moon. Shao-shan made a poem at the time. Now in the 7th month of 1873, I write this poem in response to Shao-shan's poem), *JCLST*, pp. 33–35.

39. Huang, Letter to Liang Ch'i-ch'ao, 5th month 1902, published in *Hsin-min ts'ung-pao* 13:56–57.

40. Huang, "Kan-huai" (Impressions), *JCLST*, pp. 1–4.

41. Huang, "Tsa-kan" (Impromptu), *JCLST*, pp. 14–18.

42. Liang Ch'i-ch'ao, *Intellectual Trends in the Ch'ing Period*, trans. Immanuel C. Y. Hsu (Cambridge, Mass., 1959), p. 108.

43. Huang, "Mai-shu".

44. Huang, "Pieh sui" (Farewell to the passing year), *Jen-ching-lu chi-wai-shih chi*, p. 68.

45. Huang, "Tsa-kan," *JCLST*, p. 15.

46. Ibid., pp. 15–16. Hu Shih stated that this remark of Huang's could be regarded as a declaration of revolution in poetry; *Wu-shih nien lai Chung-kuo chih wen-hsueh*, p. 42.

47. Mantaro J. Hashimoto, *The Hakka Dialect*, p. 2.

48. Huang, "Kan-huai," *JCLST*, p. 3.

49. Ibid., p. 4.

50. Ch'en Li, *Tung-shu tu-shu-chi* (prefaced 1871, Shanghai, 1930), preface, pp. 1–2.

51. Han-yin Chen Shen, "Tsung Kuo-fan in Peking, 1840–1852: His Ideas on Statecraft and Reform," *Journal of Asian Studies* 27.1:69, 78–79 (1967).

52. Huang, Letter to Liang Ch'i-ch'ao, 10th month 1902, published in *Hsin-min ts'ung-pao* 24:33 (January 1903). Interview with Huang Yen-yü, on December 30, 1969.

53. Huang, Letter to Liang Ch'i-ch'ao, 4th month 1902, in Wu T'ien-jen, *Huang Kung-tu*, p. 59.

54. Huang, "Hsiang-kang kan-huai shih-shou" (Ten verses on impressions of Hong Kong), *JCLST*, pp. 22–26.

55. Huang, "Kan Huai," *JCLST*, p. 1.

56. Huang, "Ho Chou Lang-shan chien tseng chih tso" (Response to poem presented by Chou Lang-shan), *JCLST*, p. 29.

57. Huang, "Yang-ch'eng kan-fu liu-shou" (Six verses on Canton), *JCLST*, pp. 36–39.

58. "Nien-p'u," p. 21. For early publications on the West, see Tsuen-hsuin Tsien, "Western Impact on China through Translation," *Far Eastern Quarterly* 13.3:305–327 (May 1924).

59. Huang, "Wu-ch'ing tao-chung tso" (A poem composed when traveling through Wu-ch'ing) *JCLST*, pp. 45–46.

60. Ho Ping-ti, "Chang Yin-huan shih-chi" *Ch'ing-hua hsueh-pao* 13.1:188 (1941); Fang Chao-ying, "Chang Yin-huan" in Arthur Hummel, ed., *Eminent Chinese of the Ch'ing period*, pp. 60–61; Chang Ch'i-yun et al., comps., *Ch'ing-shih*, chüan 443, pp. 4928–4929.

61. Huang, "Li Su-i hou wan-shih ssu-shou" (Four verses in memory of Li Hung-chang), *JCLST*, pp. 379–381.

62. Huang, "Yu lun-chou ti T'ien-ching tso" (Arriving at Tientsin by boat), *JCLST*, pp. 44–45. *Chuang-tzu*, "Ch'iu-shui" chapter.

63. Huang, "Shui-pin" (On the coast), *JCLST*, p. 45.

64. Huang, "Ta-yü ssu-shou" (Four verses on the Margary affair), *JCLST*, pp. 67–69; Shimada Kumiko, *Kō Junken* (Tokyo, 1963), pp. 49–51.

65. Immanuel C. Y. Hsu, *China's Entrance into the Family of Nations* (Cambridge, Mass., 1960), pp. 176–179; Lloyd E. Eastman, *Throne and Mandarins* (Cambridge, Mass., 1967), pp. 26–27.

66. Huang, "Ta-yü ssu-shou."

67. Hsueh Fu-ch'eng, *Ch'ou-yang tsou-i* (1897) in his *Yung-an ch'üan-chi* (Shanghai, 1897), 20b.

68. Liu Kuang-ching, "Cheng Kuan-ying: *I-yen*" p. 420.

69. "Nien-p'u" p. 63; Chao Erh-hsun et al., comps., *Ch'ing-shih kao* 470, 2b-3; Hsu Ta-ling, *Ch'ing-tai chüan-na chih-tu* (Peking, 1950), pp. 80–81, and attached chart.

70. K. C. Liu, "Nineteenth Century China," pp. 114–116.

71. "Nien-p'u," p. 24.

72. Ibid., pp. 23–24.

73. Immanuel C. Y. Hsu, *China's Entrance into the Family of Nations*, p. 181.

74. Liu Chin-tsao, comp., *Ch'ing-ch'ao hsu wen-hsien t'ung-k'ao* (Shanghai, 1936), chüan 142, "Chih-kuan" p. 9029.

75. *Ch'ing-ch'ao hsu wen-hsien t'ung-k'ao*, chüan 337, "Tsungli Yamen," p. 10785. *Ta-Ch'ing hui-tien shih-li*, 1899, chüan, 1220.

76. The amount of the expenses aside from the salaries was not fixed in the beginning. In 1875, because of lack of precedent, a decision was made that those expenses were to be paid according to need. Later, in 1905, a quota for an annual allowance of official expenditures was fixed for each overseas legation: the Legation in England 38,000 taels; France 30,000 taels; Germany 26,000 taels; Russia 30,000 taels; United States 28,000 taels; Japan 25,000 taels. See *Ch'ing-ch'ao hsu wen-hsien t'ung-k'ao*, chüan 141, "Chih-kuan," p. 9015. For a study using National Palace archives in Taipei, see Chuang Chi-fa, "Ch'ing-chi ch'u-shih ching-fei te ch'ou-ts'o," *Ta-lu tsa-chih* 55.2:25–33 (August 1977).

77. T'ung-tsu Ch'ü, *Local Government in China under the Ch'ing* (Cambridge, Mass., 1962), pp. 22-23, 112.
78. Note by Y. Y. Huang, 1973.
79. Huang, "Ho Chou Lan-shan chien tseng chih tso"; "Kan-huai."
80. Huang, "Yu ch'i nei-tzu" (To my wife), *JCLST,* p. 70. Azuma Bridge was built in 1874 over the River Sumida, Tokyo. "Azuma" means my wife.

2: DISCOVERY OF JAPAN: THE EASTERN FRONTIER OF THE CHINESE WORLD

1. Banno Masataka has pointed out that Japan was not listed as a tributary state but as one of the countries that had trade relations with China in the *Chia-ch'ing hui-tien* 1818 edition. Banno, *Kindai Chūgoku seiji gaikōshi,* (Tokyo, 1973), p. 372.
2. For biographies of Ho Ju-chang, see Chao Erh-hsuan et al., comps., *Ch'ing-shih-kao* (Shanghai, 1942), chüan 450; Chang Ch'i-yun et al., comps., *Ch'ing-shih* (Taipei, 1961), 6, 4937; Wen T'ing-ching, "Ch'ing chan-shih-fu shao-chan Ho kung chuan," in his *Ch'a-yang san-chia wen-ch'ao* (1925); Li Yü-shu, "Shou-jen chu-Jih kung-shih Ho Ju-chang," in Shen Chin-ting et al., eds., *Pai-nien-lai Chung-Jih kuan-hsi lun-wen chi* (Taipei, 1968), pp. 1073-1074.
3. *Tokio Times* (December 15, 1877). A clipping enclosed in despatch no. 691 from John A. Bingham, U.S. Minister in Tokyo, to Secretary of State, December 17, 1877, in "File Microcopies of Records in the National Archives: No. 133. Despatches from United States Minister to Japan" (Washington, 1949), vol. 35; Wing Yung, *My Life in China and America,* as translated by Momose Hiromu (Tokyo, 1969), Chapter 13, p. 124, notes that "Chang Shih-kuei" in the original was Chang Ssu-kuei who was then private secretary of Tseng Kuo-fan. For Chang's preface to the Japanese translation of the *Wan-kuo kung-fa,* see *Kamban bankoku kōhō* (Tokyo, 1865).
4. For the regulations governing the overseas legation, see *Ch'ing-ch'ao hsu wen-hsien t'ung-k'ao,* chüan 337, p. 10785.
5. For the list of personnel in the legation, see pp. 269-271. See also, Sanetō Keishū, *Ōkōchi monjo: Meiji Nitchū bunkajin no kōyū* (Tokyo, 1964), pp. 12-13; Ōkōchi, "Chi-mao pi-hua" (Conversations in 1879), book 15, December 5, 1879, held at Daitō Bunka Daigaku, Tokyo; Liang Chü-shih, *Liang Shih-wu hsien-sheng i-kao chi* (1960).
6. Alexander Wyle, *Memorials of the Protestant Missionaries to the Chinese* (Shanghai, 1867; Taipei reprint, 1967), pp. 135-139; Ozawa

Saburō, "Kaisei gakkō oyatoi kyōshi D. B. McCartee," *Meiji bunka* 14.12:3–4 (December 1941); "Despatches from the United States Minister to Japan," vol. 42, no. 1120 (May 20, 1880). McCartee translated into Japanese some Christian tracts which had been published in China. He himself authored tracts in Chinese: copies of *Chen-li i-chih*, and "Ling-hun pien" in *Ch'üan-shan liang-yen* are held at Harvard-Yenching library, Cambridge, Mass. For his Japanese translation of Chinese tracts, see Kokusai Kirisutokyō Daigaku, Ajia Bunka Kenkyū Iinkai, comp., *Nihon kirisutokyō bunken mokuroku*, vol. 2 (Tokyo, 1965).

7. Ho Ju-chang, "Shih-tung shu-lueh" (Brief records of mission to Japan), in *Hsiao-fang-hu-chai yü-ti ts'ung-ch'ao* (Shanghai, 1877–1897), 10, 275–275b.

8. Ho Ju-chang, "Shih-tung shu-lueh," pp. 275–277; *JPTSS* (1880), 1, 11b.

9. Ho Ju-chang, "Shih-tung shu-lueh," p. 278b.

10. Kanda Suematsu for Bōekikyoku, *Hanshin zairyū no Kashō to sono bōeki jijō*, (Overseas Chinese in the Osaka-Kobe area and their trade, 1938), p. 141.

11. Sanetō, *Ōkōchi monjo*, p. 145.

12. Kinoshita Hyō, *Meiji shiwa* (Tokyo, 1943), pp. 160–161.

13. Kinoshita, *Meiji shiwa*, pp. 355–356. For the popularity of classical Chinese literature, see also Makino Kenjirō, *Nihon kangaku shi* (Tokyo, 1943), pp. 229–237.

14. Huang, "Pu-jen-ch'ih wan-yu shih" (Poem on strolling around Lake Shinobazu in the evening), *JCLST*, pp. 79–80; *JPTSS* (1880), 2, 4–4b.

15. *PTIK*, introduction. The original records of conversations are now held at Waseda University Library and Daitō Bunka Daigaku, Tokyo.

16. Ōkōchi Teruna, preface to Ishikawa Kōsai, ed., *Shibayama isshō* (Tokyo, 1878).

17. Sanetō, *Ōkōchi monjo*, pp. 16, 34, 42.

18. Ibid., pp. 75, 86.

19. *PTIK*, pp. 29–35, 290.

20. Kawade Shobō Shinsha, publ., *Nihon rekishi daijiten* (Tokyo, 1968), 5, 274; Jiro Numata, "Shigeno Yasutsugu and the Modern Tokyo Tradition of Historical Writing," in W. G. Beardsley and E. G. Pulleyblank, eds., *Historians of China and Japan* (London, 1961), pp. 264–287; Nishimura Toshihiko, "Seisai sensei gyōjō shiryō," in *Shigeno hakushi shigaku rombunshū* (Tokyo, 1938), 1, 41.

21. Nagai Hideo, *Jiyū minken*, in *Nihon no rekishi* vol. 25 (Tokyo, 1976), p. 29.

22. Huang, "Hsu huai-jen shih" (Reminiscence of people, continued), *JCLST*, p. 209.

23. For Oka's comments on Huang, see Oka Senjin, *Zōmei sambō bun shoshū* (Tokyo, 1920), 2, 21b-23; 6, 10-11. His conversations with Huang, *PTIK*, pp. 315-326, and in Oka, *Kankō kiyū* (Tokyo, 1886), 3, 5b. His view of the contemporary Confucian studies, *Zōmei sambō bun shoshū*, 6, 11. His view of the Meiji Restoration, *Sonjō kiji* (Tokyo, 1882). Huang's letters to Oka are said to be kept by the Oka family. See, Sanetō Keishū, *Meiji Nisshi bunka kōshō* (Tokyo, 1943), p. 77.

24. Gamō Shigeaki, "Nihon-tamashii jo" (On the Japanese spirit), in Sata Hakubō, comp., *Meiji shibun* (Tokyo, 1877-1879), 24 *shū*.

25. Fuse Chisoku, *Yūki ni arawaretaru Meiji jidai no Nisshi ōrai* (Tokyo, 1938), p. 2. For Huang's poem on Ishikawa, see *JCLST*, pp. 76-78.

26. *PTIK*, p. 279; Kikuchi Takesada, preface to Kametani Kō, *Seiken shibun kō*, (Tokyo, 1902).

27. *JPTSS* (1880), 1, 37-37b.

28. Kanda Kiichirō, *Nihon ni okeru Chūgoku bungaku* (Tokyo, 1965), 1, 302, 317-320; Huang "Hsu huai-jen shih," *JCLST*, p. 208.

29. Dōjinsha, *Dōjinsha bungaku zasshi*, no. 34 (August 2, 1879), no. 41 (May 20, 1880), no. 53 (May 20, 1881), no. 62 (October 10, 1881), no. 68 (January 15, 1882) and no. 82 (September 10, 1882).

30. Wang Chung-hou, "Huang Kung-tu shih-ts'ao sai-i chu i-wen," in Cheng Tzu-yü, ed., *Jen-ching-lu ts'ung-k'ao*, p. 162.

31. Kawade Shobō Shinsha, publ., *Nihon rekishi jiten*, 3, 48-49.

32. Huang, "Hsu huai-jen-shih," *JCLST*, p. 207; *JPTSS* (1880), 1, 34. *PTIK*, pp. 34, 54, 221; Sanetō, *Ōkōchi monjo*, pp. 190-193.

33. Sin Kok-ju (Shin Kuk Ju), *Kindai Chōsen gaikōshi kenkyū* (Tokyo, 1966), pp. 114-118.

34. *JCLST*, pp. 81, 201.

35. *PTIK*, 314, 323; Ishihata Tei, *Kōshin nikki*, is cited in *Dai Nihon gaikō bunsho*, vol. 4.

36. Narahara Nobumasa, "Ryūgaku ryakki," (Sketch of study abroad) in his *Uiki tsūsan* (Tokyo, 1888), vol. 1; Tanaka Masatoshi, *"Uiki tsūsan to saikō nikki,"* in *Iwai hakushi koki tenseki kinen ronshū* (Tokyo, 1963); Tanaka Masatoshi, "Meiji shoki no kyōiku to Narahara Nobumasa, Narahara Nobumasa denkō danshō" (Early Meiji education and Narahara Nobumasa: A brief chapter of a biography of Narahara Nobumasa), in Nohara Shirō et al., eds., *Kindai Nihon ni okeru rekishigaku no hattatsu* (Tokyo, 1976), pp. 166-182.

37. Tai Shi kōrōsha denki hensankai, *Tai Shi kaiko roku* (Tokyo, 1936), 2, 1408. *Zoku tai Shi kaiko roku* (Tokyo, 1941), 2, 1309-1315.

38. *Zoku tai Shi kaiko roku*, 2, 198-205. Kuzuu Yoshihisa, comp., *Tōa senkaku shishi kiden* (Tokyo, 1936), 2, 212-303; *PTIK*, pp. 245-246.

39. *Dai ikkai Nihon teikoku tōkei nenkan* (Tokyo, 1882), pp. 10–11; Koizuka Ryū, *Yokohama kaikō gojūnen shi* (Yokohama, 1909), 2: 94, 536, 651–652; Yokohama Shiyakusho, *Yokohama-shi shi kō* (Yokohama, 1932), pp. 346–347; Yen-p'ing Hao, *The Comprador in Nineteenth Century China: Bridge between East and West* (Cambridge, Mass., 1970), pp. 54–63.

40. For the problems of the Chinatown in Yokohama, see Usui Katsumi, "Yokohama kyoryūchi no Chūgokujin," in *Yokohama-shi shi,* vol. 3b (Yokohama, 1963).

41. On the tablet of Mimeguri jinja, see the note by Toyota and Sanetō in *Nihon zatsuji shi* (Tokyo, 1943), p. 236. For Ch'en Yü-ch'ih, see Uchida Naosaku, *Nihon kakyō shakai no kenkyū* (Tokyo, 1949), p. 218. On communication between Chinese in Yokohama and the diplomats, see Ōkōchi, "Wu-yin pi-hua" (Conversations in 1878), 1878/3/26, 3/31, 5/11, and 10/19.

42. *JPTSS* (1880), 2, 30. In the 1898 edition, Huang noted other Chinese works on Japan published during the Ming period, *Jih-pen k'ao* and *Jih-pen feng-t'u chi.*

43. *JPKC,* preface, 3b–4.

44. Chou Huang, *Liu-ch'iu-kuo chih-lueh* (Taipei, 1968), facsimile reproduction of 1757 edition. See also Wang Chung-hou, "Huang Kung-tu shih-ts'ao wai-i-chu i-wen," pp. 159–160.

45. *JPKC,* "fan-li"

46. *JPTSS* (1898), preface, p. 1.

47. *JPTSS* (1880), 1, 33.

48. *JPTSS* (1880), 2, 30–30b.

49. Huang's preface to the 1885 edition of *JPTSS* is translated in Toyota and Sanetō, *Nihon zatsuji shi* (Tokyo, 1943, 1968), p. 1.

50. Chou Tso-jen, Kiyama Hideo, tr., *Nihon bunka o kataru* (Tokyo, 1973), pp. 219–220.

51. Conversation between Wang Chih-pen and Ishikawa Kōsai on June 5, 1881, in Ōkōchi, "Ch'i-yuan pi-hua" (Conversation with Wang Chih-pen), 1881/6/5.

52. Huang's preface to 1885 edition of *JPTSS.* See note 49 above.

53. Sanetō, *Ōkōchi monjo,* pp. 229–231. A photographic copy of the tablet is printed in Sanetō, *Nihon zatsuji shi* (Tokyo, 1968).

54. Huang, preface to 1885 edition of *JPTSS.* See note 49 above.

55. On Wang's visit to Japan and his association with Huang, see Cohen, *Between Tradition and Modernity* pp. 100–102, 297–298 n 30. According to an account of Cheng Hsien (pseudonym of Huang Yen-tsuan, a grandson of Huang Tsun-hsien), Huang persuaded Li Hung-chang

through a telegram to pardon Wang T'ao who had been in exile in Hong Kong because of the suspicion that he had collaborated with the Tai-pings. As a result of Huang's good offices, Wang T'ao was enabled to return to Shanghai. Otherwise, Cheng Hsien states, Huang would not have dared to let Wang T'ao publish his *Miscellaneous Poems*. Cheng Hsien, "Huang Kung-tu: Wu-hsu wei-hsin yun-tung te ling-hsiu," p. 21.

56. *JPTSS* (1898), postscript.
57. *JPTSS* (1880), 2, 30; *PTIK*, p. 284.
58. "Nien-p'u," p. 38.
59. For various editions of the *JPKC*, see Satō Saburō, "Meiji ishin igo Nisshin sensō izen ni okeru Shinajin no Nihon kenkyū", *Rekishigaku kenkyū* 10.11:86n20 (November 1940); Ishihara Michihiro, "*Nihon kokushi* to *Azuma kagami ho*," *Rekishigaku kenkyū* 8.12:62 (December (1938); Wu T'ien-jen, *Huang Kung-tu hsien-sheng chuan kao*, pp. 305–307.
60. Preface to 1885 edition of *JPTSS*. See note 49 above.
61. Tai Ch'uan-hsien (Chi-t'ao), *Jih-pen lun* (Shanghai, 1928), p. 1.
62. Chou Tso-jen, Kiyama Hideo, trans., *Nihon bunka o kataru*, pp. 35, 219, 253.
63. Takeuchi Yoshimi, "Tai Kitō no Nihon ron," (A discussion of Japan by Tai Chi-t'ao), in Tai Chi-t'ao, Ichikawa Hiroshi, trans., *Nihon ron* (Tokyo, 1972), pp. 244–245.
64. I owe the expression "cultural province of China" to Paul Cohen, *Between Tradition and Modernity*, p. 99.
65. *JPTSS* (1880), 2, 10.
66. Ibid., 1, 5–5b.
67. *JPTSS* (1880), 1, 2b–3, *JPKC*, 1, 3b. Fan Yeh, comp., *Hou Han shu*, chüan 115, "Tung-i" (Shanghai, 1927). Wei T'ing-sheng, *Hsu Fu yü Jih-pen* (Hong Kong, 1953) is an attempt by a Chinese scholar to appraise the legend of Hsu Fu. For a report on the sites of Hsu Fu, see Takeuchi Minoru, *Kikō Nihon no naka no Chūgoku* (Tokyo, 1976), pp. 3–24. As to the statement in *Liang shu* (chüan 54), that the Japanese regarded themselves as the descendants of T'ai Po (the legendary founder of the State of Wu during the Chou), Huang thought it was groundless.
68. *JCKC*, 37, 10b–11. A study by a Japanese scholar suggests the connection between religious Taoism and imperial regalia. See Fukunaga Mitsuji, "Dōkyō ni okeru kagami to tsurugi, sono shisō no genryū," *Tōhō gakuhō* 45:59–120 (1973).
69. Ueda Masaaki, "Kodai no saishi to girei," in *Iwanami kōza Nihon rekishi* (Tokyo, 1975), 1, 323–357; H. Byron Earhart, *Japanese*

Religion: Unity and Diversity (Encino, California, 1974), pp. 17–20.

70. *JPKC*, 32:3–7b. Huang's letter to Liang Ch'i-ch'ao, in the 8th lunar month of 1902, published in the *Hsin-min ts'ung-pao* 20:5 (July 1902) and printed in *Liang nien-p'u*, p. 161.

71. *JPTSS* (1880) 2, 8b–10.

72. Ibid., 2, 8b–9. Francis L. K. Hsu, *Iemoto: The Heart of Japan* (New York, 1975), p. 123.

73. *JPTSS* (1880), 2, 10b–11b.

74. Ibid., 2, 20.

75. Ibid., 2, 4.

76. Ibid., 2, 15–16; *JPTSS* (1898), 2, 8b. For a description of women entertainers on stage (*onna gidayū*), Huang adapted a chapter from Terakado Seiken, *Edo hanjō ki* (Edo, 1832–1836). See Toyota and Sanetō, *Nihon zatsuji shi*, pp. 218–219.

77. Chou Tso-jen, "Jih-pen kuan-k'ui," (Impressions of Japan), Japanese trans. in Kiyama Hideo, *Nihon bunka o kataru*, p. 21.

78. *JPKC*, 33, 1–5.

79. Huang obviously did not see all the books and made some mistakes in identifying their authors. It appears that he was not interested in Japanese scholars' interpretations of Confucianism; *JPKC*, 32, 3–15b. For Huang's mistakes, see Toyota and Sanetō, *Nihon zatsuji shi*, p. 143.

80. *JPTSS* (1880), 1, 31–32b.

81. For a discussion of pragmatic motivation in Confucianism, see Hao Chang, *Liang Ch'i-ch'ao and Intellectual Transition in China*, pp. 7–9.

82. *JPKC*, 32, 14b.

83. Ibid., 32, 14b.

84. Ibid., 32, 14b–15. Huang's message in his criticism of Japanese Confucianism (not being practical) was obviously directed against scholars in China. For a discussion of status and roles of Confucian scholars in Tokugawa Japan, see John W. Hall, "The Confucian Teacher in Tokugawa Japan," in David S. Nivison and Arthur F. Wright, eds., *Confucianism in Action* (Stanford, 1959), pp. 268–301.

85. *JPKC*, 37, 15–15b.

86. *JPTSS* (1880), 1, 21b.

87. Ibid., 1, 29–30. For a biography of Chu Shun-shui, see Ishihara Michihiro, *Shu Shunsui* (Tokyo, 1961).

88. For recent studies of the Mito School, see introductions in Imai Usaburō et al., eds., *Mitogaku* (Tokyo, 1973).

89. For discussions of Rai between Huang and the Japanese, see *PTIK*, p. 32. *Nihon gaishi* was printed in Canton (1875) and in Shanghai (1880).

See Haga Noboru, *Hihan kindai Nihon shigaku shisō shi* (Tokyo, 1974), p. 47. For a critical survey of *Nihon gaishi*, see Uete Michiari, ed., *Rai San'yō*, (Tokyo, 1977), pp. 653–668.

90. *JPTSS* (1880), 1, 11b.
91. Huang, "Chin-shih ai-kuo chih-shih ko" (Patriotic heroes in the modern age), *JCLST*, pp. 97–103.
92. Huang, "Hsi-hsiang hsing ko" (Saigō star), *JCLST*, pp. 72–76.
93. *Shimbun zasshi* 41:8 (April 1872). Numerous books have been written on the 47 by historians who attempted to clarify the causes of the incident. For a critical survey of historiography of *Chushingura*, see Matsushima Eiichi, *Chūshingura, sono seiritsu to tenkai* (Tokyo, 1964). See also, Donald Keene, *Chushingura: The Treasury of Loyal Retainers* (New York and London, 1971).
94. Huang, "Ch'ih-sui ssu-shih-ch'i i-shih-ko" (Poem on the 47 righteous samurai of Akō), *JCLST*, pp. 104–109. Aoyama Nobumitsu, *Akō shijū-shichi shi den* (prefaced 1829). Donald Keene has pointed out that there was a Chinese translation of the story published in 1794. He suggests that it was perhaps the earliest translation of Japanese literature; Keene, *Chushingura*, p. 25.
95. Huang, "Wu chih chu ko" (Poem on Wu-chu), *JCLST*, pp. 52–55.
96. Huang, "T'ien Heng tao" (The island of T'ien Heng), *JCLST*, p. 55.
97. *JPKC*, 3, 16–16b.
98. Liang Ch'i-ch'ao, *Chung-kuo chih wu-shih-tao* (Shanghai, 1904).

3: WESTERNIZATION IN EARLY MEIJI JAPAN

1. *JPTSS* (1880), 1, 6.
2. Hattori Bushō, *Tōkyō shin hanjō ki*, in *Meiji bungaku zenshū* (Tokyo, 1969), vol. 4.
3. Huang adapted some stories from Terakado Seiken, *Edo hanjō ki* (1832–1836) which was the model for the *Tōkyō shin hanjō ki*. Ōkōchi Teruna presented a copy of *Edo hangō ki* to Shen Wen-ying of the Chinese Legation; Sanetō, *Ōkōchi monjo*, p. 29.
4. *JPTSS* (1880), 2, 18–18b.
5. *JPTSS* (1880), 2, 24b–25. Edward S. Morse recorded similar impressions on the rickshaw; see *Japan Day by Day, 1877, 1878–79, 1882–83* (Boston, 1917), 1, 105.
6. *JPTSS* (1880), 2, 13. Huang had had his picture taken in China when he was about to leave for Japan, and wrote a poem about it. See *JCLST*, p. 70.
7. *JPTSS* (1880), 1, 17–17b.

8. Ibid., 2, 7b.
9. Ibid., 2, 5.
10. Ibid., 1, 13-14.
11. Ibid., 1, 17b-18.
12. Ibid., 1, 18-18b.
13. *JPKC*, chüan 15-20. In the "Treatise on Food and Money" Huang discussed population, taxation, the national budget, government bonds, currency, and foreign trade. On agricultural products and manufactured products he wrote separate treatises.
14. *JPTSS* (1880), 1, 15-16; 2, 7b. These points were amplified in *JPKC*, 15, 14; 20, 4b-6.
15. Kondō Tetsuo, "Shokusan kōgyō to zairai sangyō," pp. 232, 243-244; Unno Fukuju, "Matsukata zaisei to jinushisei no keisei," *Iwanami kōza Nihon rekishi* (Tokyo, 1976), pp. 15, 96-99.
16. *JPTSS* (1880), 2, 23b.
17. For the quantity of transactions handled by foreign traders, see"Yushutsunyū buppin kakaku naigaishō betsu," in *Dai ikkai Nihon teikoku tōkei nenkan* (Tokyo, 1882), p. 296. For contemporary discussions of the foreign domination of overseas trade, see Koizuka Ryū, *Yokohama kaikō gojūnen shi* (Yokohama, 1909), 1, 483; 2, 536, 650-652.
18. *JPKC*, 20, 28-28b.
19. *JPKC*, 20, 28b-29.
20. *JPCS*, 19, 11-12b. The quotation is from "Hsiao-ya," book 5., trans. James Legge, *Chinese Classics IV: The Sheking* (Hong Kong, 1960), p. 338.
21. Kondō Tetsuo, "Shokusan kōgyō to zairai sangyō," pp. 212-219, 239-241. For authoritative studies of the financial situation during the Meiji period, see Sawada Akira, *Meiji zaisei no kisoteki kenkyū* (Tokyo, 1934); Fujita Takeo, *Nihon shihonshugi to zaisei* (Tokyo, 1949), vol. 1.
22. *JPTSS* (1880), 1, 14-16; *JPKC*, 16, 1-19. Since the late Meiji era, salt has become an item of government monopoly. For the estimate of land tax in China, see Yeh-chien Wang, *Land Taxation in Imperial China, 1750-1911* (Cambridge, Mass., 1973), p. 128.
23. *JPKC*, 16, 19b-20b.
24. *JPTSS* (1880), 2, 25-28b.
25. In the 1870s the Japanese used the term *kōgei* (*kung-i* in Chinese, which meant handicraft arts) for modern industry. It is reported that when the Iwakura mission returned from the West in 1873, one of its members proposed that "in the age of enlightenment and civilization, the use of iron and coal must be promoted" and that it was a great mistake to identify industry (*kōgei*) with ceramics, copper ware, lacquer ware,

or the like. Kondō, "Shokusan kōgyō to zairai sangyō," p. 229.

For a study of Japanese industrialization in early Meiji Japan, see Ishizuka Hiromichi, *Nihon shihonshugi seiritsu shi kenkyū: Meiji kokka to shokusan kōgyō seisaku* (Tokyo, 1973).

26. Ohkawa and Rosovsky, "A Century of Japanese Economic Growth," in William W. Lockwood, ed., *The State and Economic Enterprise in Japan* (Princeton, 1965), pp. 53–59.

27. *JPTSS* (1880), 2, 13b–14.

28. *JPKC*, 21, 11–12. For studies of the introduction of the conscription system, see Iwai Tadakuma, "Gunji keisatsu kikō no kakuritsu," *Iwanami kōza Nihon rekishi*, 15, 185–186; Matsushita Yoshio, *Meiji gunsei shi ron* (Tokyo, 1956), 1, 268–272.

29. *JPKC*, 21, 12–20; 22, 11; 22, 13–15; 23, 3–12; 24, 2–16.

30. Koyama Hirotake, *Nihon gunji kōgyō no shiteki bunseki* (Tokyo, 1972), p. 84.

31. *JPKC*, 25, 9.

32. The *Fusō* (3,717 tons) was an iron corvette; the *Kongō* and *Hiei* (both 2,248 tons) were composite cruisers. For naval development in early Meiji Japan, see Kaigunshō, Kaigun Daijin Kambō, comp., *Kaigun gumbi enkaku* (Tokyo, 1934; reprint, 1970), pp. 12–19, and its appendix, pp. 8–13; Matsushita Yoshio, *Meiji gunsei shi ron*, 2, 198–199.

33. *JPKC*, 25, 10. For comparison of the Chinese and Japanese naval forces, see John L. Rawlinson, *China's Struggle for Naval Development, 1839–1895* (Cambridge, Mass., 1967), pp. 168–169; Matsushita, *Meiji gunsei shi ron*, 2, 207; Satō Ichirō, *Kaigun gojūnen shi* (Tokyo, 1943), pp. 127–128.

34. *JPKC*, 26, 8b–9.

35. *JPKC*, 7, 19b–21b. See also a letter from Ho Ju-chang to Liu K'un-i, in Wen T'ing-ching, *Ch'a-yang san-chia wen-ch'ao*, 3, 9–11. It was undoubtedly drafted by Huang; it is identical to Huang's discussion in *JPKC*, 7, 19b–20.

36. *JPKC* (1898), 7, 18b; 8, 28b.

37. *JPKC*, chüan 27–31. I could not find out how Huang acquired the Chinese translation of the criminal codes and the commentaries.

On *chizaihō* and *keihō*, see Kobayakawa Kingo, *Meiji hōsei shi ron: kōhō no bu* (Tokyo, 1940), 2, 999–1026; Ishii Ryōsuke, *Nihon hōsei shi* (Tokyo, 1959), pp. 101–102; Murata Tamotsu, *Keihō chūshaku*. The *chizaihō* and *keihō* were published in the *Dajōkan fukoku*, no. 37 (July 17, 1880).

It was for the purpose of providing a practical reference for legal reform in China that Huang cited the entire texts of the codes. In China, however, government efforts toward revision of the legal system did not begin until after the turn of the century. Shen Chia-pen was appointed to head the committee for the revision of the laws in 1904, which presented a draft criminal code in 1907. Chang Chih-tung recommended the policy of using the Japanese law as a model and of inviting Japanese advisors to reform the Chinese criminal code. As a result, Okada Asatarō, a law professor of Tokyo Imperial University, was invited in 1905. Long before that, in 1890, the Japanese government had promulgated a new criminal code, outdating the laws that had been cited in Huang's *Treatises*. It is not certain whether Huang's early efforts to provide a reference for reform of the criminal code had any impact on the creation of a modern legal system in China. For legal reform, see Marinus J. Meijer, *The Introduction of the Modern Criminal Law in China* (Batavia, 1949), p. 94; Shimada Masao, "Shimmatsu ni okeru keiritsu sōan no hensan ni tsuite, Okada Asatarō hakushi no gyōseki o shinonde," *Hōritsu ronsō* 39.1:2-3, reprinted in *Chūgoku kankei ronsetsu shiryō* 4.3:498-516 (1965).

38. *JPTSS* (1880), 1, 20b-21b.

39. Ibid., 1, 18b.

40. Ibid., 1, 18.

41. Ibid., 1, 6.

42. Ibid., 1, 12-13.

43. *JPKC*, chüan 13. In 1880, average wage per day of an artisan or skilled worker was 0.4 yen, and that of a farmer was 0.2 yen. (Tōkeiin, *Dai nikai Nihon teikoku tōkei nenkan*, pp. 141-146.) The price of rice per *koku* (5 bushels) was about 10 yen at the time.

44. *JPKC*, 14, 34-35b.

45. Japanese versions of *Esprit de loi* were published in 1875 under the title of *Bampō seiri*, translated by Ka Reishi, and under the title of *Ritsurei seigi*, translated by Suzuki Yuiichi. *Le contrat social*, translated by Hattori Atsushi, was published in 1877 under the title of *Min'yaku ron*. See Tokyo Daigaku Bungakubu, Bunka Kōryū Kenkyū Shisetsu Nihon Bunka Kādo Shōiinkai, comp., "Ji Keiō 4 nen shi Meiji 23 nen hon'yakusho mokuroku dai ichiji miteikō" (Tokyo, 1968), mimeographed, pp. 31, 33, 60.

46. For the most succinct and analytical account of the People's Rights movement, see Maruyama Masao, "Jiyū minken undō shi" (1948). For Japanese images of the United States, see Shunsuke Kamei, "The Sacred Land of Liberty: Images of America in Nineteenth Century Japan," in Akira Iriye, ed., *Mutual Images: Essays in American-Japanese Relations* (Cambridge, Mass., 1975).

47. *JPTSS* (1880), 1, 3-3b.
48. *PTIK*, p. 232. The conversation took place on November 16, 1878.
49. *Dōjinsha bungaku zasshi* 76:9-11 (May 10, 1882).
50. Huang, letter to Liang Ch'i-ch'ao, 5th month 1902, published in the *Hsin-min ts'ung-pao* 13:55-56 (August 1902).
51. *JPKC*, 3, 17.
52. *JPKC*, 3, 17-17b.
53. Ibid.
54. For the development of the institutions of local government, see Kikegawa Hiroshi, *Meiji chihō jichi seido no seiritsu katei* (Tokyo, 1955).
55. *JPTSS* (1880), 1, 13-13b.
56. *JPKC*, 14, 35. These comments were printed in small type at the end of the text. They were probably inserted after the printing began at the Fu-wen-chai Press, Canton, in 1890.
57. *JPKC*, 32, 20b.
58. Huang, letter to Liang Ch'i-ch'ao, 5th month 1902, published in the *Hsin-min ts'ung-pao,* no. 13.
59. *JPKC*, 40, 1b.
60. *JPKC*, 3, 1-1b.
61. *JPTSS* (1898), preface.
62. *JPKC* (1898), 3, 7b.
63. For the development of the People's Rights movement, see Gotō Yasushi, *Jiyū minken undō no tenkai,* 1966; Tōyama Shigeki, *Nihon kindai shi,* 1975, vol. 1, chap. 1.
64. *JPTSS* (1880), 1, 18b.
65. *JPTSS* (1880), 1, 6b-7. Later, Huang recognized the superiority of the Western calendar. See, *JPKC,* 9, 6b-7.
66. *JPTSS* (1880), 1, 29b-30.
67. *JPTSS* (1880), 1, 19. *JPKC,* 32, 21-22.
68. Joseph Needham, *Science and Civilization in China,* vol. 2, *History of Scientific Thought* (Cambridge, 1956), pp. 177, 183-184; vol. 4, pt. 1, *Physics and Physical Technology* (Cambridge, 1962), pp. 17-28, 81-86; vol. 1, *Introductory Orientations* (Cambridge, 1954), p. 239.
69. *JPTSS* (1880), 1, 19. *JPKC,* 32, 21b.
70. Shimada Kenji, "Shinchō makki ni okeru gakumon no jōkyō," *Kōza Chūgoku* (Tokyo, 1967), 2, 267.
71. Levenson, *Confucian China and Its Modern Fate,* 1, 76.
72. Onogawa Hidemi, *Shimmatsu seiji shisō kenkyū,* p. 45; Chang Tzu-mu, *Ying-hai lun,* 11:488-488b; Wang Chih-ch'un, *Ying-hai chih-yen,* 11:513b. Wang Chih-ch'un saw Huang's *JPTSS* in late 1879 while he was traveling in Japan. See Wang, *T'an Ying lu,* 1, 18; Ch'en Chih,

Yung-shu, "wai-pien", 8, 5b-6, 7,3b. For more about Ch'en Chih, see K. C. Liu, "Nineteenth-Century China," p. 143.

73. *JPTSS* (1880), 1, 20b.

74. *PTIK,* p. 33, 232.

75. *JPKC,* 4, 2.

76. Hattori Bushō, *Tōkyō shin hanjōki.*

77. For studies of Nakamura Keiu, see Takahashi Masao, *Nakamura Keiu* (Tokyo, 1966); Ōkubo Toshiaki, "Nakamura Keiu no shoki yōgaku shisō to *Saikoku risshihen* no yakujutsu oyobi kankō ni tsuite," *Shien* 26.2-3:153-188 (January 1966).

78. "Memorial Addressed to the Tenno," *Japan Weekly Mail,* Yokohama, May 18, 1872, p. 286. (I was able to see the copy of this newspaper at the Waseda University Library, Tokyo.) Walter E. Houghton, *The Victorian Frame of Mind* (New Haven, 1957), pp. 117, 191, 228-229, 250-251, 274.

79. Nakamura Keiu, "Saikoku risshihen jo," *Keiu bunshū* (Tokyo, 1903), 5, 6-11.

80. Nakamura Keiu, *Jiyū no ri* (Suruga, 1872), reprinted in Yoshino Sakuzō, comp., *Meiji bunka zenshū* (Tokyo, 1927), vol. 5. For critical evaluation of Nakamura's interpretation of Mill and Smiles, see H. Matsuzawa, "'Saikoku risshihen' to 'Jiyū no ri' no sekai—Bakumatsu jugaku, Bikutoria-chō kyūshinshugi, 'bummei kaika'," in Nihon Seiji Gakukai, comp., *Nihon seiji gakukai nempō, Nihon ni okeru seiō seiji shisō* (Tokyo, 1975), pp. 9-53.

81. *Keiu bunshū,* 3, 15b-17b. For a discussion of the religious thought of Nakamura, see Takahashi Masao, *Nakamura Keiu,* pp. 65-71; Jerry Fisher, "Nakamura Keiu: The Evangelical Ethic in Japan," in Robert J. Miller, ed., *Religious Ferment in Asia* (Lawrence, Kansas, 1974), pp. 37-50; A. Hamish Ion, "Edward Warren Clark and Early Meiji Japan: A Case Study of Cultural Contact," *Modern Asian Studies* 2.4:557-572 (October 1977).

82. "Memorial addressed to the Tenno," p. 286.

83. Ibid., p. 287. Nakamura's memorial to the Emperor was published in Chinese in *Chiao-hui hsin-pao (Church News),* a Shanghai missionary journal. It was signed "a Japanese." Perhaps it was one of the earliest discussions of the modernization in Japan published in Chinese; *Chiao-hui hsin-pao* (June 1872, reprint Taipei, 1968), 4, 1877-1878, 1887-1889. The reprint edition does not indicate the dates. The dates were provided in "Chiao-hui hsin-pao: Analysis of Contents" (mimeographed, Department of History, University of California, Davis, 1968).

84. Nakamura Keiu, "Katō ō nempu jo," (Preface to the chronological biography of Mr. Katō), *Keiu bunshū*, 15, 10. On publication of the memorial, see Ozawa Saburō, *Nihon Purotesutanto shi kenkyū* (Tokyo, 1964), pp. 239-248. Nakamura was converted to Christianity through the influence of an American, E. W. Clark, who taught chemistry and physics at the Tokugawa school in Shizuoka; he was baptized by a Canadian Methodist missionary, George Cackran, on Christmas Day, 1873. See Takahashi, *Nakamura Keiu*, pp. 90-95.

85. Takahashi, *Nakamura Keiu*, pp. 118-122, 128-129. D. B. McCartee taught at the Dōjinsha in 1876; see "Keiu nichijō" (Diary of Nakamura Keiu, held at the Seikadō Bunko, Tokyo) M9/2/15, 2/19, and 2/20. Wang Chih-pen also taught at the Dōjinsha; see, Sanetō, *Ōkōchi monjo*, p. 21.

86. Takahashi, *Nakamura Keiu*, pp. 155-161; *JPTSS* (1880), 1, 22-23b; Nakamura Keiu, *Keiu shishū* (Tokyo, 1926), 3, 71-72. *Dōjinsha bungaku zasshi*, 34, 8-8b (August 2, 1879) describes his visit to the normal school.

87. For literary exchanges between Nakamura and Chinese literati, see *Keiu shishū*, 3, 61b; 3, 75-78b; 4, 61-62; *Keiu bunshū*, 4, 19-20.

88. *Keiu shishū*, 4, 53b.

89. Nakamura Keiu, "Shina fukabu ron" (China should not be despised), *Meiroku zasshi* no. 35 (April 1875); reprinted in *Meiji bunka zenshū* (Tokyo, 1925), 5, 222-223.

90. A note in *Dōjinsha bungaku zasshi*, 12, 4b-6b (February 22, 1877); Nakamura, "Kangaku fukahai ron" (Learning of Chinese classics should not be abolished), in *Gakushikaiin zasshi*, May 1887.

91. *Keiu shishū*, 3, 48-48b; *Keiu bunshū*, 6, 21-21b.

92. *JPKC*, 32, 20b.

4: JAPAN'S AGGRESSION ON CHINA'S PERIPHERY

1. It could be argued that the Western model was not necessary for the Japanese to expand into Korea and China because it had been an old dream of the Japanese. For the Japanese aspiration of building a self-centered world order after the model of Sinocentric world order during the Tokugawa era, see Satō Seizaburō, "Bakumatsu Meiji shoki ni okeru taigai ishiki no sho ruikei," in Satō and R. Dingman, eds., *Kindai Nihon no taigai taido* (Tokyo, 1974), pp. 1-34.

2. Fujimura Michio, "Meiji shonen ni okeru Ajia seisaku no shūsei to Chūgoku," *Nagoya daigaku bungakubu kenkyū ronshū, shigaku* 15: 3-25 (1967).

3. For Ryukyu-Satsuma and Ryukyu-Ch'ing relations, see Robert K. Sakai, "The Ryukyu (Liu-ch'iu) Islands as a Fief of Satsuma," in Fairbank, *Chinese World Order*, pp. 112–134; Ta-tuan Ch'en, "Investiture of Liu-ch'iu Kings in the Ch'ing Period," in ibid., pp. 135–164.

4. For the most comprehensive account of the diplomatic negotiations over the Ryukyu Incident, see Ueda Toshio, "Ryūkyū no kizoku o meguru Nisshin kōshō" (Sino-Japanese negotiations disputing the sovereignty over the Ryukyu islands), *Tōyō bunka kenkyūjo kiyō* 2, 151–201 (September 1951). For a discussion of Japanese policies in handling the Ryukyu issue in a long-term perspective, see Yasuoka Akio, "Nisshin sensō zen no tairiku seisaku," in Nihon Kokusai Seiji Gakukai, *Kokusai seiji: Nihon gaikōshi kenkyū—Nisshin Nichiro sensō* (Tokyo, 1961), p. 25. For a study of the Chinese response to the Japanese annexation of Ryukyu, see Hyman Kublin, "The Attitude of China during the Liu-ch'iu Controversy, 1871–1881," *Pacific Historical Review* 18:213–231 (1949).

5. Kublin, "The Attitude of China," pp. 220–221.

6. Memorials of Ho Ching and Ting Jih-ch'ang (KH3/5/14), *Ch'ing-chi wai-chiao shih-liao*, 10, 16–18.

7. Memorial of Ho Ching and others (KH3/5/14), *Ch'ing Kuang-hsu Chung-Jih chiao-she shih-liao*, 1, 21–21b.

8. According to Huang Tsun-keng, most of the important matters in the legation were decided by Huang because Ho was an indecisive man. See "Nien-p'u," p. 25. Liang Ch'i-ch'ao saw all the draft letters sent from Ho to the Tsungli Yamen and Li Hung-chang, and stated that 70% or 80% of them were drafted by Huang, especially, according to Liang, the letters recommending strong policies. Liang, *Yin-ping-shih shih-hua*, 3, 27b.

9. The copy of the draft of Ho's letter to the Tsungli Yamen (n.d.) is included in Wen T'ing-ching, ed., *Ch'a-yang san-chia wen-ch'ao*, 2, 1–5b. Perhaps it was the draft of a letter from Ho to Li (received KH4/4/7), which was summarized in a letter from Li to the Tsungli Yamen (KH 4/5/9), in *Li Wen-chung kung i-shu han-kao*, 8, 1–1b.

10. From Ho Ju-chang to Li Hung-chang (KH4/4/28), in Li, *I-shu han-kao*, 3, 4b.

11. From Li Hung-chang to Ho Ju-chang (KH4/4/29), in Li, *I-shu han-kao*, 8, 4b–6. Gaimushō, *Nihon gaikō bunsho*, (Tokyo, 1950), 11, 269–270.

12. From Ho to Terashima, October 7, 1878, in ibid., 11, 271.

13. From Terashima to Ho, November 21, 1878, in ibid., 11, 272.

14. From Li to the Tsungli Yamen (KH5/7/22), in Li, *I-shu han-kao*, 9, 44–45; Wang Yun-sheng, *Liu-shih-nien lai Chung-kuo yü Jih-pen* (Tientsin, 1931), 1, 139.

15. Wang Yun-sheng, *Liu-shih-nien lai,* 1, 127–133.
16. For the details of the negotiations over the Ryukyu issue, see *Nihon gaikō bunsho,* 13, 369–388. For an analysis of the Japanese policy toward the Ryukyu issue, see Fujimura Michio, "Meiji shoki ni okeru Nisshin kōshō no ichi dammen."
17. Huang, "Liu-ch'iu ko," *JCLST,* pp. 115–119. The event of the Ryukyu official's visit to the Chinese delegation in the port of Kobe was reported to Li Hung-chang. See letter from Ho to Li (KH4/4/28), in Li, *I-shu han-kao,* 8, 2b.
18. For a study of the formulation of early Meiji policy toward Korea, see Mōri Toshihiko, "Meiji shoki gaikō no Chōsenkan," Nihon Kokusai Seiji Gakukai, *Kokusai seiji: Nihon gaikō no kokusai ninshiki, sono shiteki tenkai* (1974), pp. 25–42.
19. For a discussion of the economic effects of the Japanese advance in Korea, see Hō Takushū, *Meiji shoki Nikkanshin kankei no kenkyū* (Tokyo, 1969), pp. 279–292.
20. On the Kim Ki-su mission and its impact, see Sin Kok-ju, "Kōka jōki chokugo no Kan-Nichi gaikō," in Nihon Kokusai Seiji Gakukai, *Kokusai Seiji: Nikkan kankei no tenkai* (Tokyo, 1963), pp. 13–34.
21. For Huang's comments on the Japanese expedition to Korea in the past and in 1873, see *JPTSS* (1880), 1, 3b–5.
22. Ho Ju-chang's letter, which was undoubtedly written by Huang, to Li Hung-chang, in *Ch'a-yang san-chia,* 3, 3–4b. The reference to the Warring States in discussion of the world situation had been made by Chang Ssu-kuei in his preface (1864) to W. A. P. Martin's translation of Henry Wheaton's *Elements of International Law (Wan-kuo kung-fa).* The same analogy was made in the late Tokugawa Japan. See Satō, "Bakumatsu Meiji shoki ni okeru taigai ishiki no sho ruikei," pp. 14–18. For its application by Wang T'ao, see, Cohen, *Between Tradition and Modernity,* pp. 93–94.
23. Huang's proposals were mentioned in his note to "Hsu huai-jen shih" (Reminiscence of people, continued), *JCLST,* p. 210. See also, Huang, "Ch'ao-hsien t'an" (Grief over Korea), in Liang Ch'i-ch'ao, *Yin-ping-shih shih-hua,* 2, 18b–19.
24. Sin Kok-ju, *Kindai Chōsen gaikōshi kenkyū,* pp. 114–118.
25. Kim Hong-jip, "Susinsa ilgi," in Kuksa P'yŏngch'an Wiwŏnhoe, comp., *Susinsa kirok: Han'gok saryo ch'ongsŏ* (Seoul, 1958), 9, 172.
26. Ibid., pp. 176, 179, 185.
27. Huang, "Ch'ao-hsien ts'e-lueh" (Korean strategy), in ibid., pp. 160–171. Also in *Nihon gaikō bunsho,* 13, 389–396.
28. A memorial of the Tsungli Yamen (KH5/7/4) cited Ting's memorial. *Ch'ing Kuang-hsu-ch'ao Chung-Jih chiao-she shih-liao,* 1, 31b–32.

29. Imperial edict received by the Tsungli Yamen (KH5/7/4), in *Ch'ing-chi Chung-Jih-Han kuan-hsi shih-liao* (hereafter referred to as *Chung-Jih-Han*, 2, 361. The response of Li (KH5/7/17) in ibid., 2, 373–374. From Li to the Tsungli Yamen (KH5/7/13) in ibid., 2, 363 and in Li, *I-shu han-kao*, 9, 34.

30. From Li to Tsungli Yamen (KH5/11/5) in *Chung-Jih-Han*, 2, 394–395; also in Li, *I-shu han-kao*, 10, 15b–16. From Li to Tsungli Yamen (KH6/2/9) in *Chung-Jih-Han*, 2, 397. The British government encouraged China to persuade Korea to open the country because it would assist Britain's policy of containing Russian advancement in the east. In May 1880, the British Minister to Japan, Harry Parks, visited the Chinese Legation and told Ho Ju-chang that China should advise the Koreans to conclude treaties with the Western nations, emphasizing the imminent threat from Russia. The Japanese government welcomed such an action. See *Chung-Jih-Han*, 2, 332; Hirose Yasuko, "Nisshin sensō zen no Igirisu kyokutō seisaku no ichi kōsatsu: Chōsen mondai o chūshin to shite," *Kokusai seiji: Nihon gaikō no kokusai ninshiki*, pp. 129–254.

31. Hō Takushū, *Meiji shoki Nikkanshin*, p. 90. Hō stated that Huang wrote his booklet by order of Ho Ju-chang and following the opinions of Li Hung-chang; however, the document cited by Hō (p. 95) does not give information to support his point.

32. From Kim Hong-jip to Ho Ju-chang, (KH6/11/29) in *Chung-Jih-Han*, 2, 452–453.

33. From Ho Ju-chang to the Tsungli Yamen, (KH6/10/18), *Chung-Jih-Han*, 2, 437.

34. Tabohashi Kiyoshi, *Kindai Nissen kankei no kenkyū* (Seoul, 1940, reprint, Tokyo, 1963), 1, 745–746. See also, Kang Jae-ŏn, *Chōsen kindaishi kenkyū* (Tokyo, 1970), pp. 64–73; Kim Yŏng-jak, *Kammatsu nashonarizumu no kenkyū* (Tokyo, 1975), p. 96. Tabohashi suggested that the Korean King and his officials were moved by Huang's writing, although the contents of his booklet were no more than plain proposals of diplomatic tactics without any new political philosophy. Perhaps the most important reason Huang's proposal received such great response was that Kim was deeply impressed by Huang and that Kim was successful in persuading the King to accept Huang's proposals.

35. *Kojong sillok* (Seoul, 1970), 18, 5–6b; 18, 28–32b; 18, 34; 18, 35b; 18, 36b–37; Tabohashi, *Kindai Nissen kankei no kenkyū*, 1, 739–769; Kim Yŏng-jak, *Kammatsu nashonarizumu no kenkyū*, pp. 98–108; Hatada Takashi, "Kindai ni okeru Chōsenjin no Nihon kan, Eisei sekija ron o chūshin ni shite," *Shisō* 520:59–73 (October 1967).

36. Hatada, "Kindai ni okeru," pp. 60–63.
37. Hatada argued that, although the Confucian scholars did not participate in the rebellion, what they had preached was practiced by the soldiers and the populace, even though in a way not acceptable to the Confucians. Hatada, "Kindai ni okeru," p. 68.
38. Banno Masataka, *Kindai Chūgoku seiji gaikōshi*, pp. 76–78.
39. Memorial of Ying-han, Governor of Anhui, (TC9/J10/26) *Ch'ing-tai ch'ou-pan i-wu shih-mo* (Peking, 1930), III (the T'ung-chih period), 79, 7b–9.
40. Memorial of Li Hung-chang, in ibid., 79, 47–48.
41. For studies of negotiations over the Sino-Japanese Friendship Treaty of 1871, see T. F. Tsiang, "Sino-Japanese Diplomatic Relations, 1870–1894," in *The Chinese Social and Political Science Review* 17.1:1–16 (April 1933); Tabohashi Kiyoshi, "Nisshi shin kankei no seiritsu," *Shigaku zasshi* 44.2:163–199 (February 1933), 44.3:314–338 (March 1933); Fujimura Michio, "Meiji shonen ni okeru Ajia seisaku no shūsei to Chūgoku."
42. Huang, "Lu-chün kuan hsueh-hsiao k'ai-hsiao-li ch'eng-fu ch'eng Arisugawa Taruhito ch'in-wang" (On the anniversary of the Army Officers' School, I composed a poem to dedicate to Prince Arisugawa Taruhito), *JCLST*, p. 87.
43. *Tai Shi kaikoroku*, 2, 298–305. Tanaka Masatoshi, "Shin-Futsu sensō to Nihonjin no Chūgoku kan," *Shisō* 512:152, 157, 158 (February 1967); Sanetō, *Ōkōchi monjo*, pp. 69–70.
44. Kuzuu Yoshihisa, *Tōa senkaku shishi kiden*, 1, 414–416; Satō Saburō, "Kōakai ni kansuru ichi kōsatsu," *Yamagata daigaku kiyō: Jimbun kagaku* 1.4:399–412 (August 1951).
45. For changes in the Japanese attitude toward China throughout the Meiji era, see Marius B. Jansen, "Japanese Views of China During the Meiji Period," in Albert Feuerwerker, Rhoads Murphey, Mary C. Wright, eds., *Approaches to Modern Chinese History* (Berkeley and Los Angeles, 1967), pp. 163–189. Fujimura Michio, "Meiji Shoki," suggests that the expulsion of Ōkuma Shigenobu from the government in 1881 and the death of Iwakura Tomomi in 1883 contributed to the decline in the friendly approach to China, and that thereafter the Japanese government adopted hard-line policies in anticipation of a war with China.
46. Wang T'ao was one of those who was contacted by Sone in Hong Kong. See Cohen, *Between Tradition and Modernity*, pp. 102–104; Satō, "Kōakai ni kansuru ichi kōsatsu," p. 403.
47. Satō, "Kōakai ni kansuru ichi kōsatsu," pp. 401–403; Ienaga Saburō, *Ueki Emori kenkyū* (Tokyo, 1960), pp. 200–201.

48. Satō, "Kōakai ni kansuru ichi kōsatsu," pp. 403, 405; Ōkōchi Teruna, "Keng-ch'en pi-hua" (Conversations during 1880), book 4 (February 9), 14; book 5, (February 21), 29; book 6 (March 21), and book 9 (May 26).
49. Huang, "Hsu huai-jen shih" (Reminiscence of people, continued), *JCLST,* p. 207.
50. Satō, "Kōakai ni kansuru ichi kōsatsu," pp. 404–406.
51. A draft letter from Ho Ju-chang to the Tsungli Yamen (n.d.), *Ch'a-yang san-chia,* 2, 12–14. It was undoubtedly drafted by Huang.

5: CALIFORNIA, 1882-1885: CONFRONTATION WITH RACIAL ANTAGONISM

*   An earlier version of this chapter was published in the *Pacific Historical Review.* I should like to thank the University of California Press for permission to use the material without fee.

   ©1978 by The Regents of the University of California. Reprinted from *Pacific Historical Review,* Vol. XLVII, No. 2, pp. 239-260, by permission of the Regents of the University of California.

1. For a discussion of the Sinocentric world order, see Fairbank, *The Chinese World Order,* pp. 1–19.
2. Huang Tsun-hsien, "Ch'ao-hsien ts'e-lueh" (Korean strategy).
3. Huang Tsun-hsien, "Pa Mei-kuo liu-hsueh-sheng kan-fu" (On the discontinuation of the educational mission in America), in *JCLST,* pp. 109–114. William Hung, "Huang Tsun-hsien's Poem 'The Closure of the Educational Mission in America,'" *Harvard Journal of Asiatic Studies* 18: 50-73 (1955) is a complete translation of this poem and contains well-documented annotations. The quotation is from Hung's translation.
4. Huang Tsun-hsien, "Hai-hsing tsa-kan" (Impressions on traveling over the ocean), in *JCLST,* pp. 123-126. In late Ch'ing China, a diplomat was given authority to choose his subordinates, including consuls. On the appointment of Huang, see Cheng Tsao-ju to Secretary of State, March 27, 1882, "Notes from the Chinese Legation in the United States to the Department of State, 1868-1906," National Archives, vol. 1, in "File Microcopies of Record in the National Archives," no. 98 (hereafter cited as "Notes from the Chinese Legation").
5. K. C. Liu, *Americans and Chinese: A Historical Essay and a Bibliography* (Cambridge, Mass., 1963), pp. 23–24.
6. Alexander Saxton, *The Indispensable Enemy: Labor and the Anti-Chinese Movement in California* (Berkeley and Los Angeles, 1971).
7. Stuart C. Miller, *The Unwelcome Immigrant: The American Image of the Chinese, 1875-1882* (Berkeley and Los Angeles, 1969), p. 192.

8. For accounts of the negotiations, see Mary Roberts Coolidge, *Chinese Immigration* (New York; republished, Taipei, 1968), pp. 151-167.

9. *The Statutes at Large of the United States of America, From December, 1881, to March, 1883, and Recent Treaties, Postal Conventions, and Executive Proclamations* (Washington, D.C., 1883), XXII, 61. Hereafter cited as *U.S. Statutes at Large.*

10. Huang Tsun-hsien, "Sui-k'o pien" (Expulsion of the immigrants) in *JCLST*, pp. 126-128.

11. For studies of the organizations of the Chinese in San Francisco and the moral character of the Chinatown, see Stanford M. Lyman, "Conflict and the Web of Group Affiliation in San Francisco's Chinatown, 1850-1910," *Pacific Historical Review* 43:473-499 (1974); and Ivan Light, "From Vice District to Tourist Attraction: The Moral Career of American Chinatowns, 1880-1940," *Pacific Historical Review* 43:367-394 (1974).

12. Huang, "Sui-k'o pien," in *JCLST*, p. 129; and Huang's note on his autobiographical poem, "Chi-hai tsa-shih" (Miscellaneous Poems of 1899), in *JCLST*, p. 296. Huang's source of information on George Washington's ideas about racial equality is unknown.

13. Huang, "Sui-k'o pien," in *JCLST*, p. 130.

14. Huang Tsun-k'ai, "Hsien-hsiung Kung-tu hsien-sheng shih-shih shu-lueh."

15. Huang, "Sui-k'o pien," in *JCLST*, p. 130.

16. Ibid., p. 127.

17. Ibid., pp. 129-130.

18. Li Tung-hai, *Chia-na-ta- hua-ch'iao shih* (Taipei, 1967), pp. 152-158, mentions Huang's activities assisting the Chinese in Canada.

19. Hsu Shou-p'eng to Secretary of State, May 29, 1882, "Notes from the Chinese Legation."

20. *U.S. Statutes at Large,* XXII, 59-60.

21. Hsu Shou-p'eng to Secretary of State, June 8, 21, and 28, 1882, "Notes from the Chinese Legation."

22. S. W. Kung, *Chinese in American Life: Some Aspects of Their History, Status, Problems, and Contributions* (Seattle, 1962), pp. 91-92. Problems involving the reentry of the Chinese laborers who temporarily left the United States resulted in the Scott Act of 1888, which prohibited Chinese laborers who had left the United States from returning; ibid., p. 83.

23. Cheng Tsao Ju to Secretary of State, March 7, 1884; Secretary of State to Cheng Tsao Ju, March 11 and 19, in "Papers Relating to the Foreign Relations of the United States," 48 Cong., 2 sess. (1885), *H. Exec. Doc. 1,* part 1 (ser. no. 2276), 106-109. Article 2 of the 1880 Treaty states: "Chinese subjects, whether proceeding to the United States as teachers,

merchants or from curiosity, together with their body and household servants, and Chinese laborers who are now in the United States shall be allowed to go and come of their own free will and accord, and shall be accorded all the rights, privileges, immunities and exemptions which are accorded to the citizens of the most favored nation." *U.S. Statutes at Large,* XXII, 826–827.

24. *U.S. Statutes at Large,* XXIII, 115–118.

25. Tsai Kwoh Ching to Secretary of State, July 31, 1884; Acting Secretary of State to Tsai Kwoh Ching, July 31 and August 2, 1884, in *H. Exec. Doc. 1,* (1885), pp. 112–113.

26. Tsai Kwoh Ching to Secretary of State, October 4 and 8, 1884; Secretary of State to Tsai Kwoh Ching, October 17 and December 18, 1884, ibid., pp. 114–118; Treasury Dept., *Synopsis of the Decisions of the Treasury Department on the Construction of the Tariff, Navigation, and Other Laws for the Year Ended December 31, 1884* (Washington, D.C., 1885), pp. 483–484, synopsis no. 6668.

27. "Transit of Chinese Laborers over the Territory of the United States in the course of a Journey to or from other Countries," Treasury Department Circular, January 23, 1883, enclosed in note from Secretary of State to Cheng Tsao Ju, February 2, 1883, in "Papers Relating to the Foreign Relations of the United States," 48 Congress, 1 sess. (1884), *H. Exec. Doc. 1,* part 1 (ser. no. 2181), pp. 213–214; Treasury Dept., *Synopsis of the Decisions of the Treasury Department* (Washington, D.C., 1884), pp. 35–36, synopsis no. 5544.

28. Cheng Tsao Ju to Secretary of State, July 12, 1884; Secretary of State to Tsai Kwoh Ching, August 14 and December 18, 1884, in *H. Exec. Doc. 1,* (1885), pp. 111–118.

29. Miller, *The Unwelcome Immigrant,* p. 194.

30. Chang Ch'i-yun et al., *Ch'ing-shih* (Taipei, 1961), VII, 465:5051. See also Liang Ch'i-ch'ao, "Chia-ying Huang hsien-sheng mu-chih ming," in *JCLST,* pp. 10–13. When Liang Ch'i-ch'ao visited the United States more than 20 years after Huang had left, he found that the Chinese residents still remembered the episode and enthusiastically praised Huang.

31. Huang Tsun-hsien, "Hsu huai-jen shih" (Reminiscence of people, continued), in *JCLST,* p. 207. On the appointment of Bee, see Saxton, *The Indispensable Enemy,* p. 9. James B. Angell met Bee at the Chinese Legation, 917 Clay Street, San Francisco, on his way to China in June 1880. Angell, Diary, June 18, 1880, Bentley Historical Library, Ann Arbor, Mich.

32. Sing-wu Wang, "The Attitude of the Ch'ing Court toward Chinese Emigration," in *Chinese Culture* 9:62–76 (December 1968).

33. Thomas A. Metzger, *The Internal Organization of Ch'ing Bureaucracy: Legal, Normative, and Communication Aspects* (Cambridge, Mass., 1973), Chapter 1.

34. W. A. P. Martin, *Cycle of Cathay* (1900; republished, Taipei, n.d.), p. 160.

35. See note 8 above; see also Chester Holcombe, "The Restriction of Chinese Immigration," *The Outlook* 76:974 (April 23, 1904). Holcombe was a secretary of the American Legation at Peking and assisted Angell in the negotiation of the treaty revision. See also James B. Angell to Secretary of State, October 23 and November 3, 1880, "Despatches from United States Ministers to China, 1843–1906," National Archives, Vol. 47, in "File Microcopies of Records in the National Archives," No. 92.

36. Angell, Diary, November 20, 1880.

37. Chinese negotiators surprised the American commissioners with their accurate knowledge of the situation in California and the political implications of the legislation to restrict Chinese emigration in the United States. See Coolidge, *Chinese Immigration*, p. 156.

38. *Ch'ing-chi wai-chiao shih-liao*, 24, 9b–10.

39. Huang reported on his discovery to Hsueh Fu-ch'eng in 1890 while they were traveling to England to assume their duties at the Chinese Legation in London; Hsueh Fu-ch'eng, *Ch'u-shih Ying Fa I Pi ssu-kuo jih-chi* 1, 14b–15.

40. For Huang's comments on American legal institutions, see *JPKC*, 27, 1.

41. Huang Tsun-hsien, "Chi-shih" (Record of events), *JCLST*, pp. 130–135.

42. *JPKC*, 32, 1–1b.

43. Alexis de Tocqueville, *Democracy in America* (Paris, 1840; New York, 1945), 2, 107.

44. From Cheng Tsao-ju to Secretary of State, September 4, 1884, "Notes from the Chinese Legation."

45. Ibid., From Cheng Tsao-ju to Secretary of State, September 11 and 14, 1885.

46. K. C. Liu, *Americans and Chinese*, p. 25.

47. Huang, "Pa-yueh shih-wu yeh t'ai-p'ing-yang chou-chung wang yueh tso ko" (Poem composed on the ship on the Pacific on the 15th day of the 8th month), *JCLST*, pp. 141–143.

48. Huang, "Kuei kuo Jih-pen chih kan" (Impressions when passing Japan on my way home), *JCLST*, p. 143.

49. The term "yellow race" was used once in Huang's poem written in Japan. "The Western nations became stronger and more aggressive; they enslaved blacks and gradually got around to the yellow race." ("Ying-hua ko"—Cherry blossoms), *JCLST*, p. 84.

In Japan, in the early 1880s, Herbert Spencer's writings were very popular, and various versions of Japanese translations were published. However, the Japanese took his theory as a basis for liberalism and parliamentarianism and used it as a theoretical guide of the People's Rights movement. See, Matsuzawa Hiroaki, "*Saikoku risshihen* to *Jiyū no ri no sekai*," pp. 9–53; Fukuda Yoshirō, "Meiji shoki ni okeru shinkaron no sokumen," *Nihon rekishi* 14:2–10 (March 1949).

50. Huang, "Yueh-nan p'ien" (On Vietnam), *Jen-ching-lu chi-wai shih chi*, pp. 52–54.
51. Huang, "Hsi-lan-tao wo-fo" (Reclining Buddha in Ceylon), *JCLST*, pp. 163–182.
52. Huang, "Wei Lan-shih t'i tu-li t'u yun" (Note on the illustration of independence written for Lan-shih), "Nien-p'u," p. 65.
53. "Yu-chih-yuan shang-hsueh ko" (Kindergarten pupil, go to school), *Jen-ching-lu chi-wai-shih chi*, pp. 62–63. Originally published in *Hsin hsiao shuo* 1. 3 (December 1902).
54. Huang, "Hsuan-chün ko", (Military march), in ibid., p. 61.
55. Huang, "Chi-hai tsa-shih," (Miscellaneous poems of 1899), in *JCLST*, p. 289.
56. Huang, "Ping-chung chi-meng shu-chi Liang Jen-fu" (In illness I record my dream to send to Liang Ch'i-ch'ao), *JCLST*, p. 386.
57. Huang, "Chi-hai tsa-shih", *JCLST*, pp. 288–289, 295, 303.
58. K'ang Yu-wei, *Ta-t'ung-shu* (Shanghai, 1956).

6: REFORM PROPOSALS FOR CHINA: COMPLETION OF TREATISES ON JAPAN

1. "Nien-p'u," p. 32. Huang, "Chiang chih Wu-chou chih t'ung" (Painful sorrow at arriving at Wu-chou), *JCLST*, pp. 143–144.
2. Huang, preface to the 1885 edition of the *JPTSS* (trans. Toyota Minoru and Sanetō Keishū, *Nihon zatsuji shi*, Tokyo, 1943, 1968). On reprint editions of *JPTSS*, see Sanetō Keishū, "Nihon zatsuji shi," *Chūgoku bungaku* 71, 1–11 (April 1941); Chou Tso-jen, "Lun Huang Kung-tu te *Jih-pen tsa-shih-shih*," in Cheng Tzu-yü, ed., *Jen-ching-lu ts'ung-k'ao*, pp. 19–25; Ishihara Michihiro, "Kō Junken no *Nihon-koku shi* to *Nihon zatsuji shi*," in *Bungakuka ronshū* 8:25, n. 21. Besides the editions mentioned above, it was reprinted in Liang Ch'i-ch'ao, comp., *Hsin-cheng ts'ung-shu* (1896), vol. 25. Also, *Hsiao-fang-hu chai yü-ti ts'ung-ch'ao*, ts'e 52, contains Huang's commentaries on his poems.
3. "Nien-p'u," p. 33.
4. Huang, "Shao-nü" (Little girl), *JCLST*, p. 151. Translation in Shimada Kumiko, *Kō Junken* (Tokyo, 1963), pp. 83–85. Huang's second daughter was born in 1876, one year before he left for Japan.

5. *JCLST,* pp. 153-157. Trans. in Shimada, *Kō Junken.* See note 12 of Chapter 1.
6. "Nien-p'u", p. 33. Huang, "Yuan-kuei" (Coming back from afar); "Hsiang-jen i yü yuan-kuei cheng lai hsun-wen fu ts'u chih kan" (My neighbors, having heard of my returning from afar, came to see me); "Ch'un-yeh chao hsiang-jen yin" (I invited my neighbors for a drink on a spring evening), *JCLST,* pp. 146-152.
7. Huang, "Jih-pen-kuo chih shu-ch'eng chih kan" (Impressions upon the completion of *Treatises on Japan*), *JCLST,* p. 158. "Nien-p'u," p. 33.
8. *JPKC,* "fan-li," p. 4.
9. Huang, preface to *JPKC,* p. 4.
10. *JPKC,* "fan-li," p. 4.
11. *JPKC,* 4, 1b-2.
12. *JPKC,* 16, 19b; 17, 15-15b; 37, 22-22b.
13. Ibid., 32, 21b.
14. Ibid., 13, 2.
15. Ibid., 32, 22.
16. Ibid., 32, 22b.
17. Ibid., 32, 22b.
18. This point was shared by other reform advocates during the 1890s. As Charlton Lewis put it, "The conviction that the secret of China's strength lay with her own tradition was the vital heart of the reform movement." Charlton M. Lewis, *Prologue to the Chinese Revolution: The Transformation of Ideas and Institutions in Hunan Province, 1891-1907* (Cambridge, Mass., 1976), p. 57.
19. *JPKC,* 13, 1b-2.
20. Chao Feng-t'ien, *Wan-Ch'ing wu-shih nien ching-chi ssu-hsiang shih,* (Peking, 1939; reprint, Hong Kong, 1968), pp. 311-312.
21. Chung-kuo shih-hsueh-hui, comp., *Yang-wu yun-tung* (Shanghai, 1961), 2, 23-25.
22. Onogawa Hidemi, *Shimmatsu seiji shisō kenkyū* (Tokyo, 1969), p. 42. For general discussion of the use of Classics in defense of reform, see Wang Erh-min, *Chung-kuo chin-tai ssu-hsiang shih lun* (Taipei, 1977), pp. 47-55.
23. Tseng Ch'i-tse, *Tseng Hui-min kung shih-hsi jih-chi* KH5/2/23, in *Tseng Hui-min kung ch'üan-chi* (Shanghai, n.d.), 1, 12b.
24. James T. C. Liu, *Reform in Sung China, Wang An-shih (1021-1086) and His New Politics* (Cambridge, Mass., 1959), pp. 32-33.
25. *JPKC,* 13, 1-2.
26. Ibid., 27, 1.
27. Ibid., 27, 1b-2.
28. Ibid., 27, 1b-2.

29. Ibid., 38, 1b–2.
30. *JPKC*, 15, 1b.
31. Ibid., 15, 12–13b.
32. Ibid., 16, 20–21.
33. Ibid., 16, 19. The total revenue of the Japanese government in 1880 was ¥ 63,367,254 (Tōyō Keizai Shimpōsha, *Meiji Taishō zaisei shōran*, p. 2). Yeh-chien Wang has estimated that China's tax revenue of 1753 was 73,792,000 taels, and that of 1908 was 292,000,000 taels. He has pointed out that the latter amounted to merely 2 to 4 % of China's net national produce at the time. (Wang, *Land Taxation in Imperial China*, pp. 72, 74, 133.) For the exchange rate between yen and tael in 1880, see Tōkeiin, *Dai nikai Nihon teikoku tōkei nenkan*, pp. 327–329.
34. Huan K'uang, *Yen-t'ieh lun* (Shanghai, 1934).
35. Hsueh Fu-ch'eng, *Yung-an wen-pien*, in *Yung-an ch'üan-chi*, 1, 6–6b; Chao Feng-t'ien, *Wan-Ch'ing*, p. 191.
36. Cheng Kuan-ying, *Sheng-shih wei-yen* (Shanghai, 1896), 3, 9–13b. For a study of early reform proposals of Cheng, see Liu Kuang-ching, "Cheng Kuan-ying *I-yen*: Kuang-hsu ch'u-nien chih pien-fa ssu-hsiang."
37. Wang T'ao, *T'ao-yuan wen-lu wai-pien* (Hong Kong, 1883), 2, 11b–13b, "Ch'u-pi" (Eliminate abuses).
38. P'eng Tse-i, book review of Chao Feng-t'ien, *Wan-Ch'ing*, in *Chung-kuo she-hui ching-chi shih chi-k'an* 8.1 (January 1949), reprinted in Lung-men shu-tien, 1968 edition of Wan-Ch'ing, pp. 168–176. For a critical study of the economic thought in the late nineteenth century, see Albert Feuerwerker, *China's Early Industrialization: Sheng Hsuan-huai (1844–1916) and Mandarin Enterprise* (Cambridge, Mass., 1958), pp. 31–40.
39. Chao Feng-t'ien, *Wan-Ch'ing*, pp. 270–271. Onogawa Hidemi, "Ka Kei, Ko Reien no shinsei rongi," in *Ishihama sensei koki kinen tōyōgaku ronsō* (Suita, 1958), pp. 121–133.
40. Chao Feng-t'ien, *Wan-Ch'ing*, p. 271. Yen Fu, *Yuan-fu* (Discourse on wealth) in *Yen i ming-chu ts'ung-k'an* (Shanghai, 1931), pp. 834–931. See also, Schwartz, *In Search of Wealth and Power*, pp. 114–115, 117, 122.
41. *JPKC*, 17, 20b.
42. Feng Kuei-fen, "Hou yang-lien i" (Discussion of an increase in official salaries), in his *Chiao-pin-lu k'ang-i* (Yü-chang, 1884), 1, 9–10b; Cheng Kuan-ying, "Lien-feng" (Scanty salaries), in his *I-yen* (Hong Kong, 1880), 2, 40–41.

43. Ch'en Chih, "Yang-lien" (On salary), in his *Yung-shu* (Shanghai, 1898), "Nei-pien" 1, 13–14b; Chao Feng-t'ien, *Wan-Ch'ing,* pp. 288–289.

44. Ho Kai (Ch'i) and Hu Li-yuan, "Hsin-cheng lun-i" and "Hsin-cheng an-hsiang," in their *Hsin-cheng chen-ch'üan* (Hong Kong, 1900), 2, 3–3b; 4, 23–24, and preface cited in Chao Feng-t'ien, *Wan-Ch'ing,* pp. 289–290.

45. *JPKC,* 17, 15–18b.

46. Ibid., 17, 15b–16.

47. Chao Feng-t'ien, *Wan-Ch'ing,* p. 294.

48. *JPKC,* 18, 8b–10b.

49. Chao Feng-t'ien, *Wan-Ch'ing,* pp. 279–281. Cheng Kuan-ying, *I-yen,* 2, 50b–51, refers to the story of King Nan in his discussion of national bonds.

50. *JPKC,* 20, 1b.

51. Ibid., 20, 1b.

52. Ibid., 38, 1b.

53. Ibid., 20, 28b; 38, 2.

54. Feng Kuei-fen, *Chiao-pin-lu k'ang-i,* pp. 2–2b.

55. Hsueh Fu-ch'eng, "Ying-chao ch'en-yen shu" (A memorial responding to the edict, 1875), in *Yung-an wen-pien,* 1, 14–14b. Yen-p'ing Hao, "Cheng Kuan-ying: The Comprador as a Reformer," *Journal of Asian Studies* 29.1:15–22 (November 1969). For a discussion of the late Ch'ing debates on trade, see Wang Erh-min, *Chung-kuo chin-tai ssu-hsiang-shih lun,* Chapter 5.

56. *JPKC,* 21, 1b.

57. Ibid., 21, 1b.

58. Ibid., 21, 20b.

59. Ibid., 26, 8–9.

60. Ibid., 40, 1–1b.

61. Ibid., 40, 1–1b.

62. Li Hung-chang, letter to the Tsungli Yamen (1864), in *Ching-tai Ch'ou-pan i-wu shih-mo* (T'ung-chih) 25, 4–10. Hsueh Fu-ch'eng, "Ying-chao ch'en-yen shu," (1875), *Yung-an wen-pien,* 1, 13b; Hsueh Fu-ch'eng, "Chen pai kung-shuo" (Discussion for development of various industries) in *Yung-an hai-wai wen-pien,* in *Yung-an ch'üan-chi,* 3, 16b–17b.

63. *JPKC,* 33, 5–7.

64. Ibid., 33, 6.

65. Ibid., 33, 6.

66. Ibid., 33, 7.

67. *PTIK,* pp. 182–183.

68. Sogabe Shizuo, *Chūgoku shakai keizai shi no kenkyū* (Tokyo, 1966), p. 15.

69. *JPKC*, 37, 20-21.

70. Ibid., 37, 21b-22.

71. Ibid., 37, 22b.

72. Hsueh Fu-ch'eng, "Lun kung-ssu pu-chü chih ping" (Disadvantages of not developing corporations), in *Hai-wai wen-pien*, 3, 15-16; Chao Feng-t'ien, *Wan-Ch'ing*, pp. 92-94.

73. "N'ien-p'u," p. 57. See Chapter 8 for further discussion.

74. Hao Chang, *Liang Ch'i-ch'ao and Intellectual Transition in China*, pp. 95, 149-219.

75. The letters of recommendation by Li Hung-chang and Chang Chih-tung were printed in the 1890 Fu-wen-chai edition of the *JPKC*.

76. P'i Hsi-jui, *Jih-chi*, KH23/9/6, in *Hu-nan li-shih tsu-liao*, no. 4 (1958).

7: THE OTHER HALF OF THE GLOBE: REFLECTIONS IN LONDON AND SINGAPORE

1. Huang, "Tsai lun-tun hsieh-chen chih kan" (Having my picture taken in London), *JCLST*, pp. 184-185.

2. Huang, "Ch'un-yeh chao hsiang-jen yin" (I invited my neighbors for a drink on a spring evening), *JCLST*, pp. 150.

3. "Nien-p'u," pp. 36-37.

4. Ibid., pp. 37-38, 48.

5. Ibid., p. 35. Hsueh Fu-ch'eng, *Yung-an pi-chi* (Shanghai, 1937), p. 146.

6. Huang, "Chi ssu-ti" (To my fourth brother), *JCLST*, p. 41.

7. "Nien-p'u," pp. 35-36.

8. *JPKC*, 9, 1.

9. Huang, "Hsi-lan-tao wo-fo" (Reclining Buddha in Ceylon), *JCLST*, pp. 163-182.

10. Hsueh Fu-ch'eng, *Ch'u-shih Ying Fa I Pi ssu-kuo jih-chi*, chüan 1 & 2, in his *Yung-an ch'üan-chi*.

11. Huang, "Wen-tse-kung ch'ao hui" (Audience at Windsor Castle), *JCLST*, p. 182.

12. Hsueh Fu-ch'eng, *Ch'u-shih jih-chi, hsu-k'o*, (1898; reprint, Taipei, 1968), "fan-li," 1, 1b-2.

13. Huang, "Chung-wu" (Heavy fog), *JCLST*, p. 183.

14. Huang, "Lun-tun ta-wu-hsing" (On dense fog in London), *JCLST*, pp. 183-184.

15. Huang, "Chin pieh-li" (Now, in separation), *JCLST*, pp. 185-187.

16. Huang, "Sui-mo huai-jen shih" (Reminiscence of old friends at the end of the year), *JCLST*, pp. 192-202.

17. *JPTSS* (1898 edition), preface. The revised edition, not published

until 1898, contained 200 poems, whereas the original edition had 154 poems.

18. The first edition of the *JCLST* was published by his brother Huang Tsun-k'ai in Japan in 1911 with the assistance of Liang Ch'i-ch'ao. For a discussion of various editions, see Chou Tso-jen, "Lun Jen-ching-lu shih-ts'ao," in Cheng Tzu-yü, ed., *Jen-ching-lu ts'ung-k'ao* (Singapore, 1959), pp. 27–37.

19. Huang, preface to the *JCLST*. It was first published in *Hsueh-heng tsa-chih*, no. 60 (December 1926).

20. Huang, "Yü Lang-shan lun shih" (Letter to Lang-shan discussing poetry), published in *Ling-nan hsueh-pao* 2.2:184–185 (July 1931). See also, Wu T'ien-jen, *Huang Kung-tu hsien-sheng chuan-kao*, p. 381. The publisher did not give the date of the letter, but it was probably written while Huang was compiling the *JCLST*. Wu T'ien-jen identifies Lang-shan as Chou Lang-shan. According to the arrangement of the *Jen-ching-lu chi-wai-shih chi*, however, Huang's poem "K'u Chou Lang-shan" (Mourning over Chou Lang-shan) was written before Huang took the metropolitan examination.

21. Huang, "Chi-hai tsa-shih" (Miscellaneous poems composed in 1899), *JCLST*, p. 294. See Chapter 1 for a discussion of the themes of Huang's early poems.

22. For example, "Ch'ien-men" (Melancholy), *JCLST*, pp. 157–158.

23. Huang's letter to Hu Hsi (Hsiao-ts'en) 5th day of 8th month 1891 , cited in Lo Hsiang-lin, "Hu Hsiao-ts'en hsien-sheng nien-p'u," pp. 125–126.

24. Huang, "Letter to Lang-shan discussing poetry."

25. Huang did not include these colloquial-style poems in his *JCLST*.

26. Chou Tso-jen, "Jen-ching-lu shih-ts'ao" *I-ching*, no. 25 (March 5, 1937), Shanghai. Reprinted in Cheng Tzu-yü, *Jen-ching-lu ts'ung-k'ao*, p. 79. Huang began to call his poems *hsin-p'ai shih* (new-style poems) from around 1897. See "Nien-p'u," p. 55. The name reminds one of the *shintai-shi* (new-style poetry) in Japan. In August 1882, Toyama Masaichi, Yatabe Ryōkichi, and Inoue Tetsujirō published a collection of their poems under the title of *Shintai-shi shō shohen* (New-style poems, first volume). It has been regarded as the first conscious effort to create a modern form of poetry in Meiji Japan. Huang may not have seen the collection because it was published after he left Japan.

27. Huang, letter to Ch'iu Wei-yuan, published in *Hsiao-shuo yueh-pao*, 8.1 (January 1917); reprinted in "Nien-p'u," p. 75.

28. Lu Hsun, preface to "Call to Arms," in *Selected Works* (Peking, 1956).

29. Hu Shih, *Wu-shih nien lai Chung-kuo chih wen-hsueh*, p. 42.

30. Chow Tse-tsung, *The May Fourth Movement: Intellectual Revolution in Modern China* (Cambridge, Mass., 1960), p. 274.

31. "Nien-p'u," p. 54.

32. Hsueh Fu-ch'eng, *Ch'u-shih jih-chi,* in *Yung-an ch'üan-chi,* 4, 1 (KH 16/8/11); *Ch'u-shih kung-tu,* (1898; reprint, Taipei, n.d.), 1, 3–5b (KH16/8/25).

33. Hsueh Fu-ch'eng, *Hai-wai wen-pien,* 1, 5b–8b; *Ch'ing-chi wai-chiao shih-liao,* 83, 33b–38 (KH16/12/25).

34. For Hsueh's negotiations over the establishment of Chinese consulates, see Hsueh, *Ch'u-shih kung-tu,* 3, 14–19b; 3, 50; 10, 5–5b; and his *Ch'u-shih jih-chi hsu-k'o,* 1, 22–23; 1, 27–28b; 2, 16–17; 2, 51–51b.

35. Huang, "Teng Pa-li t'ieh-t'a" (Climbing up the Eiffel Tower), *JCLST,* pp. 203–205.

36. Huang, "Su-i-su ho" (Suez Canal), *JCLST,* p. 205.

37. Wen Chung-chi, "The Origins and Development of the Imperial Chinese Consulate in the Straits Settlements, 1877–1900" (MA thesis, University of Singapore, 1964). See also Michael R. Godley, "The Late Ch'ing Courtship of the Chinese in Southeast Asia," *Journal of Asian Studies* 34.2:361–385 (February 1975).

38. Huang, "Hsin-chia-p'o tsa-shih shih-erh shou" (Miscellaneous poems on Singapore, twelve stanzas), *JCLST,* pp. 210–214.

39. Huang, "Fan-k'o p'ien" (On barbarian guests), *JCLST,* pp. 218–227.

40. Hsueh Fu-ch'eng, *Ch'u-shih jih-chi hsu-k'o,* 9:9–10. The Vice-Consulate in Penang was established in early 1893. See, Hsueh, *Ch'u-shih kung-tu,* 9, 14–14b. For Chang Pi-shih, see *Biographical Dictionary of Republican China* (New York, 1976), vol. 1.

41. "Nien-p'u," p. 46. Hsueh Fu-ch'eng, *Ch'u-shih kung-tu* 7, 10–12; 7, 23.

42. In order to clarify this point, the British Minister, John Walsham, visited the Tsungli Yamen on February 28, 1889. Hsueh received a note from the Tsungli Yamen. See, Hsueh, *Ch'u-shih kung-tu,* 6, 9–9b. See also Song-ong Siang, *One Hundred Years' History of the Chinese in Singapore* (Singapore, 1967), pp. 281–282.

43. Hsueh Fu-ch'eng, *Ch'u-shih kung-tu,* 2, 40–40b.

44. *Ta-Ch'ing Te-tsung Ching (Kuang-hsu) huang-ti shih-lu,* 338, 3 (KH20/4/2).

45. Wen Chung-chi, "Origins of the Chinese Consulate."

46. Huang Yen-yü, "Financial Security," a note to the author.

47. Huang, "Fan-k'o p'ien," *JCLST,* p. 226.

48. *Ch'ing-chi wai-chiao shih-liao,* 87, 14b–18; 87, 21b–22b; Hsueh Fu-ch'eng, *Hai-wai wen-pien,* 1, 17b–20.

49. *Ch'ing-chi wai-chiao shih-liao,* 87, 17b–18; 87, 22b; Kuo T'ing-i, *Chin-tai Chung-kuo shih-shih jih-chih,* pp. 859–860.

50. Hsueh Fu-ch'eng, preface to the *JPKC.*

51. Tu Lien-che, "Hsueh Fu-ch'eng," in Hummel, *Eminent Chinese of the Ch'ing Period,* pp. 331-332.

52. Huang, "Yang-o tsa-shih" (Miscellaneous poems while recuperating from illness), *JCLST,* p. 228.

53. Huang, "I lien chü t'ao tsa-kung i-pin tso-ko" (Putting chrysanthemums, peach blossoms, and other flowers together into a vase), *JCLST,* pp. 214-217.

54. Huang, "Yang-o tsa-shih," *JCLST,* p. 229.

8: *THE SINO-JAPANESE WAR AND THE POST-WAR REFORM MOVEMENT*

1. Liang Ch'i-ch'ao, "Wu-hsu cheng-pien chi," in *Yin-ping-shih ho-chi,* (Shanghai, 1936) *chuan-chi,* vol. 1, 17, 1.

2. *Chang Wen-hsiang kung ch'üan-chi* (Peking, 1928) 76, 20b-21 ("Tien-tsou" KH20/10/11).

3. Huang, "Pei P'ing-jang" (Sorrow over Pyongyang), *JCLST,* pp. 231-232. For the accounts of the battles by historians and contemporary observers, see Fan Wen-lan, *Chung-kuo chin-tai-shih* (Shanghai, 1947), vol. 1, book 1, pp. 257-271; Yao Hsi-kuang, *Tung-fang ping-shih chi-lueh* (Wu-ch'ang, 1897); Uno Shun'ichi, *Nisshin Nichiro* (*Nihon no rekishi,* vol. 26, Tokyo, 1976), pp. 55-67. There were several editions of quick reports on the battles for general readers in Japan. For example, Kubota Beisen et al., eds., *Nisshin sentō gahō* (Tokyo, 1894-1895). For an account of Yeh Chih-ch'ao, the commander who deserted Pyongyang, see his biography in Ch'ao Erh-hsun et al., comps., *Ch'ing-shih-kao, chüan* 468 (*lieh-chuan,* 249).

4. Huang, "Tung-kou hsing," (Poem on the Yellow Sea), *JCLST,* pp. 232-233.

5. Huang, "Ai Lü-hsun" (Lament for Port Arthur), *JCLST,* pp. 233-234.

6. Huang, "K'u Wei-hai," (Weep over Weihaiwei), *JCLST,* pp. 234-235.
   See biographies of Tai Tsung-chien and Li Ping-heng in *Ch'ing-shih-kao, chüan* 466 (*lieh-chuan,* 249); *chüan* 473 (*lieh-chuan,* 254).

7. Huang, "Hsiang chiang-chün ko", (Surrendered admiral), *JCLST,* pp. 243-245. Translation in Suzuki Torao, *Chūgoku senran shi* (Tokyo, 1968), pp. 213-220. For a chronology of the battles, see Kuo T'ing-i, comp., *Chin-tai Chung-kuo shih-shih jih-chih,* vol. 2 (Taipei, 1963). Biography of Ting Ju-ch'ang appears in *Ch'ing-shih-kao, chüan* 468 (*lieh-chuan,* 249).

8. Huang's letter to Chien Hou, written in May, 1895, quoted in Mai Jo-p'eng, *Huang Tsun-hsien chuan,* p. 67.

9. Huang, "Ma-kuan chi-shih," (Event in Shimonoseki), *JCLST,* pp. 241-243.

10. Huang, "Shang Huang-ho-lou," (Yellow Crane Pavilion), *JCLST,* p. 272. For an account of the Taiwan Republic, see Harry J. Lamley, "The 1895 Taiwan Republic, A Significant Episode in Modern Chinese History," *Journal of Asian Studies* 27.4:739–762 (August 1968).

11. Huang, "Tai-wan hsing" (Poem on Taiwan), *JCLST,* pp. 245–247.

12. John K. Fairbank, Edwin O. Reischauer, and Albert M. Craig, *East Asia: The Modern Transformation* (Boston, 1965), p. 353; William Ayers, *Chang Chih-tung and Educational Reform in China* (Cambridge, Mass., 1971), pp. 103–104.

13. K. C. Liu, "Nineteenth Century China," p. 114. For a discussion of the increased importance of the private staff, see Susan Mann Jones and Philip A. Kuhn, "Dynastic Decline and the Roots of Rebellion," in John K. Fairbank, ed., *The Cambridge History of China,* vol. 10, part 1 (Cambridge, 1978), pp. 110–112; and Kenneth E. Folsom, *Friends, Guests, and Colleagues: The Mu-fu System in the Late Ch'ing Period* (Berkeley and Los Angeles, 1968), pp. 58–59.

14. *Chang Wen-hsiang kung ch'üan-chi* (Peking, 1928), 147, 26–27; 149, 5b. Memorial of Chang received on KH22/2/1 is also in "Tsung-li ko-kuo shih-wu ya-men ch'ing-tang," (KH22/2/1–2/14), at Academia Sinica, Institute of Modern History, Taipei. Lu Shih-ch'iang et al., comps., *Chiao-wu chiao-an tang,* the 5th series (Taipei, 1977), doc. no. 1314 and 1315. No report on Huang's activities is included in this series.

15. Huang Tsun-k'ai, "Hsien hsiung Kung-tu hsien-sheng shih-shih shu-lueh" in *Jen-ching-lu chi-wai-shih chi,* pp. 127–128. According to him, the French Consul General presented Huang with a bronze bust of Napoleon as a token of thanks and maintained a friendly relationship with him.

16. *Chang Wen-hsiang kung ch'üan-chi,* 42, 14 (KH21/12/29).

17. Memorial of Chang on KH22/2/1, Academia Sinica, Taipei. See note 14 above. Telegram of Liu K'un-i, KH22/2/13, 2/14, in *Ta-Ch'ing Te-tsung Ching huang-ti shih-lu,* 385, 14b (KH22/2/14). Probably it was because Huang held the official title of Expectant Circuit Intendant that the Governors General had to ask for imperial permission to get him on their private staffs.

18. Liu K'un-i, Letter to Huang Tsun-hsien, (KH22/3/14), in *Liu K'un-i i-chi* (Peking, 1959), 5, 2173. From Chinda Sutemi to Saionji Kimmochi, November 19, 1895, in unpublished archives of the Foreign Ministry of Japan. "Meiji 28–29 nen Shina kakuchi teikoku senkan kyoryū-chi settei ikken, dai 5 hen, Soshū, 1."

19. From Chinda to Saionji, in ibid.

20. From Consul Arakawa to Foreign Minister Mutsu Munemitsu, April 14, 1896, in ibid.

21. Ibid., From Foreign Minister Saionji to Arakawa, June 13, 1896.

22. Ibid., From Arakawa to Saionji, July 10, 1896.

23. Ibid., From Minister Hayashi in Peking to Foreign Minister Ōkuma, October 19, 1896. Chinese Foreign Ministry archives on Soochow negotiations are mentioned in Ting-yee Kuo and James W. Morley, *Sino-Japanese Relations, 1862–1927* (New York, 1965), p. 83.

24. Huang, "Chi-hai tsa-shih," (Miscellaneous poems of 1899), *JCLST*, pp. 298–299.

25. K'ang Yu-wei, preface to the *JCLST*, pp. 2–3.

26. Interview with Huang Yen-yu, December 30, 1969.

27. Weng T'ung-ho, *Weng Wen-kung kung jih-chi* (Shanghai, 1925), KH22/9/21. I should like to thank Chao Chung-fu of Academia Sinica in Taipei for his assistance in reading Weng's diary. The typeset edition edited by him came out from Ch'eng-wen Press, Taipei, 1970.

28. John Schrecker, "The Reform Movement of 1898 and the *Ch'ing-i*: Reform as Opposition," in Paul A. Cohen and John Schrecker, eds., *Reform in Nineteenth Century China* (Cambridge, Mass., 1976), pp. 289–305.

29. Kung-ch'üan Hsiao, "Weng T'ung-ho and the Reform Movement of 1898," *Tsing Hua Journal of Chinese Studies* n.s. 1.2:112 (April 1957).

30. Huang Tsun-hsien, "Jun-yueh yin-chi Chung-shan sung Wen yun-ko hsueh-shih chia kuei; ch'ien huai Ch'en Po-yen li-pu" (July, gathering over wine at Chungshan to bid farewell to Wen T'ing-shih who was returning home on leave, at the same time to remember Ch'en Po-yen), in *JCLST*, p. 251. Wen T'ing-shih was granted three months' leave for repairing tombs at home on KH21/4/11; see *Ta-Ch'ing Te-tsung Ching huang-ti shih-lu*, 365, 8b; Huang, *Jen-ching-lu chi-wai-shih chi*, pp. 66–67.

31. Huang, "Li Su-i hou wan-shih ssu-shou," (Eulogy for Li Hung-chang, four stanzas), *JCLST*, 379–381.

32. K'ang Yu-wei, preface to *JCLST*.

33. For an extensive discussion of K'ang's philosophy, see, Kung-ch'üan Hsiao, *A Modern China and a New World: K'ang Yu-wei, Reformer and Utopian*, Chapter 4, "Confucianism as a Philosophy of Reform and a Religion."

34. "Nien-p'u," pp. 50–51.

35. K'ang Yu-wei, "Chin-ch'eng Jih-pen Ming-chih pien-cheng-k'ao hsu," printed in Huang Chang-chien, *K'ang Yu-wei wu-hsu chen tsou-i* (Taipei, 1974), p. 499.

36. Liang Ch'i-ch'ao, "San-shih tzu-shu" (Autobiography at thirty), in

Yin-ping-shih wen-chi, 44, 27; "Tsao-pan *Shih-wu pao* yuan-wei," in *Chih-hsin pao,* no. 66. (KH24/8/11), reprinted in *WHPH* IV, 521–528. "Nien-p'u," p. 52.

37. Cheng Hsien, "Huang Tsun-hsien, Wu-hsu wei-hsin yun-tung te ling-hsiu," in *I-ching,* no. 10 (July 1936).

38. Liang Ch'i-ch'ao, "Chia-ying Huang hsien-sheng mu-chih-ming," (Tomb inscription for Mr. Huang of Chia-ying,) *JCLST,* p. 12; *Yin-Ping-shih Wen-chi,* 43, 3b–4b.

39. Huang Chang-chien, *Wu-hsu pien-fa shih yen-chiu* (Taipei, 1970), p. 5.

40. Kuo T'ing-i, *jih-chih,* p. 958.

41. "Kuang-hsu 22-nien 10-yueh fen, tung-chi tang (fang-pen shang-yü)" (Records of edicts during the 10th month, KH22 [1896], winter months), National Palace Museum Library, Taipei, includes edicts transmitted from the Grand Council to the Tsungli Yamen on 10/13 (November 17) ordering the Yamen to let Huang prepare for an imperial audience; P. 00161 "Kuang-hsu 22-nien 10-yueh fen shang-yü: hsiao-fang-pen" (Records of edicts during the 10th month of KH22: small square book), National Palace Museum Library, Taipei. The entry for 10/16 (November 20) records Huang's name as one of those who received an audience on the day. ("Nien-p'u" does not clarify the dates because there were conflicting reports about when he received an audience.)

I should like to thank Chuang Chi-fa of the National Palace Museum Library and Beatrice S. Bartlett for their generous assistance in finding these documents in the Palace Museum archives.

42. "Nien-p'u," p. 54. "Kuang-hsu 22-nien 10-yueh fen tung-chi tang (fang-pen shang-yü)" p. 00297. National Palace Museum Library, Taipei.

43. "Kuang-hsu 22-nien 10-yueh fen shang-yü: hsiao-fang-pen," KH22/10/22.

44. Schrecker, *Imperialism and Chinese Nationalism,* pp. 29–31.

45. Dispatch of German Minister in Peking, Edmund Baron von Heyking, on December 3, 1896, in *Deutsches Zentraarchiv Potsdam, Adten des Auswärtigen Amtes,* Bant 427 and 447, cited in Siegfried Behrsing, "Huang Tsun-hsien und Berlin," in Deutsche Akademie der Wisshenschaften zu Berlin, Institut für Orientforschung, publ., Veröffentlichung, Nr. 48, *Ostasiatische Studien* (Berlin, 1959), pp. 10–17. See also Weng T'ung-ho, *Jih-chi,* 35, 98b (KH22/10/26); 35, 102b (KH22/11/10).

In fact, in the process of decision-making, Huang was once considered for the position in England and finally assigned to Germany. Such a change was made in the case of Wu T'ing-fang who had been appointed to the position in England first and was later reassigned to the United States because he held British citizenship. Weng T'ung-ho wrote a footnote to his diary on November 23 (KH22/10/19, 35, 97): "Appointed four ministers to four countries. Huang Tsun-hsien originally [as Minister] to Britain, but today changed to the United States [*sic*]." About Wu T'ing-fang's appointment, see Kuo T'ing-i, *Jih-chih*, pp. 961–962.

46. Despatch of German Minister in Peking, December 3, 1896, cited in Siegfried Behrsing, "Huang Tsun-hsien und Berlin." Weng T'ung-ho, *Jih-chi,* KH22/10/27 (35, 98b).

47. Weng, *Jih-chi,* KH22/11/26 (35, 107).

48. Ibid., KH22/10/18 (35, 98).

49. *North China Herald and Supreme Court and Consular Gazette,* Shanghai, February 12, 1897, pp. 248–249. The Chinese version of the letter is cited in Ch'en Yü-sung, "Huang Tsun-hsien shih-Te ts'ao-chü shih-mo" (On the German rejection of Huang Tsun-hsien's appointment as Minister), *Nan-yang hsueh-pao* 17.1:25–28 (April 1962).

50. Weng T'ung-ho, *Jih-chi,* KH22/6/21, 9/26; KH23/2/1, 2/3, 5/30.

51. Ibid., KH23/6/15. "Nien-p'u," p. 55. K'ang Yu-wei, preface to *JCLST,* pp. 2–3. Kuo T'ing-i, *Jih-chih,* p. 970.

52. Nakamura Tadashi, "Yōmu, hempō to mimpen: 1898-nen no ryō-Ko chiku o megutte," in Nozawa Yutaka, Tanaka Masatoshi, eds., *Kōza Chūgoku kingendaishi* (Tokyo, 1978), 2, 147–175.

53. Lin Neng-shih, *Ch'ing-chi Hu-nan te hsin-cheng yun-tung* (Taipei, 1972), p. 8. Edward J. M. Rhoads pointed out that there was no comparable Reform Movement in post-war Kwangtung and suggested that the attitude of provincial officials was crucial in the post-war reform in Hunan; *China's Republican Revolution: The Case of Kwangtung, 1895–1913* (Cambridge, Mass., 1975), p. 36.

54. Lin Neng-shih, *Ch'ing-chi Hu-nan,* p. 22. Chang Chih-tung had confidence in Ch'en because he once served as the Financial Commissioner of Hupei under Chang's jurisdiction.

55. "Nien-p'u," p. 73. Onogawa Hidemi, *Shimmatsu seiji shisō kenkyū* (Tokyo, 1969), p. 186. Hu Ssu-ching, *Wu-hsu lü-hsiang-lu,* 4, 13–14b. Huang, "Shang-hai hsi-wu Ch'en Po-yen," (Delighted to meet Ch'en Po-yen [San-li] in Shanghai), *JCLST,* p. 255.

56. Onogawa, *Shimmatsu,* pp. 277–278. Lin Neng-shih, *Ch'ing-chi Hu-nan,* p. 16.

57. For a description of the reform in Hunan, see Lewis, *Prologue to the Chinese Revolution*; Onogawa, *Shimmatsu,* Chapter 5; Lin Neng-shih, *Ch'ing-chi Hu-nan*; and Hu-nan-sheng chih pien-tsuan wei-yuan-hui, comp., *Hu-nan chin pai-nien ta-shih chi-shu* (Changsha, 1959), pp. 122–

167. For the friendship between Wang Hsien-ch'ien and Ch'en Pao-chen, see Wang, *K'uei-yuan tzu-ting nien-p'u* (Changsha, 1908; Taipei reprint), pp. 281–282.

58. Ch'en Pao-chen's memorial of KH23/12/18 in *WHPFTS*, pp. 243–244.

59. Ch'en Pao-chen, "Shih-wu hsueh-t'ang chao-k'ao" (Announcement of the entrance examination of the School of Current Affairs), *WHPF*, IV, 459.

60. *Chih-hsin pao*, KH23/11/1, cited in *WHPF*, IV, 382.

61. Hsiung Hsi-ling, "Shang Yu-ming chung-ch'eng shu" (Letter to Ch'en Pao-chen) in *WHPF*, II, 585. See also Lin Neng-shih, *Ch'ing-chi Hunan*, pp. 40–41, 80 n.9.

62. Huang, *Jih-pen-kuo chih*, Fu-wen-chai (Canton), 1890; Shang-hai t'u-shu in-shu-chü (Shanghai), 1898; Che-chiang shu-chü (Chekiang), 1898; Wen-hai (Taipei), 1968, based on Shang-hai t'u-shu press edition.

63. Huang, *Jih-pen tsa-shih-shih*, Ch'ang-sha Fu-wen-t'ang (Changsha), 1898. Despite Huang's wish that only this edition be circulated and that all previous editions be destroyed, the final edition did not circulate widely. Now it is a rare book and difficult to locate. I have acquired a xerox copy thanks to the generosity of the late Takeuchi Yoshimi. Joseph Esherick, *Reform and Revolution in China: The 1911 Revolution in Hunan and Hupei*, (Berkeley, 1976), p. 14, stated that Huang suggested replacement of Chiang Piao as the Provincial Director of Education by Hsu Jen-chu. I have no evidence. The post of the Provincial Director of Education was a 3-year appointment, and Chiang Piao completed his 3-year term.

64. K'ang's speech at the opening meeting of the Pao-kuo hui, in the spring of 1898, in K'ang, "Chronological autobiography of K'ang Yu-wei," in Jung-pan Lo, ed., *K'ang Yu-wei, A Biography and Symposium* (Tucson, 1967), pp. 88–89. There is a translation of K'ang's speech by Richard C. Howard, in ibid., pp. 298–299. Richard C. Howard pointed out the conscious emulation of *shishi* by the reformers in his "Japan's Role in the Reform Program of K'ang Yu-wei," in ibid., pp. 285, 304–305. See also K'ang T'ung-wei, "Lun Chung-kuo chih shuai yu yü chih-ch'i pu-chen" (A discussion of the weakness of China from the viewpoint of the decline of the spirit of *shih*) in *Chih-hsin pao*, no. 32 (KH23/9/1). As to Liang's speeches, see "Hu-nan shi-wu-t'ang ti-i-chi" (The first collection of the School of Current Affairs at Hunan) 8b, in *Hu-nan shih-wu hsueh-t'ang ch'u-chi* (Changsha, 1898). I had a chance to see a copy of this rare book, thanks to the kindness of Professor Shimada Kenji of Kyoto University.

65. T'ang Ts'ai-ch'ang, "Pien-huo" (Refutation of erroneous arguments),

HPLT, p. 45; "Lun je-li" (On energy), ibid., p. 49; "Liu-yang hsing-suan-chi" (Establishing a school of mathematics in Liu-yang), ibid., pp. 121–122.

66. P'i Hsi-jui, "Shih-fu-t'ang wei-k'an jih-chi" (Unpublished diary of P'i Hsi-jui), in *Hu-nan li-shih tzu-liao* (Changsha, 1958), no. 4; 1959, nos. 1 and 2. Entry for KH23/9/15.

67. The idea of Hunan independence was articulated in Liang's letter to Ch'en Pao-chen, of which a draft manuscript was found at the School of Current Affairs, *WHPF,* II, 533–535.

68. For the bylaws of the Nan-hsueh-hui, see *HPLT,* pp. 493–503; P'i Hsi-jui, *Jih-chi,* KH23/9/6, 10/21; Onogawa, *Shimmatsu,* pp. 290–294. Censor Huang Chün-lung detected the concealed purpose of the association as a local assembly. See *WHPFTS,* pp. 252–253.

69. P'i Hsi-jui, *Jih-chi,* KH24/2/1.

70. "Huang Kung-tu lien-fang ti-i-tz'u chi ti-erh-tz'u chiang-i" (The first and second lectures of Huang Tsun-hsien, the Judicial Commissioner), *HPLT,* pp. 307–311; *WHPF,* IV, 423–426.

71. Ibid.

72. "Hu-nan shu nieh-ssu Huang ch'üan-yü yu-nü pu ch'an tsu shih" (Instruction of the Acting Judicial Commissioner Huang not to bind the feet of young girls), *HPLT,* pp. 736–740. P'i Hsi-jui, *Jih-chi,* KH23/10/22. "Hu-nan pu-ch'an-tsu tseng-hui chang-ch'eng," (Bylaws of the Hunan Anti-Foot-Binding Association), *HPLT,* 527–532.

73. Huang, "Chi-nü" (To my daughter), *JCLST,* pp. 257–258.

74. Liang Ch'i-ch'ao, "Chia-ying Huang hsien-sheng mu-chih-ming"; Huang, Letter to Liang, in *Liang nien-p'u,* 1, 196–197.

75. "Hu-nan t'ung-sheng k'ai-pan t'uan-lien chang-ch'eng" (Rules concerning establishing a militia in all of Hunan province), *HPLT,* pp. 569–575.

76. "Hu-nan pao-wei-chü chang-ch'eng" (Bylaws of the Police Bureau of Hunan), *HPLT,* pp. 556–569. T'an Ssu-t'ung, "Chi kuan-shen chi-i pao-wei-chü shih" (Record of a meeting of gentry members to discuss matters concerning the Police Bureau), *HPLT,* pp. 212–216. Chiang Ping-k'un, "Ch'ou-pao Hsiang-sheng ssu-i" (Private proposals for the protection of Hunan province), *HPLT,* pp. 210–211.

77. *JPKC,* 14, 30b–31. Naimushō Keiho kyoku, comp., *Chō fu ken keisatsu enkaku shi* (Tokyo, 1927), pp. 17–22. "Hu-nan pao-wei-chü chang-ch'eng." Huang, "Shang-min Yang Hsien-ta teng pin-ch'ing su-pan pao-wei-chü p'i" (Response to a letter of merchant Yang Hsien-ta requesting prompt opening of the Police Bureau), *HPLT,* pp. 749–751.

78. "Hu-nan ch'ien-shan-so chang-ch'eng" (Bylaws of the Hunan Rehabilitation Center), *HPLT,* pp. 563–569.

79. "Hu-nan shun-fu Yü Lien-san che" (Memorial of the Governor of Hunan, Yü Lien-san), KH24/12/13, *WHPFTS*, pp. 501-502. P'i Hsi-jui reports Huang's activities preparing for the opening of the system in his diary: KH23/12/13; KH24/1/20; 1/30. T'an Ssu-t'ung, "Chi kuan-shen chi-i pao-wei-chü shih"; T'ang Ts'ai-ch'ang, "Lun pao-wei-chü chih i" (Discussion of the benefits of the Police Bureau), *HPLT*, pp. 215-219; "Pien-huo," *HPLT*, pp. 41-42.

80. "Hu-nan shun-fu Yü Lien-san che"; Ayers, *Chang Chih-tung and Educational Reform in China*, p. 141.

81. "Hu-nan shang-min ch'ing su pan pao-wei-chü pin" (Hunan merchants' petition requesting quick opening of the Police Bureau), *HPLT*, 717-720.

82. Huang, "Shang-min Yang Hsien-ta . . . p'i."

83. *Hu-nan t'ung-chih*, Tseng Kuo-ch'üan et al., comps., 1885, 79:57-57b, "T'uan-lien."

84. P'i Hsi-jui, *Jih-chi*, KH24/1/30. "Hu-nan kai-ting k'o-li-kuan chang-ch'eng" (Revised bylaws of the Learning Center for Officials), *HPLT*, pp. 549-554; "Hu-nan shu nieh-ssu Huang hui-ch'ou k'o-li-kuan hsiang-wen" (Detailed regulations of the Learning Center for Officials prepared by Hunan Acting Judicial Commissioner Huang), *HPLT*, pp. 682-686.

85. P'i Hsi-jui, *Jih-chi*, KH24/1/22; 4/12; 4/15.

86. Weng T'ung-ho, *Jih-chi*, KH23/6/15.

87. Huang, "Feng-yang hsien pao Tsen Ch'ing-chien fu-tu shen-ssu chiao-shih kan-sung i an p'i" (Comment on a case reported by Feng-yang, Magistrate, on Tseng Ch'ing-chien, who committed suicide by poisoning himself, and a missionary's interference); *HPLT*, pp. 760-761. I should like to thank Chang Wei-jen of Academia Sinica, Taipei, for his assistance in reading this document.

88. "Hu-nan-sheng shen-ch'i shih-shu kung-ch'i" (An open letter by Hunan gentry), in Sasaki Masaya, *Shimmatsu no haigai undō, shiryō hen* (Tokyo, 1968), pp. 146-147; Nakamura Tadashi, "Yōmu hempō to mimpen."

89. Huang's public lecture on Christianity is mentioned in P'i Hsi-jui, *Jih-chi*, KH24/3/13.

90. "Ch'en Yu-ming ta-ch'eng ti-ch'i-tz'u chiang-i" (The seventh lecture of Governor Ch'en), *HPLT*, pp. 302-307.

91. "Hu-nan shun-fu Ch'en pao-hu yang-jen shih" (Public notice of Governor Ch'en for protection of Westerners), *HPLT*, pp. 732-734.

92. Chiang Ping-k'un, "Ch'ou pao Hsiang-sheng ssu-i."

93. For recent Chinese evaluation of the Reform of 1898, see Compilation

Group for the History of Modern China, eds., *The Reform Movement of 1898* (Peking, 1976). P'i Hsi-jui often noted the rumors concerning uprisings instigated by the Ko-lao hui, *Jih-chi*, KH24/7/5; 7/6; 7/29.

94. Letter of Pin Feng-yang to Wang Hsien-ch'ien, in Su Yü, *I-chiao ts'ung-pien*, 5, 5.

95. *Hu-nan chin pai-nien ta-shih chi-shu*, p. 151.

96. P'i Hsi-jui, *Jih-chi*, KH24/3/20; 3/29.

97. *Chang Wen-hsian kung ch'üan-chi*, 155, 20–20b.

98. Lin Neng-shih, *Ch'ing-chi Hu-nan*, pp. 111–112. Memorial of Huang Chün-lung (KH24/8/21) in *WHPFTS*, pp. 472–473.

99. "Chronological Autobiography of K'ang Yu-wei" in Jung-pang Lo, *K'ang Yu-wei: A Biography and a Symposium*, pp. 83–85; Richard C. Howard, "Japan's Role in the Reform Program of K'ang Yu-wei," in *ibid.*, pp. 294–297.

100. Weng T'ung-ho, *Jih-chi*, KH24/1/23, KH24/1/24. Kung-ch'üan Hsiao, "Weng T'ung-ho and the Reform Movement of 1898," p. 160.

101. Huang's brother, Tsung-k'ai, a magistrate in Fukien, joined the Pao-kuo hui, but Huang himself did not. See, *WHPFTS*, p. 516, and *WHPF*, IV, 403–405.

102. Hsu Chih-ching, "Pao-chien jen-ts'ai che" (Memorial recommending talented men), *Chih-hsin pao*, KH24/7/11, reprinted in *WHPF*, II, 235–238.

103. Kuo T'ing-i, *Jih-chih*, p. 1004; "Shang-yü tang (ch'ang-pen)", KH24/4/25; "Ch'i-chü-chu," KH24/4/25, National Palace Museum Library, Taipei.

104. P'i Hsi-jui, *Jih-chi*, KH24/4/29; 5/2; 5/3.

105. "Nien-p'u, p. 61; Kuo T'ing-i, *Jih-chih*, pp. 1012, 1014. Among the records of "Shang-yü tang (hsiao-fang-pen)" there is no edict on August 11 (KH24/6/24). Among "Fa-kuo chao-hui" (Correspondence with France), KH24, held at Academia Sinica, there is a note from the French Minister to the Tsungli Yamen on August 19, 1898, acknowledging the notice of Huang's appointment on KH24/6/24 (August 11). Huang's footnote to "Chi-hai tsa-shih" *JCLST*, p. 300, states that he was ill for a long time and could not begin the trip when he was appointed Minister to Japan. See also Wang Shu-huai, *Wai-jen yü wu-hsu pien-fa* (Taipei, 1965), pp. 198–199.

106. Huang, "Chi-hai tsa-shih,"; "Nien-p'u," pp. 61–62.

107. "Nien-p'u," pp. 61–62.

108. Cheng Hsien, "Huang Kung-tu." According to the account of Cheng Hsien, the Emperor intended to appoint Huang a Grand Councilor in order to consolidate the reformist position in the government.

However, Huang's rank was not high enough for such an appointment. Therefore, the Emperor planned to send him to Japan for about half a year in order to raise his rank and, at the same time, to let him negotiate for a treaty of alliance with Japan. There was a rumor in the newspapers that Huang was going to be appointed a Grand Councilor. P'i Hsi-jui, *Jih-chi*, KH24/8/11. For memorials of the Censors, see *WHPFTS*, pp. 471–476.

109. "Nien-p'u," p. 62. Wang Shu-huai, *Wai-jen*, p. 199. One of the reasons for Huang's house arrest was that he was suspected of harboring K'ang Yu-wei in his residence. According to Cheng Hsien, Huang did help K'ang to escape from Shanghai on a British gunboat. When the coup d'état took place, K'ang left Peking for Shanghai, and Liang Ch'i-ch'ao hid himself in the Japanese Legation, from where he sent a secret telegram to Huang in Shanghai asking him to inform K'ang's disciples in the city of the matter and to make an arrangement with the British Consul for K'ang's flight. Liang also asked Huang to help his family in Shanghai escape to Japan. Huang did all of this very discreetly without being noticed. Cheng Hsien, "Huang Kung-tu," pp. 19–20.

110. *Nihon gaikō bunsho*, 31, 678–679.

111. *North China Herald and Supreme Court and Consular Gazette*, October 10, 1898, p. 686. See also, October 17, 1898, p. 707.

112. "Nien-p'u," pp. 62–63. Wang Shu-huai, *Wai-jen* (pp. 199–200) suggests, based on reports of Liu K'un-i kept at the Academia Sinica, that the principal factor that forced the Chinese authorities to release Huang was a British attempt to raid the Office of Foreign Affairs to release Huang from the siege.

113. Huang, "Fang-kuei" (Released from government service); "Chiu-yueh shuo-jih ch'i-ch'eng yu Shang-hai kuei chou-chung tso" (Poem on the boat when returning from Shanghai on the 1st day of the 9th month), "Kan-shih" (Impression of the event), *JCLST*, pp. 277–283.

9: MASTER OF THE JEN-CHING-LU: HOPE FOR A NEW CHINA

1. T'ao Ch'ien (Yuan-ming), "Written While Drunk," translation by William Acker, in Cyril Birch, comp. and ed., *Anthology of Chinese Literature from Early Times to the Fourteenth Century* (New York, 1965), p. 184.

2. For the buildings of the Jen-ching-lu and the garden, see "Nien-p'u," p. 64; *JCLST*, pp. 15, 42–43, 283, and 288–289. Papaya was mentioned by Y. Y. Huang, note to the author, July 1973.

3. While in the Shanghai-Nanking area, Huang wrote a poem for his daughter

in which he told her how he was delighted with beef soup and that he was never tired of it, even after eating it for over ten years. "Chi nü" (To my daughter), *JCLST*, p. 257.

4. Note of Y. Y. Huang to the author, July 1973.

5. *JCLST*, pp. 341–349.

6. "Nien-p'u," pp. 64–65; Huang Tsun-k'ai, "Hsien-hsiung Kung-tu hsien-sheng shih-shih shu-lueh," in *Jen-ching-lu chi-wai-shih chi*, pp. 134–135; P'an Fei-sheng, *Tsai shan-ch'üan shih-hua*, in *Ku-chin wen-i ts'ung-shu* (Shanghai, 1913), 1, 6–6b.

7. Huang, "La-yueh erh-shih-ssu jih chao li huang-ssu kan-fu" (On the edict of the 24th day of the 12th month declaring the nomination of the heir apparent), *JCLST*, pp. 309–312.

8. Huang, letter to Liang, 1902, printed in "Nien-p'u," p. 74.

9. Huang, "Keng-tzu yuan-tan" (On New Year's Day, 1900), *JCLST*, pp. 313–314.

10. "Nien-p'u," p. 65. Huang wrote a series of poems on the Boxer Incident, see *JCLST*, pp. 314–356.

11. Huang, "San ai shih" (Three eulogies), *JCLST*, pp. 356–366.

12. "Nien-p'u," pp. 63–64, 75.

13. Huang, letter to Liang Ch'i-ch'ao, published in the *Hsin-min ts'ung-pao* 13:56, 57 (August 1902).

14. Huang, letter to Liang, 10th month 1902, in *Hsin-min ts'ung-pao* 24: 33 (January 13, 1903).

15. "Nien-p'u," p. 76; For Chinese students in Japan, see Sanetō Keishū, *Chūgokujin Nihon ryūgaku shi* (Tokyo, 1960), pp. 56–60.

16. Huang, Letter to Liang, KH28/11/11, in *Liang nien-p'u*, pp. 166–167.

17. Huang's pseudonyms were: Tung-hai kung, Fa-shih-shang jen-chai chu-jen, Pu-tai ho-shang, Kung-chih-t'a, and Shui-ts'ang-yen-hung-kuan chu-jen. Some letters were printed in *Liang nien-p'u*, pp. 150, 159–160, 161–162, 166–167, 167–171, 195–197, 202–204; "Nien-p'u," 68–69, 73–78; and Wu T'ien-jen, *Huang Kung-tu hsien-sheng chuan-kao*, pp. 58–72. Liang Ch'i-ch'ao published 6 letters written in 1902 in the *Hsin-min ts'ung-pao*, nos., 12, 13, 20, and 24. Wu T'ien-jen surveyed draft copies of the letters kept in the Huang family and published them in his book. They are mostly identical with the previously published letters but contain some sentences omitted in other publications.

18. Huang, letter to Liang, 4th month, KH28, *Liang nien-p'u*, p. 150.

19. Ibid.

20. Huang, letter to Liang, *Liang nien-p'u*, p. 196.

21. For Liang's article, see note 25. Huang, letter to Liang, in *Hsin-min ts'ung-pao* 12:58–61 (July 1902); also in *Liang nien-p'u*, p. 154.

22. Ibid.

23. Ibid.
24. Ibid.
25. Liang, "Pao-chiao fei so-i tsun-K'ung lun" (To "Preserve Confucianism" does not imply respect for Confucius), _Hsin-min ts'ung-pao_ 2:59–72 (February 23, 1902).
26. _Liang nien-p'u_, p. 153.
27. Wang Te-chao, "Huang Tsun-hsien yü Liang Ch'i-ch'ao" (Huang Tsun-hsien and Liang Ch'i-ch'ao), in _Hsin-ya shu-yuan hsueh-shu nien-kan_ (New Asia College Annual) 11:1–31 (September 1969).
28. Huang, letter to Liang, 7th month, 1902, in _Hsin-min ts'ung-pao_ 20:51 (November 1902); also in _Liang nien-p'u_, p. 161. Letter to Liang, KH30/7/4, in _Liang nien-p'u_, p. 197.
29. Kōsaka Masaaki, _Meiji bunka shi, 4, Shisō genron hen_ (Tokyo, 1955), pp. 663–664.
30. Huang, letter to Liang, 8th month 1902, in _Liang nien-p'u_, pp. 161–162.
31. Ibid.
32. Huang, letter to Liang, 5th month 1902, in _Liang nien-p'u_, pp. 159–160. Yano handed in his credentials on July 4, 1897, and Huang left Peking on July 13. See, Kuo ting-i, _Chin-tai Chung-kuo shih-shih jih-chih_, p. 970.
33. Huang, letter to Liang, KH30/7/4, in _Liang nien-p'u_, pp. 195–197.
34. Onogawa, _Shimmatsu seiji shisō_, pp. 264–268. Chang P'eng-yuan, _Liang Ch'i-ch'ao yü Ch'ing-chi ko-ming_, pp. 81–118.
35. Huang, letter to Liang, 11th month 1902, in _Hsin-min ts'ung-pao_ 24:35–47 (January 1903). Also in _Liang nien-p'u_, pp. 167–171.
36. Ibid.
37. Ibid.
38. Ibid.
39. Onogawa, _Shimmatsu seiji shisō_, pp. 273–274; Liang Ch'i-ch'ao, "Pi-jen tui-yü yen-lun-chieh chih kuo-ch'ü chi chiang-lai" (My view of journalism; its past and future), in _Hsin-min ts'ung-pao_, no. 49 (June 1904).
40. _Liang nien-p'u_, p. 191; Chang P'eng-yuan, "Huang Tsun-hsien te cheng-chih ssu-hsiang chi ch'i tui Liang Ch'i-ch'ao te ying-hsiang," _Chung-yang yen-chiu-yuan chin-tai-shih yen-chiu-so chi-k'an_ 1:217–237 (August 1969).
41. Liang Ch'i-ch'ao, "Hsin-min shuo" (On the new people), _Hsin-min ts'ung-pao_, no. 1 (February 1902).
42. Schwartz, _In Search of Wealth and Power_, pp. 69–73.
43. Huang, draft letter to Yen Fu, in "Nien-p'u," pp. 70–71.

44. Huang, letter to Liang, 11th month 1902, in *Hsin-min ts'ung-pao* 24:37.
45. Wu T'ien-jen, *Huang Kung-tu hsien-sheng chuan-kao*, p. 63. Huang, "Ch'u-chün ko" (Military march), "Chün-chung ko" (A song of military camps), "Hsuan-chün ko" (Military march), in *Jen-ching-lu chi-wai-shih chi*, pp. 57–62. "Ch'u-chün ko" was published in *Hsin-hsiao-shuo* 1.1 (October 1902). They were all printed in Liang Ch'i-ch'ao, *Yin-ping-shih shih-hua*, 2, 1b–3b.
46. Huang, "Ch'u-chün ko" (Military march), *Jen-ching-lu chi-wai-shih chi*, pp. 57–58.
47. Huang, "Chün-chung ko" (A song of military camps), in ibid., pp. 59–60.
48. Huang, letter to Liang, KH30/7/4, *Liang nien-p'u*, p. 196.
49. Huang, letter to Liang, KH31/1/18 in ibid., p. 203.
50. Huang, "Yu-chih-yuan shang-hsueh ko" (Kindergarten pupil, go to school), in *Hsin-hsiao-shuo* 1.3 (December 1902). Also in *Jen-ching-lu chi-wai-shih chi*, pp. 62–63.
51. Huang, "Hsiao-hsueh-hsiao hsueh-sheng hsiang-ho ko" (A chorus for primary school students), in *Jen-ching-lu chi-wai-shih chi*, pp. 64–66.
52. Huang, "Ping-chung ch'i-meng shu-chi Liang Jen-fu" (In illness I record my dream to send to Liang Ch'i-ch'ao), *JCLST*, pp. 384–388.
53. "Nien-p'u," p. 79.

CONCLUSION

1. Folsom, *Friends, Guests, and Colleagues*, p. 194.
2. Hao Chang, *Liang Ch'i-ch'ao and Intellectual Transition in China*, p. 298.
3. Schwartz, *In Search of Wealth and Power*, p. 19.
4. Paul Cohen, *Between Tradition and Modernity*, pp. 134, 232. Cheng Kuan-ying, *I-yen*, 1, 4. In his statement criticizing the concept of the Middle Kingdom and encouraging an open-minded attitude toward foreign culture, Cheng Kuan-ying remarked: "When their religion is introduced [to China] , then it will result in the introduction of our teaching to their land. Once the air is opened up, nothing will stop the current [of cultural influences]. Once the *tao* of the sages is extended to the barbarians, there will be no living creatures who will not respect their parents. Thus, civilization and teaching [of the sages] will reach out to the remote areas."

Bibliography

Angell, James B. "Diary, 1880-1881" (original handwriting and typescript) among "Papers, including materials on his mission to Peking, 51 boxes, 1866-1816" held at Bentley Historical Library, Ann Arbor, Michigan.

Aoyama Nobumitsu 青山延光 . *Akō shi-jū-shichi shi den* 赤穂、四十七士傳 (Biographies of the forty-seven retainers of Akō). Prefaced 1829.

Arimoto Masao 有元正雄 . "Chiso kaisei to chihō seiji" 地租改正と地方政治 (Reform of land tax and local government), *Iwanami kōza Nihon rekishi,* Volume 14. Tokyo, Iwanami Shoten, 1975.

Aritaka Iwao 有高巖 . "*Nihon kokushi* ni tsuite" 「日本國志」について (On *Jih-pen-kuo chih*), *Shichō* 8:4.

Ayers, William. *Chang Chih-tung and Educational Reform in China.* Cambridge, Harvard University Press, 1971.

Banno Masataka 板野正高 . *Kindai Chūgoku gaikōshi kenkyū* 近代中國外交史研究 (Studies of the diplomatic history of modern China). Tokyo, Iwanami Shoten, 1970.

——. *Kindai Chūgoku seiji gaikōshi—Vasco da Gama kara goshi undō made* 近代中国政治外交史 — ヴァスコダガマから五四運動まで (Political and diplomatic history of modern China: From Vasco da Gama to the May Fourth movement). Tokyo, Tokyo Daigaku Shuppankai, 1973.

Bays, Daniel H. *China Enters the Twentieth Century: Chang chih-tung and the Issues of a New Age, 1895-1909.* Ann Arbor, University of Michigan Press, 1978.

Behrsing, Siegfried. "Huang Tsun-hsien und Berlin," in Deutsche Akademie der Wissenschaften zu Berlin, Institut für Orientforschung, Veröffentlichung, No.

48, *Ostasiatische Studien.* I. L. Kluge, ed., Akademie-Verlag. Berlin, 1959.

Birch, Cyril, comp. and ed. *Anthology of Chinese Literature from Early Times to the Fourteenth Century.* New York, Grove Press, 1965.

Campbell, George. "Origin and Migrations of the Hakkas," in *Chinese Recorder* 43.8 (August 1912).

Chang Chih-tung 張 之 洞 . *Chang Wen-hsiang kung ch'üan-chi* 張文襄公全集 (Collected works of Chang Chih-tung). 120 ts'e. Peking, Wen-hua-chai, 1928.

Chang, Hao. *Liang Ch'i-ch'ao and Intellectual Transition in China: 1890–1907.* Cambridge, Harvard University Press, 1971.

Chang P'eng-yuan 張朋圓 . "Huang Tsun-hsien te cheng-chih ssu-hsiang chi ch'i tui Liang Ch'i-ch'ao te ying-hsiang" 黃遵憲的政治思想及其對梁啓超的影響 (The political thought of Huang Tsun-hsien and his influence on Liang Ch'i-ch'ao), *Chung-yang yen-chiu-yuan chin-tai-shih yen-chiu-so chi-k'an* 中央研究院近代史研究所集刊 (Bulletin of the Institute of Modern History, Academia Sinica) 1:217–237 (August 1969).

Chang Tzu-mu 張自牧 . *Ying-hai lun* 瀛海論 (A discourse on the sea powers), in *Hsiao-fang-hu-chai yü-ti ts'ung-ch'ao.* 60 ts'e. 11, 483–495.

Chang Yuan-chi 張元濟 . "Wu-hsu cheng-pien te hui-i" 戊戌政變的回憶 (Recollection of the Reform of 1898), *Hsin chien-she* 新建設 (Reconstruct) 1.1:18–20 (October 6, 1949). Reprinted in Chung-kuo shih-hsueh hui 中國史學會 comp., *Chung-kuo chin-tai-shih tzu-liao ts'ung-k'an: Wu-hsu pien-fa* 中國近代史資料叢書戊戌變法 (A collection of materials on history of modern China: the Reform of 1898). Shanghai, Shen-chou Kuo-kuang-she, 1953, Volume 4.

Chao Erh-hsun. See *Ch'ing-shih kao.*

Chao Feng-t'ien 趙豐田 . *Wan-Ch'ing wu-shih nien ching-chi ssu-hsiang shih* 晚清五十年經濟思想史 (Economic thought during the last fifty years of the Ch'ing period). Hong Kong, Lung-men shu-tien, 1968. Facsimile reproduction of 1939, Peking, Ha-fo Yen-ching-she edition.

Ch'en Chih 陳熾 . *Yung-shu* 庸書 (Utilitarian discourse). Taipei, T'ai-lien kuo-feng ch'u-pan-she, 1970. Facsimile reproduction of 1898, Shanghai, Shen-chi Shu-chuang edition.

Ch'en Li 陳澧 . *Tung-shu tu-shu-chi* 東塾讀書記 (Notes from reading). Prefaced 1871. Shanghai. Commercial Press, 1930.

Ch'en P'an 陳槃 . "Huang Kung-tu p'ing-chuan hsu" 黃公度評傳序 (A note on an autobiography of Huang Tsun-hsien), *Chuan-chi wen-hsueh* 傳記文學 (Biographical works) 17.4 (December 1970).

Ch'en San-li 陳三立 . "Hsun-fu hsien-fu-chün hsing-chuang" 巡府先府君行狀 (A biography of Ch'en Pao-chen), in his *San-yuan ching-she wen-chi* 散原精舍文集 (Collected essays of Ch'en San-li). Taipei, Chung-hua Shu-chü, 1961.

Ch'en, Ta-tuan. "Investiture of Liu-ch'iu Kings in the Ch'ing Period," in John K. Fairbank, ed., *The Chinese World Order.*

Ch'en Yen 陳衍 . *Shih-i-shih shih-hua* 石遺室詩話 (Essays on poems by Ch'en Yen). Shanghai, Commercial Press, 1929.

Ch'en Yü-sung (Tan Yeok Seong) 陳育崧 . "Hsin-chia-p'o Chung-kuo ling-shih she-chih shih" 新嘉坡中國領事設置史 (A history of the Chinese Legation in Singapore), *Nan-yang tza-chih* 南洋雜誌· (The Nanyang miscellany) 1.6:122–123.

——. "Chi Lin Wen-ch'ing i kou-jou ch'i Huang Tsun-hsien shen-o shih" 記林文慶以狗肉起黃遵憲·沉痾事(Dr. Lim Boon Keng cured Hwang Tzuen Shiann's tuberculosis by dog's meat), in *Nan-yang hsueh-pao* 南洋學報 (Journal of the South Seas Society) 17.1 (April 1962).

——. "Huang Tsun-hsien shih-Te ts'ao-chü shih-mo" 黃遵憲·使德· 遭拒始末 (On the German rejection of Huang Tsun-hsien's appointment as minister), in *Nan-yang hsueh-pao* 17.1:25–28 (April 1962).

Cheng Hsien 正先 . "Huang Kung-tu: Wu-hsu wei-hsin yun-tung te ling-hsiu" 黃公度 ：戊戌維新運動的領袖 (Huang Tsun-hsien: the leader of the Reform of 1898), *I-ching: Wen-shih pan-yueh k'an* 逸經：文史半月刊 (Semi-monthly journal of literature and history) 10:16–21 (July 1936). [Cheng Hsien is a pseudonym of Huang Yen-tsuan, a grandson of Huang Tsun-hsien. I learned his identity from Huang Yen-yu (note to the author, June 17, 1973).]

Cheng Kuan-ying 鄭觀應 . *I-yen* 易言 (Easy words). Hong Kong, Chung-hua in-wu tseng-chü, 1880. Microfilm copy at the Harvard-Yenching Library, Harvard University.

——. *Sheng-shih wei-yen* 盛世危言 (Warning to the seemingly prosperous world). 5 chüan. Shanghai, 1896.

Cheng Tzu-yu 鄭子瑜 . "T'an Huang Kung-tu te nan-yu-shih" 談黃公度的南游詩 (On Huang Tsun-hsien's poems during his sojourn in the South Seas), in Cheng Tzu-yü, ed., *Jen-ching-lu ts'ung-k'ao* 人境廬叢考 . (Studies on Huang Tsun-hsien) Singapore, Commercial Press, 1959.

Cheng Tzu-yü and Satō Keishū 實藤惠秀 , comps. *Huang Tsun-hsien yü Jih-pen yu-jen pi-t'an i-kao* 黃遵憲與日本友人筆談遺稿 (Records of written conversations between Huang Tsun-hsien and his Japanese friends). Tokyo, Waseda Daigaku, Tōyō Bungaku Ken-kyūkai, 1968.

Ch'eng Kuang-yü 程光裕 . "Huang Tsun-hsien yü Joh-pen-jen chih ch'ing-i chi ch'i *Jih-pen-kuo chih*" 黃遵憲與日本人之情誼及其日本國志 (Friendship between Huang Tsun-hsien and the Japanese and his *Treatises on Japan*), in Shen Chin-ting 沈覲鼎 et al., eds., *Pai-nien lai Chung-Jih kuan-hsi lun-wen chi.*

Chia-ying chou-chih. See *Kuang-hsu Chia-ying chou-chih.*

Chiao-an shih-liao pien-mu 敎案史料編目 (Materials on anti-missionary cases). Wu Sheng-te 吳盛德、 and Ch'en Tsung-hui 陳增輝 comps. Peking, Yen-ching University, 1942.

Chiao-hui hsin-pao 敎會新報 (*Church News*). Lin Lo-chih 林樂知 (Young John Allen), ed. 1868–1874. Reprint edition, Taipei, Ching-hua Shu-chü, 1968.

"Chiao-hui hsin-pao: Analysis of Contents." Mimeographed. Department of History, University of California, Davis, 1968.

Ch'ien Mu 錢穆 . *Chung-kuo chin san-bai-nien hsueh-shu shih* 中國近三百年學術史 (An intellectual history of China during the past three hundred years). Shanghai, Commercial Press, 1937.

Ch'ien O-sun (Chung-lien) 錢萼孫 （仲聯 ）, comp. "Huang Kung-tu hsien-sheng nien-p'u" 黃公度先生年譜 (A chronological biography of Huang Tsun-hsien), in *JCLST.*

Ch'ing-ch'ao hsu wen-hsien t'ung-k'ao 清朝續文獻通考 (A survey of history of the Ch'ing dynasty). Liu Chin-tsao, 劉錦藻 comp. Taipei, Hsin-hsing shu-chü, 1965 Facsimile reproduction of Shanghai Commercial Press edition of 1936.

Ch'ing-chi Chung-Jih-Han kuan-hsi shih-liao 清季中日韓關係史料 (Sources on the relations among China, Japan, and Korea during the late Ch'ing period). Kuo T'ing-i 郭廷以 et al., comps. Taipei, Chung-yang yen-chiu-yuan Chin-tai-shih Yen-chiu-so, 1972.

Ch'ing-chi wai-chiao shih-liao 清季外交史料 (Diplomatic archives during the late Ch'ing). Wang Yen-wei 王彥威 , comp. Reproduction of Peiping 1932–1935 edition. Taipei, Wen-hai Press, 1964.

Ch'ing Kuang-hsu-ch'ao Chung-Jih chiao-she shih-liao 清光緒朝中日 交涉史料 (Documents of Sino-Japanese relations during the reign of Kuang-hsu), 56 chüan. Taipei. Reproduction of 1932 Palace Museum edition.

Ch'ing-shih 清史 (History of the Ch'ing dynasty). Chang Ch'i-yun 張其昀 et al., comps. 8 vols. Taipei, Kuo-fang Yen-chiu-yuan, 1961.

Ch'ing-shih kao 清史稿 (Draft history of the Ch'ing dynasty). Chao Erh-hsun 趙爾巽 et al., comps. 2 vols. Shanghai, Lien-ho Shu-tien, 1942.

Ch'ing-tai ch'ou-pan i-wu shih-mo 清代籌辦夷務始末 (A complete account of the management of barbarian affairs during the Ch'ing period), Wen Ch'ing 文慶 et al., comps. Series I, Tao-kuang reign (1836–1850), 80 chüan; Series II, Hsien-feng reign (1851–1861), 80 chüan; Series III, T'ung-chih reign (1861–1874), 100 chüan. Photographic reproduction. Peking, Palace Museum, 1929–1930.

Chou Huang 周煌 . *Liu-ch'iu-kuo chih-lueh* 琉球國志略 (Brief treatises of Liu-ch'iu). Taipei, Hua-wen shu-chü, 1968. Facsimile reproduction of 1757 edition.

Chou Tso-jen 周作人 , Kiyama Hideo 木山英雄 , trans. *Nihon bunka o kataru* 日本文化を語る (Essays on Japanese culture). Tokyo, Chikuma Shobō, 1973.

Chow, Jen-hwa. "The History of Chinese Diplomatic Mission in Japan, 1877–1911." A thesis submitted to Australian National University, 1971.

Chow, Tse-tsung. *The May Fourth Movement: Intellectual Revolution in Modern China*. Cambridge, Harvard University Press, 1960.

Ch'ü T'ung-tsu. *Local Government in China under the Ch'ing*. Cambridge, Harvard University Press, 1962.

Chuang Chi-fa 莊吉發 . "Ch'ing-chi ch'u-shih ching-fei te ch'ou-ts'o" 清季出使經費的籌措 (Arrangement for the expenses for overseas legations in the late Ch'ing period), *Ta-lu tsa-chih* 55.2:25–33 (August 1977).

Cohen Myron. "The Hakka or 'Guest People': Dialect as a Sociocultural Variable in Southeastern China," *Ethnology* 15.3:237–292 (summer 1968).

Cohen, Paul A. *Between Tradition and Modernity: Wang T'ao and Reform in Late Ch'ing China*. Cambridge, Harvard University Press, 1974.

—— and John Schrecker, eds. *Reform in Nineteenth Century China*. Cambridge, East Asian Research Center, Harvard University, 1976.

Coolidge, Mary Roberts. *Chinese Immigration*. New York; republished, Taipei, 1968.

Dai ikkai Nihon teikoku tōkei nenkan 第一回日本帝國統計年鑑 (The first annual statistics of the Japanese empire). Tokyo, Naikaku Tōkei-kyoku, 1882.

Dai Nihon shi 大日本史 (History of great Japan). Tokugawa Mitsukuni 徳川光圀 et al., comps. 17 vols. Tokyo, Yūbenkai, 1928-29.

de Tocqueville, Alexis. *Democracy in America*. Paris, 1840. New York, 1945.

Dōjinsha bungaku zasshi 同人社文學雜誌 (Literary journal of the Dōjinsha). Tokyo, Dōjinsha, 1876-1883.

Drake, Fred W. *China Charts the World: Hsu Chi-yu and His Geography of 1848*. Cambridge, East Asian Research Center, Harvard University, 1975.

Earhart, H. Byron. *Japanese Religion: Unity and Diversity*. Encino, California, 1974.

Eastman, Lloyd E. *Throne and Mandarins: Chinese Search for a Policy during the Sino-French Controversy, 1880-1885*. Cambridge, Harvard University Press, 1967.

Esherick, Joseph W. *Reform and Revolution in China: The 1911 Revolution in Hunan and Hupei*. Berkeley and Los Angeles, University of California Press, 1976.

Fairbank, John K., ed. *The Chinese World Order: Traditional China's Foreign Relations*. Cambridge, Harvard University Press, 1968.
——. *The Cambridge History of China*, Volume 10. Cambridge University Press, 1978.
——, Edwin O. Reischauer, and Albert M. Craig. *East Asia: The Modern Transformation*. Boston, Houghton Mifflin, 1965.

Fan Wen-lan 范文瀾 . *Chung-kuo chin-tai-shih* 中國近代史 (History of modern China). Shanghai, Tu-shu ch'u-pan-she, 1947.

Fan Yeh 范曄 , comp. *Hou Han shu* 後漢書 (History of the Later Han dynasty). Shanghai, Chung-hua Shu-chü, 1927.

Feng Kuei-fen 馮桂芬 . *Chiao-pin-lu k'ang-i* 校邠廬抗議 (Protests from the Chiao-pin studio). Yü-chang, Feng family edition, 1884.

Feuerwerker, Albert. *China's Early Industrialization: Sheng Hsuan-huai (1844-1916) and Mandarin Enterprise*. Cambridge, Harvard University Press, 1958.

Fisher, Jerry. "Nakamura Keiu: The Evangelical Ethic in Japan," in Robert J. Miller, ed., *Religious Ferment in Asia*. Lawrence, Kansas, University of Kansas Press, 1974.

Folsom, Kenneth E. *Friends, Guests, and Colleagues: The Mu-fu System in the Late Ch'ing Period.* Berkeley and Los Angeles, University of California Press, 1968.

Fu Yun-lung 傅雲龍 . *Yu-li Jih-pen t'u-ching* 遊歷日本圖經 (Illustrated record of travel in Japan). 30 chüan. 1889. Microfilm copy of the collection of Keishū Sanetō at Hibiya Library, Tokyo.

Fujimura Michio 藤村道生 . "Meiji ishin gaikō no kyū kokusai kankei e no taiō, Nisshin shūkō jōki no seiritsu o meggutte" 明治維新外交の旧国際関係への対応・　一日清修好条規の成立をめぐって (The Meiji Government's response to the traditional international relationship in East Asia; on the conclusion of the Sino-Japanese Friendship Treaty of 1871), *Nagoya daigaku bungakubu kenkyū ronshū, shigaku* 14 (March 1966).

————. "Meiji shonen ni okeru Ajia seisaku no shūsei to Chūgoku, Nisshin shūkō jōki sōan no kentō" 明治初年における アジア政案の修正と中国　一日清修好条規草案の検討 (Revision of Japan's policies toward Asia in the early Meiji era, an examination of the drafts of the friendship treaty with China), *Nagoya daigaku bungakubu kenkyū ronshū, shigaku* 15:3–25 (1967).

————. "Meiji shoki ni okeru Nisshin kōshō no ichi dammen, Ryūkyū buntō jōyaku o megutte" 明治初期における日清交渉の一断面　一琉球分島条約をめぐって (An aspect of Sino-Japanese diplomacy in the early Meiji era; On the treaty concerning the division of the Ryukyu Islands), *Nagoya daigaku bungakubu kenkyū ronshū, shigaku* 16 (1968).

Fujita Takeo 藤田武夫 . *Nihon shihonshugi to zaisei* 日本資本主義と財政 (Capitalism in Japan and financial administration). Tokyo, Jitsugyō-no-Nihon sha, 1949.

Fukuda Yoshirō 福田芳郎 . "Meiji shoki ni okeru shinkaron no sokumen" 明治初期における進化論の側面 (Theory of evolution in early Meiji Japan), *Nihon rekishi* 14:2–10 (March 1949).

Fukunaga Mitsuji 福永光司 . "Dōkyō ni okeru kagami to tsurugi, sono shisō no genryū" 道教における鏡と剣　一その思想の源流 (Mirror and sword in Taoism: their ideological origins), *Tōhō gakuhō* 45:59–120 (1973).

Fumoto Yasutaka 麓保孝 . "Shimmatsu no Kō Kōdo no mitaru Nihon" 清末の黄公度の観たる日本 (Japan as seen by Huang Kung-tu of the late Ch'ing), *Rekishi kyōiku* 8.1 (January 1960).

Fuse Chisoku 布施知足 . *Yūki ni arawaretaru Meiji jidai no Nisshi* ōrai 遊記に現はれたる明治時代の日支往來   (Sino-Japanese exchanges as revealed in the travel records [by Chinese]). Tōa Kenkyūkai 東亞研究會 , Tōa kenkyū kōza 東亞研究會講座 (Series on East Asia), no. 84. 1938.

Gaimushō 外務省 . Dai Nihon gaikō bunsho 大日本外交文書 , Nihon gaikō bunsho 日本外交文書 (Documents on the foreign relations of Japan). Tokyo, Nihon Kokusai Rengō Kyōkai, 1947- .

———. "Meiji 28–29 nen Shina kakuchi teikoku senkan kyoryūchi settei ikken: Dai 5 hen Soshū (1)" 明治二十八〜二十九年支那各地帝國專管居留地設定一件第五編蘇州（一） (On exclusive Japanese settlements in China during 1895–1896 [unpublished archive of the Foreign Ministry]).

Godley, Michael R. "The Late Ch'ing Courtship of the Chinese in Southeast Asia," *Journal of Asian Studies* 34.2:361–385 (February 1975).

Gotō Yasushi 後藤靖 . Jiyū minken undō no tenkai 自由民權運動の展開 (Development of the People's Rights movement). Tokyo, Yūhikaku, 1966.

Haga Noboru 芳賀登 . Hihan kindai Nihon shigaku shisō shi 批判近代日本史学思.想.史 (A critical study of modern Japanese historical thought). Tokyo, Kashiwa Shobō, 1974.

Hall, John W. "The Confucian Teacher in Tokugawa Japan," in David S. Nivison and Arthur F. Wright, eds., *Confucianism in Action*. Stanford, Stanford University Press, 1959.

Hao, Yen-p'ing. "Cheng Kuan-ying: The Comprador as Reformer," *Journal of Asian Studies* 29.1:15–22 (November 1969).

———. *The Comprador in Nineteenth Century China: Bridge Between East and West*. Cambridge, Harvard University Press, 1970.

Hashimoto, Mantaro J. *The Hakka Dialect: A Linguistic Study of Its Phonology, Syntax, and Lexicon*. Cambridge, Cambridge University Press, 1973.

Hatada Takashi 旗田巍 . "Kindai ni okeru Chōsenjin no Nihon kan, Eisei sekija ron o chūshin ni shite" 近代における朝鮮人の日本観衛正斥邪論を中心にして (Korean views of Japan in the modern age), *Shisō* 520:59–73 (October 1967).

Hattori Seiichi (Bushō) 服部誠一（撫松） . Tōkyō shin hanjō ki 東京新繁昌記 (A new description of the prosperity of Tokyo), in *Meiji bungaku zenshū*. Tokyo, Chikuma Shobō, 1969.

Hirose Yasuko 広瀬靖子 . "Nisshin sensō zen no Igirisu kyokutō

seisaku no ichi kōsatsu: Chōsen mondai o chūshin to shite" 日清戦争前のイギリス極東政策の一考察 —朝鮮問題を中心として (British attitudes towards the opening of Korea), *Kokusai seiji: Nihon gaikō no kokusai ninshiki, sono shiteki tenkai* 国際政治: 日本外交の国際認識, その史的展開 (Japanese views of international relations in its diplomatic policies). Nihon Kokusai Seiji Gakukai, 1974.

Ho Ju-chang 何如璋 . "Shih tung shu-lueh" 使東述略 (Brief records of mission to Japan), in *Hsiao-fang-hu-chai yü-ti ts'ung-ch'ao,* 52 ts'e (10,309–333b).

Ho Kai (Ch'i) 何啓 and Hu Li-yuan 胡禮垣 . *Hsin-cheng chen-ch'üan* 新政眞詮 (Essentials of new government). Hong Kong (?), Chung-kuo Pao-kuan, 1900.

Ho Ping-ti 何炳棣 . "Chang Yin-huan shih-chi" 張蔭桓事蹟 (The career of Chang Yin-huan), *Ch'ing-hua hsueh-pao* 清華學報 (Tsing Hua Journal of Chinese Studies) 13.1: 185–210 (1941).

Hō Takushū (P'eng Tse-chou) 彭澤周 . *Meiji shoki Nikkanshin kankei no kenkyū* 明治初期日韓清関係の研究 (Relations among Japan, Korea, and China in the late nineteenth century). Tokyo, Hanawa Shobō, 1969.

——. *Chūgoku no kindaika to Meiji ishin* 中国の近代化と明治維新 (The modernization of China and the Meiji Restoration). Kyoto, Dōbōsha, 1976.

Holcombe, Chester. "The Restriction of Chinese Immigration," *The Outlook* 76:971–977 (April 23, 1904).

Houghton, Walter E. *The Victorian Frame of Mind.* New Haven, Yale Paperbound, 1957.

Howard, Richard C. "Japan's Role in the Reform Program of K'ang Yu-wei," in Jung-pang Lo, ed., *K'ang Yu-wei: A Biography and Symposium.* Tucson, The University of Arizona Press, 1967.

Hsiang-pao lei-tsuan 湘報類纂 (Classified compilation of *Hsiang pao*). Taipei, Ta-t'ung Shu-chü. Reproduction of 1902 Shanghai, Chung-hua Pien-i In-shu-kuan edition.

Hsiao-fang-hu-chai yü-ti ts'ung-ch'ao 小方壺齋輿地叢鈔 (Collected essays on the geography of the little-square-kettle studio). Wang Hsi-ch'i 王錫祺 , comp. Shanghai, Chu-i-t'ang, 1877–1897.

Hsiao, Kung-ch'üan, "Weng T'ung-ho and the Reform Movement of 1898," *Tsing Hua Journal of Chinese Studies* n.s. 1.2:111–245 (April 1957).

——. *A Modern China and a New World: K'ang Yu-wei, Reformer and*

Utopian, 1858–1927. Seattle and London, University of Washington Press, 1975.

Hsieh Kuo-chen 謝國珍 . *Chia-ying p'ing-k'ou chi-lueh* 嘉應平寇 紀略 (Records of suppression of the rebels in Chia-ying), in Hsiao-yuan ts'ung-shu 嘯圓叢書 ts'e 28. Prefaced 1879.

Hsin-min ts'ung-pao 新民叢報 (New citizen journal) nos. 12, 13, 20 and 24. Yokohama, 1902–1903.

Hsiu-hsin-shih chi-lu 修信使記錄 . *See* Kim Hong-jip.

Hsu Ch'ang-an 許常安 . "Ban Shin 'shikai kakumei' shi no yōgo ni tsuite—tokuni sono Nihongo teki na mono" 晚清「詩界革命」詩 の用語について — 特にその日本語的なもの (On vocabulary in the late-Ch'ing poems, particularly on words adopted from the Japanese), *Shibun* (Journal of Sinology) 44:19–30 (January 1966).

Hsu, Francis L. K. *Iemoto: The Heart of Japan.* New York, J. Wiley, 1975.

Hsu, Immanuel C. Y. *China's Entrance into the Family of Nations.* Cambridge, Harvard University Press, 1960.

Hsu Ta-ling 許大齡 . *Ch'ing-tai chüan-na chih-tu* 清代捐納 制度 (The system of purchasing offices by contribution during the Ch'ing). Yenching Journal of Chinese Studies, Monograph Series, no. 22. Peking, 1950.

Hsueh Fu-ch'eng 薛福成 . *Yung-an ch'üan-chi* 庸盦全集 (Collected works of Hsueh Fu-ch'eng). Shanghai, Tsuei-liu-t'ang, 1897. Includes: *Yung-an wen-pien* 庸盦文編 (Collected essays), 4 chüan; *Hsu-pien* 續編 (Supplements), 2 chüan; *Wai-pien* 外編 (Extra supplements), 4 chüan; *Hai-wai wen-pien* 海外文編 (Essays abroad), 4 chüan; *Ch'ou-yang ch'u-i* 籌洋芻議 (Discussions on foreign affairs), 1 chüan; *Ch'u-shih Ying Fa I Pi ssu-kuo jih-chi* 出使英法義比四國 日記 (Diary of my mission to four countries: England, France, Italy, and Belgium), 6 chüan.

———. *Ch'u-shih kung-tu* 出使公牘 (Official correspondences of the mission abroad). Taipei, Chung-hua wen-shih ts'ung-shu. Reproduction of 1898 Chuan-ching-lou edition.

———. *Ch'u-shih jih-chi hsu-k'o* 出使日記續刻 (Diary of the mission abroad, continued). Taipei, Chung-hua wen-shih ts'ung-shu, 1968. Reproduction of 1898 Chuan-ching-lou edition.

———. *Yung-an pi-chi* 庸庵筆記 (Essays by Hsueh Fu-ch'eng). 6 chüan. 1898. Reproduction, Shanghai, Commercial Press, 1937.

Hu-nan chin pai-nien ta-shih chi-shu 湖南近百年大事紀述 (Major events in Hunan during the last one hundred years). Hu-nan-

sheng chich Pien-tsuan Wei-yuan hui 湖南省志·編纂委員會 ,
comp. Tokyo, Daian, 1966. Reprint of 1959 Changsha edition.

Hu-nan li-shih tzu-liao 湖南历史資料 (Historical materials
on Hunan). Hu-nan li-shih tzu-liao Pien-chi Wei-yuan hui 湖南历史資料
編輯委員会 , comp. 1958 no. 4; 1959 nos. 1–2. Hu-nan
Jen-nin ch'u-pan she.

Hu-nan shih-wu hsueh-t'ang ch'u-chi 湖南時務學堂初集 (The
first collection of writings at the School of Current Affairs in Hunan).
Changsha, 1898.

Hu-nan t'ung-chih 湖南通誌· (A history of Hunan). Tseng Kuo-ch'üan
曾國荃 et al., comps. Fu-hsueh tsun-ching-ko 1885 edition.

Hu Shih 胡適 . *Wu-shih nien lai Chung-kuo chih wen-hsueh* 五十年來
中國之文學 (Chinese literature during the last fifty years). [n.p.]
Hsin-min-kuo shu, 1929.

Hu Ssu-ching 胡思敬 . *Wu-hsu lü-hsiang lu* 戊戌履霜錄
(An aftermath account of the Reform of 1898). Nan-ch'ang, 1913.

Huan K'uang 桓寬 . *Yen-t'ieh lun* 鹽鐵論 (Discourse on salt and
iron). Shanghai, Commercial Press, 1934.

Huang Chang-chien 黃彰健 . *Wu-hsu pien-fa shih yen-chiu* 戊戌變法
史研究 (Studies of the history of the 1898 Reform). Taipei, Chung-
yang Yen-chiu-yuan Li-shih Yü-yen Yen-chiu so, 1970.

———. *K'ang Yu-wei wu-hsu chen tsou-i* 康有爲戊戌眞奏議
(True memorials of K'ang Yu-wei in 1898). Taipei, Chung-yang Yen-chiu-
yuan Li-shih Yü-yen Yen-chiu-so, 1974.

Huang Tsun-hsien. *Jih-pen tsa-shih-shih* 日本雜事詩 (Miscellaneous
poems on Japan). Tokyo, Iijima Yūnen, 1880. Ch'ang-sha, Fu-wen-t'ang,
1898. Japanese translation by Sanetō Keishū and Toyota Minoru 豐田
穰 . *Nihon zatsuji shi.* Tokyo, Seikatsusha, 1943. Revised edition,
Tokyo, Heibonsha, 1968.

———. *Jih-pen-kuo chih* 日本國志· (Treatises on Japan). Canton, Fu-
wen-chai, 1890. Taipei, Wen-hai Press, 1968. Reproduction of 1898, Shanghai T'u-shu Chi-ch'eng Tu-shu-chü edition.

———. Letter to Ch'iu Wei-yuan (Shu-yuan) 邱煒菱 （萩園). A
photocopy published in *Hsiao-shuo yueh-pao* 8.1 (January 25, 1917).

———. "Yü Lang-shan lun shih" 與朗山論詩 (Letter to Lang-
shan discussing poetry). Published in *Ling-nan hsueh-pao* 領南學報
2.2:184–185 (July 1931).

———. *Jen-ching-lu shih-ts'ao chien-chu* 人境廬詩草箋註 (Collection of poems by Huang Tsun-hsien, annotated), annotation by Ch'ien

O-sun. Shanghai, Ku-tien Wen-hsueh Press, 1957.

——. *Jen-ching-lu chi-wai shih chi* 人境廬集外詩輯 (Poems of Huang Tsun-hsien not included in the collections prevously published. Pei-ching Ta-hsueh Chung-wen hsi Chin-tai shih yen-chiu hsiao tsu 北京大學中文系近代詩研究小組 , comp. Peking, 1960.

Huang's official letters and public announcements in Hunan were published in *HPLT*.

A comprehensive list of Huang's writings including unpublished manuscripts is in Yang T'ien-shih 杨天石 , *Huang Tsun-hsien*, in Ch'en Chiu-lu 陈旭麓 , comp., Chung-kuo chin-tai shih ts'ung-shu 中国近代史丛平 (Series on modern Chinese history). Shang-hai Jen-min ch'u-pan-she, 1979.

Huang Tsun-k'ai 黃遵楷 . "Hsien-hsiung Kung-tu hsien-sheng shih-shih shu-lueh" 先兄公度先生事實述略 (Brief biography of my brother, the late Huang Tsun-hsien), in Huang Tsun-hsien, *Jen-ching-lu chi-wai-shih chi*. Peking, 1960. Originally published in mimeograph by Lai Po-t'ao 賴伯陶 in Singapore in 1957 as an appendix to Huang Tsun-hsien, *Jih-pen tsa-shih-shih* (reprint of 1898 edition), which has been reprinted in Taipei in the series comp. by Shen Yun-lung 沈雲龍 , *Chin-tai Chung-kuo shih-liao ts'ung-k'an hsu-pien* 近代中國史料叢刊續編 (A series of historical materials on modern China, 2nd series), Volume 95.

Hummel, Arthur W., ed. *Eminent Chinese of the Ch'ing Period*. 2 vols. U. S. Government Printing Office, 1943.

Hung, William. "Huang Tsun-hsien's Poem 'The Closure of the Educational Mission in America'," *Harvard Journal of Asiatic Studies* 18:50–73 (1955).

Ichiko Chūzō 市古宙三 . *Kindai Chūgoku no seiji to shakai* 近代中国の政治と社会 (Studies of government and society of modern China). Tokyo, Tokyo Daigaku Shuppankai, 1971.

Ienaga Saburō 家永三郎 . *Ueki Emori kenkyū* 植木枝盛研究 (A study of Ueki Emori). Tokyo, 1960.

Imai Usaburō 今井宇三郎 , Seya Yoshihiko 瀨谷義彥 , Bitō Masahide 尾藤正英 , eds. *Mitogaku* 水戸学 (Mito School), in series Nihon shisō taikei 日本思想大系 . Tokyo, Iwanami Shoten, 1973.

Inoue Nobumasa 井上陳政 . *See* Narahara Nobumasa.

Ion, A. Hamish. "Edward Warren Clark and Early Meiji Japan: A Case Study of Cultural Contact," *Modern Asian Studies* 2.4:557–572 (October 1977).

Ishihara Michihiro 石原道博 . *"Nihon kokushi* to *Azuma kagami ho"* 日本國志と吾妻鏡補 (The *Treatises on Japan* and *Supplement to the History of The Eastern Provinces*), *Rekishigaku kenkyū* 歷史學研究 8.12 (December 1938).

——. *"Kō* Junken no *Nihon-koku shi* to *Nihon zatsuji shi"* 黄遵憲ノ 日本国志と日本雜事詩 (*Treatises on Japan* and *Miscellaneous poems on Japan* by Huang Tsun-hsien), *Ibaraki daigaku jimbungakubu kiyō, Bungakuka ronshū*, Nos. 7, 8, & 9 (1974, 1975, 1976).

——. *Shu Shunsui* 朱舜水 (Chu Shun-shui). Tokyo, Yoshikawa Kōbunkan, 1961.

Ishii Ryōsuke 石井良助 et al., eds. *Meiji bunka shi 2: Hōsei hen* 明治文化史 2: 法制編 (Cultural history of the Meiji era). Tokyo, 1954.

——. *Nihon hōsei shi* 日本法制史 (A history of legal institutions in Japan). Tokyo, Seirin Shoin, 1959.

Ishikawa Ei (Kōsai) 石川英 (鴻齋) ed. *Shibayama isshō* 芝山 一笑 (Jubilation at Mt. Shiba). Tokyo, Kumagaya Shōshichi, 1878. Microfilm copy of the Sanetō collection at Hibiya Library.

Ishizuka Hiromichi 石塚裕道 . *Nihon shihonshugi seiritsu shi kenkyū: Meiji kokka to shokusan kōgyō seisaku* 日本資本主義成立史研究 : 明治国家と殖産興業政策 (A study of the establishment of capitalism in Japan: The Meiji state and its policies for development of industries). Tokyo, Yoshikawa Kōbunkan, 1973.

Iwai Tadakuma 岩井忠熊 . "Gunji keisatsu kikō no kakuritsu" 軍事 警察機構の確立 (Establishment of the military and police systems), *Iwanami kōza Nihon rekishi,* Volume 15. Tokyo, 1976.

Jansen, Marius B. "Japanese Views of China During the Meiji Period," in Albert Feuerwerker, Rhoads Murphey, Mary C. Wright, eds., *Approaches to Modern Chinese History.* Berkeley and Los Angeles, University of California Press, 1967.

——. *Japan and China: From War to Peace 1894–1972.* Chicago, Rand McNally College Publishing Co., 1975.

Jones, Susan Mann, and Philip A. Kuhn, "Dynastic Decline and the Roots of Rebellion," in John K. Fairbank, ed., *The Cambridge History of China,* Volume 10. Cambridge, Cambridge University Press, 1978.

Jung Hung. *See* Yung Wing.

Kaigunshō, Kaigun Daijin Kambō 海軍省海軍大臣官房 , comp. *Kaigun gumbi enkaku* 海軍軍備沿革 (A history of the naval forces of Japan). Tokyo, 1934. Reprint, Gannandō Shoten, 1970.

Kamban bankoku kōhō 官版萬國公法 (Official edition of Elements of international law). [Tokyo], Kaiseisho, 1865.

Kamei, Shunsuke. "The Sacred Land of Liberty: Images of America in Nineteenth Century Japan," in Akira Iriye, ed., *Mutual Images: Essays in American-Japanese Relations.* Cambridge, Harvard University Press, 1975.

Kametani Kō (Seiken) 亀谷行 (省軒). *Seiken shi bun kō* 省軒 詩文稿 (Essays and poems by Kametani Seiken). Tokyo, 1902.

Kanda Kiichirō 神田喜一郎 . *Nihon ni okeru Chūgoku bungaku 1: Nihon tenshi shiwa* 日本における中国文学 1 ：日本 塡詞史話 (Chinese literature in Japan; a history of *tz'u*). Tokyo, 1965.

Kanda Suematsu 神田末保 , for Bōekikyoku 貿易局 . *Hanshin zairyū no Kashō to sono bōeki jijō* 阪神在留ノ華商ト 其ノ貿易事情 (Overseas Chinese in the Osaka-Kobe area and their trade). 1938.

Kang Jae-ŏn 姜在彦 . *Chōsen kindaishi kenkyū* 朝鮮近代史 研究 (Studies of modern Korean history). Tokyo, Nihon Hyōronsha, 1970.

K'ang Yu-wei 康有為 . *Jih-pen Ming-chih pien-cheng-chi (k'ao)* 日本 明治變政記 [考](A record [study] of Meiji Restoration in Japan). Microfilm copy, reprinted in Huang Chang-chien, *K'ang Yu-wei Wu-hsu chen tsou-i.*

——. *Ta-t'ung-shu* 大同書 (Book of grand harmony). Shanghai, Kutien Press, 1956.

——. *K'ang Yu-wei shih-wen hsuan* 康有為詩文選 (Collection of poems and essays of K'ang Yu-wei). Peking, Jen-min Wen-hsueh Press, 1958.

Kao Wei-lien 高維廉 . "Huang Kung-tu chiu-jen Hsin-chia-po tsung-lingshih k'ao" 黄公度就任新嘉坡總領事考 (Huang Tsun-hsien as the Consul General in Singapore), in Cheng Tzu-yü, *Jen-ching-lu ts'ung-k'ao.*

Keene, Donald, trans. *Chushingura: The Treasury of Loyal Retainers.* New York and London, Columbia University Press, 1971.

Kikegawa Hiroshi 亀封川浩 . *Meiji chihō jichi seido no seiritsu katei* 明治地方自治制度の成立過程 (The development of the system of local government during the Meiji period). Tōkyō Shisei Chōsakai 東京市政調査会 , 1955.

Kim Hong-jip 金弘集 , "Susinsa ilgi" 修信使日記

(Diary of the friendship commissioner), in Kuksa P'yŏngch'an Wiwŏnhoe 國史編纂委員會 , comp., *Susinsa kirok* 修信使記錄 (Records of the friendship commissioner), in *Han'gok saryo ch'ongsŏ* 韓國史料叢書 (A study of the modern diplomatic history of Korea), Volume 9. Seoul, 1958.

Kim Yŏng-jak 金榮作 . *Kammatsu nashonarizumu no kenkyū* 韓末ナショナリズムの研究 (Studies of nationalism in the late Han period in Korea), Tokyo, Tokyo Daigaku Shuppankai, 1975.

Kinoshita Hyō 木下彪 . *Meiji shiwa* 明治詩話 (Essays on poetry during the Meiji). Tokyo, Bunchūdō, 1943.

Ko Kung-chen 戈公振 . *Chung-kuo pao-hsueh shih* 中國報學史 (A history of journalism in China). Taipei, 1964.

Kobayakawa Kingo 小早川欣吾 . *Meiji hōsei shi ron: kōhō no bu* 明治法制史論 : 公法の部 (A history of legal institutions during the Meiji: public law). Tokyo, 1940.

Koizuka Ryū 肥塚龍 for Yokohama Shōkōkaigisho 横濱商工會議所 , *Yokohama kaikō gojūnen shi* 横濱開港五十年史 (Fifty-year history of Yokohama since the opening of the port). 2 vols. Yokohama, 1909.

Kojima Shinji 小島晋治 . "Meiji ishin to Chūgoku" 明治維新と中國 (The Meiji Restoration and China). *Iwanami kōza Nihon rekishi geppō* 岩波講座日本歴史月報 no. 4 (August 1975).

Kojong sillok 高宗實錄 (Veritable records of the reign of Kojong). Oda Shōgo 小田省吾 et al., comps. Reprint in *Kojong Sunjong sillok* 高宗純宗實錄 (Veritable records of the reigns of Kojong and Sunjong). Seoul, 1970.

Kondō Tetsuo 近藤哲生 . "Shokusan kōgyō to zairai sangyō" 殖産興業と在末産業 (Industrialization and indigenous industries), *Iwanami kōza Nihon rekishi*, Volume 14. Tokyo, 1975.

Kōsaka Masaaki 高坂正顯 . *Meiji bunka shi 4: Shisō genron hen* 明治文化史4: 思想言論篇 (Cultural history of the Meiji era: Thoughts and journalism). Tokyo, 1955.

Koyama Hirotake 小山弘健 . *Nihon gunji kōgyō no shiteki bunseki* 日本軍事工業の史的分析 (Historical analysis of military industries in Japan). Tokyo, Ochanomizu Shobō, 1972.

Kuang-hsu-ch'ao tung-hua hsu-lu 光緒朝東華續錄 Chu Shou-p'eng 朱壽朋 , comp. Shanghai, 1909.

Kuang-hsu Chia-ying-chou chih 光緒嘉應州志 (History of Chia-ying department compiled in the Kuang-hsu period). Wen Chung-ho

溫仲和   et al., comps. 32 chüan. 1898. Facsimile reproduction by
Mei Hsien T'ung-hsiang-hui 梅縣同鄉會   . Taipei, 1962.

Kublin, Hyman. "The Attitude of China during the Liu-ch'iu Controversy,
1871–1881," *Pacific Historical Review* 18:213–231 (1949).

Kubota Beisen 久保田米僊   et al., eds. *Nisshin sentō gahō* 日清
戰鬪畫報 (Pictorial report on the battles in the Sino-Japanese War).
Tokyo, Ōkura Shoten, 1894–1895.

Kuhn, Philip A. "Origins of the Taiping Vision: Cross-Cultural Dimensions of
Chinese Rebellion," *Comparative Studies in Society and History* 19.3:
350–366 (July 1977).

Kung, S. W. *Chinese in American Life: Some Aspects of Their History, Problems, and Contributions.* Seattle, University of Washington Press, 1962.

Kuo Ting-yee and James W. Morley. *Sino-Japanese Relations, 1862–1927.* New
York, Columbia University, East Asian Institute, 1965.

Kuo T'ing-i 郭廷以   , comp. *Chin-tai Chung-kuo shih-shih jih-chih*
近代中國史事日誌· (Day-by-day chronicle of the historical
events in modern China). 2 vols. Taipei, Academia Sinica, 1963.

Kurata Sadayoshi 倉田貞美   . *Shimmatsu minsho o chūshin to shita
Chūgoku kindai shi no kenkyū* 清末民初を中心とした
中国近代詩の研究 (A study of Chinese poetry during the
late Ch'ing and early Republican periods). Tokyo, Taishūkan Shoten, 1969.

Kuzuu Yoshihisa 葛生能久   , comp. *Tōa senkaku shishi kiden*
東亞先覺志·士記傳 (Biographies of the activists in Japan's expansion in Asia). Tokyo, Kokuryūkai, 1933–1936.

Lamley, Harry J. "The 1895 Taiwan Republic, A Significant Episode in Modern Chinese History," *Journal of Asian Studies* 27.4:739–762 (August
1968).

Legge, James. *Chinese Classics.* 5 vols. Hong Kong, Hong Kong University
Press, 1960.

Levenson, Joseph R. *Confucian China and Its Modern Fate: A Trilogy.* Berkeley and Los Angeles, University of California Press, 1968.

Lewis, Charlton M. *Prologue to the Chinese Revolution: The Transformation
of Ideas and Institutions in Hunan Province, 1891–1907.* Cambridge, East
Asian Research Center, Harvard University, 1976.

Li Hung-chang 李鴻章   . *Li Wen-chung kung i-shu han-kao* 李文忠·
公譯署函稿 (Letters to the Tsungli Yamen), in his *Li
Wen-chung kung ch'üan-chi* 李文忠·公全集 (Collected works
of Li·Hung-chang), Wu Ju-lun 吳汝綸   , comp. Taipei, Wen-hai Press,

1962. Reproduction of 1921 Shanghai Commercial Press edition.

Li Tung-hai 李東海 . *Chia-na-ta hua-ch'iao shih* 加拿大華僑 史 (A history of overseas Chinese in Canada). Taipei, Chung-hua Ta-tien Pien-in-hui, 1967.

Li Yü-shu 李毓澍 . "Shou-jen chu-Jih kung-shih Ho Ju-chang" 首任 駐日公使何如璋 (Ho Ju-chang, the first Minister to Japan), in Shen Chin-ting et al., eds., *Pai-nien-lai Chung-Jih kuan-hsi lun-wen chi.*

Liang Ch'i-ch'ao 梁啓超 . *Chung-kuo chih wu-shih-tao* 中國之 武士道 (The *bushidō* in China). Shanghai, Kuang-chih Shu-chü, 1904.

——. *Yin-ping-shih shih-hua* 飲冰室詩話 (Essays on poetry). Shanghai, Shang-hai shu-chü, 1910.

——. *Yin-ping-shih wen chi* 飲冰室文集 , *Yin-ping-shih ho-chi* 飲冰室合集 (Collected works of Liang Ch'i-ch'ao). Shanghai, Chung-hua Shu-chü, 1936.

——. *Intellectual Trends in the Ch'ing Period.,* Immanuel C. Y. Hsu, trans. Cambridge, Harvard University Press, 1959.

——. "Chia-ying Huang hsien-sheng mu-chih ming" 嘉應黃先生墓誌· 銘 (Tomb inscription for Mr. Huang of Chia-ying), in *JCLST,* pp. 10–13.

Liang Chü-shih (Shih-wu) 梁居實 (詩五). *Liang Shih-wu hsien-sheng i-kao chi* 梁詩五先生遺稿集 (Collected works of Liang Chü-shih). [Taipei?]. 1960.

Light, Ivan. "From Vice District to Tourist Attraction: The Moral Career of American Chinatowns, 1880–1940," *Pacific Historical Review* 43:367–394 (1974).

Lin Ch'uan-fang 林傳芳 . "Hakka to Chūgoku no kindai" 客家 と中国の近代 (Hakka and modern China), *Ryūkoku shidan* 71:1–23 (September 1973).

Lin Neng-shih 林能士 . *Ch'ing-chi Hu-nan te hsin-cheng yun-tung* 清季湖南的新政運動 (Reform Movement in Hunan in the late Ch'ing period). Taipei, Taiwan University, 1972.

Lin Ta-ch'üan 林達泉 . "K'o-shuo" 客說 (A treatise on Hakka) in Wen T'ing-ching, comp., *Ch'a-yang san-chia wen-ch'ao.* Reprinted in Shen Yun-lung, comp., *Chin-tai Chung-kuo shih-liao ts'ung-k'an, ti 3 chi* 4:2–4 (1967).

Liu, James T. C. *Reform in Sung China: Wang An-shih (1021–1086) and His New Politics.* Cambridge, Harvard University Press, 1959.

Liu, K. C. *Americans and Chinese. A Historical Essay and a Bibliography.* Cambridge, Harvard University Press, 1963.

——. "Nineteenth-century China: The Disintegration of the Old Order and the Impact of the West," in Ping-ti Ho and Tang Tsou, eds., *China in Crisis*. Chicago, University of Chicago Press, 1968.

——. "The Confucian as Patriot and Pragmatist: Li Hung-chang's Formative Years, 1823–1866," *Harvard Journal of Asiatic Studies* 30:5–47 (1970).

Liu Kuang-ching 劉廣京 . "Cheng Kuan-ying *I-yen:* Kuang-hsu ch'u-nien chih pien-fa ssu-hsiang" 鄭觀應易言 －光緒初年之變法思想 (Cheng Kuan-ying's *I-yen:* Reform proposals of the early Kuang-hsu period), *Ch'ing-hua hsueh-pao* 8.1–2:373–416, English summary 417–425 (August 1970).

Liu K'un-i 劉坤一 . *Liu K'un-i i-chi* 劉坤一遺集 (Collected works of Liu K'un-i). 6 vols. Peking, Chung-hua Shu-chü, 1959.

Lo Hsiang-lin 羅香林 . *K'o-chia yen-chiu tao-lun* 客家研究導論 (An introduction to the study of Hakka in their ethnic, historical, and cultural aspects). [Kwangtung], Hsing-ning, Hsi-shan Shu-tsang, 1933.

——. "Hu Hsiao-ts'en hsien-sheng nien-p'u" 胡曉岑先生年譜 (Chronological biography of Hu Hsi 胡曦), in *Chung-yang yen-chiu-yuan li-shih yen-yü yen-chiu-so chi-k'an wai-pien, ti 4 chung, Ch'ing chu Teng Tso-pin hsien-sheng 65 sui lun-wen-chi* 中央研究院歷史語言研究所集刊外篇第四種 －慶祝董作賓先生六十五歲論文集 (The Bulletin of the Institute of History and Philology, Academia Sinica, Extra Volume No. 4, Part I; Studies Presented to Tung Tso-Pin on His Sixty-Fifth Birthday). Taipei, 1960.

——. "Huang Kung-tu hsien-sheng chuan-kao hsü" 黃公度先生傳稿序 (A note on the draft biography of Huang Tsun-hsien), *Ta-lu tsa-chih* 43.5 (November 1971).

Lo, Jung-pang, ed. *K'ang Yu-wei: A Biography and Symposium*. Tucson, The University of Arizona Press, 1967.

Lu Hsun. *Selected works of Lu Hsun*. Yang Hsien-yi et al., trans. 2 vols. Peking, 1956–1957.

Lu Shih-ch'iang 呂實強 et al., comps. *Chiao-wu chiao-an tang* 教務教案檔 (Archives on diplomatic issues on missionaries and missionary cases), the 5th series (1887–1895). 4 vols. Taipei, Chung-yang Yen-chiu-yuan Chin-tai-shih Yen-chiu-so, 1977.

Lyman, Stanford M. "Conflict and the Web of Group Affiliation in San Francisco's Chinatown, 1850–1910," *Pacific Historical Review* 43:473–499 (1974).

Maeda Katsutarō 前田勝太郎 . "Shin-dai no Kanton ni okeru nō-

min tōsō no kiban" 清代の広東における農民闘争の
基盤 (Bases of peasants' struggle in Canton during the Ch'ing period),
Tōyō gakuhō 51.4:1-38 (1968).

Mai Jo-p'eng 麥若鵬 . *Huang Tsun-hsien chuan* 黃遵憲傳 (A
biography of Huang Tsun-hsien). Shanghai, Ku-tien Wen-hsueh Press, 1957.

Makino Kenjirō 牧野謙次郎 . *Nihon kangaku shi* 日本漢學
史 (A history of Chinese learning in Japan). Tokyo, Sekaidō Shoten,
1943.

Martin, W. A. P. *Cycle of Cathay*. New York, Fleming H. Revell Co., 1900.
Republished, Taipei, Ch'eng-wen Press, n.d.

Maruyama Masao 丸山真男 , "Jiyū minken undō shi" 自由民権
運動史 (A history of the People's Rights movement), 1948, in
his *Senchū to sengo no aida* 戦中と戦後の間 (Collection of essays written during and after the war). Tokyo, Misuzu Shobō, 1976.

Masuda Wataru 増田渉 . *Chūgoku bungakushi: Bungaku kakumei to
sono zenya no hitobito* 中国文学史, 文学革命とその
前夜の人々 (A history of Chinese literature: the literary revolution and its prelude). Tokyo, Iwanami Shoten, 1970.

Matsui Kiyoshi 松井清 , ed. *Kindai Nihon bōeki shi* 近代日本
貿易史 (A history of foreign trade of Japan in the modern period).
Tokyo, Yūhikaku, 1959.

Matsushima Eiichi 松島栄一 . *Chūshingura, sono seiritsu to tenkai*
忠臣蔵 − その成立と展開 (Chūshingura, its origins and
development). Tokyo, 1964.

Matsushita Yoshio 松下芳男 . *Meiji gunsei shi ron* 明治軍制
史論 (A history of the military system during the Meiji period).
2 vols. Tokyo, Yūhikaku, 1956.

Matsuzawa H. 松沢弘陽 . "'Saikoku risshihen' to 'Jiyū no ri' no sekai—Bakumatsu jugaku, Bikutoria-chō kyūshinshugi, 'bummei kaika'"
「西国立志編」と「自由之理」の世界 −幕末儒学,
ビクトリア朝急進主義 [文明開化] (The World of *Saiko-
ku risshihen* and of *Jiyū no ri*—late Tokugawa Confucianism, Victorian
radicalism, and Meiji enlightenment,) in Nihon Seiji Gakukai, comp., *Nihon seiji gakukai nempō, Nihon ni okeru seiōseiji shishō* 日本政治
学会年報, 日本における西欧政治思想 . Tokyo, 1975.

Meijer, Marinus J. *The Introduction of the Modern Criminal Law in China*.
Batavia, 1949.

Meiji bunka zenshū 明治文化全集 . Yoshino Sakuzō
吉野作造 et al., comps. Tokyo, Nihon Hyōronsha, 1927-1928.

Metzger, Thomas A. *The Internal Organization of Ch'ing Bureaucracy: Legal,*

Normative, and Communication Aspects. Cambridge, Harvard University Press, 1973.

Miller, Stuart Creighton. *The Unwelcome Immigrant: The American Image of the Chinese, 1785-1882.* Berkeley and Los Angeles, University of California Press, 1969.

Milner, Jocelyn Valery. "The Role of Huang Tsun-hsien in the Reform Movement of the Nineteenth Century." MA thesis, University of Hong Kong, October 1962.

——. "The Reform Ideas of Huang Tsun-hsien's 'History of Japan' and Its Influence on the Hundred Days' Reform," *Nan-yang hsueh pao* 17:49-94 (November 1963).

Mōri Toshihiko 毛利敏彦 . "Meiji shoki gaikō no Chōsenkan" 明治初期外交の朝鮮観 (A view of Korea in early Meiji Government), *Kokusai seiji: Nihon gaikō no kokusai ninshiki, sono shiteki tenkai.* Kokusai Seiji Gakukai, 1974.

Morse, Edward S. *Japan Day by Day, 1877, 1878-79, 1882-83.* Boston, Houghton Mifflin, 1917.

Murata Tamotsu 村田保 . *Keihō chūshaku* 刑法註釋 (Annotation to the keihō). Tokyo, Uchida Seieidō, 1880.

——. *Chizaihō chūshaku* 治罪法註釋 (Annotation to the chizaihō), 8 kan. Tokyo, Uchida Seieidō, 1880.

Nagai Hideo 永井秀夫 . "Tōitsu kokka no seiritsu" 統一国家の成立 (Establishment of the unified state), *Iwanami Kōza Nihon rekishi,* Volume 14. 1975.

——. *Jiyū minken* 自由民権 (Freedom and People's Rights). in *Nihon no rekishi* 日本の歴史 (History of Japan), Volume 25. Tokyo, Shōgakukan, 1976.

Naimushō Keiho kyoku 內務省警保局 , comp. *Chō fu ken keisatsu enkaku shi* 廳府縣警察沿革史 (History of the police system in the central and local governments). Tokyo, 1927. Reprint, Hara Shobō, 1973.

Naitō Shigenobu 內藤戊申 . "Ō Kōnen denkō" 汪東年傳稿 (A draft biography of Wang K'ang-nien), *Tōyōshi kenkyū* 17.3:14-26 (December 1959); 19.9 (March 1961).

Nakae Chōmin 中江兆民 . *San suijin keirin mondō* 三醉人經綸問答 (A discourse on politics by three gentlemen), in his *Nakae Chōmin shū* 中江兆民集 . Tokyo, Chikuma Shobō, 1967.

Nakamura Masanao (Keiu) 中村正直 (敬宇). *Saikoku risshi hen*

西國立志·編 (Stories of self-made men in the West). Tokyo, Shichishoya Zōhan, 1877.

——. *Seiyō hinkō ron* 西洋品行論 (On Western ethics). Tokyo, Nakamura Masanao, 1878.

——. "Keiu nichijō 敬宇日乘 (Diary of Nakamura Keiu). Book 1 (February–August, 1876); Book 2 (January–July, 1882); Book 3 (July, 1882–January, 1883). Held at Seikadō Bunko, Tokyo.

——. "Kangaku fukahai ron" 漢學不可廢論 (Learning of Chinese Classics should not be abolished), *Gakushikaiin zasshi,* May 1887.

——. *Keiu bunshū* 敬宇文集 (A collection of essays by Nakamura Keiu). Tokyo, Yoshikawa Kōbunkan, 1903.

——. "Shina fukabu ron" 支那不可侮論 (China should not be despised), *Meiroku zasshi* 35 (April 1875). Reprinted in *Meiji bunka zenshū (zasshi hen),* Tokyo, 1925.

——. *Keiu shishū* 敬宇詩集 (A collection of poems by Nakamura Keiu). Tokyo, Keiu Shishū Kankō Hakkōsho, 1926.

——. *Jiyū no ri* 自由之理 (On liberty). Surugaya, 1872. Reprinted in Yoshino Sakuzō, comp., *Meiji bunka zenshū.* Tokyo, 1927.

Nakamura Mitsuo 中村光夫 . *Meiji bungaku shi* 明治文学史 (A history of literature during the Meiji period). Tokyo, 1963.

Nakamura Tadashi 中村義 . "Yōmu, hempō to mimpen: 1898 nen no ryō-Ko chiku o megutte," 洋務·変法と民変 — 1898年の両湖地已をめぐって (Westernization, reform, and mass uprising: Hunan and Hupei in 1898), in Nozawa Yutaka 野沢豊 and Tanaka Masatoshi, 田中正俊 , eds., *Kōza Chūgoku kingendaishi* 講座中国近現代史 (Series of studies on modern and contemporary China), Volume 2. Tokyo Daigaku Shuppankai, 1978.

Narahara Nobumasa 楢原陳政 . "Ryūgaku ryakki" 留學略記 (A brief record of my study in China), in his *Uiki tsūsan* 禹域通纂 (General survey of China). Tokyo, Ōkurashō, 1888.

National Archives. "Notes from the Chinese Legation in the United States to the Department of State, 1868–1906," in "File Microcopies of Record in the National Archives," Washington, D.C. No. 98.

——. "Despatches from the United States Minister to Japan to the Department of State." In ibid., No. 133.

——. "Despatches from United States Ministers to China to the Department of State, 1843–1906." In Ibid, No. 92.

National Palace Museum Library, Taipei. "Shang-yü tang" 上諭檔 (Records of edicts): *fang-pen* 方本 (square book). *hsiao-fang-pen* 小

方本 (small square book). I saw the books for the period from Kuang-hsu 21st to 24th year.

———. "Chün-chi-ch'u tang-an" 軍機處檔案 (Grand Council archives: copies of edicts kept at the Grand Council). For the years, Kuanghsu 7 and 23.

Needham, Joseph. *Science and Civilization in China.* Volume 1 *Introductory Orientations,* 1954. Volume 2 *History of Scientific Thought,* 1956. Volume 4 Pt. 1 *Physics and Physical Technology,* 1962. Cambridge, Cambridge University Press.

Nihon keizai tōkei sōkan 日本經濟統計總觀 (A collection of statistics on the Japanese economy). Tokyo, Asahi Shimbunsha, 1930.

Nihon kirisutokyō bunken mokuroku 日本キリスト敎文献目録 (Bibliographies of archives on Christianity in Japan). Kokusai Kirisutokyō Daigaku, Ajia Bunka Kenkyū Iinkai 國際基督敎大學 アジア文化研究委員會 , comp. 2 vols. Tokyo, 1965.

Nihon rekishi daijiten 日本歷史大辞典 (A dictionary of Japanese history). Tokyo, Kawade Shobō, 1968.

Nishimura Tokihiko 西村時彦 . "Seisai sensei gyōjō shiryō" 成齋先生行狀資料 , in *Shigeno hakushi shigaku rombunshū* 重野博士史學論文集 (Collection of works in history by Dr. Shigeno). Tokyo, 1938.

Niu Yang-shan 牛仰山 . *Huang Tsun-hsien.* Peking, 1961.

Numata Jirō. "Shigeno Yasutsugu and the Modern Tokyo Tradition of Historical Writing," in W. G. Beasley and E. G. Pulleyblank, eds., *Historians of China and Japan.* London, Oxford University Press, 1961.

Ohkawa, Kazushi and Rosovsky, Henry, "A Century of Japanese Economic Growth," in William W. Lockwood, ed., *The State and Economic Enterprise in Japan.* Princeton, Princeton University Press, 1965.

Oka Senjin 岡千仭 . *Sonjō kiji* 尊攘紀事 (Record of the Meiji Restoration). 8 kan. Tokyo, 1882.

———. *Kankō kiyū* 觀光紀遊 (Records of sightseeing [in China]). Tokyo, 1886.

———. *Zōmei sambō bun shoshū* 藏名山房文初集 (Collected essays of Oka Senjin). 6 kan. Tokyo, 1920.

Ōkōchi Teruna 大河內輝聲 , "Hitsuwa" 筆話 (Records of conversations in writing). Unpublished notebooks held at Waseda University and Daitō Bunka Daigaku, Tokyo.

———. "Ragenchō (Lo-yuan-t'ieh)," 羅源帖 18 books (1 missing), contain conversations during 1875–1876.

——. "Teichū hitsuwa (Ting-ch'ou pi-hua)" 丁丑筆話 , 7 books (6 missing), contain conversations during 1877.

——. "Boen hitsuwa (Wu-yin pi-hua)" 戊寅筆話 , 26 books (1 missing), 1878.

——. "Kibō hitsuwa (Chi-mao pi-hua)" 己卯筆話 , 16 books (14 missing), 1879.

——. "Kōshin hitsuwa (Keng-ch'en pi-hua)" 庚辰筆話 , 10 books, 1880.

——. "Shitsuen hitsuwa (Ch'i-yuan pi-hua)" 桼園筆話 , 17 books, 1880–1881.

——. "Kanjin hitsuwa (Han-jen pi-hua)" 韓人筆話 , 1 book.

——. "Shoga hitsuwa (Shu-hua pi-hua)" 書畫筆話 , 1 book.

Ōkubo Toshiaki 大久保利謙 "Nakamura Keiu no shoki yō-gaku shisō to *Saikoku risshihen* no yakujutsu oyobi kankō ni tsuite" 中村敬宇の初期洋学思想と西国立志編の訳述及び刊行について (Nakamura Keiu's view of Western learning in early years and his translation and publication of *Self-Help*), *Shien* 26.2–3: 153–188 (January 1966).

Ōno Jitsunosuke 大野實之助 , "Keitaimen kara mita Kō Junken no shi" 形態面から觀た黄遵憲の詩 (Poems of Huang Tsun-hsien from the morphological point of view), *Chūgoku koten kenkyū* 中國古典研究 (Waseda Daigaku Chūgoku Koten Kenkyūkai) 12:55–69 (December 1964).

Onogawa Hidemi 小野川秀美 . "Ka Kei, Ko Reien no shinsei rongi" 何啓胡禮垣の新政論議 (On Hsin-cheng lun-i by Ho Ch'i and Hu Li-yuan), in *Ishihama sensei koki kinen tōyōgaku ronsō* 石濱先生古稀記念東洋學論叢 (Collection of articles in Oriental studies dedicated to Professor Ishihama at his 70th birthday). Suita, 1958.

——. *Shimmatsu seiji shisō kenkyū* 清末政治思想研究 (Studies on the political thought of the late Ch'ing). Tokyo, Misuzu Shobō, 1969.

Ozawa Saburō 小澤三郎 . "Kaisei gakkō oyatoi kyōshi D. B. McCartee" 開成學校御傭教師マックカーテー (D. B. McCartee, a visiting professor at the Kaisei School), *Meiji bunka* 14.12:3–4 (December 1941).

——. *Nihon Purotesutanto shi kenkyū* 日本プロテスタント史研究 (A study of the history of Protestantism in Japan). Tokyo, 1964.

P'an Fei-sheng 潘飛聲 . *Tsai shan-ch'üan shih-hua* 在山泉詩話

(Essays on poems), in Ku-chin wen-i ts'ung-shu 古今文藝叢書, series 3, 4–5 ts'e. Shanghai, Kuang-i Shu-chü, 1913.

Pao Tsun-p'eng 包遵彭 . *Chung-kuo hai-chün shih* 中國海軍史 (The history of the Chinese navy). Taipei, Chinese Naval Publication Office, 1951.

P'i Hsi-jui 皮錫瑞 . "Shih-fu-t'ang wei-k'an jih-chi" 師伏堂未刊日記 (Unpublished diary of P'i Hsi-jui), in *Hu-nan li-shih tzu-liao* 1958 no. 4; 1959 no. 1, no. 2.

Price, Don. *Russia and the Roots of the Chinese Revolution*. Cambridge, Harvard University Press, 1974.

Rai Jō (San'yō) 賴襄 , (山陽). *Nihon gaishi* 日本外史 (Unofficial history of Japan). Tokyo, Rai Fukujirō, 1875.

——. *Nihon seiki* 日本政記 (The record of governments of Japan) Rai shi zōhan, n.d., n.p.

Rawlinson, John L. *China's Struggle for Naval Development, 1839–1895*. Cambridge, Harvard University Press, 1967.

The Reform Movement of 1898. Compilation Group for the History of Modern China, eds. Peking, Foreign Language Press, 1976.

Rhoads, Edward J. M. *China's Republican Revolution: The Case of Kwangtung 1895–1913*. Cambridge, Harvard University Press, 1975.

Sakai, Robert K. "The Ryukyu (Liu-ch'iu) Islands as a Fief of Satsuma," in John K. Fairbank, *Chinese World Order*.

Sakamoto Tarō 坂本太郎 . *Nihon no shūshi to shigaku* 日本の修史と史学 (Historical compilation and historical studies in Japan). Tokyo, Shibundō, 1958.

Sanetō bunko mokuroku 實藤文庫目録 (Catalogue of the Sanetō collection), Tokyo Toritsu Hibiya Toshokan 東京都立日比谷図書館 . Tokyo, 1966.

Sanetō Keishū 實藤惠秀 . *Kindai Nisshi bunka ron* 近代日支文化論 (Cultural contact between Japan and China in modern times). Tokyo, Daitō Shuppansha, 1941.

——. "Nihon zatsuji shi" 日本雜事詩 (On *Miscellaneous poems on Japan*), in *Chūgoku bungaku*, Nos. 71, 72, 73 (April–June 1941).

——. *Meiji Nisshi bunka kōshō* 明治日支文化交渉 (Cultural intercourse between Japan and China during the Meiji period). Tokyo, Kōfūkan, 1943.

——. *Chūgokujin Nihon ryūgaku shi* 中國人日本留學史 (A

history of Chinese students in Japan). Tokyo, Kuroshio Shuppan, 1960.

——. *Ōkōchi monjo: Meiji Nitchū bunkajin no kōyū* 大河内文書 明治日中文化人の交遊 (The Ōkōchi documents: Social intercourse between intellectuals of Japan and China during the Meiji period). Tokyo, Heibonsha, 1964.

—— and Toyota Minoru, trans. *Nihon zatsuji shi* 日本雜事詩 (Miscellaneous poems on Japan). Tokyo, Heibonsha, 1968. A revised edition of Toyota Minoru and Sanetō Keishū, trans., *Nihon zatsuji shi,* Seikatsusha, 1943.

Sasaki Masaya 佐々木正哉 . *Shimmatsu no haigai undō, shiryō hen,* (jōkan) 清末の排外運動・資料篇 (上巻) (Anti-foreign movements in the late-Ch'ing, source materials, Volume 1). Tokyo, Gannandō Shoten, 1968.

Sata Hakubō 佐田白芽 , comp. *Meiji shibun* 明治詩文 (A collection of prose and poems of the Meiji era). Tokyo, Okada Bunsuke, 1877–1879.

Satō Ichirō 佐藤市郎 . *Kaigun gojūnen shi* 海軍五十年史 (A fifty-year history of the Navy). Tokyo, Masu Shobō, 1943.

Satō Saburō 佐藤三郎 . "Meiji ishin igo Nisshin sensō izen ni okeru Shinajin no Nihon kenkyū" 明治維新以後日清戰爭以前に於ける支那人の日本研究 (Chinese studies of Japan from the Meiji Restoration to the Sino-Japanese War of 1894–1895), *Rekishi gaku kenkyū* 10.11 (November 1940).

——. "Kōakai ni kansuru ichi kōsatsu" 興亞會に關する一考察 (A study of the Kōakai), *Yamagata daigaku kiyō Jimbun kagaku* 1.4 (August 1951).

——. "Chūgokujin to Azuma kagami" 中國人と吾妻鏡 (Chinese and *Azuma kagami*), *Nihon rekishi* 188:45–47 (January 1964).

——. "Meiji shoki ni okeru Chūgokujin no Meiji ishin seiji ni taisuru mikata ni tsuite," 明治初期における中國人の明治維新政治に對する見方について (On Chinese views of the government of early Meiji Japan), *Yamagata daigaku kiyō* 8.4:1–26 (February 1977).

Satō Seizaburō 佐藤誠三郎 . "Bakumatsu Meiji shoki ni okeru taigai ishiki no sho ruikei" 幕末明治初期における対外意識の諸類型 (Patterns of consciousness toward the outside world during the late Tokugawa and early Meiji eras), in Satō and R. Dingman, eds., *Kindai Nihon no taigai taido* 近代日本の対外態度 (The Japanese attitude toward the outside world in the modern era). Tokyo, Tokyo Daigaku Shuppankai, 1974.

Sawada Akira 澤田章 . *Meiji zaisei no kisoteki kenkyū* 明治財政

の基礎的研究 (Basic studies of the financial administration during the Meiji). Tokyo, Hōbunkan, 1934.

Saxton, Alexander. *The Indispensable Enemy: Labor and the Anti-Chinese Movement in California.* Berkeley and Los Angeles, University of California Press, 1971.

Schrecker, John E. *Imperialism and Chinese Nationalism: Germany in Shantung.* Cambridge, Harvard University Press, 1971.

Schwartz, Benjamin. *In Search of Wealth and Power: Yen Fu and the West.* Cambridge, Harvard University Press, 1964.

Shang Yen-liu 商衍鎏 . *Ch'ing-tai k'o-chü k'ao-shih shu-lu* 清代科舉考試述錄 (A study of the civil service examination system during the Ch'ing period). Peking, Sheng-ho Tu-shu Hsin-chih San-lien Shu-tien, 1958.

Shen Chin-ting 沈覲鼎 et al., eds. *Pai-nien-lai Chung-Jih kuan-hsi lun-wen chi* 百年來中日關係論文集 (Articles on Sino-Japanese relations during the last hundred years). Taipei, 1968.

Shen, Han-yin Chen. "Tsung Kuo-fan in Peking, 1840–1852: His Ideas on Statecraft and Reform," *Journal of Asian Studies* 27.1 (1967).

Shimada Kenji 島田虔次 . "Shinchō makki ni okeru gakumon no jōkyō" 清朝末期における学問の情況 (Trends in scholarship during the late Ch'ing period), in *Kōza Chūgoku* 2. Tokyo, Chikuma Shobō, 1967.

Shimada Kumiko 島田久美子 . *Kō Junken* 黃遵憲、 (Huang Tsun-hsien): *Chūgoku shijin senshū 2 shū* 中国詩人選集 (Selected works of Chinese poets, second series). Tokyo, Iwanami Shoten, 1963.

Shimada Masao 島田正郎 . "Shimmatsu ni okeru keiritsu sōan no hensan ni tsuite, Okada Asatarō hakushi no gyōseki o shinonde" 清末における刑律草案の編纂について―岡田朝太郎博士の業蹟をしのんで (On the compilation of the draft criminal code in the late-Ch'ing, in memory of the late Dr. Asatarō Okada), *Hōritsu ronsō* 39.1:2–3.

Shimbun shūsei Meiji hennen shi 新聞集成明治編年史 (Chronological history of the Meiji period based on newspaper articles). Tokyo, Tokyo Zaisei Keizai Gakkai, 1941.

Shimbun zasshi 新聞雜誌、 (Newspaper magazine). Seki Tokusuke 關篤輔、 et al., publishers. Tokyo, 1871–1874.

Siang, Song Ong. *One Hundred Years' History of the Chinese in Singapore.* Singapore, University of Malaya Press, 1967.

Sin Kok-ju 申國柱 . "Kōka jōki chokugo no Kan-Nichi gaikō"

江華条規直後の韓日外交　(Diplomatic relations between Korea and Japan immediately after the Kanghwa Treaty), in *Kokusai Seiji: Nikkan kankei no tenkai* 國際政治：日韓關係の展開　(Developments in Japanese–Korean relations). Kokusai Seiji Gakukai, 1963.

——. *Kindai Chōsen gaikōshi kenkyū* 近代朝鮮外交史研究 (Studies in the modern diplomatic history of Korea). Tokyo, Yūshindō, 1966.

Sogabe Shizuo 曾我部静雄　. *Chūgoku shakai keizai shi no kenkyū* 中国社会経済史の研究　(Studies of Chinese socio-economic history). Tokyo, Yoshikawa Kōbunkan, 1966.

Su Yü 蘇輿 . *I-chiao ts'ung-pien* 翼敎叢編　(The collection of writings for promoting sacred teachings). 3 ts'e. [Wu-ch'ang?], 1898.

Suzuki Torao 鈴木虎雄　. *Chūgoku senran shi* 中国戦乱詩 (Chinese poems on warfare). Tokyo, Chikuma Shobō, 1968.

Ta Ch'ing hui-tien shih-li 大清會典事例　(Cases and precedents of the collected statutes of the Ch'ing dynasty). Reprint of 1899 edition. 24 vols. Taipei, Hsin-wen-feng Press, 1976.

Ta Ch'ing Te-tsung Ching (Kuang-hsu) huang-ti shih-lu 大清德宗景（光緒　）皇帝實錄　(Veritable records of the reign of the Kuang-hsu Emperor). Ch'en Pao-ch'en 陳寶琛　et al., comps. Taipei, Hsin-wen-feng Press reproduction, 1978.

Tabohashi Kiyoshi 田保橋潔　. "Nisshi shin kankei no seiritsu" 日支新關係の成立　(The establishment of the new relationship between China and Japan), *Shigaku zasshi* 44.2 (February 1933); 44.3 (March 1933).

——. *Kindai Nissen kankei no kenkyū* 近代日鮮關係の研究　(A study of Japan–Korea relations in the modern era). Tokyo, Bunka Shiryō Chōsakai. Reproduction of 1940 Seoul edition, 1963.

Tai Ch'uan-hsien (Chi-t'ao) 戴傳賢（李陶　）. *Jih-pen-lun* 日本論 (A discussion of Japan). Shanghai, Min-chih Shu-chü, 1928.

Tai Shi Kōrōsha Denki Hensankai 對支功勞者傳記編纂會 , comp. *Tai Shi kaiko roku* 對支回顧錄　(Reminiscent records of development towards China). Tokyo, 1936.

——. *Zoku tai Shi kaiko roku* 續對支回顧錄　(continued). Tokyo, 1941.

Takahashi Masao 高橋昌郎　. *Nakamura Keiu* 中村敬宇　(A biography of Nakamura Keiu). Tokyo, Yoshikawa Kōbunkan, 1966.

Takeuchi Minoru 竹内実　. "Meiji kangakusha no Chūgoku kikō"

明治漢学者の中国紀行 (Travel diaries of Sinologists of the Meiji era), *Nihonjin ni totte no Chūgoku zō* 日本人にとっての 中国像 (Japanese images of China). Tokyo, Shunjūsha, 1966.

————. "Shikōtei no mukashi yori—Jo Fuku densetsu no ato" 始皇帝の 昔より —徐福伝説のあと (From the time of the Ch'in Shih-huang-ti—the sites of the legend of Hsu Fu), in *Kikō Nihon no naka no Chūgoku* 紀行日本のなかの中国 (Travel notes: China in Japan). Tokyo, Asahi Shimbunsha, 1976.

Takeuchi Yoshimi 竹内好 . "Tai Kitō no Nihon ron," 戴季陶 の日本論 (A discussion of Japan by Tai Chi-t'ao), in Tai Chi-t'ao and Ichikawa Hiroshi 市川宏 , trans., *Nihon ron* 日本論 (A discussion of Japan). Tokyo, 1972.

Tamura Eitarō 田村栄太郎 . *Akō rōshi: sono shiteki haikei to ningensei* 赤穂浪士 —その史的背景と人間性 (The Akō samurai, the historical background and their personalities). Tokyo, Shunjūsha, 1964.

T'an Hsien 譚獻 . *Fu-t'ang jih-chi* 復堂日記 (Diary of T'an Hsien), in T'an T'ing-hsien 譚廷獻 , comp., *Pan-an ts'ung-shu* 半厂叢書 . 13–14 ts'e. 1889. Reprint, Taipei, Hua-wen Shu-chü.

T'an Ssu-t'ung 譚嗣同 . *T'an Ssu-t'ung ch'üan-chi* 譚嗣同 全集 (Collected works of T'an Ssu-t'ung). Peking, Sheng-ho Tu-shu Hsin-chi San-lien Shu-tien, 1954.

————. "T'an Ssu-t'ung i-mo hsu-k'an" 譚嗣同遺墨續刊 , in *Hu-nan li-shih tzu-liao* 1959 no. 1 (March 1959).

Tanaka Akira 田中彰 . *Meiji ishin to rekishi kyōiku* 明治維新 と歴史教育 (Meiji Restoration and historical education). Tokyo, Aoki Shoten, 1970.

Tanaka Masatoshi 田中正俊 . "*Uiki tsūsan to Saikō nikki*" 禹域 通纂と西行日記 (*Uiki tsūsan* and *Saikō nikki*), in *Iwai hakushi koki kinen tenseki ronshū* 岩井博士古稀記念・典籍論集 (A collection of articles on books to commemorate the seventieth birthday of Dr. Iwai). Tokyo, 1963.

————. "Shin-Futsu sensō to Nihonjin no Chūgoku kan" 清仏戦争と 日本人の中国観 (The Sino–French War and the Japanese view of China), *Shisō* 512 (February 1967).

————. "Meiji shoki no kyōiku to Narahara Nobumasa: Narahara Nobumasa denkō danshō" 明治初期の教育と楢原陳政 — 楢原陳政伝稿断章 (Early Meiji education and Narahara Nobumasa: A brief chapter of a biography of Narahara), in Nohara Shirō et al., eds., *Kindai Nihon ni okeru rekishigaku no hattatsu* 近代日本における歴史学の発達 (Development of historical studies in modern Japan), Volume 1. Tokyo, Aoki Shoten, 1976.

T'ang Chih-chün 湯志鈞 . *Wu-hsu pien-fa shih lun-ts'ao* 戊戌變法史論叢 (Collection of articles on the Reform of 1898). Wu-han, Hu-pei Jen-min ch'upan-she, 1957.

———. *Wu-hsu pien-fa jen-wu chuan-kao* 戊戌變法人物傳稿 (Biographies of the people who were involved in the Reform of 1898). Peking, Chung-hua Shu-chü, 1961.

T'ang Ts'ai-ch'ang 唐才常 . *Chueh-tien-ming-chai nei-yen* 覺顛冥齋內言 (Private remarks of the Chueh-tien-ming studio). Taipei, Wen-hai Press, 1969. Facsimile reproduction of 1898 Ch'ang-sha edition.

Teng, S. Y. and John K. Fairbank. *China's Response to the West.* Cambridge, Harvard University Press, 1954.

Terakado Seiken 寺門靜軒 . *Edo hanjō ki* 江戶繁昌記 (Prosperity of Edo). Edo, 1832–1836. Reproduction, Tokyo, Heibonsha, 1974–1976.

Ting Wen-chiang 丁文江 , comp. *Liang Jen-kung hsien-sheng nien-p'u ch'ang-pien ch'u-kao* 梁任公先生年譜長編初稿 (First draft of a chronological biography of Liang Ch'i-ch'ao). Taipei, Shih-chieh Shu-chü, 1959.

Tōkeiin 統計院 . *Dai nikai Nihon teikoku tōkei nenkan* 第二回日本帝國統計年鑑 (The second annual statistics of the Japanese Empire). Tokyo, 1883.

Tokyo Daigaku Bungakubu, Bunka Kōryū Kenkyū Shisetsu Nihon Bunka Kādo Shoiinkai 東京大學文學部文化交流研究施設日本文化カード小委員会 , comp. "Ji Keiō 4 nen shi Meiji 23 nen hon'yakusho mokuroku dai ichiji miteikō" 自慶應四年至明治二十三年飜訳書目録第一次未定稿 (Bibliography of books translated into Japanese between 1867 and 1890, first draft). Mimeographed. Tokyo, 1968.

Tōyama Shigeki 遠山茂樹 . *Nihon kindai shi* 日本近代史 (History of modern Japan). Tokyo, Iwanami Shoten, 1975.

Tōyō Keizai Shimpōsha 東洋經濟新報社 , comp. *Nihon bōeki seiran* 日本貿易精覽 (Statistics of Japanese trade). Tokyo, 1935.

———. *Meiji Taishō zaisei shōran* 明治大正財政詳覽 (Statistics of finance during the Meiji and Taisho periods). Tokyo, 1929.

Toyota Minoru 豐田穰 and Sanetō Keishū 實藤惠秀 . *Nihon*

zatsuji shi 日本雜事詩   (Miscellaneous poems on Japan. Translation of Huang Tsun-hsien, *JPTSS.*). Tokyo, Seikatsusha, 1943.

Tseng Ch'i-tse 曾紀澤   . *Tseng Hui-min kung ch'üan-chi* 曾惠敏公全集 (Collected works of Tseng Ch'i-tse). Shanghai, Shanghai Shu-chü, n.d.

Tsiang, T. F. "Sino–Japanese Diplomatic Relations, 1870–1894," *The Chinese Social and Political Science Review* 17.1:1–16 (April 1933).

Tsien, Tsuen-hsuin. "Western Impact on China through Translation," *Far Eastern Quarterly* 13.3:305–327 (May 1924).

Tso Tsung-t'ang 左宗棠   . *Tso Wen-hsiang kung ch'üan-chi* 左文襄公全集 (Collected works of Tso Tsun-t'ang). Taipei, Wen-hai Press, 1964. Reproduction of 1890 edition.

Uchida Naosaku 内田直作   . *Nihon kakyō shakai no kenkyū* 日本華僑社會の研究 (A Study of the overseas Chinese community in Japan). Tokyo, Dōbunkan, 1949.

Ueda Masaaki 上田正昭   . "Kodai no saishi to girei" 古代の祭祀と儀礼 (Religious services and rituals in ancient times), in *Iwanami kōza Nihon rekishi*. Tokyo, 1975.

Ueda Toshio   植田捷雄   . "Ryūkyū no kizoku o meguru Nisshin kōshō," 琉球の歸屬を繞る日清交渉 (Sino–Japanese negotiations disputing sovereignty over the Ryukyu islands), *Tōyō bunka kenkyūjo kiyō* 2:151–201 (September 1951).

Uete Michiari 植手通有   ed. *Rai San'yō* 賴山陽   in series, Nihon shisō taikei 日本思想大系   . Tokyo, Iwanami Shoten, 1977.

Unno Fukuju 海野福寿   . "Matsukata zaisei to jinushisei no keisei" 松方財政と地主制の形成   (Matsukata's administration of finance and the formation of the landlord system), *Iwanami kōza Nihon rekishi*, Volume 15. Tokyo, 1976.

Uno Shun'ichi 宇野俊一   . *Nisshin Nichiro* (*Nihon no rekishi*, Volume 26) 日清日露   (日本の歴史   ) (The Sino–Japanese and Russo–Japanese Wars, *History of Japan*, Volume 26. Tokyo, Shōgakukan, 1976.

Usui Katsumi 臼井勝美   , "Yokohama kyoryūchi no Chūgokujin" 横浜居留地の中国人   (Chinese in the foreign settlement in Yokohama), in Yokohama-shi, *Yokohama-shi shi* 横浜市史 (History of Yokohama city), Volume 36. Yokohama, 1963.

Wan-kuo kung fa 萬國公法 . W. A. P. Martin, trans. See *Kamban bankoku kōhō.*

Wang Chih-ch'ün 王之春 . *Ying-hai chih-yen* 瀛海厄言 (Miscellaneous talks on the sea powers), in *Hsiao fang-hu-chai yü-ti ts'ung-ch'ao,* 62 ts'e (11:509–522b).

———. *T'an ying lu* 談瀛錄 (Records of a trip to Japan). 4 chüan. Ching-k'ou, 1880.

Wang Chung-hou 王仲厚 . "Huang Kung-tu shih-ts'ao wai-i chu i-wen" 黃公度詩草外遺著佚聞 (Miscellaneous information on the collection of poems of Huang Tsun-hsien), in Cheng Tzu-yü, ed., *Jen-ching-lu ts'ung-k'ao.*

Wang Erh-min 王爾敏 . "Ch'ing-chi wei-hsin jen-wu te t'o-ku kai-chih lun" 清季維新人物的託古改制論 (Late Ch'ing reformers' discussions using the classics), *Ta-lu tsa-chih* 21.6:14–19 (September 1960).

———. *Wan-Ch'ing cheng-chih ssu-hsiang-shih lun* 晚清政治思想史論 (Studies of political thought during the late Ch'ing era). Taipei, Wang Erh-min, 1969.

———. *Chung-kuo chin-tai ssu-hsiang shih-lun* 中國近代思想史論 (Studies of the modern intellectual history of China). Taipei, Wang Erh-min, 1977.

Wang Hsien-ch'ien 王先謙 . *Jih-pen yuan-liu k'ao* 日本源流考 (A study of the history of Japan). Changsha, Ssu-hsien Shu-chü, 1902.

———. *Hsu-shou-t'ang shu-cha* 虛受堂書札 (A collection of essays by Wang Hsien-ch'ien). Taipei, Wen-hai Press. Facsimile reproduction of 1907 edition.

———. *K'uei-yuan tzu-ting nien-p'u* 葵園自訂年譜 (Chronological autobiography of Wang Hsien-ch'ien). Changsha, 1908. Reproduction, Taipei, Wen-hai Press.

Wang Shu-huai 王樹槐 . *Wai-jen yü wu-hsu pien-fa* 外人與戊戌變法 (Foreigners and the Reform of 1898). Taipei, 1965.

Wang, Sing-wu. "The Attitude of the Ch'ing Court toward Chinese Emigration," *Chinese Culture* 9:62–76 (Taipei, December 1968).

Wang T'ao 王韜 . *Fu-sang yu-chi* 扶桑遊記 (Records of travel in Japan), in *Hsiao-fan-hu-chai yü-ti ts'ung-ch'ao.* 52 ts'e. (10,274–280b).

———. *T'ao-yuan chih-tu* 弢園尺牘 (Letters of Wang T'ao). [n.p.], Nan-t'ien tun-chü, 1880.

———. *T'ao-yuan wen-lu wai-pien* 弢園文錄外編 (Collected essays of Wang T'ao, supplement). Hong Kong, T'ao-yuan Lao-min, 1883.

Wang Te-chao 王德昭 . "Huang Tsun-hsien yü Liang Ch'i-ch'ao" 黄遵憲與梁啓超 (Huang Tsun-hsien and Liang Ch'i-cha'ao), *Hsin-ya shu-yuan hsueh-shu nien-k'an* 新亞書院學術年刊 Hong Kong, New Asia College Annual 11:1–31 (September 1969).

Wang Yeh-chien. *Land Taxation in Imperial China, 1750–1911.* Cambridge, Harvard University Press, 1973.

Wang Yun-sheng 王芸生 . *Liu-shih-nien lai Chung-kuo yü Jih-pen* 六十年來中國與日本 (Sino–Japanese relations during the past sixty years). Tientsin, Ta-kung-pao, 1931.

Wei T'ing-sheng 衛挺生 . *Hsu Fu yü Jih-pen* 徐福與日本 (Hsu Fu and Japan). Hong Kong, 1953.

Wen Chung-chi. "The Origins and Development of the Imperial Chinese Consulate in Straits Settlements, 1877–1900." MA thesis, University of Singapore, 1964.

Wen Chung-ho. *See Kuang-hsu Chia-ying-chou chih.*

Wen T'ing-ching 溫廷敬 . *Ch'a-yang san-chia wen-ch'ao* 茶陽三家文鈔 (A collection of writings by three men from Chia-yang). [n.p.], Pu-tu-shu-lu, 1925.

Wen T'ing-shih 文廷式 . *Yun-ch'i-hsien tz'u-ch'ao* 雲起軒詞鈔 (A collection of essays by Wen T'ing-shih). 1911.

——. *Wen T'ing-shih ch'üan-chi* 文廷式全集 (Collected works of Wen T'ing-shih). 9 vols. Taipei, Ta-hua In-shu-kuan, 1969.

Weng T'ung-ho 翁同龢 . *Weng Wen-kung kung jih-chi* 翁文恭公日記 (Diary of Weng T'ung-ho). Shanghai, Commercial Press, 1925. Photographic reproduction. *Weng T'ung-ho jih-chi pai-yin-pen, fu, so-yin* 翁同龢日記排印本附索引 (Typeset edition of the diary of Weng T'ung-ho, and index), transcribed and ed. by Chao Chung-fu 趙中孚 . Taipei, Chinese Materials and Research Aids Service Center, 1970–.

Wright, Mary C. *The Last Stand of Chinese Conservatism: The T'ung-chih Restoration, 1862–1874.* Stanford, Stanford University Press, 1957.

Wu-hsu pien-fa 戊戌變法 . Chung-kuo Shih-hsueh-hui 中國史學會 , comp. *Chung-kuo chin-tai-shih tzu-liao ts'ung-k'an* 中國近代史資料叢刊 (A collection of materials on history of modern China). 4 vols. Shanghai, 1953.

Wu-hsu pien-fa tang-an shih-liao 戊戌變法檔案史料 (Archival materials on the Reform of 1898). Kuo-chia tang-an-chü Ming Ch'ing tang-an kuan 國家檔案局明清檔案館 , comp. Peking, Chung-hua Shu-chü, 1958.

Wu T'ien-jen 吳天任 . *Huang Kung-tu hsien-sheng chuan kao* 黃公度 先生傳稿 (A draft biography of Huang Tsun-hsien). Hong Kong, Chung-wen Ta-hsueh, 1972.

Wyle, Alexander. *Memorials of the Protestant Missionaries to the Chinese.* Shanghai, American Presbyterian Mission Press, 1867. Reprint, Taipei, Ch'eng-wen Press, 1967.

Yamaguchi Kazuo 山口和雄 . *Meiji zenki keizai no bunseki* 明治前期経済の文析 (Analysis of the Japanese economy during the early Meiji period). Tokyo, Tokyo Daigaku Shuppankai, 1956.

Yanagita Izumi 柳田泉 . *Meiji shoki no bungaku shisō* 明治初期 の文学思想 (Literary thought during the early Meiji). Tokyo, Shunjūsha, 1965.

Yang Shou-ching 楊守敬 . *Lin-su lao-jen nien-p'u* 鄰蘇老人 年譜 (A chronological biography of Yang Shou-ching). Shanghai, Ta-lu Shu-chü, 1933.

Yang T'ien-shih 杨天石 . *Huang Tsun-hsien* 黃遵憲 . Shanghai, Jen-min ch'u-pan-she, 1979.

Yang T'ing-fu 楊廷福 . *T'an Ssu-t'ung nien-p'u* 譚嗣同年譜 (A chronological biography of T'an Ssu-t'ung). Peking, Jen-min ch'u-pan-she, 1957.

Yang-wu yun-tung 洋務運動 (The Westernization movement). Chung-kuo Shih-hsueh-hui, comp. Shanghai, Jen-min ch'u-pan-she, 1961.

Yao Hsi-kuang 姚錫光 . *Tung-fang ping-shih chi-lueh* 東方兵事 紀略 (A brief account of the war with Japan). 5 vols. Wu-ch'ang, 1897.

Yasuoka Akio 安岡昭男 . "Nisshin sensō zen no tairiku seisaku" 日清戦争前の大陸政策 (Continental policy of Japan before the Sino-Japanese War), in Nihon Kokusai Seiji Gakukai, *Kokusai seiji: Nihon gaikōshi kenkyū—Nisshin Nichiro sensō* 国際政治：日本外交 史研究 —日清日露戦争 (International politics: Studies in the history of Japanese diplomacy, Sino–Japanese and Russo–Japanese Wars). Tokyo, Yūhikaku, 1961.

Yen Fu 嚴復 . *Yen i ming-chu ts'ung-k'an* 嚴譯名著叢刊 (Translations by Yen Fu). 8 vols. Shanghai, Commercial Press, 1931.

Yokohama Shiyakusho 橫濱市役所 , comp. *Yokohama-shi shi kō* 橫濱市史稿 (Draft history of the city of Yokohama). Yokohama, 1932.

Yuan Ch'ang (Shuang-ch'iu) 袁昶 (爽秋). *Yü-hu hsiao-chi* 于湖

小集　　　(A collection of writings of Yuan Shuang-ch'iu). Shanghai, Commercial Press, 1937.

Yung Wing (Jung Hung 容閎　). *My Life in China and America.* New York, 1909. Trans. and annot. Momose Hiromu 百瀬弘　. *Seigaku tōzen ki: Yō Kō jiden* 西學東漸記容閎自傳　. Tokyo, Heibonsha, 1969.

Glossary

This list does not include place names. Personal names are not included for persons listed in Appendix A, Appendix B, and the Bibliography, except in those cases where it is here useful to note their *tzu*.

Aikokusha 愛國社

Aizawa Yasushi (Seishisai)
會澤安（正志齋）

Ajia Kyōkai 亞細亞協會

Aoyama Nobutoshi (Kikyō)
青山延壽（李卿）

Aoyama Nobuyuki (Sessai)
青山延于（拙齋）

Arai Hakuseki 新井白石

Arakawa Motoji 荒川己次

Arima Michisumi
有馬道純

Arisugawa Taruhito
有栖川熾仁

Ashikaga Takauji 足利尊氏

Azuma kagami 吾妻鏡

Bampō seiri 萬法精理

bummei kaika 文明開化

bushidō 武士道

busshitsu no gaku 物質の學

Chang Chien 張謇

Chang Chung-hsin 張仲炘

Chang Hsiao-ch'ien
張孝謙

Chang K'en-te 張坤德.

Chang Pi-shih (Chen-hsun)
張弼士（振勳）

Chang Ping-lin 張炳麟

Chang Tsu-t'ung 張祖同

Chang Tz'u-fang 張慈昉

Chang Wen-ch'eng 張文成

Chang Yin-huan (Ch'iao-yeh)
張陰桓（樵野）

Ch'ang-yen pao 昌言報

chao-chien 召見

Ch'ao-hsien-kuo chi
朝鮮國記

Ch'en Lan-p'in (Li-ch'iu)
陳蘭彬（荔秋）

Chen-li i-chih 眞理易知

Ch'en Pao-chen (Yu-ming)
陳寶箴（右銘）

Ch'en Sung-sheng 陳松生

Ch'en Yü-ch'ih 陳玉池

Cheng 鄭

cheng 徵

Cheng Ch'eng-kung 鄭成功

cheng-chiao 政敎

cheng li-shih kuan 正理事官

Cheng Tsao-ju (Yü-hsuan)
鄭藻如（玉軒）

Ch'eng-Chu 程朱

Chia I 賈誼

Chiang Piao (Chien-hsia)
江標（建霞）

Chiang Ping-k'un 姜炳坤

Chiang T'ung 江統

Ch'iang-hsueh hui
強學會

Ch'iang-hsueh pao
強學報

chiao 敎

Chiao-ching shu-yuan
校經書院

chiao-hua 敎化

chien-ai 兼愛

Chien-hou 建侯

chih-li chou 直隸州

ch'ien-shan so 遷善所

chin-shih 進士

chin-wen 今文

ch'in-ch'ai ta-ch'en
欽差大臣

Chinda Sutemi 珍田捨己

chindai 鎭台

ching 經

Ching-pao 京報

ching-shuo 經說

ching-t'ien 敬天

ch'ing-i 淸議

Ch'ing-i pao 淸議報

ch'ing-liu 淸流

Ch'iu Feng-chia (Chung-yen)
邱逢甲（仲閼）

"Ch'iu-shui" 秋水

chizaihō 治罪法

Ch'oe Ik-hyŏn 崔益鉉

chou 州

Chou Han 周漢

Chou Lang-shan 周朗山

Chou-li 周禮

Ch'ou-chang chü
籌賬局

Ch'ou-hai t'u-pien 籌海圖編

Chu Chih-yü (Lu-yü, Shun-shui Shu Shunsui) 朱之瑜（魯興，舜水）

Chu Chu-ch'a 朱竹坨

Chu Hsi 朱熹

Chu Yun 朱雲

ch'u-shih 處士

ch'u-shih ta-ch'en 出使大臣

chü-jen 舉人

Ch'üan-shan liang-yen 勸善良言

Chuang-tzu 莊子

chün 均

chün-ch'üan 君權

chün-hsien 郡縣

chün-min kung-chu 君民共主

ch'ün 群

chung-hsueh 重學

Chung Kuei-t'ien 鍾貴添

Chung t'ai-shu-jen 鍾太淑人

Chung Yung-ho 鍾用龢

Dai Nihon hennenshi 大日本編年史

Dajōkan fukoku 太政官布告

datsu A 脫亞

dōbun dōshu 同文同種

Dōjinsha 同人社

fa 法

fan-p'ing 藩屏

Fa-shih-shang jen-chai chu-jen 法時尚任齋主人

Fang La 方臘

fang-shih 方士

feng-chien 封建

feng-tseng 封贈

Feng-hu shu-yuan 豐湖書院

Fukuzawa Yukichi 福澤諭吉

gagaku 雅樂

Gamō Shigeaki (Kyōsai) 蒲生重章（絅齋）

Gamō Shūjitsu (Kumpei) 蒲生秀實（君平）

Genrōin 元老院

Gesshō 月照

Hai-an 海安

Hakka (k'o-chia) 客家

hakurai 舶來

han 藩

han-ō 藩王

Han shu 漢書

Han Yü 韓愈

Hattori Atsushi 服部德

Hayashi Shihei 林子平

Heirinji 平林寺

Heng Fa Tang 恒發當

Himiko 卑彌呼

Ho Ching 何璟

ho-ch'ün 合羣

Ho Shun-yang 何順養

Ho Ti-shan (T'ing-ch'ien)
何地山（廷謙）

Hong Jae-hak 洪在鶴

Hou Han shu 後漢書

hsi-fa 西法

hsi fan-i 西翻譯

Hsiang-hsueh pao 湘學報

Hsiang pao 湘報

hsiao-hsing-jen 小行人

"Hsien-k'ao Ssu-en-kung shu-
    lueh"
先考思恩公述略

hsien-shih 縣試

"Hsien-tsu Jung-lu-kung shu-
    lueh"
先祖榮祿公述略

Hsin-cheng lun-i 新政論議

"Hsin Chung-kuo wei-lai
    chi"
新中國未來記

Hsin hsiao-shuo pao
新小說報

Hsin-hsueh wei-ching k'ao
新學偽經考

"Hsin-min shuo" 新民說

hsin-p'ai shih 新派詩

hsing-erh-hsia 形而下

hsing-erh-shang 形而上

Hsiung Hsi-ling 熊希齡

Hsu Chih-ching 徐致靖

Hsu Ching-ch'eng 許景澄

Hsu Chueh (Ching-shan)
許珏（靜山）

Hsu Fu 徐福

Hsu Hsu-tseng 徐旭曾

Hsu Hung-ju 徐鴻儒

Hsu Jen-chu 徐仁鑄

Hsu Shen 許慎

Hsu Shou-p'eng 徐壽朋

Hsu Shu-ming 徐樹銘

hsueh-cheng 學政

Hsueh-chi i-te 學計一得

Hsueh-hai-t'ang 學海堂

Hsun-huan jih-pao
循環日報

Hsun-tzu 荀子

Hu Hsi (Hsiao-ts'en)
胡曦（曉岑）

Hu Hsuan-tse (Huang-p'u)
胡璇澤（黃浦）

Hu Li-yuan 胡禮垣

Hu Lin-i 胡林翼

Hu Yung-hsiang 胡永祥

hua 化

Huai Su 懷素

Huang Ch'ao 黃巢

Huang Chi-sheng (Yun-ch'u)
黃際昇（允初）

Huang Chün-lung 黃均隆

Huang Fang-yü 黃芳玉

Huang Hsueh-shih (Tz'u-hai)
黃學詩（詞海）

Huang Hung-hsien 黄洪憲.

Huang Hung-tsao (I-nung, Yen-pin)
黄鴻藻 (逸農. 硯賓)

Huang Jun (P'u-ch'uan)
黄潤 (樸泉)

Huang Kuei-yun 黄桂鋆

Huang Mien (Po-yuan)
黄冕 (伯元)

Huang Ping-li 黄炳離

Huang-shu 黄書

Huang Shao-chi 黄紹箕

Huang Tsun-hsien (Kung-tu)
黄遵憲 (公度)

Huang Tsun-k'ai (Yung-ta)
黄遵楷 (牖達)

Huang Tsun-keng (Yu-fu)
黄遵庚 (由甫)

Huang Tsun-lu (Kung-wang)
黄遵路 (公望)

Huang Tsun-mo (Ts'ai-t'ing)
黄遵模 (采汀)

Huang Tsun-shih (Shih-fu)
黄遵實 (實甫)

Huang Yen-yü 黄延毓

Hung Hsiu-ch'üan 洪秀全

Hung-lou meng 紅樓夢

Hung Shih-wei 洪士偉

i 易

i 義

I ching 易經

I Nai 易鼐

I-nung pi-chi 逸農筆記

Iijima Yūnen 飯島有年

Inoue Kaoru 井上馨

Inoue Tetsujirō
井上哲次郎

Ishihata Tei 石幡貞

Itagaki Taisuke 板垣退助

Itō Hirobumi 伊藤博文

Iwakura Tomomi
岩倉具視

Iwaya Shū 巖谷脩

jen 仁

Jen-ching-lu 人境廬

jen-ch'üan 人權

jen-min 仁民

jen-tao 人道

jen-ts'ai 人材

Jih-pen feng-t'u chi
日本風土記

Jih-pen k'ao 日本考

Jih-pen ti-li ping-yao
日本地理兵要

Jimmu 神武

Jingū 神功

jiyū 自由

Jiyūtō 自由黨

ju 儒

Ju 儒

Jung-lu-ti 榮祿第

jusha 儒者

Ka Reishi 何禮之
Kaisei Gakkō 開成學校
Kaishintō 改進黨
Kamo no Mabuchi 賀茂眞淵
"Kan huai" 感懷
kana 假名
kangaku 漢學
kanshi 漢詩
"Kao-tsu-pi Chung t'ai-shu-jen shu-lueh"
高祖妣鐘太淑人述略
"Kao-tsu P'u-ch'üan fu chün shu-lueh"
高祖樸泉府名述略
"K'ao-kung chi" 考工記
Katō Hiroyuki 加藤弘之
Katō Ki (Ōrō)
加藤熙(櫻老)
Kawada Yōkō 川田甕江
Kawashima Naniwa
川島浪速
keihō 刑法
keiji soshō hō
刑事訴訟法
keijijō no gaku
形而上の學
keijika no gaku
形而下の學
Keiō Gijuku 慶應義塾
"Keiten aijin setsu"
敬天愛人說

Kido Takayoshi 木戸孝允
Kihara Genrei 木原元禮
Kikuchi Takesada 菊池武貞
Kim Ki-su 金綺秀
Kim P'yong-muk 金平默
kō A 興亞
Ko-lao hui 哥老會
K'o-chia yuan-liu tiao-ch'a-hui
客家源流調查會
K'o-chia yuan-liu yen-chiu-hui
客家源流研究會
K'o-li-kuan 課吏館
K'o-li-t'ang 課吏堂
k'o-t'ung 客童
Kōakai 興亞會
Kōbushō 工部省
kōgei 工藝
Kōda Rohan 幸田露伴
Kojō Teikichi 古城貞吉
kokugaku 國學
Kokushi ryaku 國史略
Kōmei 孝明
Kōyōkan 紅葉館
"Ku-hsiang-ko shih-chi hsu"
古香閣詩集序
Ku-i ts'ung-shu 古逸叢書
Ku Yen-wu 顧炎武
kuan-ch'üan 官權
Kuan Chung 管仲
Kuan T'ien-p'ei 關天培

Kuan Yü 關羽
Kuang-hsueh hui 廣學會
Kuang-tung hsiang-t'u li-shih
廣東鄉土歷史
Kuang-tzu 管子
Kuga Katsunan 陸羯南
Kumano 熊野
Kung Chao-yuan 龔照瑗
Kung-chih-t'a 公之它
kung-i 工藝
kung-te 公德
k'ung-t'an 空談
K'ung-tzu kai-chih-k'ao
孔子改制考
kuo 國
kuo-chia 國家
kuo-hsueh 國學
kuo-shih 國勢
Kuo Sung-t'ao 郭嵩燾
kuo-ts'ui 國粹
Kuo-yü 國語
Kurimoto Joun 栗本鋤雲
Kusakabe Tōsaku
日下部東作
Kusunoki Masashige 楠正成
kyōgen 狂言
Kyōwatō 共和黨
Kyūusha 舊雨社

Lang-shan 朗山
Lao-tzu 老子
Lat pau 叻報

li 理
li 禮
Li Ching-hsi 李經羲
Li Chung-hsuan 李仲璇
li-hsueh 禮學
Li Hsueh-yuan (Po-t'ao)
李學源 (伯陶)
Li Shu-ch'ang 黎庶昌
Li t'ai-fu-jen 李太夫人
Li Wei-ko 李維格
Li Yen-kung 李言恭
Liang-Hu 兩湖
Liang Ting-fen (Hsing-hai)
梁鼎芬 (星海)
Lien-ch'ih 蓮池
lien-ho li 聯合力
lin-shan-sheng 廩膳生
Ling-hun p'ien 靈魂篇
Liu Ch'i-hsiang 劉麒祥
Liu Hsi-hung 劉錫鴻
Liu Hsin 劉歆
Liu T'ui 劉蛻
Lo Feng-lu 羅豐祿
Lo Shao-shan 羅少珊
Lu Hsun 魯迅
Luan-yang tsa-yung
灤陽雜咏

Ma Chien-chung 馬建忠
Ma Chien-ts'ai 馬兼才
Ma Ko-li (Ch'ing-ch'en)
馬格里 (清臣)

Matsuda Michiyuki 松田道之
Matsudaira Yoshinaga (Shun-gaku) 松平慶永 (春岳)
Mei-shui shih-chuan 梅水詩傳
Meiroku zasshi 明六雜誌‧
Min 閔
min-chu 民主
min-ch'üan 民權
Min Tzu-ch'ien 閔子騫
Minamoto Shōbyō 源松苗
Ming-shih 明史
ming-te 明德‧
minji 民事
Min'yaku ron 民約論
Mishima Chūshū 三島中州
Miyajima Daihachi 宮島大八
Miyajima Seiichirō (Zokkō) 宮島誠一郎 (栗香)
Miyamoto Shōichi 宮本小一
Mo-ti 墨翟
Mo-tzu 墨子
Mori Kainan 森槐南
Mori Rochoku (Shuntō) 森魯直 (春濤)
Motoori Norinaga 本居宣長
mu-fu 幕府
Mukōyama Kōson 向山篁村

Murata Tsuneyoshi 村田經芳
Mutsu Munemitsu 陸奥宗光

Na San (Hua-chu) 那三 (革祝)
Nagaoka Moriyoshi 長岡護美
Naitō Chisō 內藤耻叟
Nakamuraya 中村屋
Namma Kōki 南摩綱紀
Nan 枏
Nan-hsueh hui 南學會
Nan Sung tsa-shih shih 南宋雜事詩
Naruse On (Taiiki) 成瀬溫 (大域)
Nihon bunshō kihan 日本文章規範
"Nihon tamashii jo" 日本魂序
Noguchi Tadakame 野口忠龜
Nü Kua 女媧

O ta Pi-te pien-fa chi 俄大彼得變法記
Ogyū Sorai 荻生徂徠
Okada Asatarō 岡田朝太郎

Ōkōchi Teruna (Minamoto Kei-
　kaku)
　大河內輝聲（源桂閣）
Ōkubo Toshimichi
　大久保利通
Ōkuma Shigenobu
　大隈重信

Ōmachi Keigetsu 大町桂月
onna gidayū 女義太夫
Ono Chōgen 小野長愿
Ōnuma Atsushi (Chinzan)
　大沼厚（枕山）
Ou-yang Hsiu 歐陽修

pa-kung-sheng 拔貢生
P'an Chui 樊錐
P'an Ku 盤古
Pao Ch'ao 鮑超
pao-chia 保甲
Pao-chia chü 保甲局
Pao-huang hui 保皇會
Pao-kuo hui 保國會
Pao-wei chü 保衛司
P'eng Tse-i 彭澤益
Po I 伯夷
Pu-tai ho-shang 布袋和尚
Punti 本地

Reitakusha 麗澤社
Rikkentō 立憲黨
Risshi 立志

Risshisha 立志社
Ritsurei seigi 律例精義
Ro Gempō 鱸元邦

Saigō Takamori 西鄉隆盛
Sakuma Shōzan 佐久間象山
Sakura Sōgorō 佐倉宗五郎
Sanjō Sanetomi 三條實美
seigaku 西學
seirei no gaku 精靈の學
Seishitsu shobun
　請筭所聞
Seiyō jijō 西洋事情
Shan-hai ching 山海經
shan-ko 山歌
shang-t'ung 尚同
she-hui 社會
Shen Chia-pen 沈家本
Shen Nan-p'in 沈南蘋
Shen Pao-chen 沈葆楨
Shen Tseng-chih 沈曾植
Shen Tseng-t'ung 沈曾桐
sheng-yuan 生員
Shigeno Yasutsugu (Seisai)
　重野安繹（戌齋）
Shih Chen-chi 石鎮吉
Shih chi 史記
shih-hsueh 實學
shih-shih 時勢
shih-shih ch'iu-shih
　實事求是

Shih Ta-k'ai 石達開

shih-t'ien 事天

shih-wu 時務

Shih-wu hsueh-t'ang
時務學堂

Shih-wu pao 時務報

Shimada Kōsen 島田篁村

Shin-A sha 振亞社

Shimbun shi 新文詩

Shinobu Joken 信夫恕軒

shinritsu kōryō 新律綱領

shintai-shi 新體詩

Shintai-shi shō shohen
新體詩抄初篇

shishi 志士

Shōheikō 昌平黌

Shōhō kaigisho
商法會議所

Shōkōkan 彰考館

"Shu Lin T'ai-p'u k'o-shuo hou"
書林太僕客説後

Shu Ch'i 叔齊

Shui-ts'ang yen-hung kuan chu-
jen 水蒼雁紅館主人

shun-t'ien hsiang-shih
順天鄉試

Soejima Taneomi 副島種臣

Sone Toshitora 曾根俊虎

Ssu-en tsa-chu 思恩雜著

Ssu-hui hsien-chih 四會縣志

Ssu-ma Ch'ien 司馬遷

Su Shih (Tung-p'o) 蘇軾(東坡)

sui-yuan 遂員

Sujin 崇神

Su Wu 蘇武

Sugawara Michizane 菅原道眞

Sun Chia-nai 孫家鼐

Sun I-jang 孫詒讓

Suzuki Yuiichi 鈴木唯一

ta-t'ung 大同

Taewŏn'gun 大院君

t'ai-p'ing 太平

T'ai Po 泰伯

taigi 大義

Takayama Hikokurō (Seishi)
高山彦九郎 (正之)

Takezoe Shin'ichirō
竹添進一郎

T'ang Chen 湯震

T'ang Ching-sung 唐景崧

tao 道

tao-yuan 道員

T'ao Ch'ien (Yuan-ming)
陶潛 (淵明)

T'ao Shu 陶澍

t'ao-yuan 桃源

Tendō sogen 天道朔源

Terashima Munenori
寺島宗則

t'i 體

T'ien-chu chiao 天主教

T'ien Heng 田橫

t'ien-hsia 天下

Ting Jih-ch'ang (Yü-sheng) 丁日昌 (雨生)

Ting Ju-ch'ang 丁如昌

t'ing-shih 廷試

Tōa Dōbunkai 東亞同文會

Tokugawa Iesato 德川家運

Tokugawa Ieyasu 德川家東

Tokushi yoron 讀史餘論

Toyama Masaichi 外山正一

Toyotomi Hideyoshi 豐臣秀吉

"Tsa-kan" 雜感

Ts'ai Wen-pao 蔡文寶

ts'an-tsan 參贊

Tseng Kuo-ch'üan 曾國荃

Tseng Kuo-fan 曾國藩

"Tseng-tsu Tz'u-hai fu chün shu lueh" 曾祖詞海府君述略

Tso-chuan 左傳

Tso Hsiao-t'ung 左孝同

Tso Ping-lung 左東隆

Tso Tsung-t'ang 左宗棠

Tsou Po-ch'i 鄒伯奇

Tsou Tai-chün 鄒代鈞

"T'u-k'o yuan-liu k'ao" 土客源流考

Tuan 端

T'uan-fang chü 團防局

T'ui-ssu-shu-wu shih-wen chi 退思書屋詩文集

tung fan-i 東翻譯

Tung-hai kung 東海公

Tung-shan 東山

tung t'ung-shih 東通事

t'ung 同

t'ung 桐

T'ung-ch'eng 桐城

t'ung-hsiang 同鄉

T'ung-wen kuan 同文館

t'ung-wen t'ung-chung 同文同種

t'ung-yang-hsi 童養媳

Uchida Masao 內田正雄

Uchimura Nobuyuki (Suisho) 內邨宣之 (綏所)

Ueki Emori 植木枝盛

Uemura Seigi (Roshū, Shijun) 植村正義 (蘆州·子順)

wai-fu 外府

wai-shih-shih 外史氏

Wang An-shih 王安石

Wang Fu-chih 王夫之

Wang Hai-yang 汪海洋

Wang Jen-kan (T'i-chai) 王仁乾 (惕齋)

Wang K'ang-nien 汪康年

Wang Mang 王莽

Wang Wen-shao 王文韶

Wang Yang-ming 王陽明

Watanabe Kazan 渡邊革山

Wei Yuan 魏源

Wei-yen 危言

Wen Sheng (Shu-lai) 文晟(叔來)

wijŏng ch'ŏksa 衛正斥邪

Wo-jen 倭仁

Wu Ta-ch'eng 吳大澂

Wu Te-hsiao (Chi-ch'ing)
吳德潚(季清)

Wu-ti 武帝

Wu T'ing-fang 伍廷芳

Ya-hsi-ya 亞細亞

Ya-su chiao 耶蘇教

Yamagata Masasada
山縣昌貞

Yanagiwara Sakimitsu
柳原前光

Yang Ch'ung-i 楊崇伊

Yang Jui 楊銳

Yang-wu chü 洋務局

yang-yuan 洋員

Yano Fumio 矢野文雄

Yao Wen-tung 姚文棟

Yasui Sokken 安井息軒

Yatabe Ryōkichi 矢田部良吉

Yeh Ming-ch'en 葉名琛

Yeh Pi-hua (Jung-sheng, Wan-shan)
葉璧華(潤生, 婉山)

Yeh Te-hui 葉德輝

Yen K'ung 演孔

Yi Man-son 李晚孫

Yi Tong-in 李東仁

Yi Yu-wŏn 李裕元

yin-chien 引見

Ying-han 英翰

Yochi shiryaku 輿地誌略

Yoshida Shōin 吉田松陰

Yoshino Kinryō 芳野金陵

Yü-keng 裕庚

Yü Lien-san 俞廉三

Yü Yueh 愈樾

yuan-shih 院試

Yuan Shih-k'ai 袁世凱

Yūbin hōchi 郵便報知

yueh 約

Yueh Fei 岳飛

Zenrin Shoin 善鄰書院

Zenshintō 漸進黨

Index

Harvard East Asian Monographs

90. Noel F. McGinn, Donald R. Snodgrass, Yung Bong Kim, Shin-Bok Kim, and Quee-Young Kim, *Education and Development in Korea*

91. Leroy P. Jones and Il SaKong, *Government, Business, and Entrepreneurship in Economic Development: The Korean Case*

92. Edward S. Mason, Mahn Je Kim, Dwight H. Perkins, Kwang Suk Kim, David C. Cole et al., *The Economic and Social Modernization of the Republic of Korea*

93. Robert Repetto, Tai Hwan Kwon, Son-Ung Kim, Dae Young Kim, John E. Sloboda, and Peter J. Donaldson, *Economic Development, Population Policy, and Demographic Transition in the Republic of Korea*

94. Parks M. Coble, *The Shanghai Capitalists and the Nationalist Government, 1927–1937*

95. Noriko Kamachi, *Reform in China: Huang Tsun-hsien and the Japanese Model*

96. Richard Wich, *Sino-Soviet Crisis Politics: A Study of Political Change and Communication*

DATE DUE

GAYLORD   PRINTED IN U.S.A.